GATEWAYS TO ART

Debra J. DeWitte • Ralph M. Larmann • M. Kathryn Shields

GATEWAYS TO ART

Understanding the Visual Arts

With 1013 illustrations, 865 in color

Thames & Hudson

First published in 2012 in paperback in the United States of America by Thames & Hudson Inc., 500 Fifth Avenue, New York, New York 10110

thamesandhudsonusa.com

Reprinted 2012

Library of Congress Catalog Card Number 2011922637

ISBN 978-0-500-28956-3

Designed by Geoff Penna

Printed and bound in China by C&C Offset Printing Ltd

FRONT COVER

Henri Matisse, *Icarus*, Plate VIII from *Jazz*, 1943–47. The Museum of Modern Art, New York.
The Louis E. Stern Collection. 930.1964.8. Digital image, The Museum of Modern Art, New York/Scala, Florence.
© Succession H. Matisse/DACS 2012

BACK COVER

Above, left to right:

Katsushika Hokusai, "The Great Wave off Shore at Kanagawa," from *Thirty-Six Views of Mount Fuji*,
1826–33 (printed later). Library of Congress, Washington, D.C.

Artemisia Gentileschi, *Judith Decapitating Holofernes*, *c.* 1620. Uffizi Gallery, Florence

Raphael, *The School of Athens*, 1510–11. Stanza della Segnatura, Vatican City

Dorothea Lange, *Migrant Mother, Nipomo, California*, 1936. Library of Congress, Washington, D.C.

The Great Pyramid of Khufu, Giza, *c.* 2,500 BC. Photo Heidi Grassley © Thames & Hudson Ltd, London

Francisco De Goya, *The Third of May, 1808*, 1814. Museo Nacional del Prado, Madrid

Below:

Colossal Head, Olmec, Basalt, 1500–1300 BCE. Museo de Antropología, Veracruz, Mexico.
Photo Irmgard Groth-Kimball © Thames & Hudson Ltd, London

Contents

How to Use *Gateways to Art: Understanding the Visual Arts*

Gateways to Art is a new introduction to the visual arts, divided into four parts: Fundamentals, the essential elements and principles of art that constitute the "language" of artworks; Media, the many materials and processes that artists use to make art; History, the forces and influences that have shaped art throughout the course of human history; and Themes, the major cultural and historical themes that have motivated artists to create. Each of these parts is color coded to help you move easily from one section to the next.

Gateways to Art gives you complete flexibility in finding your own pathway to understanding and appreciating art. Once you have read the Introduction, which outlines the core knowledge and skills you will need to analyze and understand art, you can read the chapters of our book in any order. Each chapter is entirely modular, giving you just the information you need when you need it. Concepts are clearly explained and definitions of terminology in the margins ensure that you are never at a loss to understand a term.

This means that you can learn about art in the order that works best for you. You can, of course, read the chapters in the order that they are printed in the book. This will certainly tell you all you need to know to

appreciate art. But you can also choose your own path. For example, in the Introduction we discuss how art can be defined and what it contributes to our lives. This might be a great time to read chapter 2.8, "The Tradition of Craft," which deals with media that artists have used for centuries to create artworks, but which in our Western culture have sometimes been considered less important than "fine art." You could also read the discussion of Japanese art in chapter 3.3, "Art of India, China, and Japan," where you will discover that in Japan an expertly made kimono (an item of traditional clothing), for example, is appreciated as much as a painting or a print that in our culture are usually considered more prestigious. After considering the contrast between human proportion in the art of Ancient Greece and of Africa in chapter 1.7, " Scale and Proportion," you could next read chapter 4.9, "The Body in Art," to understand how some artists have attempted to devise rules to portray the "perfect" body, while others have represented the human body as they see it in daily reality, challenging traditional notions of beauty.

Gateways to Art aims to demonstrate how rewarding it is to look at a great work of art many times and always discover something new because there are many ways of seeing and analyzing an artwork. That is why our book takes its title from a unique new feature, not found in any other art appreciation textbook: what we call the "Gateways to Art." Through eight iconic works of world art (introduced on pp. 16–25), we will invite you to come back to these Gateways and look again to discover something new: about the design characteristics of the work; the materials with which it was made; the historical era and culture that influenced its creation; or how the work expressed something personal (for example the artist's character, gender, or political views). These discussions also sometimes provide a comparison with another work on the same subject, or consider what the artwork tells us about the great mysteries of our existence, such as spirituality or the cycle of life and death. We hope this will encourage you to revisit not only our Gateways, but also other works, and continue to enjoy them for years to come.

Our Gateways to Art boxes are just one of numerous features we provide to help you in your studies. In many chapters you will find Perspectives on Art boxes, in which artists, art historians, critics, and others involved in the world of art explain how diverse people involved in art think and work. Other boxes will, for example, help you to focus in depth on a single artwork, or alternately to compare and contrast artworks that deal with a similar subject or theme.

The Authors

Debra J. DeWitte
has studied art history at the University of Texas Arlington, Southern Methodist University, and the University of Texas at Dallas. She has devised an award-winning online art appreciation course at UT Arlington.

Ralph M. Larmann
has a BFA from the University of Cincinnati and an MFA from James Madison University. He currently teaches at the University of Evansville and is a past President of Foundations in Art: Theory and Education.

M. Kathryn Shields
has a PhD in art history from Virginia Commonwealth University and has taught at the University of Texas Arlington and at Guilford College.

Resources for Instructors

- The authors of *Gateways to Art* have written an Instructors' Manual that is

1 Fifteen media and process videos made by art educators at Bowling Green State University demonstrate how art is made.

2 Twenty videos examine individual artworks in depth or set a work in a broader context.

available in print and digital form. In addition, they have created a test bank that is available in print, on disk with free software, and also as a download from our instructors' website.

- Images from the book are available as Jpegs and PowerPoint slides. Contact your W. W. Norton representative for details.
- The authors have worked with a team of art educators and digital art specialists at the Bowling Green State University to create a range of high-quality media to enrich your teaching:

  50 multimedia animations to demonstrate key elements and principles of art

  15 videos demonstrating how art is made

  20 video presentations that provide a multimedia presentation of key works of world art.

For full details of all instructors' resources go to thamesandhudsonusa.com/college.

Resources for Students

Our student website offers a wide range of review materials designed to improve your understanding and your grades: self-test quizzes; flash cards; chapter summaries; a glossary; multimedia demonstrations of key concepts; and videos that explain how art is made. Other content-rich resources for students include an audio glossary of foreign-language terms and artists' names.

For full details of our student resources go to http://www.wwnorton.com/college/art/gatewaystoart.

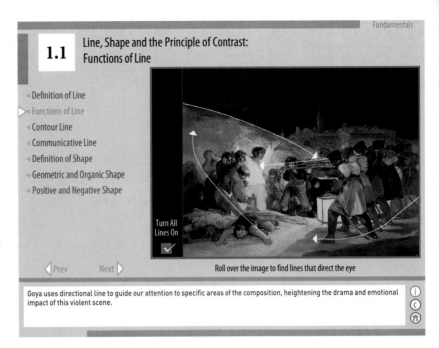

3 Fifty-one Interactive Exercises help students to understand the elements and principles of art.

4 A free and open student website presents an array of review opportunities, using the analytical framework of the text throughout

Department of Art and Design—
Appreciating and Celebrating the Visual Arts

In 2010, 8.5 million people visited the Louvre in Paris to see among other artworks da Vinci's *Mona Lisa*, (Matthews 2011) over 4 million went to the Vatican in Rome to look at Michelangelo's ceiling of the Sistine Chapel (Golden 2010) and 3.09 million visited New York's Museum of Modern Art, with Monet's *Water Lilies* drawing the largest crowd for the year (Orden 2010). Over 850 million people visit American museums each year, making them one of the top three family vacation destinations in the United States (www.speakupformuseum.org/docs/Museum%20Facts.pdf). Whether we acknowledge it or not, it is the visual arts that determine our perception of the world. Every building we enter, every object we look at or hold in our hands, and every printed or painted image we see has a major impact on our daily lives. If art, design and architecture directly add to the quality of our cultural experiences then it is our responsibility as citizens to become knowledgeable in this field of study.

This textbook is a condensed version of *Gateways To Art: Understanding the Visual Arts*. It was customized to better suit the needs of the art appreciation course at Troy University. Offered in the General Studies Program, ART 1133 Visual Arts is a course of study in the fine and applied arts for the non-art major. This course addresses the

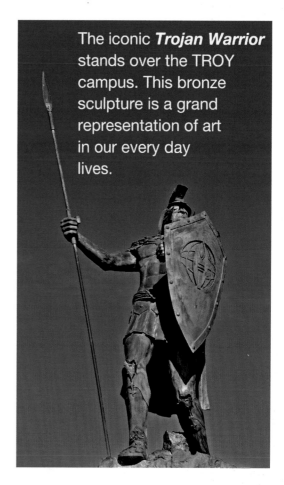

The iconic *Trojan Warrior* stands over the TROY campus. This bronze sculpture is a grand representation of art in our every day lives.

visual arts as it relates to our human needs and aspirations.

The General Studies Program at TROY is designed to provide a fundamental basis for lifelong learning and advanced studies. The desire of the Department of Art and Design is to provide non-art majors with the keys to understanding the visual arts, to challenge

A critical step in the process of visual arts is the actual production. Although creativity is a significant factor that makes art so varied and interesting, quality production is also an important aspect of making art. The *Trojan Warrior* statue that stands on four of the TROY campuses was part of an extended and exhaustive creative process. Shown above are sections of the molds that were used in constructing the larger than life, symbol of TROY, the *Trojan Warrior*.

them to become advocates of the arts or better yet, discover their own "artist" within. There are four concepts that the student should keep in mind while learning about the visual arts:

(1) **Art is organized.**

It is important that students learn something about the fundamentals of art, such as the principles of design and visual elements. Strong art has structure, even if it appears chaotic; there is usually an underlined structure or a constant element that holds it together. For example, Early Renaissance painters developed an underneath structure based on geometry, called the armature. It is the armature that was the basis of their compositions (Bouleau 1963). Understanding how something is made can lead to a better understanding of what the artwork or artist is attempting to say. Learning the process that an artist takes to make art is witnessing creativity at its best and most basic function. A little bit of knowledge will keep one from jumping to conclusions when looking at art and possibly misreading the artists' intentions.

(2) **Art is of its own culture and of its own time.**

Rarely does anything make sense out-of-context. Therefore, it is important to understand where, when and why something was designed, created or made. Look at it this way, everything we do, how we react, is based on our culture, environment and past experiences. This is no different for the artist. To understand the culture or times in which an artist lived and worked is to gain insight into the artist's role in history and the value of their contributions to society. No one sees things the same way but we can learn to empathize: putting one's self into "the artist's" shoes will help the observer see clearer the intent of the work and its importance.

(3) **Art is about People.**

Learn about all the People in the arts—even what role that *you* might play. Some of these identifiable roles are obvious such as the artist, art critic, art historians and art dealers. These people are significant in determining the success of artists and their place in history. But never underestimate the crucial role of average citizens who attend museums, become patrons of the arts and purchase artwork for investment or personal enjoyment. These people are extremely important in the art world for they are the voice of the public

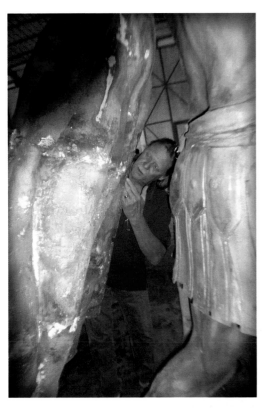

TROY alumnus and sculptor—Larry Strickland—inspects the foundry work being done for his rendition of the *Trojan Warrior*. The casting was done in X'ian, People's Republic of China.

and can make political decisions that determine the fate of the visual arts on all levels—city, state, national and international.

The field of art has become a huge industry with many diverse paths and directions. If you do an Internet search you will discover hundreds of identified jobs, professions and opportunities in art. Artists are no longer stigmatized by the feared lifestyle of the "Starving Artist" or Mencken's cliché, "Those who can – do. Those who can't – teach." Today art majors are looking at highly successful careers in design—graphic, fashion, interior, furniture, automobile to name a few, as well as becoming art directors, museum curators or art coordinators. Societies newfound interest in the arts has spawned fields in art services—creative management, arts management, art therapy, art law, art insurance and many more.

We are all participants in the field of art. Gaining better understanding and appreciation of the visual arts can aid in determining what role we will choose to play.

(4) Art is the pathway to creativity and innovation.

What are our needs as humans? What motivates us to strive to achieve? Abraham Maslow introduced the concept of a hierarchy of needs in a 1943 paper called *A Theory of Human Motivation*. In this paper he suggested that people are motivated to fill basic needs before moving on to other more advanced needs. Maslow offers five levels of motivational need: Physiological, Safety, Love/Belonging, Esteem and Self-actualization. Many believe this is a rather humanistic point of view; maybe true. If you follow the theory of Maslow he places the need for "creativity" in the highest category—Self-actualization (Maslow 1943). In the quest to acquire success or fulfill the highest motivational needs we strive to broaden our search for knowledge in all fields of study as lifelong learners. Whether a scientist, a writer, a mathematician, an entrepreneur or other, one cannot escape the necessity of critical thinking and imagination, which are at the core of art and humanity.

The following books (below) on the subject of creativity have been recommended reading for majors in the College of Communication and Fine Arts as part of the Major Reading Initiative Program at TROY. It is obvious that visual artists are creative people and many of these books are just reaffirming what most art majors already realize about themselves. This selection of books would also be beneficial reading for non-art majors especially anyone wanting to discover how to become more creative, better understand the creative process and/or learn how the business world capitalizes on the innovations of creative thinkers.

- *The Creative Habit, Learn It And Use It For Life* by Twyla Tharp
- *A Whole New Mind, Why Right-brainers Will Rule The World* by Daniel H. Pink
- *Talent is Overrated, What Really Separates World-Class Performers from Everybody Else* by Geoff Colvin
- *Imagine, How Creativity Works* by Jonah Lehrer

ART1133 Visual Arts is just an introduction to the visual arts. If you are interested, TROY offers an array of relevant and timely programs of study in the disciplines of art and design. In the right column of the next page is a list of the available programs.

We wish you great success in this course and hope that as you become more exposed to the arts your life will be enhanced for the better. Please remember in your worldly travels to visit museums, public arts and architectural landmarks throughout the United States and the World. Art can forever change how you see.

Pamela S. Allen, Chairman
TROY Department of Art and Design
www.troy.edu
(334) 670-3391

Troy University is a public university with its main campus located in Troy, Alabama. Website: www.troy.edu

REFERENCES:

Bouleau, Charles, *The Painter's Secret Geometry*, New York: Harcourt, Brace & World, INC, 1963. Book

Golden, Fran, *Tourist Numbers Threaten Vatican's Sistine Chapel*, 2010. Article. http://news.travel.aol.com/2010/09/10/tourist-numbers-threaten-vatican-s-sistine-chapel/

Maslow, A. H., *A Theory of Human Motivation, Psychological Review*, 50. 370-396. 1943 Article

Matthews, Lyndsey, *World's Most Visited Museums*, 2011. Article. www.travelandleisure.com/articles/worlds-most-visited-museums

Orden, Erica, MoMa Attendance Hits Record High, 2010. Article. www.online.wsj.com/article/SB10001424052748703964104575335301840480246.html

www.speakupformuseums.org/docs/Museum%20Facts.pdf

ART/DESIGN PROGRAMS
AT TROY UNIVERSITY:

Bachelor of Science:
- 2D Studio Art
- 3D Studio Art
- Photo Studio Art
- <<dti>> (graphic design

Bachelor of Fine Arts (professional degree):
- 2D Studio Art
- 3D Studio Art
- Photo Studio Art
- Digital Studio Art

Bachelor of Science in Education:
- Art Education (P–12)

Master of Education:
- Art Specialization

. . . .

*<<dti>> (Design, Technolo and Innovation) is an innov tive graphic design progra unique to TROY. <<dti>> s dents are required to hybri their design studies with a other discipline such as ma communication, intercultur communication, multimedia design, music industry, technical theatre, informati systems, advertising, forei languages, or select from many other options. Progra of study can be customize address the students' care interests while still meeting accreditation standards.

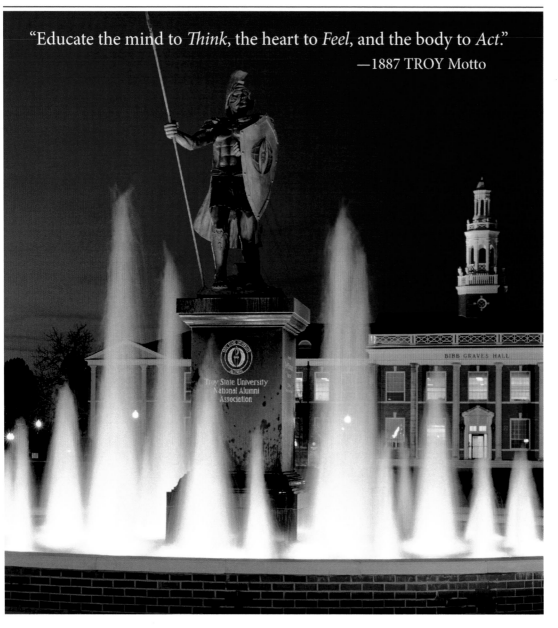

"Educate the mind to *Think*, the heart to *Feel*, and the body to *Act*."
—1887 TROY Motto

Introduction

What Is Art?

The Japanese artist Katsushika Hokusai (1760–1849) is said to have created a painting, titled *Maple Leaves on a River*, by dipping the feet of a chicken in red paint and letting the bird run freely on a sheet of paper he had just covered in blue paint. Although we know that Hokusai

was an unconventional character, we cannot be certain that the story is true, because *Maple Leaves on a River* no longer exists. If we think about this curious story for a while, however, we can begin to understand the most basic question addressed in this book: What is art? This question is not an easy one to answer, because people define art in many individual ways. In Hokusai's case, he wanted to make viewers of his work feel the peaceful sensations of a fall day by a river, without actually showing them what a real river and real leaves look like. In this instance, art communicated a sensation to its audience.

In nineteenth-century Japan, art could be a means to encourage the quiet contemplation of nature, but to an Egyptian artist almost 3,000 years earlier, art would have meant something very different. The Egyptian who in the tenth century BCE decorated the wooden coffin of Nespawershefi with a painting of the Sun god Re had a quite different idea of rivers in mind from the one Hokusai conceived. For ancient Egyptians, rivers were important for survival. The Egyptians depended on the flooding of the River Nile to grow their crops. Rivers also had religious significance. Egyptians believed that during the daytime Re sailed across a great celestial ocean in his day boat. By night, the Sun god traveled in his evening boat along a river in

0.1 *The Journey of the Sun God Re*, detail from the inner coffin of Nespawershefi, Third Intermediate Period, 990–969 BCE. Plastered and painted wood. Fitzwilliam Museum, Cambridge, England

0.2 William G. Wall, *Fort Edward*, from *The Hudson River Portfolio*, 1820. Hand-colored aquatint, 14½ × 21⅜"

Medium: the material on or from which an artist chooses to make a work of art
Print: a picture reproduced on paper, often in multiple copies

the underworld, but before he could rise again he had to defeat his enemy, the serpent Apophis, which in **0.1** can be seen swimming in the river. Here the river is again suggested rather than being realistically portrayed. It is a place of danger, not of contemplation, and if Re does not emerge victorious, the world will be deprived of the life-giving light of the Sun. Re, who in the image is seated, is protected by another god carrying a spear. He travels with several attendants, including a baboon. The choice of this subject was appropriate for a coffin: no doubt Nespawershefi hoped to emerge from the underworld to live a happy afterlife, just as Re rose again every morning. For the painter of this coffin, art was a way to express profound religious ideas and to invoke beliefs in a happy life after death.

Both of the works we have examined so far are paintings, even though they were painted on different materials for different purposes. If we consider another **medium**, a **print**, we can see how another artist from a different era and

continent could depict a river in yet another way. For William Wall (1792–1864), working in the United States in the early nineteenth century, rivers and the landscape of which they formed part were a vehicle for expressing nationalistic sentiment and a way of celebrating the expansion and development of America. Wall published the first book that made Americans aware of the sublime beauty of their own scenery. The work shown here is *Fort Edward* (**0.2**). Wall produced an attractive scene, but this was not all he wanted to communicate to his audience. His print recalls the struggles of empire- and nation-building that took place on this site. As the artist noted: "The ploughshare now peacefully turns up the soil moistened by the blood of thousands: the dust of the merciless Indian and the ambitious European repose in awful amity together." As if to remind us that the time of the Indian has been replaced by new ways of life, a lone Indian woman passes in front of prosperous European farmsteads. Although

Wall painted an original **watercolor** of this scene, the print was made by another artist, John Hill.

Finally, before we try to come to some conclusions about the definition of art, consider a work by Louise Nevelson (1899–1988) that also features a river, or, more precisely, a waterfall (**0.3**). Nevelson constructed twenty-five painted rectangular and square wooden sections inside an overall rectangular frame, measuring 18 × 9 ft. Inside some of the rectangles we can see undulating curved forms that suggest a cascading waterfall or the froth of white water. Other forms in the upper right of the square resemble squirming fish. Clearly, Nevelson's purpose in this artwork is not to show to us an instantly recognizable likeness of a waterfall full of fish. Instead we are invited to examine closely her carefully constructed work and to feel the sensations of watching water cascade and fish swimming.

If we go back to our original question, what is art?, can our consideration of these four very different works help us to find a quick and simple definition that will tell us whether we are looking at something called art? These four works certainly do not have much in common in terms of their appearance. The definition also cannot include a common range of materials (in fact, art can be made from almost anything). We cannot define art in terms of the kind of choices an artist makes: very few artworks involve a live chicken, but Hokusai used one to make his painting. Nor do these works have a common purpose. The Egyptian coffin painting has a clear religious message. Wall's print portrays a beautiful landscape but also carries a powerful message of nationalism and colonial conquest. Hokusai's painting used very simple means to convey restful sensations. Nevelson's work also focuses on communicating the sensations of being by a river, but in her case with a meticulously constructed geometric suggestion of one.

Perhaps the works do have some things in common, however. We can see that artworks

0.3 Louise Nevelson, *White Vertical Water*, 1972. Painted wood, 18 × 9′. Solomon R. Guggenheim Museum, New York communicate ideas and emotions (religious feelings or the sensation of watching beautiful fall foliage, for example). The communication of ideas by visual means can help us see the world in new and exciting ways and strengthen our understanding. In other words, art is a form of language. In our contemporary world, some people hold the opinion that art has no boundaries, and that anything can be a work of art. In this book we will examine about 750 artworks made over thousands of years and in all parts of the world, but there will still be many kinds of art that we will not have space to include. The language of art is a living entity that is constantly evolving and changing. Perhaps the most important qualities an artwork can possess are the ability to move the spectator; to convey a message; or to inspire thoughts a person would not otherwise have had.

Where Is Art?

Although so far we have examined only four works of art, you have probably already figured out that there is no single place in which we can find art. We can discover it in a coffin, a book, or a museum. In the modern world we go to museums and art galleries—institutions established specifically to display and care for artworks. If we visit a major museum, such as the Metropolitan Museum of Art in New York or the British Museum in London, we will see that visitors have come from just about every country in the world. But if we consider only works that are displayed in museums and galleries, we will ignore many works that are certainly art. In fact, a great deal of art exists outside such institutions.

You almost certainly have some art in your home: perhaps a painting in the living room, a poster in your bedroom, or a beautifully made flower vase. In parks or other public spaces in most cities there are sculptures and memorials. From 1921 to 1954 Simon Rodia built seventeen interconnected structures on a residential lot in a neighborhood of Los Angeles (**0.4**). Rodia's work is now known as the Watts Towers, although he named it *Nuestro Pueblo* (Spanish for "our

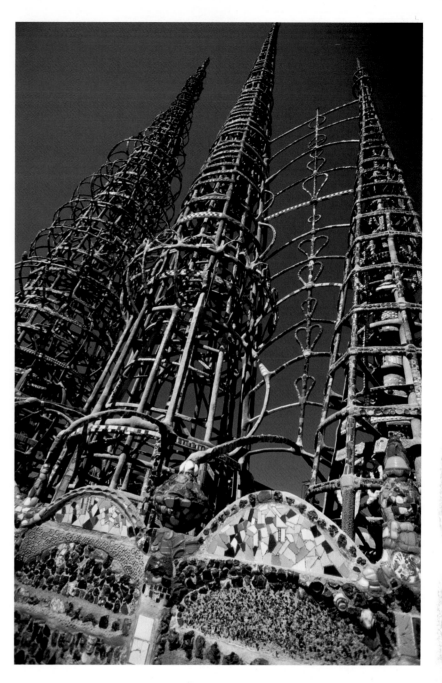

town"). Rodia, a construction worker, made his structures out of materials he found or that local people brought to him. The towers are made of steel rods and pipes, wire mesh, and mortar, and decorated with bits of broken glass and pottery. Rodia's neighbors and the City of Los Angeles did not approve of his work, and efforts were made to destroy it, but in 1990 it was named a National Historic Landmark.

In most American cities there are civic buildings (such as the courthouse or the Capitol) that were designed to impress and to communicate something about the strength of

0.4 Simon Rodia, Watts Towers, 1921–54. Seventeen mortar-covered steel sculptures with mosaic, 99½' high at tallest point. 1761–1765 East 107th Street, Los Angeles, California

Watercolor: transparent paint made from pigment and a binder dissolved in water

0.5 Thomas Jefferson, Virginia State Capitol Building, 1785–8, Court End District, Richmond, Virginia

the Republic and its institutions. The Virginia State Capitol (**0.5**), designed by Thomas Jefferson, was modeled closely on a famous ancient Roman temple in Nîmes, France, built 1,800 years before Jefferson's building. It thereby drew on the symbolic power of ancient Rome.

Who Makes Art?

Who decides what an artwork looks like? The simple answer might seem to be the artist who makes it. We know that art has been made for thousands of years: at least since humans first painted images on the walls of caves, and probably long before then. Much artwork made in the past has not survived, however, so we do not know what it looked like. Even when art did survive, we often have no idea who made it.

The great temples of ancient Egypt, Greece, and Rome were certainly not the work of one person, and in some cases, we cannot tell if their overall design was the idea of a single individual. Archaeologists have discovered in the Valley of the Kings in Egypt an entire village, Deir el-Medina, which was occupied by artisans who made the great monuments that we admire today. The cathedrals of **medieval** Europe were the result of the skills of many different artists and artisans: stone carvers, the makers of stained-glass windows, and carpenters who made the furniture. These skilled workers remain mostly anonymous, except for a very few whose names have been found in manuscripts or carved on works of art—for example, the sculptor Gislebertus carved his name on sculptures that adorn the cathedral of Autun, France. But though we may never identify most of these early artists, it is clear that humans have always wanted to make art. This urge is part of our nature, just like our need to eat and sleep.

In the nineteenth and twentieth centuries in the Western world, the popular idea of the artist was of a lone individual creating his or her own work to express something very personal. In these centuries it became more common for artists to create their own work, and, in their search for new forms of self-expression, to make art that was often very controversial. But for many centuries before this, very few artists worked alone. **Renaissance** artists created workshops staffed by artist assistants who carried out most of the work involved in turning their master's design into a work of art. In nineteenth-century Japan, the eccentric Hokusai was famous around the world for his prints, but he could not have made them alone. A wood carver cut his designs into blocks from which a printer manufactured copies. Even today, some famous artists, such as Jeff Koons, employ other artists to realize their ideas (**0.6**).

In other words, there is no simple definition to enable us to tell who is an artist and who is

0.6 Jeff Koons, *Rabbit*, 1986. Stainless steel, 41 × 19 × 12". Edition of 3 and artist's proof

Medieval: relating to the Middle Ages; roughly, between the fall of the Roman Empire and the Renaissance
Renaissance: a period of cultural and artistic change in Europe from the fourteenth to the seventeenth century

not. If we take a global view, we certainly cannot define an artist by what he or she made. In Western culture during some eras of history, particularly since the Renaissance, painting and sculpture have been considered to be the most important categories of art ("high art"), while others, such as ceramics and furniture, have been considered less important. The term craft was usually applied to such works, and their makers were considered less skilled or of lower status than painters and sculptors. This distinction arose partly because the cost of producing a fine painting or a beautifully carved marble statue was high. Therefore, those became status symbols of the rich and powerful. In other cultures the relative importance of different forms of art was quite different. The people of ancient Peru seem to have placed special value on wool, and those who made fine woolen textiles were likely considered as skillful as a painter would be in our society. In China the art of **calligraphy** (elegantly painted lettering) was considered one of the highest forms of art. A Chinese encyclopedia of 624 CE included calligraphy and painting in "Skills and arts," alongside, for example, archery and chess.

For centuries, in Japan, such **ceramic** objects as tea bowls have been highly esteemed for their beauty. The bowl seen in **0.7** would have been prized for its subtle variations of color, the pleasant tactile sensations of its slightly irregular surface, and its shape. It was designed to be appreciated slowly as the user sipped tea. The artist who made this bowl worked at roughly the same time as the Italian Renaissance artist Leonardo da Vinci (1452–1519), but the two had different ideas of what it meant to be an artist. The Japanese maker of the tea bowl worked in a society that valued tradition. Japanese artists followed with supreme skill the established methods of working and making. Leonardo, however, became famous in an era in Europe that valued individual ingenuity. He was a supremely talented artist whose visionary interests and inventions extended far beyond the visual arts, to engineering and science. Between 1500 and 1503 he created a portrait that is probably the most famous painting in the world. Leonardo was not content to create a likeness of the subject (Lisa Gherardini, wife of a silk merchant in Florence). The *Mona Lisa* smiles and looks out at the viewer, inviting us to seek in her face, her pose, and the surrounding landscape a meditation on the human soul (**0.8**). Both the tea cup and the portrait are great works of art, but they display very different ideas of what it means to be an artist.

We must also consider that artworks are not only the result of the work of those who made them, but are also influenced by the input of others: the **patrons** who employ an artist

0.7 Tea bowl, 16th century. Stoneware with red glaze (Karatsu ware), 3 × 19⅞". Indianapolis Museum of Art

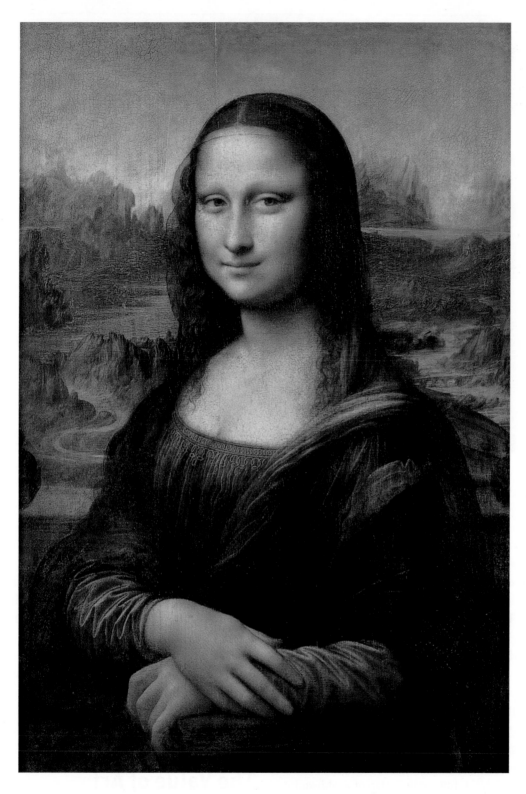

0.8 Leonardo da Vinci, *Mona Lisa*, 1503. Oil on wood, 30⅜ × 20⅞". Musée du Louvre, Paris, France

to make a work; the collectors who buy it; and the dealers and gallery owners who sell it. In contemporary times, both the publicist who presents artworks and the critic who reviews them in a newspaper, on TV, or on the Internet help to make an artist's work well known and desirable. All of these people, not just the artist, help to determine what art we see, and to some extent they can influence what we consider to be art. By controlling access to those who buy art, the places where art is displayed, and the media that inform the public about art and artists, they also often influence what kind of art an artist actually produces.

0.9 Titian, *Isabella d'Este*, 1536. Oil on canvas, 40¼ × 25¼". Kunsthistorisches Museum, Vienna, Austria

One individual who greatly impacted the production and presentation of art was Isabella d'Este (1474–1539), Marchesa of the city of Mantua, Italy, and the wife of the ruler of the city, which she governed in her husband's absence. As an influential patron of the arts, Isabella funded a variety of artists to create luxurious objects for her collections, including such things as gems, musical instruments, **manuscripts**, and ceramics. Her money and tastes therefore played an important part in determining what art was produced in Mantua. Titian's (1485–1576) portrait of the Marchesa presents her as a formidable woman who enjoys the finer things in life (**0.9**). This elegant woman wears a turban she designed, fine embroidered clothes, and a white ermine stole (a sign of wealth and refinement) over her shoulder. Although the Marchesa was in her sixties when she commissioned this painting, Titian portrays her as a youthful beauty.

Fame and success do not always come in an artist's lifetime. Perhaps the most famous example of this is the Dutch painter Vincent van Gogh (1853–1890). In his ten years as an active artist, Van Gogh produced about 1,000 drawings, sketches and watercolors, as well as around 1,250 other paintings. Very few people saw his work in his lifetime, however; he received only one favorable notice in a newspaper; his work was shown in only one exhibition; and he sold only one painting. Yet today his work is extraordinarily famous, it sells for millions of dollars, and in his native Netherlands an entire museum is devoted to his work.

The training of artists also helps to determine who makes art and what art is shown in galleries and museums. For example, traditional training for painters in China focused on the passing of artistic skill from a master to his students, who learned by copying his works and those of other famous artists. Only scholars and government officials could become professional painters. Other painters were considered to be just craftspeople whose work was of lower status. In medieval Europe, only those trained in associations of craftsmen called **guilds** were allowed to make works of art. For example, there were guilds of carpenters, glassmakers, and goldsmiths. The system in Europe changed in the sixteenth century. Schools called **Academies** were organized (first in Italy) to train artists in a very strict curriculum devised by specialized teachers. It was very difficult to succeed as an artist without being trained in an Academy. In modern Europe and North America, most practicing artists are trained in art schools, which are sometimes independent schools, but often part of a university or college that teaches many different subjects. It is possible, but more difficult, for artists who have not been formally trained in this way to succeed in having their work displayed and sold.

The Value of Art

On November 8, 2006 a sale at Christie's auction house in New York City broke records by selling 491 million dollars' worth of artworks. The most expensive item for sale that evening was a portrait of Adele Bloch-Bauer II (**0.10**), painted in 1912 by the Austrian artist Gustav Klimt (1862–

1918). It sold for $135 million. Klimt made a comfortable living from painting portraits of the wives and sisters of wealthy Austrian businessmen, but in his own lifetime he was certainly never paid anything like the enormous sum for which his portrait of Mrs Bloch-Bauer sold in 2006. One reason for the painting's increase in price was its controversial history. In 1938 it had been looted by the Nazis, who had occupied Austria, and the work later became the subject of a lawsuit by the heirs of the Bloch-Bauer family.

0.10 Gustav Klimt, *Adele Bloch-Bauer*, 1912. Oil on canvas, 6'2⁷⁄₈" × 3'11¼". Private collection

Manuscripts: handwritten texts
Guilds: medieval associations of artists, craftsmen, or tradesmen
Academies: institutions training artists in both the theory of art and practical techniques

Perspectives on Art: Robert Wittman
What Is the Value of an Artwork?

A work of art will usually attract a high price if works by the artist who made it are rarely available for sale. Some artists' works are so rare that thieves will go to great trouble to steal them. Special Agent Robert Wittman is a former FBI investigative expert for stolen artworks. Here he explains how criminals valued a self-portrait by Dutch artist Rembrandt van Rijn (1606–69).

Value can be defined as the price that a willing buyer will pay to a willing seller. But that value changes as a result of the circumstances surrounding an artwork. One needs only to look at auction records to determine the value of a painting. These prices are records of what a willing buyer paid to a willing seller to obtain a work of art that had a good **provenance** and title that could be transferred on the market.

These are the legitimate prices in the art world, but there are other prices that have no basis in legitimacy. These others are the prices that are paid when an artwork is stolen and sold on the black market. Even criminals need a basis to place a value on their ill-gotten gains and that is usually about ten percent of the legitimate market value of the stolen artwork; but even that sum is usually not paid.

For example, in December 2000 a Rembrandt self-portrait (**0.11**) was stolen from the Swedish National Museum in Stockholm. Three men entered the museum wielding machine guns. After placing the guards, visitors, and guides on the floor, two of the men raced around the museum and stole three paintings: two by Auguste Renoir, and the Rembrandt. The *Self-portrait* was painted in 1630 and is very rare: it is the only known portrait by the Dutch master painted on copper. Its market value is $35 million. The men had set two car bombs off in the city to snarl traffic and prevent the police from responding. They made their escape in a motorboat moored to a pier near the entrance of the museum.

It was not until nearly five years later, in September 2005, that the Rembrandt self-portrait was recovered in a multi-national police undercover operation in Copenhagen, Denmark. The thieves attempted to sell it to me when I posed as an art expert working for the Mafia. The price was $250,000, or less than one percent of the market value of the artwork. Stolen art has no real value: the lack of good title, improper provenance, and inability of a buyer to sell the painting in the future all decrease the value of an artwork. As most thieves eventually learn, the true art in an art theft is in the selling, not the stealing.

0.11 Rembrandt van Rijn, *Self-portrait*, 1630. Oil on copper, 6⅛ × 4¾". Nationalmuseum, Stockholm, Sweden

When we read that some works of art sell for large amounts of money while others do not, we quite reasonably ask ourselves why such a high financial value is placed on a single work. Works of art by famous artists of the past tend to be valued at a high price, especially if they are very rarely available.

In our modern society art is often valued by its sale price, but there are many other ways of valuing it. When we visit art museums and see artworks displayed inside glass cases or at a distance from the viewer who must not touch, the care to preserve them in perfect condition is an indication that these works are highly valued. Sometimes a work is valued because it is very old or rare, or indeed unique.

In many societies, however, artworks were not made to be sold or displayed where they cannot be touched. As we have seen, the Japanese made fine tea bowls. These bowls were to be used as part of a ceremony, involving other fine objects, good conversation, and, of course, excellent tea. The tea bowl was valued because it formed part of a ritual that had social and spiritual significance. Similarly, in the African art section of many museums we can see masks displayed that were originally made to form part of a costume that, in turn, was used in a ceremony involving other costumed figures, music, and dancing. In other words, the mask often had some kind of spiritual or magic significance for its original creators: but they would have regarded it as holding this value only when used as intended, not when displayed in isolation in a museum.

So we see that price is, of course, not the only measure of the value of an artwork. We might place a high value on a work because it is aesthetically pleasing or because its creation involved great skill. This can be true even if there is no possibility of our owning it. Many museums organize large exhibitions of the work of famous artists because they know that great numbers of people will pay to see the work. Enthusiasts will travel long distances, even to other continents, to visit such exhibitions. In 2007, for example, 796,000 people visited an exhibition of the work of Leonardo da Vinci at the Tokyo National Museum, Japan.

Artworks can also acquire great religious, cultural, or political significance. For example, the Lincoln Memorial in Washington, D.C., was dedicated in 1922 to honor a president who had become a symbol of American values and identity. The memorial was the work of three artists. Architect Henry Bacon (1866–1924) designed in the form of an ancient Greek temple the building that houses Lincoln's statue (**0.12**). Daniel Chester French (1850–1931) made the over-life-sized statue of Lincoln, while Jules Guerin (1866–1946) painted the **murals** (*Reunion* and *Emancipation*) on the interior walls.

Provenance: the record of all known previous owners and locations of a work of art
Mural: a painting executed directly on to a wall

0.12 The Lincoln Memorial statue by Daniel Chester French, 1920. Marble, 19' high. The Mall, Washington, D.C.

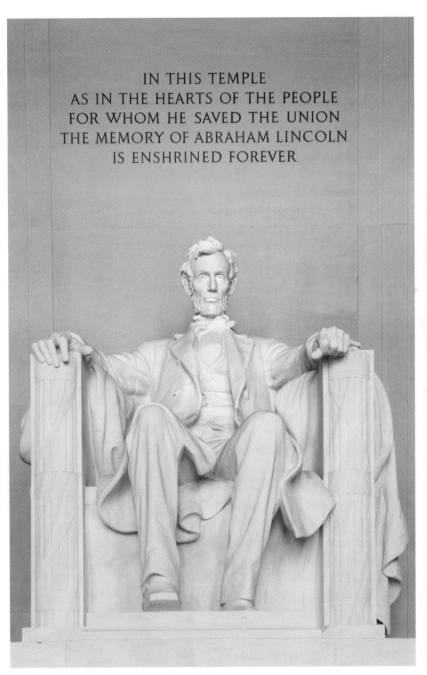

IN THIS TEMPLE
AS IN THE HEARTS OF THE PEOPLE
FOR WHOM HE SAVED THE UNION
THE MEMORY OF ABRAHAM LINCOLN
IS ENSHRINED FOREVER

Perspectives on Art: Tracy Chevalier
Art Inspires a Novel and a Movie

Art can have value as a source of inspiration. Tracy Chevalier is the author of the bestselling novel Girl with a Pearl Earring *(1999), which in turn inspired a movie (2003) starring Scarlett Johansson and Colin Firth. Tracy tells how her novel was inspired by a poster of the famous painting by the Dutch painter Johannes Vermeer.*

I first saw the painting *Girl with a Pearl Earring* (0.13) when I was nineteen and visiting my sister in Boston for spring break. She'd hung a poster of it in her apartment. I was so struck by it—the color! the light! the girl's look!—that the next day I bought a poster of it myself. That same poster has accompanied me for twenty-nine years, hanging in my bedroom or— as it does now—in my study.

Over the years I've hung many other paintings on my walls. But most art, even great art, loses its punch after a while. It becomes part of the space designated for it; it becomes decorative rather than challenging. It turns into wallpaper. Occasionally someone will ask a question about one of the paintings in my house, or I'll notice one's crooked and straighten it, and I'll look at it again and think, "Oh yeah, nice painting. I forgot about you."

Girl with a Pearl Earring is not like that. She has never become wallpaper. I have never grown tired or bored of her. I notice her all the time, even after twenty-nine years. Indeed, you'd think I'd have nothing left to say about the painting. But even after writing a whole novel about her, I still can't answer the most basic question about the girl: Is she happy or sad?

That is the painting's power. *Girl with a Pearl Earring* is unresolved, like a piece of music that stops on the penultimate chord. Vermeer draws us in with his technique—his remarkable handling of light and color—but he holds us with her. He has somehow managed the impossible, capturing a flickering moment in a permanent medium. You would think that, with the paint static, the girl would be too. But no, her mood is always changing, for we ourselves are different each time we look at her. She reflects us, and life, in all its variations. Few paintings do that so well, which is why *Girl with a Pearl Earring* is a rare masterpiece.

0.13 Johannes Vermeer, *Girl with a Pearl Earring, c.* 1665. Oil on canvas, 17½ × 15⅜". Mauritshuis, The Hague, Netherlands

0.14 Marc Quinn, *Self*, 1991. Blood (artist's), stainless steel, perspex, and refrigeration equipment, 81⅞ × 24¾ × 24¾". Private collection

Censorship of Art

Art can be a form of expression and communication so powerful that those who are challenged or offended by it wish to censor it. If we examine the history of the censorship of art, we find many reasons for attacking, destroying, or preventing the display of artworks. Art may be censored because some consider it pornographic; because it offends religious beliefs; because of objections to the political message of a work; or because it represents values that somebody considers offensive or improper. For example, in 1999 the Brooklyn Museum held an exhibition of contemporary British art titled

Sensation. The mayor of New York, Rudolph Giuliani, objected to a painting by Chris Ofili, *The Holy Virgin Mary.* When the museum refused to remove the work from public display, the mayor attempted to evict the Brooklyn Museum from the building it had occupied for 106 years and to withhold city funding. He then objected that the exhibition included many works that offended religious sensibilities, were sexual in nature, or were in some other way offensive. One, titled *Self,* was a self-portrait by Marc Quinn made from nine pints of his frozen blood (**0.14**). The city argued that the museum had violated the terms of its lease by holding an exhibition that was not appropriate for the citizens of New York, and in particular young people. A federal court protected the museum's right to hold the exhibition and prevented the city from evicting it or from withdrawing funding.

In Germany in the 1930s, the Nazi regime of dictator Adolf Hitler launched a systematic and large-scale attack on modern art that did not conform to Nazi party goals. The Nazis initially confiscated around 5,000 works of art from museums; they subsequently took a further 16,500 from private collections. Some 4,000 of these were then burned, while others became the property of Nazi collectors, or were sold to foreign collectors for Nazi profit. The artists who had made them were banned from working. The Nazis also dismissed museum directors, closed art schools, such as the famous **Bauhaus**, and burned books. On July 19, 1937 the Nazis opened an exhibition of "Great German Art." The next day they opened a display of 730 works labeled "Degenerate Art" to suggest that these were the work of mentally deficient artists. Works were deliberately displayed awkwardly and labels on the walls ridiculed the artworks. One read: "We act as if we were painters, poets, or whatever, but what we are is simply and ecstatically impudent. In our impudence we take the world for a ride and train snobs to lick our boots!"

One of the artists whose work was ridiculed in the exhibition was Otto Dix (1891–1969). Dix had been a machine-gunner in the German army during World War I from 1914 to 1918. He made many sketches of war scenes, and the experience of war became the main subject of his work until the 1930s. The Nazis dismissed him from his teaching position at the Prussian Art Academy in 1933. They then confiscated his paintings from museums and banned him from exhibiting his work because his paintings were "likely to adversely affect the military will of the German people." Dix's drawing *War Cripples* (**0.15**) was one of the works that was included in the Degenerate Art Exhibition. Dix was then forced to join the government's Chamber of Fine Arts and to promise to paint only landscapes. He was drafted into the German army in 1945 and taken prisoner by the French.

0.15 Otto Dix, *Kriegeskrueppel (War Cripples)*, 1920. Drypoint, 12¾ × 19½" (sheet size). MOMA, New York

Thus the Degenerate Art Exhibition not only affected the lives of artists, but also restricted what art Germans were allowed to see and how they would view it. Ironically, however, Hitler's attempt to censor art backfired: five times as many visitors attended the Degenerate Art Exhibition as the show of Great German Art. Very few records survive to reveal what viewers really thought of the art in this propaganda spectacle.

Why Do We Study Art?

Finally, why take a course that teaches you how to look at art? Surely we all have eyes and we all see the same thing when we look at a work of art, so we can decide what we like or dislike about it. In fact, it is not quite that simple. Our interpretations of works of art may differ from other people's according to our perceptions, beliefs and ideas. Art is also a form of language; one that can communicate with us even more powerfully than written language. Art

communicates so directly with our senses (of sight, touch, even smell and sound) that it helps us to understand our own experiences. By learning to see, we experience new sensations and ideas that expand our horizons beyond our daily lives.

Let us consider an artwork and the fact that we may not see the work the way it was seen when it was first made. *Prisoners from the Front* (**0.16**) by American artist Winslow Homer was painted in 1866. We can tell immediately that the subject is war and that it involves men from two armies. But there are many ways in which we can discover and learn more from this painting: how *really* to look at it. We can begin by examining the way Homer organizes different aspects of the painting to direct our eyes and to communicate with us. How has he placed the figures in the painting and what first attracts our attention? Perhaps we look first at the group of soldiers dressed in gray (especially the one standing in the center of the work)—but does the gaze of this group then direct us to the officer standing alone on the right? What colors did Homer

Bauhaus: design school founded in Weimar, Germany, in 1919

0.16 Winslow Homer, *Prisoners from the Front*, 1866. Oil on canvas, 24 × 38". Metropolitan Museum of Art, New York choose, why, and what impact do they have? What medium did the artist select? In this case, Homer chose **neutral tones** of **oil paint**, which has the advantage that it dries very slowly and allows the artist to make alterations almost without limit. Scientific studies have shown that Homer made many changes to his work. Is the date of the painting (1866) significant? This was one year after the end of the Civil War. Homer had witnessed and recorded the war personally. This painting was made during the period of Reconstruction, when the victorious Union troops forced changes on the slave-owning South, represented here by Confederate soldiers in gray uniforms. The officer standing to the right is Homer's distant cousin: once we know this, it causes us to ask whether all these men are real historical figures. In other words, Homer was not simply showing his audience a dramatic scene, but was also commenting on the important issues that arose after the end of the war. Finally, what is the painting about in a more general sense? It is a painting about war and history, but also about social concerns, and the artist's desire for reconciliation after a devastating conflict. If we study other paintings that address these themes, we will see that some aspects of the way Homer depicted this event are

0.17 Eugène Delacroix, *The Massacre at Chios*, 1824. Oil on canvas, 13'8" × 11'7⅜". Musée du Louvre, Paris, France

similar to paintings by other artists. If we compare such works with *Prisoners from the Front* we might learn more about portrayals of history and war in general and about Homer's works in particular.

A very contrasting view of war and the treatment of prisoners is found in a painting by Eugène Delacroix (1798–1863) (**0.17**). The island of Chios was ruled by the Ottomans of Turkey, but for centuries the majority of the population had been Greek. In 1822 Greeks from a nearby island attacked the Turks on Chios and destroyed mosques. The Turks responded by killing thousands of Greek residents of Chios. Delacroix portrays the victims as helpless: most are women and are partially nude, which emphasizes their helplessness. As in Homer's painting, a victorious soldier is seen to the right, but in Delacroix's painting he shows no pity, cutting down a woman with his curved sword. He and the faceless Turkish soldier behind the Greek civilians wear exotic turbans, as if to make them even more fearsome to Delacroix's European audience.

0.18 Carved ivory mask-shaped hip pendant, mid-16th century. Ivory inlaid with iron and bronze, 9⅝ × 5 × 2⅜". British Museum, London, England

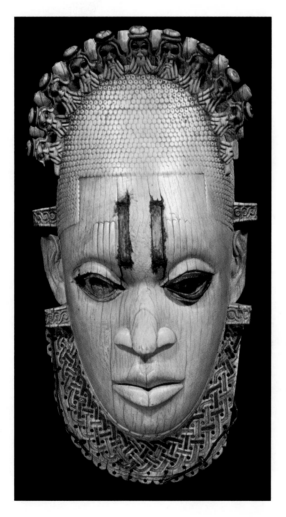

Thus, if we know what questions to ask about a work of art, we can learn more about it than we probably expected when we first saw it. What happens if a work is several centuries old and comes from a completely different culture? The head of an African woman shown here (**0.18**) was made in the mid-sixteenth century and comes from Benin in West Africa. The artist has made the woman's face a perfect and pleasing oval shape. Everything in the figure, from the faces on the woman's headdress to the eyes that look down and the shape of the nose and mouth, seems to direct our eyes downward. The effect is to concentrate on the beauty of the woman's features. The artist chose as materials **ivory**, iron, and bronze, rare items in Benin, so presumably the head was made for someone wealthy. Although we now see this work in a glass case in a museum, this was not how it was used in Benin. Research into its history tells us that this was a decoration worn on the belt of a king. Therefore, it formed part of the presumably impressive finery of the king: the artist did not design it to be seen alone in a glass case. We know that the king maintained groups of specialist artists (including ivory-carvers) and paid them in food, slaves, and wives. Anybody who made ivory objects without the king's permission was severely punished. Therefore, we can tell that this was an object of great luxury intended to show the wealth and power of a ruler. Finally, the head also tells us something about the history of Africa and the religion of Benin. Those odd-looking heads around the top of the headdress represent the faces of men from Portugal, which was then a powerful European trading nation that had conquered some parts of Africa. The Portuguese were important in Benin because they had worked with the king, whose power had grown as a result. Alternating with the Portuguese heads are mudfish that had sacred significance, and were symbolically connected to the god of the sea, Olukun. This pendant from Benin means much more to us if we take the time and effort to understand and analyze it.

Similarly, if we learn how to look at art, we will discover how exciting it can be. This book aims to help you not just to get a good grade in your course, but also to begin a lifetime of enjoying and being inspired by art.

FUN

Art is a form of visual language, and much as we use vocabulary and grammar to communicate verbally, artists use a visual vocabulary (the elements of art) and rules similar to grammar (the principles of art.) When we study an artwork, we can use the same elements and principles to analyze the work: a process called visual analysis. In this part you will learn about the elements and principles and will be shown how to apply them in a visual analysis. You will also learn how to use two other concepts when you analyze a work of art: style and content.

PART 1

DAMENTALS

The ten elements of art are:	The ten principles of art are:
Color	Balance
Form	Contrast
Line	Emphasis
Mass	Focal Point
Shape	Pattern
Space	Proportion
Texture	Rhythm
Time and Motion	Scale
Value	Unity
Volume	Variety

1.1

Art in Two Dimensions: Line, Shape, and the Principle of Contrast

Just as we use the principles of grammar to turn vocabulary into sentences, so the language of art consists of **elements** (the basic vocabulary of art) and **principles** (the "grammar" that artists apply to turn the elements into art). The principles of design are a set of rules that explain how the elements of a work of art are organized.

Two-dimensional art is a remarkably elegant way to express ideas and share our mental pictures of the world. A two-dimensional object, such as a drawing of a triangle, is flat. It has height and width, but not depth. It can be made very simply, for example with a pencil on paper. The first plans for the grandest of designs can be drawn up on a cocktail napkin with a few squiggles of a pen. As well as drawing and painting, two-dimensional arts include the graphic arts: printmaking, graphic design, and photography.

In this chapter we will look at **line** and **shape**, basic elements of any kind of two-dimensional artwork. We will then see how to apply them to the understanding of works of art by using the principle of **contrast**.

Line

Lines are the most fundamental element artists use. They are there in almost every work of art or design. Lines organize the visible world. Without line, an artist hardly knows where to begin.

The ancient designs known as the Nazca Lines, located on the high desert plains of Peru,

include some of perhaps the most unusual drawings in the world. They can show us much about line and shape.

In the spider "drawing," lines define the shape onto the landscape at such an enormous scale that it can only be seen from the sky (**1.1**). (In fact, the Nazca Lines were first discovered in modern times by overflying commercial aircraft.) Unlike most drawings, the Nazca Lines cannot be rolled up in a tube or carried off in a portfolio. First of all, they are too huge: the spider shown here is 150 feet long; side by side, two such spiders would nearly fill up a football field. Second, they are hardly "drawings" at all. Instead, they were made by scraping off the layer of dark gravel that covers the flat Nazca plain, to expose the white gypsum that lies just beneath the surface. In this sense, they are a sort of incision or engraving.

The lines are mysterious. Why would such huge designs, so huge they can hardly be understood at ground level, be made? What was their purpose? The designs resemble symbolic decorations found on local pottery made at least 1,300 years ago. We do not know what they were used for, but their size suggests they played an important part in the lives of the people who made them. How were they made? There are postholes found at intervals along their edges—perhaps strings from post to post formed guidelines for the scraping of the pathway. Notably, the Nazca Lines do not cross over themselves—in the photo, the parallel tracks intersecting with the spider were made

Elements: the basic vocabulary of art—line, form, shape, volume, mass, color, texture, space, time and motion, and value (lightness/darkness)
Principles: the "grammar" applied to the elements of art—contrast, balance, unity, variety, rhythm, emphasis, pattern, scale, proportion, and focal point
Two-dimensional: having height and width
Line: a mark, or implied mark, between two endpoints
Shape: the two-dimensional area the boundaries of which are defined by lines or suggested by changes in color or value
Contrast: a drastic difference between such elements as color or value (lightness/darkness)

1.1 Spider, *c.* 500 BCE–500 CE, Nazca, Peru

Outline: the outermost line of an object or figure, by which it is defined or bounded
Plane: a flat surface

by off-road vehicles. The lines define the **outline** of a shape.

Definition and Functions of Line

A line can be a mark that connects two points, like the strings that must have run from post to

post at Nazca. Artists can use lines to define the boundaries between **planes** in a two-dimensional work of art: notice how the lines at Nazca divide one area of the gravel surface of the land from another. In two-dimensional art, line can also define shapes (in this case the shape of a giant spider). A line may direct our eyes to look at

1.2a (left) A modern photo of the Ducal Palace and Piazzetta in Venice; **1.2b** (below) Canaletto, *The Maundy Thursday Festival before the Ducal Palace in Venice*, 1763/6. Pen and brown ink with gray wash, heightened with white gouache, 15⅛ × 21¾". National Gallery of Art, Washington, D.C. Lines drawn on the Canaletto image indicate his use of line to define planes something the artist particularly wants us to notice. Finally, line can convey a sense of movement and energy, even the movement of a giant spider. We can see many of these uses of line in two very different artworks, one from eighteenth-century Italy and the other from modern Japan.

In Figs. **1.2a** and **1.2b** we see a modern photograph of the Ducal Palace in Venice, Italy, and a drawing, *The Maundy Thursday Festival before the Ducal Palace in Venice*, by Italian artist Canaletto (1697–1768). Canaletto uses line both to differentiate one part of the building from another and to mark the boundary between the building and its surroundings. Although line is two-dimensional, with line the artist points out where one plane meets another, and creates an impression of three dimensions. Line is thus a tool for describing, in a simple way and in two dimensions, the boundaries and edges of three-dimensional surfaces. For example, in the photo we see the division between the top of the building and the blue sky, but there is no line as such. Canaletto uses line to define where the pointed tracery at the top of the building ends and the sky begins.

Some of Canaletto's lines also give the viewer a sense of the surface. The artist accentuates the patterned surface (which can barely be seen in the photograph) with diagonal lines that fall across the **facade** of the building. Canaletto uses line to emphasize surface information that perhaps we overlook at first glance.

Besides demarcating boundaries and surface changes, line can also communicate direction and movement. The page from the manga (Japanese comic/cartoon book) *Tsubasa RESERVoir CHRoNiCLE* (**1.3**) is divided into two major sections. A close-up sketch of a character is compressed into the bottom, and a larger action scene occupies the upper two-thirds of the page. In this section directional lines converge on a light area in the upper right of the page, then our attention is redirected to the left, where a figure is being blasted away by an explosion. The mangaka (group of manga artists) CLAMP has cleverly used the strong diagonals to add an intense feeling of movement to the page.

47

Lines to Regulate and Control

The variety of different types of line is virtually infinite. Whether straight or curved, a line can be regular and carefully measured. Regular lines express control and planning and impart a sense of cool-headed deliberation and accuracy. Such lines are effective for communicating ideas that must be shared objectively by groups of people, such as the plans an architect provides to guide builders.

American **conceptual artist** Mel Bochner (b. 1940) uses ruled line in his work *Vertigo*

1.3 CLAMP, page from the *Tsubasa RESERVoir CHRoNiCLE*, volume 21, page 47

Facade: any side of a building, usually the front or entrance
Conceptual art: a work in which the ideas are often as important as how it is made

1.4 Mel Bochner, *Vertigo*, 1982. Charcoal, Conté crayon, and pastel on canvas, 9' × 6'2". Albright-Knox Art Gallery, Buffalo, New York

(**1.4**). By using a regular line drawn with the aid of a straightedge, Bochner speaks in the language of mechanical planning. However, he seems to contradict the use of regular line to convey a sense of control. The repetitious diagonal movement and hectic crossing and overlapping of his lines impart a sense of motion in disarray, as if his machine has somehow gone out of whack.

The British sculptor Barbara Hepworth (1903–75) utilized regulated line in the preliminary drawings she made for her sculptures. The lines she uses are crisp and clear. They combine to represent feelings or sensations that Hepworth wants to make visible in her sculpture. Hepworth said, "I rarely draw what I see. I draw what I feel in my body."

In **1.5**, the artist has projected four views of a future sculpture. As she rotates this imaginary sculpture in her mind's eye, the precision of her line helps her comprehend the complexity of her sensations. Like a dancer who responds to the

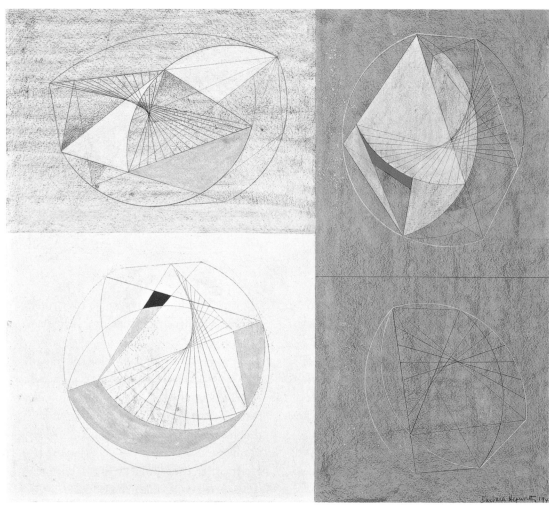

1.5 Barbara Hepworth, *Drawing for Sculpture (with color)*, 1941. Pencil and gouache on paper mounted on board, 14 × 16". Private collection

rhythm of music, Hepworth has revealed the kind of lines that she feels, rather than sees, and has translated them into a visual "dance." Like an architect preparing the blueprints of a real building, Hepworth uses regulated line to translate her feelings into drawing and then, finally, into a real sculpture.

Lines to Express Freedom and Passion

Lines can also be irregular, reflecting the wildness of nature, chaos, and accident. Such lines—free and unrestrained—seem passionate and full of feelings otherwise hard to express.

Some artists decide to use irregular lines to reflect their drawing and thinking process. French artist André Masson (1899–1987) wanted to create images that expressed the depths of his subconscious. Sometimes he would go for days without food or sleep in an attempt to force himself to explore deeper-rooted sources of creativity and truth. His **automatic** drawings look spontaneous and free, and also perhaps unstructured and rambling (**1.6**).

The drawings of French artist Jean Dubuffet (1901–85) are uninhibited in **style**. Their lines

1.6 André Masson, *Automatic Drawing*, 1925–6. Ink on paper, 12 × 9½". Musée National d'Art Moderne. Centre Georges Pompidou, Paris, France

appear irregular and loose. At first sight, his *Suite with 7 Characters* may seem chaotic and unpredictable, even scribbled, but the overall composition is controlled and orderly (**1.7**).

Regular and Irregular Lines

Although line can be either regular or irregular, most art exhibits a combination of both. American artist George Bellows (1882–1925) uses both varieties of line in his work *Woodstock Road, Woodstock, New York, 1924* (**1.8**). He contrasts

1.7 Jean Dubuffet, *Suite avec 7 Personnages*, 1981. Ink on paper, 13¾ × 16⅞". Private collection

Automatic: suppressing conscious control to access subconscious sources of creativity and truth

Style: a characteristic way in which an artist or group of artists uses visual language to give a work an identifiable form of visual expression

1.8 (right) George Bellows, *Woodstock Road, Woodstock, New York, 1924*. Black crayon on wove paper, image 6⅛ × 8⅞", sheet 9¼ × 12⅜". Collection of Mr. and Mrs. Paul Mellon, National Gallery of Art, Washington, D.C.

the natural and organic lines of landscape and sky with the restrained and regular line of the man-made and architectural features. It seems that Bellows made this drawing as a preliminary sketch for another work. In the center at the bottom is the inscription, "all lights as high as possible / get color out of shadows." He wrote this to remind himself later of ideas he had while sketching the scene.

Implied Line

The lines we have discussed so far can be clearly seen as continuous marks. We can call these lines

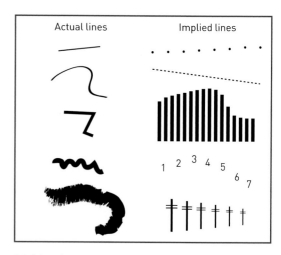

1.9 (above) Actual and implied lines

1.10 (left) Franco-German hand, *Pentateuch with Prophetical Readings and the Five Scrolls*, 13th–14th century. Illustrated manuscript. British Library, London, England

1.11 (above) Detail of *Pentateuch with Prophetical Readings and the Five Scrolls*

A. **Sylvester** (an innocent kid)
B. **Randolph** (Sylvesters best friend)
C. **The Evil Reverend Skull**
D. **Robert** (could have been any dog)
E. **Birdboy** (still not able to fly)
F. **Harold**
G. **Adrian** (PhD)
H. **Maybelle**

1.12 Sauerkids, *The Devil Made Me Do It*, 2006. Digital image, 16½ × 8¼"

Actual line: a continuous, uninterrupted line
Implied line: a line not actually drawn but suggested by elements in the work
Rhythm: the regular or ordered repetition of elements in the work
Etching: a printmaking process that relies on acid to bite (or etch) the engraved design into the printing surface

actual lines. But line can also be implied by series of marks. An **implied line** gives us the impression we are seeing a line where there is no continuous mark (**1.9**).

Implied line is important in the Jewish art of micrography, the creation of designs using very small writing. At first glance, the text border in **1.10** appears to be an ornate line drawing that has been used to help embellish the text. In fact, the ornate frame is made from tiny Hebrew letters and words. If we look at the detail in **1.11** it becomes more obvious there is no line at all, but an implied line created by the skillful arrangement of the lettering. The "microscopic" text has been added as a guide (called a masorah) that provides advice about pronunciation and intonation.

Implied line is used in a more freeform way in the work by Sauerkids, the Dutch graphic designers Mark Moget (b. 1970) and Taco Sipma

(b. 1966). *The Devil Made Me Do It* uses implied line to influence visual **rhythms** that add to the excitement of the design (**1.12**). The many dashes and the grid of dots at the bottom of the work imply vertical and horizontal lines. Even the title of the work is spelled out using implied line.

Directional Line

An artist can use line to direct our attention to something he or she wants us to notice (see Gateway Box: Goya, **1.13**, p. 54). An example of directional line occurs in the American artist James Allen's (1894–1964) **etching** of Depression-era construction workers. They are depicted working in New York City on the Empire State Building, which was to become the tallest building in the world. In *The Connectors*, the steel girders are closer together at the bottom

Using Line to Guide the Viewer's Eye

1.13 Francisco Goya, *The Third of May, 1808*, 1814. Oil on canvas, 8′4⅜″ × 11′3⅞″. Museo Nacional del Prado, Madrid, Spain

Directional lines can be either actual or implied. Painters often use implied line to guide a viewer's eye as it scans the canvas. In Goya's *Third of May, 1808*, the artist portrays the execution of Spaniards who had resisted the occupation of their country by the French army of Emperor Napoleon (1.13). Goya uses contrast to draw our attention to a particular line (A)—created in the place where the dark background sky meets and contrasts with the lighted hillside—that separates the two areas of value. Our attention is drawn downward and to the right toward an area where there is more visual activity. Goya holds our attention by using other directional lines; (B), for example, follows the line implied by the feet of the soldiers. Then a shadowed area (C) at the bottom of the page directs our eye to the left, where other lines such as (D) and (E) draw our gaze up toward the area of high contrast (A). Goya is keen to keep our attention on the atrocities committed by the army of Napoleon. The strong horizontal of the rifles is so distinct that our eye is pulled toward the group of victims: we identify not with the line of executioners, but with the victims.

1.14 James Allen, *The Connectors*, 1934. Etching, 12⅞ × 9⅞". British Museum, London, England

1.15 Egon Schiele, *Portrait of the Artist's Wife, Standing, with Hands on Hips*, 1915. Black crayon on paper, 18 × 11¼". Private collection

of the picture than at the top; they direct the viewer's eye downward in order to accentuate great height (**1.14**). The narrowing lines showing the buildings in the **background** of the print help reinforce the same effect.

Contour Line

A contour is the outer edge or profile of an object. Contour lines can suggest a **volume** in **space** by giving us clues about the changing character of a surface.

Portrait of the Artist's Wife, Standing, with Hands on Hips, by Austrian painter Egon Schiele (1890–1918), is drawn almost entirely using contour lines (**1.15**). The lines of the fingers and shirtsleeves express the pose with utmost economy; their simplicity is a sign of Schiele's superb drafting skills. Compare the regularity of lines that indicate the clothing with those depicting the contours of the hair. The lines in the hair vary in thickness and regularity. They suggest an organic surface that contrasts with the machine-like print of the clothing.

Communicative Line

The directions of lines (whether they go up, across, or diagonally) both guide our attention and suggest particular feelings. Vertical lines tend to communicate strength and energy; horizontal lines can suggest calmness and passivity; diagonal lines are associated with action, motion, and change.

Graphic designers use the communicative qualities of directional line when creating logos (**1.16**, p. 56). To convey the strength of government or the stability of a financial

Background: the part of a work depicted furthest from the viewer's space, often behind the main subject matter
Volume: the space filled or enclosed by a three-dimensional figure or object
Space: the distance between identifiable points or planes

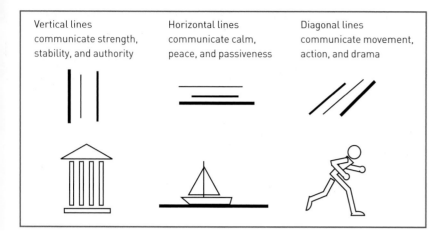

Vertical lines communicate strength, stability, and authority

Horizontal lines communicate calm, peace, and passiveness

Diagonal lines communicate movement, action, and drama

1.16 Communicative qualities of line

1.17 Carolyn Davidson, Nike Company logo, 1971

institution, they may choose verticals. Logos for vacation resorts often have horizontal lines to communicate peaceful repose. Diagonals can express the excitement of athletic activity. For example, Carolyn Davidson's (b. *c.* 1943) distinctive Nike "swoosh" conveys action with a shape comprising a stylized, diagonal line (**1.17**).

Line gives an unsettling energy to a painting of the bedroom (**1.18**) of the Dutch artist Vincent van Gogh (1853–90). Most of the lines that make

up the room are strong verticals. This suggests that van Gogh's bedroom was not a calm place of rest, as horizontal lines might imply. The floor also nervously changes **color** and value. The varying width of the vertical lines communicates the anxiety van Gogh may have felt in the months leading up to his suicide in 1890. The strength of the verticals combined with the agitation of the emphatic diagonals makes for a powerful sense of unease. Yet van Gogh may also have been trying to ground himself in the here-and-now by painting the simple room where he slept—the same room in which he died a year later.

1.18 Vincent van Gogh, *The Bedroom*, 1889. Oil on canvas, 28¾ × 36¼". Art Institute of Chicago

Color: the optical effect caused when reflected white light of the spectrum is divided into a separate wavelength

Shape

A shape is a two-dimensional area the boundaries of which are defined by lines or suggested by changes in color or value.

Geometric and Organic Shapes

Shapes can be classified into two types: geometric and organic. Geometric shapes are composed of regular lines and curves. Organic shapes, however, as the examples in the right-hand part of **1.19** show, are made up of unpredictable, irregular lines that suggest the natural world. Organic shapes may seem unrestrained and sometimes chaotic, reflecting the never-ending change characteristic of living things.

Geometry is a branch of mathematics dating back more than 2,000 years. It is concerned with space, area, and size. Traditionally defined, a geometric shape is mathematically regular and precise. The simple shapes we know—circle, square, triangle—are all examples of geometric shapes. Geometric shapes can be created by plotting a series of points and connecting them with lines, or simply enclosing a space using regulated and controlled line. Although artists can draw by hand something similar to a geometric shape, they often use tools to control and regulate the preciseness of the line. For example, an artist may use a ruler to create perfectly straight lines, or alternatively a computer graphics application can be used to generate a clean sharp edge. In both cases the artist adds a layer of control that gives the shape greater predictability.

While line may be the most fundamental element of art, often shape is the element we see. The **collage** by Canadian-born feminist artist Miriam Schapiro (b. 1923) illustrates differences between geometric and organic shapes (**1.20**).

1.19 Geometric and organic shapes

In *Baby Blocks*—also the name of a traditional quilting pattern—images of flowers and children's clothes overlap a tiling of orange, blue, and black diamond shapes. The work's title suggests a **pattern** of diamond shapes creating an illusion of cubes. The organic shapes of the flowers are clearly distinct from the hard geometric shapes of the "blocks" and the red frame; they overflow the boundaries of both.

The stylized floral designs, derived from old-fashioned wallpaper and upholstery patterns, are simplified representations of real flowers. Even so, the shapes have an irregularity that reflects the kind of shapes we find in living things.

The interlocked blue and yellow blocks are so predictable and regular that we can even envision the pattern where it disappears behind the flowers. This geometric regularity acts as a foil to the organic shapes casually arranged "on" it.

By incorporating doll clothes, home decorations, and sewing materials into her "femmages" (homages to the work of women), Schapiro opens our eyes both to the remarkable artistry of much traditional "women's work," and to the cultural forces that undervalue it.

1.20 Miriam Schapiro, *Baby Blocks*, 1983. Collage on paper, 29⅞ × 30". University of South Florida Collection, Tampa

Collage: a work of art assembled by gluing materials, often paper, onto a surface. From the French *coller*, to glue
Pattern: an arrangement of predictably repeated elements

of positive and negative, any color combination can work the same way. Sometimes, too, the lighter color becomes the positive shape.

We can see the interlock of positive and negative shape in the work of American Shepard

AT&T

1.22 Saul Bass, Bass & Yager, AT&T logo, 1984

Implied Shape

Most shapes are defined by a visible boundary, but we can also see a shape where no continuous boundary exists. Just as line can be implied, so too can shape (**1.21**).

The AT&T logo, created in the 1980s by American graphic designer Saul Bass (1920–96), uses horizontal lines to imply a sphere or globe (**1.22**). Twelve horizontal lines are trimmed to form a circle. By constricting the width of nine of these lines, a **highlight** appears on the circular shape, implying the swell of a globe. This logo communicates the idea of an expansive telecommunication network operating all over the globe. The image is simple, creating an appropriately meaningful and readily recognizable symbol for a global company.

Contrast

When an artist uses two noticeably different states of an element, he or she is applying the principle of contrast. For example, lines can be both regular and irregular, or shapes can be both geometric and organic. Strong differences in the state of an element can be a very useful effect for an artist to use; it is especially effective to use opposites.

Positive and Negative Shapes

In everyday life, positive and negative are opposites: one needs the other for contrast and comparison. Without positives, negatives would not exist and vice versa. When we speak of positive and negative in visual form it is most often represented by black and white. The words on this page, for example, are **positive shapes** of printed black ink that we can see on the **negative space** of the white paper. The space supports the solidity of the placement of the word or shape. Although black and white are common examples

Highlight: an area of lightest value in a work
Positive shape: a shape defined by its surrounding empty space
Negative space: an empty space given shape by its surround, for example the right-pointing arrow between the **E** and **x** in **FedEx**

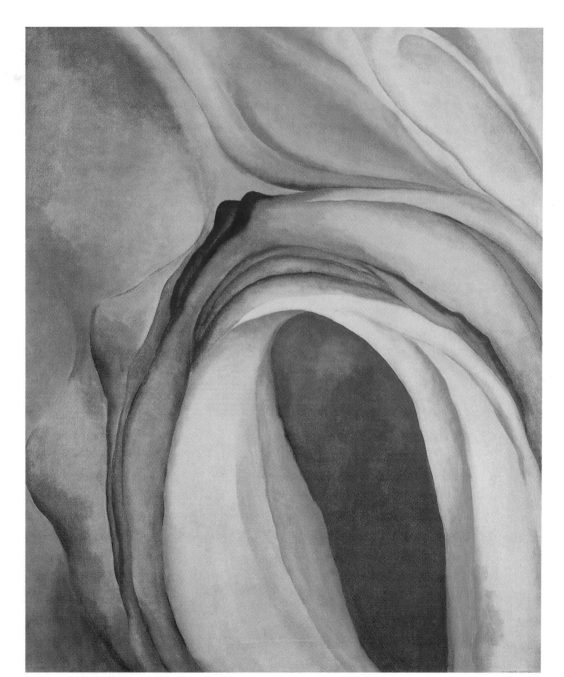

1.23a and **1.23b** (left)
Shepard Fairey, *Obey*, 1996.
Campaign poster and a view
of the posters as they were
installed in public

1.24 Georgia O'Keeffe,
Music—Pink and Blue II, 1919.
Oil on canvas, 35 × 29⅛".
Whitney Museum of American
Art, New York

Abstract: art imagery that
departs from recognizable
images from the natural world

Fairey (b. 1970). The black features and the blank
white space contrast with and complement each
other, intensifying the design of this poster
(**1.23a** and **1.23b**). Fairey wants strong impact
because, as a street artist, he needs to catch his
audience's attention quickly as they pass by. In
this case, the image is of the professional wrestler
Andre the Giant (Fessick in the movie *The
Princess Bride*), captioned by the word "Obey."
Without seeking prior permission, Fairey posts
these images in public spaces as an expression
of guerrilla marketing and street theater. The

tension between contrasting positive and negative
shapes draws our attention, while the cryptic
slogan makes us wonder what it is all about.

The works of the American artist Georgia
O'Keeffe (1887–1986) often play upon the
relationship between positive and negative
shape. Her **abstract** shapes derive from a close
observation of organic objects. In the painting
Music—Pink and Blue II, O'Keeffe puts emphasis
on the negative blue shape in the bottom right
of the picture (**1.24**). That negative shape
initially draws our attention into a deep interior

so that the positive shape of the pink arc above it carries us back to the surface through a maze of tender folds. O'Keeffe's paintings use landscape and flower shapes to make associations to the female body. The interplay of positive and negative space becomes symbolic of the erotic and life-giving nature of womanhood.

Sometimes graphic designers use negative shape to convey information subtly. For example, when the Big Ten Conference—ten major universities competing in many different sports—expanded to eleven teams, they needed a logo that announced the change. The only problem was that they wanted to retain the name, "Big Ten," rather than use eleven and change the conference title. The graphic designer Al Grivetti ingeniously inserted the number "11" in the negative space on either side of the capital "T"

1.25 Al Grivetti, Big Ten logo, 1991

(**1.25**). We can discern both messages (Big Ten and 11) as we view the logo. The alternation of positive and negative shape communicates the new and old titles of the conference in a single image.

In the **woodcut** *Sky and Water I* the Dutch artist M. C. Escher (1898–1972) applies many of the concepts we have been exploring in this chapter (**1.26**). The negative shape changes from white in the upper part of the picture to

1.26 M. C. Escher, *Sky and Water I*, 1938. Woodcut, 17⅛ × 17⅜". The M. C. Escher Company, Netherlands black in the lower. The most refined version of each animal occurs at the top and bottom extremes of the image. As we follow each transition upward or downward, each animal becomes more simplified until it forms part of the background negative shape. Strong geometric patterns change into the organic shapes of animals. The woodcut, where removed material prints white and preserved material prints black, is conducive to exploring **figure–ground reversal**, which is the very essence of Escher's technique here.

Conclusion

Artists use line, shape, and contrast to communicate in two dimensions. By combining these different characteristics, artists can communicate visual ideas with elegance and razor-edged efficiency. They can describe the beautiful and ugly details of our world, and express the deepest emotional experiences of the human soul. Within two dimensions we can communicate nearly every interaction in mankind's history of understanding.

The *Banner of Las Navas de Tolosa* (**1.27**), a thirteenth-century Islamic tapestry, exemplifies the themes of this chapter. Made during the time when Spain was under Islamic rule, it is supposed to have been captured in battle from the Muslim occupying forces. To this day, patterns from Islamic art can be found in the designs and architecture of Spain.

The banner is composed of a central medallion surrounded by several **concentric** shapes. Within the circular medallion, squares are rotated to create a series of concentric eight-pointed stars. These star shapes are encircled by a large round shape with a border of smaller circles. These circles in turn are surrounded by a square that sits inside another square.

Along the margins at the top and bottom are inscriptions in ornate Arabic calligraphy. The free-flowing and vigorous letterforms create strong horizontal implied lines. This ornamental writing style is often used in Islamic art to communicate words—in this case from the Koran—richly and expressively.

1.27 *Banner of Las Navas de Tolosa*, 1212–50. Silk and gilt thread tapestry, 10'10" × 7'2⅝". Monasterio de las Huelgas, Museo de Telas Medievales, Burgos, Spain

The banner also uses contrasting positive and negative shapes as a series of patterned organic shapes weave in and out of the enclosed central spaces. The line, principal shape, and contrasting shapes are used to great effect. A central square that meets the left and right edges of the banner encloses a series of other shapes. Just inside the edges of the square is a series of round medallions that create another implied square. That same implied square spills into a centered circular shape that subdivides the square and leaves almost-triangular shapes in the corners. Centered within the circle is another series of shapes that are superimposed and subdivided again. This multitude of simple shapes combines to create a masterpiece of complexity that attests to the power and majesty of Allah. From humblest simplicity to the boldest intricacies, the basics of two dimensions provide us with great visual communicative power.

Woodcut: a print created from an incised piece of wood
Figure–ground reversal: the reversal of the relationship between one shape (the figure) and its background (the ground), so that the figure becomes background and the ground becomes the figure
Concentric: identical shapes stacked inside each other sharing the same center, for example the circles of a target

1.2

Three-Dimensional Art: Form, Volume, Mass, and Texture

Three-dimensional: having height, width, and depth
Elements: the basic vocabulary of art—line, form, shape, volume, mass, color, texture, space, time and motion, and value (lightness/darkness)
Two-dimensional: having height and width
Shape: the two-dimensional area the boundaries of which are defined by lines or suggested by changes in color or value
Form: an object that can be defined in three dimensions (height, width, and depth)
Scale: the size of an object or artwork relative to another object or artwork, or to a system of measurement
Volume: the space filled or enclosed by a three-dimensional figure or object
Mass: a volume that has, or gives the illusion of having, weight, density, and bulk
Space: the distance between identifiable points or planes
Texture: the surface quality of a work, for example fine/coarse, detailed/lacking in detail

In 1802 a French artist and archaeologist described his impression of the great pyramids of Egypt:

> On approaching these colossal monuments, their angular and inclined form diminishes the appearance of their height and deceives the eye…but as soon as I begin to measure …these gigantic productions of art, they recover all their immensity…

(Vivant Denon, *Travels in Upper and Lower Egypt*)

The massive structures that so impressed Denon have three dimensions, like every object in our world, which can be expressed as their height, width, and depth (**1.28**). Because the pyramids can be measured in these three dimensions they are classified as **three-dimensional** works of art, and like all the art discussed in this chapter they possess four of the visual **elements**: form, volume, mass, and texture. We need to understand these terms in sequence so that we can analyze and understand three-dimensional art.

Form

A **two-dimensional** object, such as a drawing of a triangle, is called a **shape**. Shapes are flat. A three-dimensional object, such as a pyramid, is called a **form**. Forms are tactile; we can feel them with our hands. Some forms are so tiny they cannot be seen with the naked eye, while others are as large as a galaxy. When artists and designers create forms, they consider how we will experience them in three dimensions. Architects usually make buildings that accord with our physical size, in proportions that are convenient and easy to live in, but sometimes they might build to a larger **scale** in order to leave us in awe. A jeweler makes objects at a small scale that few people can experience at once: we are drawn closer to examine the work more intimately.

Forms have two fundamental attributes: **volume** and **mass**. Volume is the amount of **space** a form occupies. Mass is the expression that a volume is solid and occupies space, whether it is enormous like a pyramid or relatively small like a piece of jewelry.

The surface of a form can be cool and slick, rough and jagged, soft and warm. Such sensations arise from the **texture** of the form. Texture can be experienced directly, but we can also imagine how the surface of a form may feel simply by looking at it. Some hand-made objects, like ceramics or basketry, attract our touch naturally. They were touched by the hands that formed them, and they fit in our hands just as they used to fit in the hands of the artist. Some machine-made forms reflect the crisp precision of mechanical perfection; their smooth, shiny forms seduce our senses. Artists and designers create forms with full knowledge that they can evoke our memories of other three-dimensional objects in the world and allow us to experience our own world in a richer way.

The forms created by artists in the ancient world reflected the everyday experiences of people of that time. For example, stone was a common material in ancient Egypt, easily accessible and so durable that artists must have thought it would last for a very long time—a correct assumption, as we can still see.

The Great Sphinx of Giza guards the tombs of the Egyptian kings at Giza, near Cairo (**1.29**). The Great Sphinx is the largest carving in the world made from a single stone. The sculpture stands as a symbol of the power to change our surroundings. The Egyptians who created this work changed the very earth by sculpting the living rock. We do not know what the Egyptians called this half-man, half-lion, but we have come to call it a "sphinx" after the creature from Greek

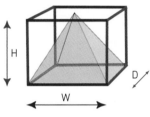

1.28 (above) Three dimensions: height, width, and depth

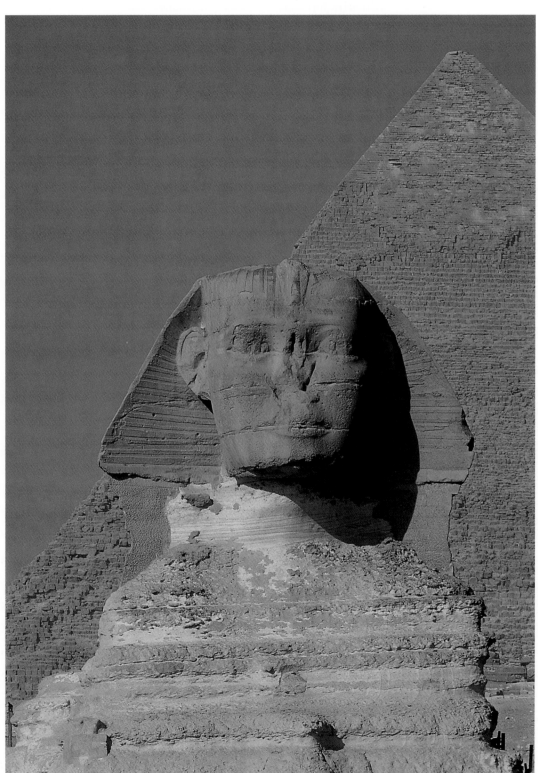

1.29 Great Sphinx of Giza, c. 2650 BCE, Giza, Egypt

mythology with the body of a lion, the wings of an eagle, and the head of a woman.

There are two types of form: geometric and organic.

Geometric Form

Geometric forms are regular and are readily expressible in words or numbers: cubes, spheres, cylinders, cones, and pyramids are simple examples. The Great Pyramid of Khufu is a stunning example of geometric form in architectural design (see Gateway Box: The Great Pyramid of Khufu, **1.30**).

Like the ancient Egyptians, the American sculptor David Smith (1906–65) also relied on geometric forms to create his compositions. In *Cubi XIX*, made of stainless steel, Smith

Gateway to Art: The Great Pyramid of Khufu
The Importance of Geometric Form

1.30 Great Pyramid of Khufu, *c.* 2560 BCE, Giza, Egypt

The regulated and controlled geometric form of the Great Pyramid at Khufu in Giza, Egypt, stands as a monument to the engineering and construction skills of the ancient Egyptians (**1.30**). The base of Khufu's pyramid is level to within less than an inch, and the greatest difference in the length of the sides is 1¾ inches. The pyramids at Giza (there are three) were originally encased in fine white limestone: the simplicity of their geometry must have stood out like gigantic crystals in the desert sands. They point to the sky, the realm of the sun god. Just as we can calculate the result of a mathematical equation, if we view a pyramid from its eastern side, we can predict what its northern, southern, and western sides will look like. Egyptian art and architecture exhibit carefully ordered and controlled characteristics. The work of these artists was governed by a canon, or set of rules, that is also expressed in the strict formality of ancient Egyptian art.

uses cubes, cuboids, and a thick disk (**1.31**). Smith learned welding in an automobile factory and became expert while fabricating tanks of thick armor plate during World War II. The late works of his Cubi series combine geometric forms in angular relationships. The diagonal angles imply movement, giving these basic geometric forms a visual energy. Smith burnished their surfaces to create a counterpoint between industrial and natural form.

Organic Form

The form of most things in the natural world is organic: it is irregular and unpredictable. Living things, such as plants and animals, change constantly, and their forms change too. Artists accentuate the irregular character of organic form for expressive effect.

The human figure gives an artist a subject that can communicate the rich experience of humanity and organic form in a way we can all understand. The human body, like other organic forms, constantly changes in concert with its surroundings. Forms representing the human figure can provide the artist with a subject conveying symmetry and balance. But by visually contradicting such order, an artist can make a work seem uncomfortable or uneasy to look at. The unknown artist who carved the work *Vesperbild* in the fourteenth century expresses the agony of death and grief by making the bodies of Jesus and Mary irregular, awkward, and distorted (**1.32**).

The suffering of torture is made shocking by the disjointedness of the lifeless Jesus. Stiffly angular, he is stretched across the lap of his mother Mary. Prickly thorns, gushing wounds, and crumpled drapery give texture to pain and anguish. The disproportionate size of Mary's twisted face makes her unbearable sorrow all the more inescapable.

1.31 David Smith, *Cubi XIX*, 1964. Stainless steel, 113¼ × 21⅝ × 20⅝"

1.32 *Vesperbild* (Pietà), Middle Rhine region, *c.* 1330. Wood, 34½" high. Rheinisches Landesmuseum, Bonn, Germany

1.33 Lino Tagliapietra, *Batman*, 1998. Glass, 11½ × 15½ × 3½"

The expression of vigor and uplift in Italian glass artist Lino Tagliapietra's *Batman* (**1.33**) contrasts with the expression of death and despair in *Vesperbild*. Tagliapietra (b. 1934) wanted to convey the idea of "a creature who emerges from his dark cave to share goodness and light." He has enhanced the positive emotion of this **abstract** image by using bright **color** and stretching the extreme edges upward as if this were a growing, living object. Rather than having hard, angular distortions, the artist uses a form that is lively and organic. The natural energy of light is captured in the glowing transparency of the glass. Tagliapietra, a master of glassblowing technique, wants the form to allude, without making a literal reference, to the idea behind the character Batman. Thus we are free to revel in the life,

energy, and power of the superhero through an expressive form, rather than a carefully depicted, lifelike representation. Tagliapietra says of the work, "I imaged pieces that allow the viewer to see both the reality and fantasy of Batman's world."

Form in Relief and in the Round

An artist who works with three-dimensional form can choose to create a work in **relief** or **in the round**. A relief is a work in which forms project from a flat surface. It is designed to be viewed from one side only. A form in the round can be seen from all sides.

Facade: any side of a building, usually the front or entrance
Foreground: the part of a work depicted as nearest to the viewer
High relief: a carved panel where the figures project with a great deal of depth from the background
Bas-relief: a sculpture carved with very little depth
Stela (plural **stele**): upright stone slab decorated with inscriptions or pictorial relief carvings
Plane: a flat surface
Composition: the overall design or organization of a work

Forms in relief combine aspects of two-dimensional and three-dimensional works of art. Like a two-dimensional work, a relief can be mounted on a wall or other surface.

Although relief may appear to limit the work's potential visual impact, in fact the sculptor can create the illusion of a three-dimensional space, with dramatic results.

In the relief sculptures on the south **facade** of the Ara Pacis (Latin for Altar of Peace) in Rome, Italy, a sculptor chose to fit many figures into a limited space (**1.34**). The unknown artist uses the depth of the carvings to suggest that some areas of the composition are further away from us than others. The figures in the **foreground** are deeply carved (in **high relief**) so that the

1.35 Stela with supernatural scene, Mexico or Guatemala, 761 CE. Limestone, 92 × 42 × 3". Fine Arts Museums of San Francisco

folds in their togas are strongly delineated by shadows. But the artist wanted to imply a large crowd rather than just a line of people. The figures behind those in the foreground are also carved in relief, but not quite so deeply. They appear to be further away because there is less shadow defining their shape. The artist suggests even greater depth by using a third group of figures who are carved in shallow relief, so that there is no shadow at all to make them stand out. This effect is clear in the upper left-hand corner, where the carving overlaps and diminishes in height.

The Maya artist who carved **1.35** in **bas-relief** worked in a tradition quite different from that of the Roman sculptor of the Ara Pacis, with its deeply incised figures. On the Maya **stela** all the carving is carefully arranged on the same **plane**. The sculptor has created a large figure of a Maya ruler, shown wearing a highly detailed and elaborate costume. The Mayan writing to the left of the figure seems to be of equal visual weight; the sculptor intended the viewer to read every element of the **composition**.

1.36 Volume and mass

Volume

Three-dimensional objects necessarily have volume. Volume is the amount of space occupied by an object. Solid objects have volume; so do objects that enclose an empty space. Mass, by contrast, suggests that something is solid and occupies space (**1.36**). Architectural forms usually enclose a volume of interior space to be used for living or working. For example, some hotel interiors feature a large, open atrium that becomes the **focal point** of the lobby. Some sculptures accentuate weight and solidity rather than openness. Such works have very few open spaces that we can see. The presence of mass suggests weight, gravity, a connection to the earth. The absence of mass suggests lightness, airiness, flight. Asymmetrical masses—or masses that cannot be equally divided on a central **axis**—can suggest dynamism, movement, change.

Open Volume

When artists enclose a space with materials that are not completely solid, they create an open volume. In *Ghostwriter*, Ralph Helmick (b. 1952) and Stuart Schechter (b. 1958) use carefully suspended pieces of metal to make an open volume that, when looked at as a whole, creates the image of a large human head (**1.37a** and **1.37b**). The small metal pieces, which represent letters of the alphabet and other objects, are organized so that they delineate the shape of the head but do not enclose the space. In the stairwell where the piece hangs, the empty space and the "head" are not distinct or separate, but the shape is nonetheless implied.

1.37a (top right) Ralph Helmick and Stuart Schechter, *Ghostwriter*, 1994. Cast metal/stainless cable, 36 × 8 × 10ʹ. Evanston Public Library, Illinois
1.37b (right) Detail of *Ghostwriter*

The Russian artist Vladimir Tatlin's (1885–1953) *Monument to the Third International* was intended to be a huge tower with rooms housing the offices and chamber of delegates of the Communist International. It was going to commemorate the triumph of Russia's Bolshevik Revolution. Never built, it would have been much higher than the Eiffel Tower in Paris, France. In its form as we see it in **1.38**, the spiraling open volume of the interior, and its proposed novel use of such materials as steel and glass, symbolize the modernism and dynamism of Communism. Tatlin believed that art should support and reflect the new social and political order.

Open volume can make a work feel light. *In the Blue*, a collaborative work by American sculptors Carol Mickett (b. 1952) and Robert Stackhouse (b. 1942), was created to imply the presence of water (**1.39**). By creating **negative space** (the openings between the wooden slats) with crowds of horizontal members, the artists make the work seem to float. Mickett and Stackhouse also curve the pieces and place them at irregular intervals to create many subtle changes in direction. This arrangement gives a

1.38 Vladimir Tatlin, Model for *Monument to the Third International*, 1919

feeling of motion like the gentle ripples of flowing water. The artists hope that viewers will experience a feeling of being surrounded by water as they walk through the passage.

1.39 Carol Mickett and Robert Stackhouse, *In the Blue (Crest)*, 2008. Painted cypress, 24 × 108 × 11'. Installation at St. Petersburg Art Center, Florida

Focal point: the center of interest or activity in a work of art, often drawing the viewer's attention to the most important element
Axis: an imaginary line showing the center of a shape, volume, or composition
Negative space: an empty space given shape by its surround, for example the right-pointing arrow between the **E** and **x** in **FedEx**

Mass

Mass suggests that a volume is solid and occupies space. Every substance has mass. Our perception of mass influences how we react to and what we feel about that substance (see Gateway Box: Colossal Olmec Heads, **1.40**). We can feel the weight of a pebble in the palm of our hand, or the heaviness of a chair as we pull it away from a table. Our perception of mass in large objects is derived from our imagination, our previous experience with smaller objects, and our understanding of the forces of nature. Artists tap into these various intuitions when they create a work of art.

Mass can suggest weight in a three-dimensional object. Some artists imply mass (without it necessarily being there) to give us the impression that the object we are looking at is very heavy. In movies, special-effect artists use boulders made of foam to give the impression of great weight.

Gateway to Art: Colossal Olmec Heads
Mass and Power

The monumental quality of some artworks is directly related to their mass. The eight-foot-high Olmec sculpture of a Colossal Head has an imposing physical presence (**1.40**). The sheer size of the work was almost certainly intended to impress and overwhelm. At La Venta, in Mexico, three heads were positioned in a "processional arrangement" requiring the viewer to walk from one head to another, which must have increased their visual impact. Some of the Olmec colossal heads are flat at the back because they had been carved out of earlier monuments known as "altars," although they may in fact have been thrones. The flat back to the head was the base of the altar. While a similar head could be carved on a pebble that would fit in the palm of the hand, the massive scale of this head makes an imposing statement. Its intimidating size suggests the power of a mighty ruler or an important ancestor. The full lips and nose amplify the head's massive scale.

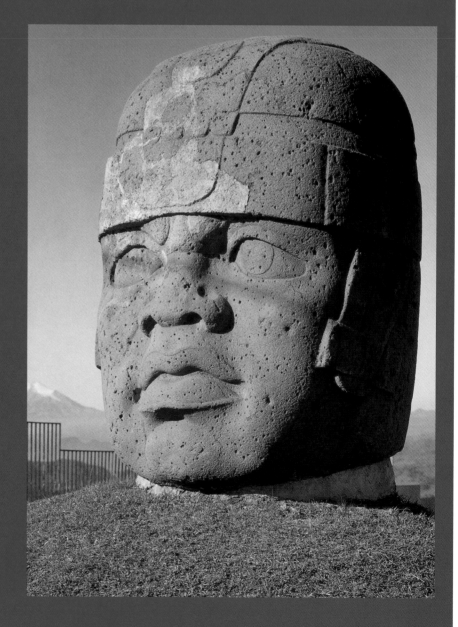

1.40 Colossal Head, Olmec, 1500–1300 BCE. Basalt. Museo de Antropología, Veracruz, Mexico memorial of its former self. Whiteread has taken the volume of this building's interior and transformed it into a lasting memorial of the lives of the people who used to live in it, and in other houses just like it. We not only comprehend the weight of the concrete, but the related associations of life and death, memory and change.

The sculpture of Father Damien by the Venezuelan-born artist Marisol (b. Maria Sol Escobar, 1930) stands as an immovable object against an irresistible force (**1.42**). It depicts

1.42 Marisol (Escobar), *Father Damien*, 1969. Bronze. State Capitol Building, Honolulu, Hawaii

1.41 Rachel Whiteread, *House*, 1993. Concrete. Bow, London, England (demolished 1994)

Mass does not necessarily imply heaviness, only that a volume is solid and occupies space.

The mass of British sculptor Rachel Whiteread's *House* suggests great weight and solidity (**1.41**). To create this work, Whiteread (b. 1963) filled the interior space of a house with tons of concrete before demolishing the exterior walls and windows. The empty volume that was once filled with the happy and sad moments of ordinary domestic life has been turned into a the courage of a humanitarian hero. Father Damien was a Catholic missionary who supervised a leper colony on the Hawaiian island of Molokai during the nineteenth century. His steadfast compassion is suggested by the four-square mass of Marisol's work, while his upright correctness is reflected in its vertical lines—in the cane, in the cape, and in the straight row of buttons. The stout form communicates stability and determination. Father Damien, who himself died of leprosy while serving its victims, exemplified such heroism that the Hawaiian legislature voted to place this memorial to him in front of the State Capitol Building in Honolulu.

1.43 Nam June Paik, *TV Buddha*, 1974. Closed circuit video installation with bronze sculpture, monitor, and video camera, dimensions vary with installation. Stedelijk Museum, Amsterdam, Netherlands

Texture

Any three-dimensional object that can be touched and felt has texture, the tactile sensation we experience when we physically encounter a three-dimensional form. Textures vary, from the slick, cold surface of a finely finished metal object, to the rough-hewn splintery character of a broken branch, to the pebbly surface of a rocky beach.

When you hold this book in your hands, you feel the surface of the pages and feel its weight. We mostly rely on the impressions we receive from our hands when we think of texture, and

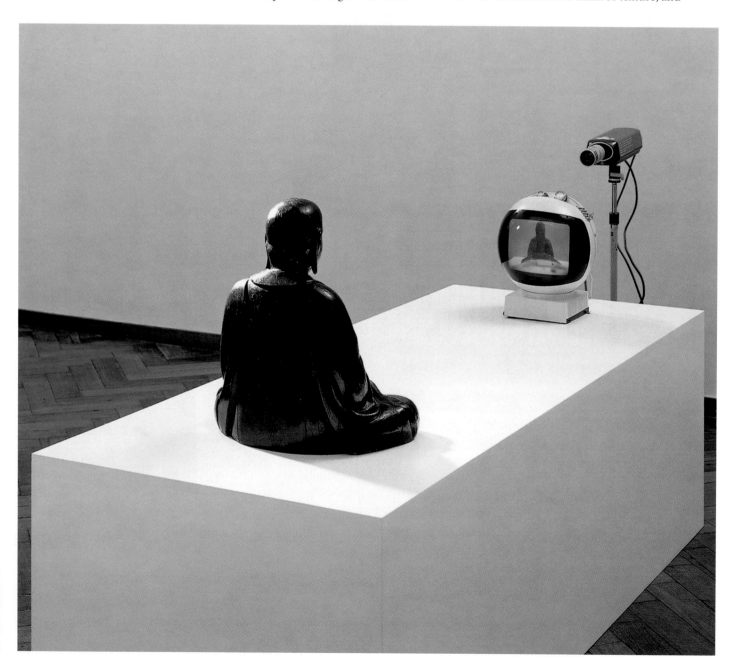

these tactile experiences influence the way we look at art.

Even if we do not touch three-dimensional works of art, we can still think of them as having "actual texture." We know what polished stone feels like (cool and smooth), so when we look at a highly polished marble sculpture we can imagine how its texture feels, based on our past experience. Our experience of it will be different, though, if we look at a picture of it in a book or if we stand next to it in the same room.

Viewers of Korean artist Nam June Paik's sculpture *TV Buddha* experience actual texture when they see and touch the work (**1.43**). We understand the tactile sensations of touching a bronze sculpture, or a television screen, or a video camera. Paik (b. 1932) presents us with a visual image of the Buddha contemplating the world and meditating through modern electronics. The artist successfully draws on our past tactile experiences to give us a fuller experience of the artwork. The low-tech sense of touch contrasts with the high-tech process of capturing a visual image and projecting it onto a screen. A camera installed in the work shoots video of the actual texture and translates it into an image that can only be experienced from our tactile memory. The texture can then be implied by the two-dimensional image on the screen.

Subversive Texture

A subversive texture contradicts our previous tactile experience. Some types of cactus appear to have a soft, furry covering, but touching them will be painful. Artists and designers use the contradictions and contrasts of subversive texture to invite viewers to reconsider their preconceptions about the world around them.

In the early twentieth century, artists calling themselves **Surrealists** created work that drew on ideas and images from dreams and the unconscious mind. The Swiss Surrealist Méret Oppenheim (1913–85) used texture to contradict the conscious logical experiences of viewers. In her sculpture *Object*, Oppenheim takes a cup, saucer, and spoon, normally hard and cool to the touch, and instead makes them soft and furry (**1.44**). The idea of sipping tea from this object conjures up an unexpected sensation of fur tickling our lips. The artist is counting on our tactile memory to conflict with the actual experience of sipping tea from a shiny teacup. In this case, the form is recognizable, but the associated experience is not.

Surrealist: an artist belonging to the Surrealist movement in the 1920s and later, whose art was inspired by dreams and the subconscious

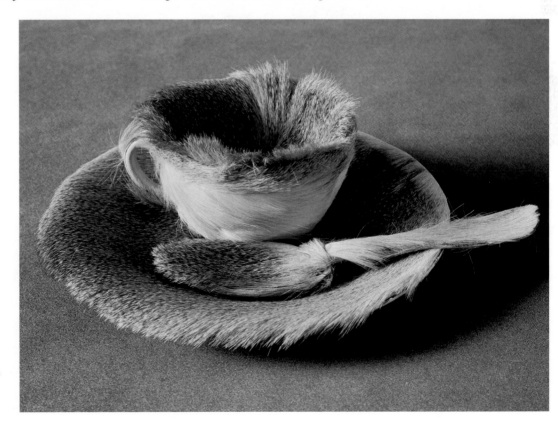

1.44 Méret Oppenheim, *Object*, 1936. Fur-covered cup, saucer, and spoon, 2⅞" high. MOMA, New York

The Guggenheim Museum, Bilbao

The American architect Frank Gehry (b. 1929) designed the Guggenheim Museum, located between a river and a motorway, in Bilbao, Spain; it was completed in 1997 (1.45). Bilbao was once a center for ship-building, and the undulating surfaces of Gehry's creation suggest ships and ship construction. Gehry's design uses contrasts in geometric and organic form. Historically, architectural design has relied on geometric form. Organic forms, by comparison, are more difficult to visualize and plan in advance; curved and irregular structures are difficult to survey, measure, plumb, and level. But Gehry used computer programs originally invented for aerospace design to plan buildings that contradict our preconceived ideas about architecture as geometric form. Most of the walls of the Guggenheim Museum consist of irregular, curving organic forms that rise and fall unpredictably. The undulating surfaces give a sense of movement and life to the structure.

This could make some visitors feel disoriented, but Gehry counters this at critical junctures by using strongly geometric form. At the entrance, for instance, the reassurance of geometric form encourages even the most apprehensive visitor to enter the building.

Gehry employs both sculptural relief and in-the-round forms. The surfaces of the organic portion of the building are covered with titanium tiles. The subtle changes to the surfaces of this material resemble an abstract bas-relief. But the entire building is also like a sculpture in-the-round that the viewer can stroll around to appreciate its unexpected juts and curves.

Gehry's museum has reshaped its location. The interior space, designed to meet the changing needs of art and artists in the future, can also be extended or reduced, creating interesting exhibition opportunities. The complex shapes of the building extend out into space like a huge boat, emphasizing its relationship to the

1.45 Frank Gehry, Guggenheim Museum, 1997, Bilbao, Spain

1.46 Louise Bourgeois, *Maman*, 1999 (cast 2001). Bronze, stainless steel, and marble, 29′4³⁄₈″ × 32′9¹⁄₈″ × 38′1″. Guggenheim Museum, Bilbao, Spain

nearby River Nervión. The building stands in stark contrast to the surrounding urban landscape, offering an optimistic vision in a deteriorating industrial district of Bilbao.

The shimmering titanium tiles of Gehry's building are complemented by a sculpture that stands beside the museum, *Maman* (1.46; meaning "Momma" in French), by French artist Louise Bourgeois (1911–2010). The Guggenheim's apparently solid mass is contrasted with the spindly form and open volume of *Maman*. The negative space surrounding its legs and body imparts lightness. The subtle variations of angle in the legs imply movement. The wobbly vulnerability of the spider contrasts with the massive solidity of the building. Even though this spider is made of bronze, the effect is one of lightness. And by suspending below the central body a container of marble spheres like an egg sac, Bourgeois wants to suggest both the tenderness and fierce protectiveness of motherhood.

Conclusion

We see a three-dimensional work of art in terms of its height, width, and depth. The term form is used to describe any three-dimensional work. Three-dimensional forms can be geometric or organic. They also have volume (the amount of space occupied by the form) and mass (the impression that the volume is solid and occupies space). The surface of the form can be described in terms of its texture. Artists can use the language of three-dimensional art to express many ideas and emotions. Méret Oppenheim playfully tests our assumptions about everyday objects with a furry teacup and saucer. On a much larger scale, the creators of the Colossal Olmec Heads express the power of their rulers or ancestors, while the fourteenth-century sculptor of *Vesperbild* communicates the terrible sorrow of Mary as she holds the lifeless form of Jesus.

1.3

Implied Depth: Value and Space

Three-dimensional: having height, width, and depth
Two-dimensional: having height and width
Value: the lightness or darkness of a plane or area
Space: the distance between identifiable points or planes
Perspective: the creation of the illusion of depth in a two-dimensional image by using mathematical principles
Surrealist: an artist belonging to the Surrealist movement in the 1920s and later, whose art was inspired by dreams and the subconscious

1.47 René Magritte, *The Treachery of Images ("This is not a pipe")*, 1929. Oil on canvas, 23¾ × 32". LACMA

Reality is merely an illusion, albeit a very persistent one.

(Albert Einstein, physicist and Nobel Prize winner)

When Albert Einstein suggested that not everything we see is real, he probably did not have art in mind. But artists readily understand his remark, because when they create a picture of real space on a flat surface they know they are creating an illusion. When we watch a magician perform a trick, we instinctively wonder how the magic was achieved. In this chapter we will reveal some of the secrets that artists rely upon to create the appearance of **three-dimensional** depth in a **two-dimensional** work of art.

The techniques artists use to imply depth—**value**, **space**, and **perspective**—evoke our past visual experiences and the way we see. **Value**, the lightness or darkness of a surface, emulates the effects of light and shadow, and can be used to suggest solidity. Artists have a variety of techniques based on the optics of vision that enable them to create the illusion of pictorial space. One of these is called atmospheric perspective, a method that mimics our visual perceptions of color, clarity, and form at a distance. Linear and isometric perspective are drawing methods that can express the idea of three-dimensional space on a two-dimensional surface. In this chapter we will introduce these methods of creating the illusion of space and discuss why some artists choose to use them.

In *The Treachery of Images*, Belgian **Surrealist** artist René Magritte (1898–1967) uses value and perspective to imply depth (**1.47**). The pipe is painted in varying values (light and dark tones), which gives the appearance of shadows that suggest depth. The top of the pipe bowl (where the tobacco would be stuffed) is composed of two concentric ellipses, which is how circles appear in perspective. We know what a real pipe looks like in real space, and Magritte understands our habits of visual perception. He paints a picture of a pipe that "feels" solid, but then playfully invites us to re-examine our habits of mind.

In this painting, Magritte tells us that painting is a visual trick. By writing "Ceci n'est pas une pipe" ("This is not a pipe"), Magritte wants us to recognize that what appears to be a pipe is not really a pipe: it is an illusion, nothing more than paint on a flat surface.

Ceci n'est pas une pipe.

Value

Value refers to lightness and darkness. An artist's use of value can produce a sense of solidity and influence our mood. For example, detective movies of the 1940s were filmed in such dark tones that they had their own **style** called *film noir*, French for "dark film." The serious mood of these mysteries was enhanced by the filmmaker's choice of dark values. Artists use dark and light values as tools for creating depth.

Artists learn to mimic the appearance of things by observing the effects of light as it illuminates a surface. The Art Dome, formerly used as a sculpture studio at Reed College in Portland, Oregon, demonstrates the effect of light on planes in varying locations (**1.48**). Many triangular flat planes make up this surface. Each of these planes has a different value, the relative degree of lightness or darkness of the **plane** according to the amount of light shining on it. The light source (high and to the left of the dome) hits some of the triangular planes of the Art Dome more directly than others. The planes that have a lighter value are facing the light source; the darker ones are facing away.

Value changes often occur gradually. If you look at the Art Dome, you will notice that the relative dark values increase as the planes get further away and face away from the light (see also **1.49**). These changes occur on any object. There are subtle value changes even in a white object.

1.48 Buckminster Fuller, Geodesic Dome (Art Dome), 1963–79, Reed College, Portland, Oregon

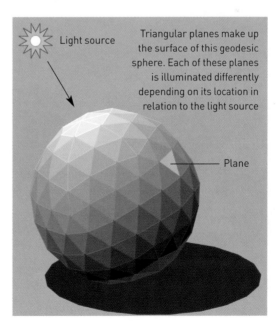

Triangular planes make up the surface of this geodesic sphere. Each of these planes is illuminated differently depending on its location in relation to the light source

Light source

Plane

1.49 Values and planes of a geodesic sphere, vector graphic

Style: a characteristic way in which an artist or group of artists uses visual language to give a work an identifiable form of visual expression
Plane: a flat surface

A value range refers to a series of different values. In the image of the geodesic sphere (see p. 77) there is a value range of black, white, and eight values of gray. Black and white are the values at the extreme ends of this value range.

Chiaroscuro

Chiaroscuro (Italian for "light-dark") is a method of applying value to a two-dimensional piece of artwork to create the illusion of a three-dimensional solid form (**1.50**).

The illusion of solidity and depth in two dimensions can be achieved by using an approach devised by artists of the Italian **Renaissance**. Using a sphere as their model, Renaissance artists identified five distinct areas of light and shadow. A **highlight** marks the point where the object is most directly lit. This is most often depicted as bright white. From the highlight, moving toward the shadow, progressively less light is cast on the object until the point is reached where the surface faces away from the light. Here there is a more sudden transition to darker values, or core shadow. At the bottom of the sphere a lighter value is produced by shadow mixed with light reflected from the surrounding environment. This lighter value defines the bottom edge of the sphere. In contrast, the sphere casts a shadow

1.50 Diagram of chiaroscuro

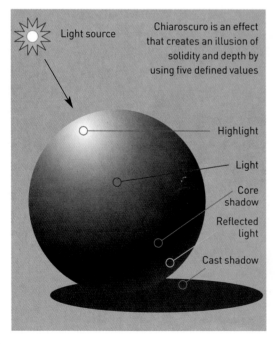

Light source

Chiaroscuro is an effect that creates an illusion of solidity and depth by using five defined values

Highlight

Light

Core shadow

Reflected light

Cast shadow

Highlight

Light

Core shadow

Reflected light

Cast shadow

1.51 Chiaroscuro graphic applied to Pierre-Paul Prud'hon, *Study for La Source,* *c.* 1801. Black and white chalk on blue paper, 21¾ × 15¼". Sterling and Francine Clark Art Institute, Williamstown, Massachusetts

away from the direction of the light source. Near the edge of the cast shadow, as light from the surrounding environment increases, the shadow becomes lighter.

In *Study for La Source*, the French artist Pierre-Paul Prud'hon (1758–1823) uses chiaroscuro in the drawing of a female figure (**1.51**). If you look carefully at the figure's upper left leg (the leg on the viewer's right), you

Renaissance: a period of cultural and artistic change in Europe from the fourteenth to the seventeenth century

Highlight: an area of lightest value in a work

can see that the chiaroscuro is being used just as it is in **1.50**. There is an area of highlight on the knee transitioning to the lighted thigh. Under the knee and thigh there is a strong core shadow: reflected light can be seen on the calf and the underside of the thigh. The reflected light is accentuated by the dark cast shadow behind the calf. Prud'hon's use of black and white chalk on a gray paper allows him to accentuate the lightest and darkest areas, the chiaroscuro.

Dramatic effects can be achieved through the use of chiaroscuro, especially if it is exaggerated. *The Calling of St. Matthew* by the Italian artist Caravaggio (1571–1610) uses strongly contrasting values to convert a quiet gathering into a pivotal and powerful event (**1.52**). The intense difference between lights and darks places extra **emphasis** on Christ's hand as he singles out Matthew, who points to himself in response. The light also frames Matthew and highlights the surprised looks of the others in the room as Matthew is called to become one of Christ's disciples.

1.52 Caravaggio, *The Calling of St. Matthew, c.* 1599–1600. Oil on canvas, 11'1" × 11'5". Contarelli Chapel, San Luigi dei Francesi, Rome, Italy

Emphasis: the principle of drawing attention to particular content in a work

Hatching: the use of non-overlapping parallel lines to convey darkness or lightness

Medium (plural **media**): the material on or from which an artist chooses to make a work of art, for example canvas and oil paint, marble, engraving, video, or architecture

Cross-hatching: the use of overlapping parallel lines to convey darkness or lightness

Shape: the two-dimensional area the boundaries of which are defined by lines or suggested by changes in color or value

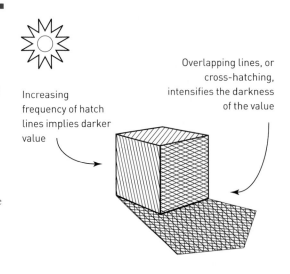

Increasing frequency of hatch lines implies darker value

Overlapping lines, or cross-hatching, intensifies the darkness of the value

1.53 Creating value using hatching and cross-hatching

1.54 Michelangelo, *Head of a Satyr*, c. 1520–30. Pen and ink on paper, 10⅝ × 7⅞". Museé du Louvre, Paris, France

Hatching and Cross-Hatching

Artists also use a method called **hatching** to express value (**1.53**). Hatching consists of a series of lines, close to and parallel to each other. **Media** that demand a thin line, for example engraving or pen-and-ink drawing, do not allow much variation in the width of the line. Here an artist may choose hatching or **cross-hatching** (a variant of hatching in which the lines overlap) to suggest values that create a greater sense of form and depth.

The Italian artist Michelangelo (1475–1564) uses cross-hatching in his pen-and-ink drawing *Head of a Satyr* (**1.54**). Cross-hatching gives the face of the satyr solidity and depth. By building up layers of brown ink, Michelangelo overcomes the restrictions created by the thin line of the pen. For example, if we look carefully at the cheekbone of the satyr it appears to be jutting out toward us. This effect is created by hatching and cross-hatching. The bright white highlight uses no lines; the surrounding hatch lines define the transition from bright light to a darker value. As we move our gaze downward and to the right of the highlight we notice that a second layer of overlapping hatching lines intersects the diagonals bordering the highlight. Then, as we continue to scan downward and to the right we see more layers of hatching lines crossing over the previous. As the hatching lines cross over and over, the value appears to get darker. Michelangelo communicates three-dimensional depth by using narrow and two-dimensional lines.

Space

Value is just one of a variety of strategies artists use to communicate the idea of depth in a work of art. The strategies are techniques whereby an artist creates a sense of depth and the illusion of space.

Size, Overlapping, and Position

In a work of art, the size of one **shape** compared to another often suggests that the larger object is closer to us. Another way to create the illusion of depth is to overlap shapes. If one shape appears to

Gateway to Art: Hokusai, "The Great Wave off Shore at Kanagawa"
Methods for Implying Depth

1.55 Katsushika Hokusai, "The Great Wave off Shore at Kanagawa", from *Thirty-Six Views of Mount Fuji*, 1826–33 (printed later). Print, color woodcut. Library of Congress, Washington, D.C.

The Japanese artist Katsushika Hokusai (1760–1849), one of the great masters of drawing and printmaking, uses several devices to indicate depth in "The Great Wave off Shore at Kanagawa" (1.55). The artist makes one boat shape smaller than the others, so by *size comparison* we see the boat that is smallest as furthest. Hokusai also gives us other clues about depth. The shape of the wave *overlaps* the two largest boat shapes (on the bottom). In this way, the artist tells us that the water is closer to us than the boat shapes. The *relative positions* of the shapes in the print also imply depth. By placing the wave shape at the lowest point on the page, the artist suggests that it is closest to the viewer. As the shapes get higher in the composition, they appear to be further

away. Hokusai then draws our attention back to the foreground with the enormous white-capped wave shape that gives the piece its title. The placing of Mount Fuji lower than the top of the waves deliberately confuses the composition of the picture space, but it also adds to our sense of the size of the wave that towers over it. At first glance the mountain seems like just another wave, but once we realize it is the far-off Mount Fuji we get a sense of distance. We can then assume the boats are far off shore, and this contributes to our feeling of unease regarding the fate of these mariners in a churning, violent sea.

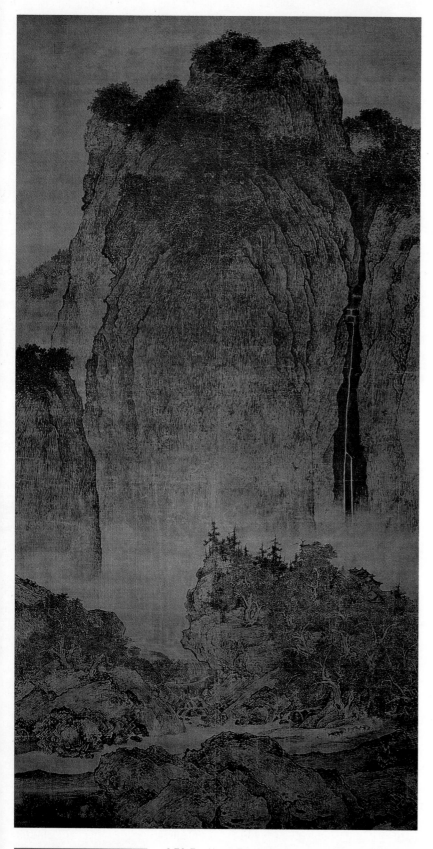

overlap another, the shape in front seems closer than the shape that is partially covered. Position in the **picture plane** is also an effective device for implying depth. A shape lower in the picture plane appears to be closer.

Alternating Value and Texture

The illusion of depth in two dimensions is often influenced by the arrangement of value and texture. Artists intersperse value and visual texture to create a sense of **rhythm**. Look at *Travelers among Mountains and Streams* (**1.56**), by Chinese painter Fan Kuan (*c.* 990–1020). From the bottom up, we first confront a large boulder, followed by a light opening (a road with travelers), and then some trees and foliage clinging to a rocky landscape. After this section there is another light area, after which the values gradually darken as our view climbs the face of a mountain. Finally, the sky is lighter, although somewhat darkened, completing the alternating rhythm from bottom to top. Each area of light and dark occupies different amounts of space, making the design more interesting. We can also note the change in visual texture from bottom to top. The texture appears to be extremely rough and detailed near the bottom. From this point it progressively becomes less precise. As Fan Kuan's landscape rises it also appears to recede. These visual layers create a sense of depth.

Brightness and Color

Brightness and color can both be used to suggest depth in a work of art. Lighter areas seem to be closer as dark areas appear to recede. This is especially true of color. For example, we are more likely to think that a green that is very pure and intense is closer to us than a darker green. American painter Thomas Hart Benton (1889–1975) used brightness and color to create a sense of distance in his painting *The Wreck of the Ole '97* (**1.57**). In the green areas we see the bright pure greens come forward as the darker, less intense greens fall away. The greens in the lower central portion of the work are more intense than the greens on the far left. Because

1.56 Fan Kuan, *Travelers among Mountains and Streams*, Northern Sung Dynasty, 11th century. Hanging scroll, ink and colors on silk, 81¼ × 40⅝". National Palace Museum, Taipei, Taiwan

Picture plane: the surface of a painting or drawing
Rhythm: the regular or ordered repetition of elements in the work

we perceive color that is more intense as being closer, this difference in color **intensity** helps us to feel we are at a safe distance from the terrible train wreck.

Atmospheric Perspective

Some artists use atmospheric perspective to create the illusion of depth. Distant objects lack contrast, detail, and sharpness of focus because the air that surrounds us is not completely transparent. The effect makes objects with strong color take on a blue-gray middle value as they get farther away: the atmosphere progressively veils a scene as the distance increases. Contemporary filmmakers use this atmospheric effect to give the illusion of great depth, just as traditional artists have always done.

In **1.58** the Greek temple to the left appears to be closer to the viewer than the other temples because its colors are brighter and its shape is more sharply defined. The smallest temple lacks detail and is tinged blue-gray, making it seem the

1.57 Thomas Hart Benton, *The Wreck of the Ole '97*, 1943. Egg tempera and oil on canvas, 28½ × 44½". Hunter Museum of Art, Chattanooga, Tennessee

1.58 The effects of atmospheric perspective

Intensity: the relative clarity of color in its purest raw form, demonstrated through luminous or muted variations

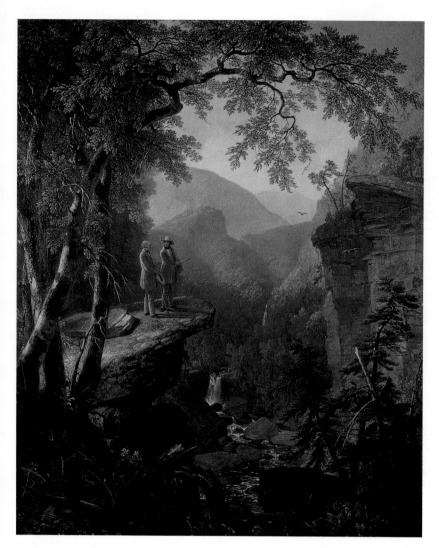

1.59 Asher Brown Durand, *Kindred Spirits*, 1849. Oil on canvas, 44 × 36". Crystal Bridges Museum of American Art, Bentonville, Arkansas

Isometric perspective: a system using diagonal parallel lines to communicate depth
Linear perspective: a system using converging imaginary sight lines to create the illusion of depth

parallels to communicate depth, while **linear perspective** relies on a system where lines appear to converge at points in space. Both forms of perspective tap into some of the ways we see the world and think about space.

Isometric Perspective

Isometric perspective arranges parallel lines diagonally in a work to give a sense of depth. The word isometric derives from the Greek meaning "equal measure." The system has been used by artists in China for more than a thousand years. It was particularly suitable for painting on scrolls, which can be examined only in sections. Since Chinese landscape painters were never really interested in portraying space from a single viewing point—they preferred to convey multiple viewpoints simultaneously—isometric perspective was their chosen technique to convey the illusion of space in the structural lines of architecture and other rectilinear objects. A section from the painting *The Qianlong Emperor's Southern Inspection Tour, Scroll Six: Entering Suzhou and the Grand Canal* by Xu Yang shows this system in action (**1.60**). The parallel diagonal lines that define the small L-shaped building in the center of the work suggest a three-dimensional object (**1.61**). Xu Yang, a Chinese artist working in the 1770s, uses this method to give the architecture along the Grand Canal the illusion of depth. This method of implying depth is not "realistic" according to the Western tradition, but the artist makes use of other spatial devices to help us understand how the space is structured. For example, the diminishing size of the trees as they recede into the distance reinforces the sense of depth.

Isometric perspective is now common in contemporary computer graphics as well. The computer game *The Sims* (**1.62**) is designed to express depth with a perspective method similar to the one Xu Yang used in 1770. The designers have created the architecture of the game using parallel diagonal lines to make "tiles." The tiles allow uniform objects to remain the same size, yet as they move around the game field they still imply depth. The game designers' choice

farthest away. American Asher Brown Durand (1796–1886) used comparable effects in his painting *Kindred Spirits* (**1.59**). The trees in the foreground are detailed and bright green, but as the trees recede into the landscape behind the two figures they become a lighter gray and increasingly out of focus. Lines and shapes also become less distinct as the illusion of distance increases. By using atmospheric perspective, Durand conveys an impression of the vastness of the American landscape.

Perspective

Artists, architects, and designers who wish to suggest the illusion of depth on a two-dimensional surface use perspective. They have the choice of several ways to do this, of which two are the most common. **Isometric perspective** uses diagonal

1.60 Xu Yang, *The Qianlong Emperor's Southern Inspection Tour, Scroll Six: Entering Suzhou and the Grand Canal*, Qing Dynasty, 1770 (detail). Handscroll, ink and color on silk, 2'3⅛" × 65'4½". Metropolitan Museum of Art, New York

Lines are drawn parallel and diagonal to create depth in isometric perspective

1.61 (above) Graphic detailing isometric perspective in scroll image

1.62 Screenshot from *The Sims*, a computer simulation game, 2000

of isometric perspective allows players to manipulate the architecture without distortion because the individual tiles remain the same size.

Linear Perspective

Linear perspective is a mathematical system that uses lines to create the illusion of depth in a two-dimensional artwork. (The "lines" can be **actual lines**, for example of buildings, or **implied lines** of figures or shapes.) The linear perspective systems used by artists are based on observation of space in the world we see around us: the two sides of a straight railway line or road appear to converge as they recede into the distance, even though in reality they are parallel.

Origins and History

The history of linear perspective begins in the fifth century BCE when the Chinese philosopher

Mozi observed that a pinhole of light projected on a wall in a dark room would also project an image. Later, around the year 1000, an Arabic mathematician named Alhazen theorized that, like the pinhole projection discovered by Mozi, light funnels into the eye so that we can see the world. He also used what we now know as a camera obscura (Latin for "dark room") to demonstrate the effects of projected light. This device, combined with the knowledge that light enters the eye, created a theoretical basis for the later development of linear perspective. The Renaissance artist and architect Leon Battista Alberti (1404–72) made use of these theories and his own observations to write his treatise *On Painting*.

Alberti proposed to emulate the image projected through a camera obscura in order to create a sense of depth in works of art. Other Renaissance artists began to use the device to explore the possibilities of naturalistic illusion

1.63 The effect of convergences: Edith Hayllar, *A Summer Shower*, 1883. Oil on panel, 21 × 17⅜". Private collection

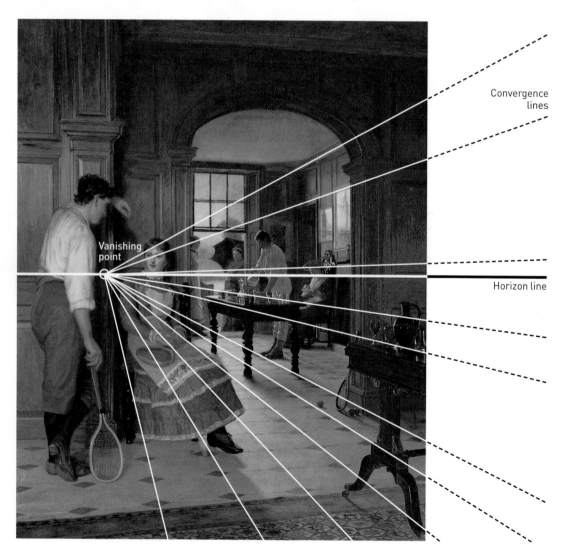

Convergence lines

Vanishing point

Horizon line

Actual line: a continuous, uninterrupted line
Implied line: a line not actually drawn but suggested by elements in the work

and the re-creation of reality. The artist would stand in a darkened room with a small hole in one wall. Sunlight would pass through the hole and project a full-color upside-down image of the objects outside the room onto the opposite wall. The artist could then draw the projected image or trace the image directly onto paper or canvas. The Italian Filippo Brunelleschi (1377–1446) was the first artist to apply the tenets that had been explored by Alberti and others to create works of art using linear perspective. Later artists would use the process to give realistic depth to their works.

The British artist Edith Hayllar (1860–1948) exhibited many works at the Royal Academy (a rare honor for a woman artist at the time) between 1882 and 1897. The enhanced photograph of her painting *A Summer Shower* shows the basis for linear perspective (**1.63**). The converging lines represent planes that are parallel to each other in reality. Notice how, if we were to draw lines from the right side of the image and continue them until they intersect, these parallel lines would appear to converge on one single point in front of the male tennis player

on the left of the painting. This is the **vanishing point**. These converging parallel lines are also known as **orthogonals**; the artist uses them here to create a composition that reflects the orderly life of upper-middle-class Victorian England.

There are a number of variations of linear perspective—one-point, two-point, and multi-point—depending on the effect the artist wants to achieve. These formal approaches to conveying a sense of depth are important tools.

One-Point Perspective

The **one-point perspective** system has some limitations. Although the system makes it possible to represent "real" space, certain rules have to be followed. Since one-point perspective relies on a single vanishing point, the scene must be directly in front of the artist and receding. The effect is something like standing on an empty highway facing an underpass (**1.64**). The sides of the road and the inside of the underpass appear to follow converging paths to a single point on the horizon. But if you redirect your gaze to the right or left of the underpass, the edges of the roadway and underpass are out

Vanishing point: the point in a work of art at which imaginary sight lines appear to converge, suggesting depth
Orthogonals: in perspective systems, imaginary sightlines extending from forms to the vanishing point
One-point perspective: a perspective system with a single vanishing point on the horizon

One-point linear perspective

Vanishing point

Horizon   line

Orthogonals

1.64 Applying one-point perspective technique

Vanishing
point

Horizon line

1.65 Use of one-point
perspective: Masaccio, *Trinity*,
c. 1425–6. Fresco, 21′10¹/₂″ ×
10′4⁷/₈″. Santa Maria Novella,
Florence, Italy

of direct sight and it is not as easy to see the
recession of space.

One of the first artists to use one-point
perspective was the Italian Masaccio (1401–28).
In his **fresco** of the *Trinity*, Masaccio places the
horizon line, an imaginary line that mimics the
horizon, at the viewer's eye level (note the figure)
and centers the vanishing point in the middle of
that line (**1.65**). The horizon line represents our
eye level and is the basis for the setting-out of a
perspective drawing. The orthogonals create an
illusion that the background is an architectural
setting. The end result is an effective illusion of
depth on a two-dimensional surface that must

have amazed visitors at the church of Santa Maria
Novella in Florence, Italy.

Two-Point Perspective

The one-point perspective system worked for
Masaccio because his composition relied on the
viewer standing directly in front of the vanishing
point. But if the vanishing point is not directly
(or near directly) in front of a viewer, or if the
objects in the work are not all parallel, one-point
perspective does not create a believable illusion
of depth. The Italian artist Raphael (1483–1520)
dealt with this problem in his famous painting
The School of Athens (**1.66a** and **1.66b**).

Fresco: a technique where
the artist paints onto freshly
applied plaster. From the Italian
fresco, fresh

Gateway to Art: Raphael, *The School of Athens*
Perspective and the Illusion of Depth

1.66a Raphael, *The School of Athens*, 1510–11. Fresco, 16'8" × 25'. Stanza della Segnatura, Vatican City

In *The School of Athens* Raphael combines one-point perspective and two-point perspective in one composition (**1.66a** and **1.66b**). The figure in the foreground is leaning against an object set at an angle that is not perpendicular and parallel to the rest of the architectural setting. Consequently, it cannot depend on the central vanishing point that has been determined following the rules of one-point perspective, or it will be distorted. Raphael deals with this situation by introducing two additional vanishing points. Notice that both these new vanishing points fall on the horizon line, following the established rules of perspective (vanishing points must fall on the horizon line). One vanishing point is positioned to the left of the central vanishing point that anchors the architecture, and the right vanishing point is outside of the picture. The block in the center is the only object in the composition that uses these two vanishing points, because the viewer is not perpendicular or parallel to it. Since it is turned at an angle, Raphael had to integrate another level of perspective into the work. All of the objects and architectural spaces depicted in this painting rely on one of these two perspective points.

1.66b (below) Applying two-point perspective: detail from Raphael, *The School of Athens*

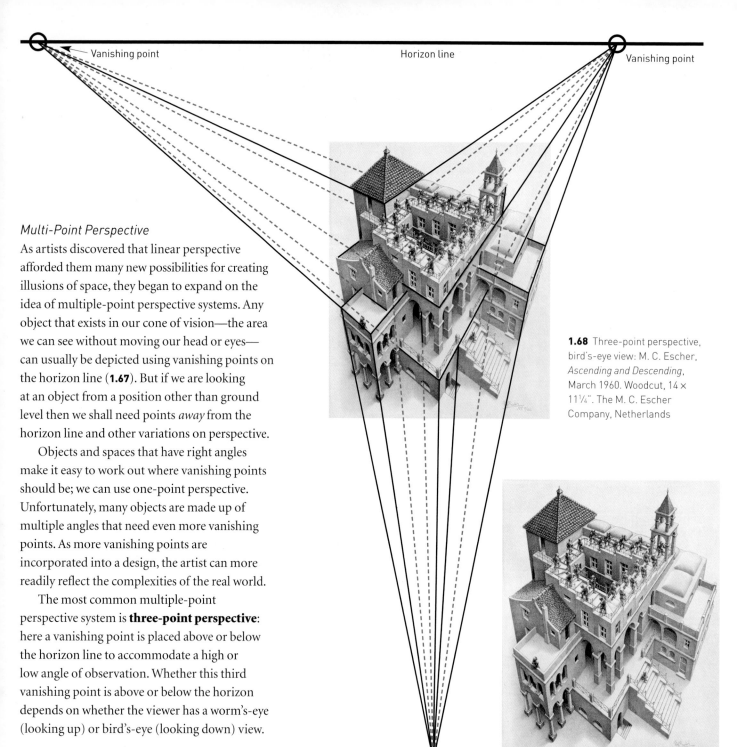

Vanishing point

Horizon line

Vanishing point

Multi-Point Perspective

As artists discovered that linear perspective afforded them many new possibilities for creating illusions of space, they began to expand on the idea of multiple-point perspective systems. Any object that exists in our cone of vision—the area we can see without moving our head or eyes—can usually be depicted using vanishing points on the horizon line (**1.67**). But if we are looking at an object from a position other than ground level then we shall need points *away* from the horizon line and other variations on perspective.

Objects and spaces that have right angles make it easy to work out where vanishing points should be; we can use one-point perspective. Unfortunately, many objects are made up of multiple angles that need even more vanishing points. As more vanishing points are incorporated into a design, the artist can more readily reflect the complexities of the real world.

The most common multiple-point perspective system is **three-point perspective**: here a vanishing point is placed above or below the horizon line to accommodate a high or low angle of observation. Whether this third vanishing point is above or below the horizon depends on whether the viewer has a worm's-eye (looking up) or bird's-eye (looking down) view.

1.68 Three-point perspective, bird's-eye view: M. C. Escher, *Ascending and Descending*, March 1960. Woodcut, 14 × 11¼". The M. C. Escher Company, Netherlands

1.67 Cone of vision

Vanishing point

Peripheral vision

Cone of vision

Cone of vision is the area one can see when focusing on a single point in space. The brim of a man's hat is outside of the cone of vision in an area of peripheral vision. He can only see things in this area if he moves his eyes.

Dutch graphic artist M. C. Escher (1898–1972) uses a third vanishing point in *Ascending and Descending*; we can see three distinct vanishing points (**1.68**). Two of the vanishing points are placed on the horizon line, but one is well below it. This gives us a bird's-eye view of the building that allows us to see the sides of the structure while looking down on it as if from above.

Three-point perspective: a perspective system with two vanishing points on the horizon and one not on the horizon

1.69 Albrecht Dürer, *Draftsman Drawing a Recumbent Woman*, 1525. Woodcut. Graphische Sammlung Albertina, Vienna, Austria

Foreshortening: a perspective technique that depicts a form at a very oblique (often dramatic) angle to the viewer in order to show depth in space
Woodcut: a print created from an incised piece of wood

1.70 Andrea Mantegna, *The Lamentation over the Dead Christ*, c. 1480. Tempera on canvas, 26¾ × 31⅞". Pinacoteca di Brera, Milan, Italy

Foreshortening

Foreshortening results when the rules of perspective are applied to represent unusual points of view. The German artist Albrecht Dürer (1471–1528), in his **woodcut** *Draftsman Drawing a Recumbent Woman*, portrays an artist at work drawing a figure (**1.69**). At this oblique angle the usual proportions of different parts of the body do not apply. The artist has a fixed lens or aperture in front of him to make sure he always views from the same point. As he looks through the gridded window he can see the coordinates, in relation to the grid, of the different parts of the model's body. He can then transfer those coordinates onto the similar grid marked on the piece of paper in front of him. The gridded screen in the illustration helps the artist to translate a three-dimensional form into a foreshortened two-dimensional composition.

A painting by the Italian artist Andrea Mantegna (1431–1506), *The Lamentation over the Dead Christ*, also illustrates foreshortening (**1.70**). The figure of Christ is oriented so that the wounded feet are placed in the extreme foreground, with the rest of the body receding away from the viewer back into space. Mantegna only slightly enlarges the feet, and depicts the body in shortened sections. Like perspective in general, foreshortening has the effect of grabbing our interest. In this work, we feel as if we are standing at the foot of the slab where they have put down Christ's dead body.

Conclusion

The depiction of space in a work of art is more than just an illusion, trick, or device. By means of a rich and creative variety of techniques, artists through the ages and across the world have given us clues we can connect with things we have seen and the ways in which we have seen them.

Artists anticipate the effects of light on an object by subtle variations in value. By noting how we see light and shadow the artist can use chiaroscuro or hatching to remind us of solid objects similar to those we have seen.

When an artist overlaps different shapes, or contrasts their sizes in a particular way, we begin to imagine something that is not there. The artist, from observation of the real world, mimics variations in texture, brightness, color intensity, and atmospheric perspective. These effects create an illusion that increases our ability to perceive space. The right method can help even the simplest graphic convey depth.

Different systems of perspective organize and distribute lines and forms in two-dimensional space, allowing artists to create a new and convincing sense of depth.

Implied depth has been a powerful tool for artists since the first created image. The ability to make a two-dimensional surface look as if it opens up into a new space expands our imagination and enhances our experience of the world.

1.4

Color

Color: the optical effect caused when reflected white light of the spectrum is divided into a separate wavelength
Primary colors: three basic colors from which all others are derived
Secondary colors: colors mixed from two primary colors
Pigment: the colored material used in paints. Often made from finely ground minerals
Hue: general classification of a color; the distinctive characteristics of a color as seen in the visible spectrum, such as green or red
Value: the lightness or darkness of a plane or area
Tint: a color lighter in value than its purest state

The first colors that made a strong impression on me were bright, juicy green, white, carmine red, black and yellow ochre. These memories go back to the third year of my life. I saw these colors on various objects which are no longer as clear in my mind as the colors themselves.

(Vasily Kandinsky, Russian painter)

Color is the most vivid element of art and design. By its very essence, color attracts our attention and excites our emotion. Just as personality and mood vary from one person to the next, our perceptions of color are personal and subjective. Few other phenomena touch our innermost feelings as deeply and directly.

Ancient Greek philosophers speculated that color was not a state of matter but a state of mind. Today, physicists tell us that an object's color is determined by the wavelengths of light it reflects. The refraction of light through a prism shows that we can think of white light as composed of constituent colors of different wavelengths (**1.71**). The colors we see are those portions of the light spectrum that a surface fails to absorb, and reflects instead. Physiologists, meanwhile, explain that this reflected light excites nerve cells that line the back of our eyes, and that their nerve signals are reprocessed and interpreted as color

in our brains. In natural sunlight, the color of an object we see is, in fact, a reflected fraction of light. When we see someone wearing a blue sweater, the blue we see is the portion of the spectrum that is reflected back to our eyes; the rest of the light is absorbed by the sweater.

Because color is so essential to our experience of seeing, it is deeply associated with the psychological and expressive aspects of our lives. That simple blue sweater may have many complex associations. We will explore and explain the complexities of color in this chapter.

Light and Color

The colors of the color wheel are the building blocks of most color combinations (**1.72**). The traditional **primary colors**—red, yellow, blue—cannot be mixed from any other two colors. The **secondary colors** are colors, such as orange (a blend of red and yellow) and green (a blend of yellow and blue), which can be mixed from two primary colors. In the color wheel the secondary colors are located between the primary colors because they naturally fall between them in the visible spectrum.

Colors of light and colors of **pigment** behave differently. You see this in action when you mix all the colors of paint together and get a muddy middle gray instead of white. There are two ways of working with color mixtures, known as subtractive and additive. When subtractive colors are mixed they make a darker and duller color because more of the visible spectrum is

1.71 White light can be separated into the visible spectrum using a prism

Light

Prism

Visible spectrum

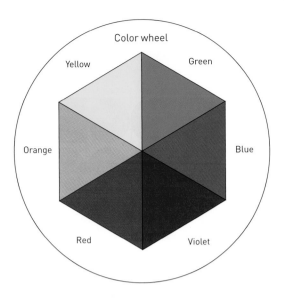

1.72 Traditional color wheel (red, yellow, blue primaries)

Color wheel

Yellow

Green

Orange

Blue

Red

Violet

1.73 Kane Kwei, *Coffin in the Shape of a Cocoa Pod*, *c.* 1970. Polychrome wood, 2'10" × 8'6" × 2'5". Fine Arts Museums of San Francisco

absorbed. When additive colors are mixed they make colors even lighter.

Dimensions of Color

All colors have three basic properties: hue, value, and saturation. By manipulating these three properties painters can achieve an endless range of visual effects.

Hue

Hues are the basic colors of the spectrum, the same as those in a rainbow: red, orange, yellow, green, blue, and violet. In addition, there are a

number of other hues we can see when white light is divided into the spectrum, for example blue-green or yellow-orange.

Color is such an important aspect of a coffin created by the African sculptor Kane Kwei (1922–92) that it is sometimes known as *Coffin Orange* (**1.73**). Kwei's coffin is painted with a brilliant middle-orange hue, the color of a half-ripened cocoa pod. Although cocoa pods are orange, the brightness of color used for this coffin is exaggerated. In Ghana, Kwei's native country, funerals are celebratory, loud affairs where bright color adds to the festive mood. Ghanaians believe that having lots of happy people at a funeral gives solace to the family of the deceased, reminding them that they still have many friends. Kwei got started in his career when his dying uncle asked Kwei to build him a boat-shaped coffin. It was such a hit in the community that others began to ask for coffins made in interesting shapes. *Coffin in the Shape of a Cocoa Pod* was commissioned by a cocoa farmer who wanted to tell everybody about his lifelong passion at his last party on earth.

Value

Each hue has a **value**, meaning its relative lightness or darkness compared to another hue. For example, a pure yellow has a light value and a pure blue has a dark value. Similarly, different colors of the same hue vary in terms of their value: there are light reds and dark reds. **Tints** are

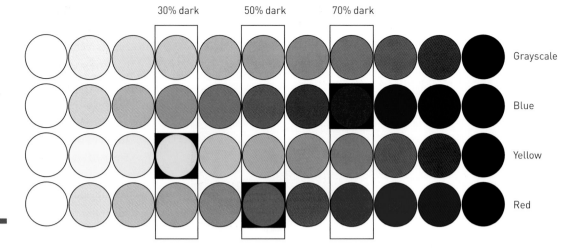

30% dark   50% dark   70% dark

Grayscale

Blue

Yellow

Red

Shade: a color darker in value than its purest state

Neutral: colors (such as blacks, whites, grays, and dull gray-browns) made by mixing complementary hues

Monochromatic: having one or more values of one color

Cubism: a twentieth-century art movement that favored a new perspective emphasizing geometric forms

Collage: a work of art assembled by gluing materials, often paper, onto a surface. From the French *coller*, to glue

Palette: the range of colors used by an artist

colors that are lighter than their basic hue; **shades** are colors that are darker. **1.74** shows relative values of red, blue, and yellow. The purest values, compared with those visible in the spectrum, are indicated by the black outline. **1.74** also shows the grayscale values; these are described as **neutral**, meaning there is an absence of color.

A work that uses only one hue is called **monochromatic**. An artist can give variety to such a work by using a range of values. Creating dramatic differences in the values of a color allows for ordered transitions from one value

to another. Many of American Mark Tansey's (b. 1949) large paintings are monochromatic. In *Picasso and Braque*, Tansey depicts two figures, whom he refers to as "Orville and Wilbur," a reference to aviators the Wright Brothers (**1.75**). He is also referring wryly to Pablo Picasso's (1881–1973) and Georges Braque's (1882–1963) habit of referring to each other as Orville and Wilbur during the pioneering days of **Cubism**. The two figures here have created a flying machine that resembles an early Cubist **collage**. The monochromatic **palette** is

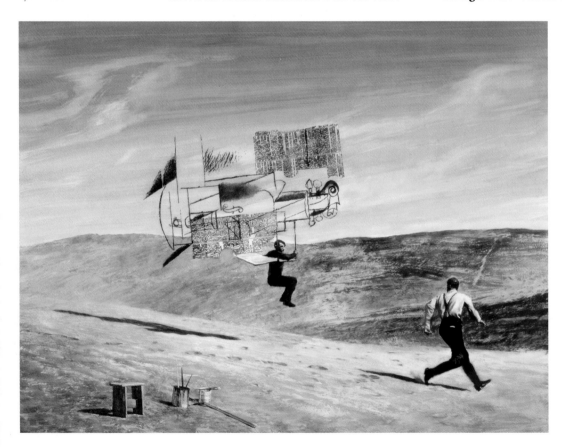

1.75 Mark Tansey, *Picasso and Braque*, 1992. Oil on canvas, 5'4" × 7'

reminiscent of the black-and-white photos of the Wright Brothers' experiments with flight, and the blue tone refers to an early **style** of Picasso's known as his Blue Period. Tansey uses humor to comment on historic discoveries in art and flight within a single monochromatic composition.

Saturation

When we think of the color yellow, we often imagine something strong, bright, and intense. Many shades of yellow exist, but we tend to associate a color with its purest state, or its highest level of **saturation**. A color at its most intense is said to have a high saturation. The color mustard yellow, which has a brownish tone, is said to have a lower level of saturation.

Saturation describes the purity of a hue as it is derived from pure white light. A red at the height of saturation is closest to its pure state in the spectrum (**1.76**). There are no tints or shades when a color is fully saturated. A color that is almost gray has a low saturation. Therefore a muted color, whatever its value, is less saturated as it gets further from the purity of its color in the spectrum. A pastel tone and a dark tone would each have a low saturation of color, but a grayed middle value of red would also have a low saturation of color; saturation is not related to value.

Works such as *Vir Heroicus Sublimis* (Latin for "heroic sublime man") by the American painter

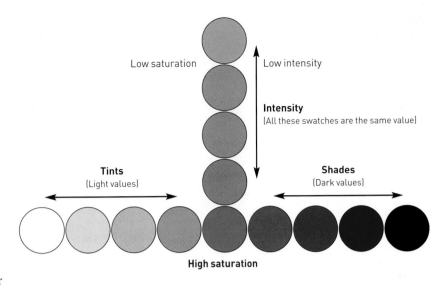

1.76 High and low saturation in a red hue

Barnett Newman (1905–70) rely for their visual impact on the value and saturation of color (**1.77**). The alternating colors of the narrow vertical lines (which Newman calls "zips") break up a broad red **plane**. The white zip makes a gap, while the maroon zip seems to meld into the red field. Subtle variations in the saturation of the red tones create the sensation that parts of the painting are separately lit. Newman wants viewers to stand close to the canvas, engulfed by color, meeting the artwork as one might another person. The square area in the center of this painting suggests

Style: a characteristic way in which an artist or group of artists uses visual language to give a work an identifiable form of visual expression
Saturation: the degree of purity of a color
Plane: a flat surface

1.77 Barnett Newman, *Vir Heroicus Sublimis*, 1950–51. Oil on canvas, 7'11⅜" × 17'8¼". MOMA, New York

1.78 André Derain, *The Turning Road, L'Estaque*, 1906. Oil on canvas, 4′3″ × 6′4¾″. Museum of Fine Arts, Houston, Texas

Newman's idealistic vision of the perfectibility of humankind.

The French painter André Derain (1880–1954) was a great advocate of highly saturated color. In his work *The Turning Road, L'Estaque*, his use of strong bright color makes the entire scene glow with energy and vitality (**1.78**). Derain was a member of the **Fauves** (French for "wild beasts"). The Fauves delighted in the new and brighter colored pigments made available by advances in industrial manufacturing. They used colors in their purest and strongest states as an act of defiance against the Academy, a state-sponsored school of art that set rigid rules for acceptable standards for art and artists at the turn of the century. The Fauves' fierce colors challenged the Academy and Western artistic conventions generally and earned the artists their nickname. Derain's painting is energized by deeply saturated color and color opposites, colors that intensify each other when seen close together.

Color Schemes

The color wheel displays important color relationships. It is a kind of color "map" that allows us to assess quickly the attributes of colors as they relate to each other. Colors opposite each other on the color wheel are called **complementary colors**. Complementary colors contrast strongly with each other. Colors adjacent to each other on the color wheel are called **analogous colors**. These colors do not contrast strongly with each other.

Complementary Color

When complementary colors are mixed, they produce gray; they tend to desaturate one another. However, when two complementary colors are painted side by side, these "opposite" colors create visual anomalies: they intensify one another, and each seems more saturated. This happens because complementary colors have markedly different wavelengths, creating an illusion (in the photoreceptors of the eye) of vibrating movement where their edges meet (**1.79**).

When the eye tries to compensate for the different wavelengths of two complementary colors, we tend to see color more intensely than when we see the colors separately. So when red is present, greens tend to appear more vibrantly green. Henri Matisse was a Fauve (like Derain) and explored the bold contrasts of black and

1.79 Color combinations, color complements, and vibrating boundaries

Primary/secondary analogous combinations

Primary/secondary and tertiary complements

Vibrating boundaries

Gateway to Art: Matisse, *Icarus*
The Artist's Fascination with Color

Throughout the whole of his career, the French artist Henri Matisse (1869–1954) explored the expressive potential of color. He often painted in southern France, and the kind of bright light he experienced there seems to emanate from his paintings. As a Fauve he used colors so bright that some viewers considered them violent. Much later, in the 1940s, Matisse began to excel in creating artworks by using scissors to cut out pieces of brightly painted paper. In part this was a response to his ill-health—he could not hold a brush up to a canvas for hours at a time. As he commented:

> Paper cutouts allow me to draw in color. For me, that simplifies matters. Instead of drawing an outline and then adding color— which means that line and color modify one another—I can draw directly with color ... the simplification means that the two means of expression can be united.
>
> (Matisse, 1951)

Matisse was interested in using vibrant colors to evoke an emotional response. To make his cutouts, he had his assistants pre-paint the paper in vivid colors. He found many creative ways to use these cutouts. In the case of *Icarus* (**1.80**), Matisse made a stencil of the cutout to print the image in his artist's

book *Jazz*. Subsequently, he used some of the images in *Jazz* as an inspiration for large tapestries that he designed by arranging cutouts on the wall of his apartment. Matisse found the process of designing with cutouts an ideal way to study different color relationships.

In *Jazz*, *Icarus* is accompanied by handwritten text, which reads: "At this moment we are so free, shouldn't we make young people who have finished their studies take a grand trip by plane." Matisse uses the myth of youthful exuberance to encourage young people to experience the world first hand—if not with wings, as the mythological young Icarus did, then by airplane.

1.80 Henri Matisse, *Icarus*, from *Jazz*, 1943–7. Page size 16⅞ × 12⅞". MOMA, New York

1.81 Frederic Edwin Church, *Twilight in the Wilderness*, 1860. Oil on canvas, 40 × 64". Cleveland Museum of Art, Ohio

white against the intensity of primary colors (see Gateway Box: Matisse, **1.80**, p. 97).

American landscape painter Frederic Edwin Church (1826–1900) used complementary colors for dramatic effect. In *Twilight in the Wilderness*, the intense red-orange clouds complement swathes of the blue-green evening sky, giving magnificence to a quiet landscape (**1.81**). The powerful color of the sky and its reflection in the water below reveal Church's awe and respect for the American landscape.

Analogous Color

Analogous colors are similar in wavelength, so they do not create optical illusions or visual vibrations the way complementary colors do. Painters use analogous color to create color unity and harmonies to steer viewers toward a particular attitude or emotion. By keeping the color within a similar range, artists avoid jarring, contrasting combination of colors and moods.

In *The Boating Party* by Mary Cassatt (1844–1926), her color palette creates a harmonious effect (**1.82**). This is the result of using analogous colors that are next to one another on the

1.82 Mary Cassatt, *The Boating Party*, 1893–4. Oil on canvas, 35⅜ × 46⅛". National Gallery of Art, Washington, D.C.

color wheel. In this painting, yellows, greens, and blues predominate. These colors have relatively similar wavelengths and do not intensify each other when placed in close proximity. Cassatt's color seems relaxed, reinforcing her theme. Cassatt was one of the few female (and only American) members of the **Impressionists**, a group of artists who shared an interest in the effects of light and color on the natural world, which they depicted in their paintings of everyday life.

In *Interior with Figures*, by British artist Howard Hodgkin (b. 1932), pinkish verticals on each side of the scene make a frame of analogous colors for the saturated reds in the space between

(**1.83**). Deep crimsons, fleshy pinks, and countless dabs of scarlet fill this scene with heat. Red is dominant here and heightens our response to an enigmatically erotic encounter.

Our Perceptions of Color

Our experiences of color are sometimes evocative or physical. Some colors are associated with emotional states: if we say we are feeling "blue," we are describing a psychological state of mind. Blue is also associated with cold, and red with hot: an association known as color **temperature**.

1.83 Howard Hodgkin, *Interior with Figures*, 1977–84. Oil on wood, 54 × 60". Private collection

Impressionism: a late nineteenth-century painting style conveying the impression of the effects of light
Temperature: a description of color based on our associations with warmth or coolness

Color can also affect the way we see. Because of color saturation, our eyes cannot fully comprehend all the colors we see, so our brain translates (or distorts) the incoming information. This is the basis of an illusion known as optical color, when boundaries between complementary colors seem to "vibrate" as our eyes struggle to compensate for differences between them.

Color Temperature

We associate color with temperature because of our previous experiences. We may have been burned by something red-hot, or chilled by cool blue water. Our perception of the temperature of a color can be altered if it is placed next to an analogous color. For example, green, a color we might associate with coolness, can be warm if we see it next to a cooler color like blue. A yellow-green would be warmer than a blue-green. Color temperature is relative to the other colors nearby. Artists use such associations to communicate physical and emotional states.

The colors chosen for the underglaze-painted lamp from the Islamic shrine the Dome of the Rock, in Jerusalem, are blue and green, on a white **ground** for contrast (**1.84**). They reflect the kind of color influence valued in the meditative atmosphere of a holy place. The choice of colors is cool and peaceful. Many people associate green and blue with water, plant life, a clear sky. Our life experiences with blue and green things can easily be associated with passive environments. The color green has positive associations in Islamic art and supports the peacefulness of prayer.

Optical Color

Sometimes our brains receive so much information that they simplify it. Optical colors are colors our minds create based on the information we can perceive. In **1.85** the square on the left contains so many red and blue dots that our brain mixes them so that we see a purple color. In the square on the right, red and yellow dots create an orange tone.

The French painter Georges Seurat (1859–91) used the optical qualities of color to create a

1.84 Mosque lamp from the Dome of the Rock in Jerusalem, 1549. Iznik pottery, 15" high. British Museum, London, England

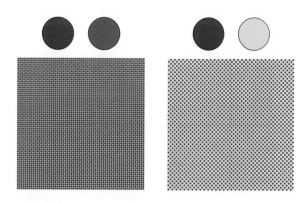

1.85 (above) Two squares, one filled with red and blue dots and the other with red and yellow dots to create optical color mixing effect

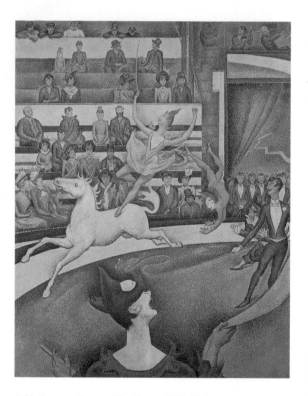

1.86 Georges Seurat, *The Circus*, 1890–91. Oil on canvas, 6'7⅞" × 4'11⅞". Musée d'Orsay, Paris, France

new style of painting, called **pointillism** because it relied on small dots (or points) of color. In *The Circus* Seurat paints a scene of lively entertainment, imbued with bright color and texture through the use of small dots (**1.86**, **1.87**). Because these dots are so close together, the colors we see are different from the actual colors of the dots. This optical mixing makes the colors more intense because they have retained their individual saturation, whereas if they were mixed on the palette they would appear more subdued. *The Circus*'s jewel-like diffusion of light and vibration of color make it visually exciting.

Color in Design

Artists who design images for commercial printing or to display on videoscreens take a different approach to color than such painters as Seurat and Hodgkin. In this section we will look at how color is used in print and electronic displays.

Color in Print

Most printed color images—from posters, to magazines, to this book—rely on four separate colors to create the range of colors that we see. Commercial printers use three primary colors—cyan (a kind of light blue-green), magenta (a light red-violet), and yellow—plus black, or key; the color wheel for printing is referred to as CMYK (**1.88**). An image is scanned and separated into the four colors. **1.89** shows a typical set of color separations. The image is re-created when the separated colors are printed in sequence, overlapping each other. The four colored inks are printed on paper as dots in a regular pattern ("screen"): the smaller the dot, the less of each color is printed. In the darkest colors the dots are nearly joined together. If you look very closely (using a magnifying lens) at the pictures in this book, you will be able to see the dots. Because the

pictures are divided into tiny dots of color, optical color mixing also plays a role in the control and perception of CMYK color, in a similar way to Seurat's Pointillist paintings.

Color in Electronic Displays

A computer-generated image produces color very differently. First, the digital display is illuminated by three different colored light cells, called phosphors, which project the primary colors of red, green, and blue (the color wheel is referred to as RGB) (**1.90**). Then, the electronic monitor turns a combination of phosphors on or off to produce the colors the designer wants. If the red and blue phosphors are on, the color on the display will be magenta, a secondary color. If all three of the primaries are on, the combination will result in white light (**1.91**). Complex combinations of these color lighting cells will result in millions of color possibilities.

The brilliant illuminated color of a video display is a seductive **medium** for computer artists. The digital artist Charles Csuri (b. 1922) has been creating imagery on computers since 1963. In *Wondrous Spring*, the RGB primaries create a dazzling illuminated array of colors reminiscent of a modern-day stained-glass window (**1.92**). A pioneer in the merging of art with scientific innovations in computer

1.88 Color wheel for commercial printing inks

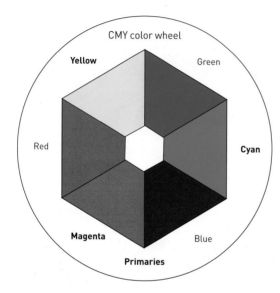

CMY color wheel

1.89 Subtractive color mixtures using CMY primaries, CMYK color separation, and image with exaggerated color print screen

1.90 Color wheel for light using red, green, and blue primaries

RGB Color wheel

1.91 Additive color mixtures using RGB primaries

1.92 (above) Charles Csuri, *Wondrous Spring*, 1992. Computer image, 4′ × 5′5″

technology, Csuri has explored and helped develop the digital realm as a viable art medium. The organic flow and brilliant color of *Wondrous Spring* remind us of growth and positive change. Digital works have a glow and rich color that bring new dimensions of color to art and design, and they attract a growing number of artists. This is a medium that will surely continue to prosper.

Color and the Brain

Color affects how we think and feel. Studies by Faber Birren, a color psychologist, have shown that when people are constantly exposed to red light they become loud, grow argumentative, and eat voraciously: red seems to bring out aggression in our behavior. We also make associations between colors and language—calling a coward "yellow," telling "white" lies—that can make our meaning clearer and affect how we feel about those colors.

Advertisers can reach their audience better by knowing how people respond to color. The most visible color is lime yellow because it lies near the middle of the visible spectrum. For this reason some advertisers use lime yellow in designing product packaging, to attract the attention of consumers.

Colors also have traditional symbolic values. Green has positive associations for Muslims; Confucius and Buddha wore yellow or gold; Jews and Christians associate the color blue with God. Our cultural beliefs about color also affect the way we think and feel.

The Psychology of Color

Color affects us physiologically because it alters our psyche. In Western cultures we associate love with red and sadness with blue. Some ancient cultures, like the Egyptians and Chinese, engaged in chromotherapy, or the use of colors for healing.

Artists understand that color affects the way we think and react to the world. Some of these reactions are culturally based: brides wear red in Asia, but white in the West. But there do appear to be some universal psychological associations. As we have seen, red (which we can easily associate with blood) can arouse feelings of anxiety, aggression, passion, eroticism, and anger. Green, a color we associate with growing plant life,

encourages restfulness, but it also suggests decay and illness.

The Dutch painter Vincent van Gogh (1853–90) was enormously affected by color, and studied its psychological effects. Van Gogh was plagued by periods of deep depression and was hospitalized on many occasions; through his treatment he learned a great deal about psychology. The colors in his painting *The Night Café* are carefully chosen to elicit emotional responses from viewers (**1.93**). In a letter to his brother Theo, van Gogh writes about the work, "I have tried to express with red and green the terrible passions of human nature." The color intensifies the psychological implications of the scene, in a seedy nightspot in Arles, France, as we wander into this menacing place as an outsider.

1.93 Vincent van Gogh, *The Night Café*, 1888. Oil on canvas, 28½ × 36¼". Yale University Art Gallery, New Haven, Connecticut

Expressive Aspects of Color

Artists like van Gogh wanted a viewer of a work to "feel" an artwork, rather than merely to understand it. Color in particular can express a wide range of emotions. Artists and designers know that the bright yellow of a happy-face symbol attracts our attention and lifts our spirits. They can use color to engage the viewer, whether it is the use of blue around the image of a political candidate to suggest traditional values, or green as an identifier of environmental awareness.

The French painter Paul Gauguin (1848–1903) used yellow for its uplifting associations when he painted *The Yellow Christ* (**1.94**). Gauguin painted this scene—a deliberately populist portrayal of folk spirituality—while in Brittany, France. In it, three women in traditional Breton dress appear to attend the crucifixion. Although Gauguin is known to have been inspired by a woodcarving in a local chapel, his choice of color is primarily symbolic. Through color he connects the crucifixion of Christ to the seasons of Earth and the cycle of life. Here, yellows and browns correspond to the colors of the surrounding autumnal countryside, harvested fields, and turning leaves. Gauguin's color palette relates the background natural world to the body on the cross, so that our gaze too is drawn in and upward. By using bright color, Gauguin creates a simple and direct emotional connection with the viewer. While depicting death, Gauguin chose colors that yet express the optimism of rebirth.

Conclusion

Artists must understand color. The terms hue, value, and saturation are essential. Other attributes of color, such as complementary and analogous color, allow artists to control how colors combine. Some colors seem warm or cool to us: we refer to this as their temperature. Sometimes, our physiological ability to perceive color can be challenged when there is too much color information. Optical color is our mind's response to this kind of sensory overload.

"Artists' color" is the name for the basic theory about color based on the three primary colors

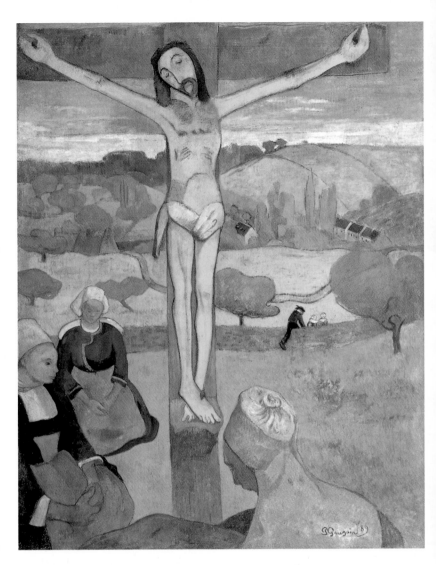

1.94 Paul Gauguin, *The Yellow Christ*, 1889. Oil on canvas, 36¼ × 27⅞". Albright-Knox Art Gallery, Buffalo, New York

(red, yellow, and blue). It was developed to help artists paint. However, modern four-color printing is based on the mixing of four inks: cyan, magenta, yellow, and black: CMYK color. In both artists' color and CMYK color, hues and values are mixed by adding pigments together. Modern video, digital cameras, and liquid crystal diode (LCD) computer monitors operate in yet another color space mixing red, green, and blue light, called RGB color. In RGB color, hues and values are modulated by controlling tiny projectors of red, green, and blue light. Interestingly, when all the hues of RGB color are mixed, white light is the result; whereas when all the pigments of artists' color or CMYK color are mixed, the theoretical result is black.

Artists have used color to express feelings—and have been exploring the human response to it—for thousands of years.

1.5

Time and Motion

Moving images are part of our daily experience of life in the twenty-first century. We see them on our TV and computer screens, on displays in stores, and on the street. But if we could travel back in time little more than a century, our visual experience would be quite different: all art images were still.

Time and **motion** are closely linked elements in art. Most of the traditional art **media** are inherently motionless and timeless. Paintings, for example, are static, holding a moment so that it can be experienced through the ages. But artists who work in static media have found imaginative ways to indicate the passage of time and the appearance of motion. And film and video have gradually overturned the conventions of traditional art, as new technology and media have evolved that allow artists to capture and express time and motion.

Time

Since events necessarily take place over time, any artwork that deals with events must show how time goes by. Stories of gallant deeds and heroic moments—and stories of life's ordinary moments too—unfold over time in chronologies of events. Writers use chapters, episodes, and other tools to give us a sense of how events unfold. Artists also find ways to communicate

the passage of time and to remind us of its influence on our lives.

The Passage of Time

Artists often seek to tell a story. When painters in the workshop of the fifteenth-century artist known as the Master of Osservanza illustrated *The Meeting of St. Anthony and St. Paul*, they solved the problem of how to tell a story in a single painting by merging a series of episodes into one picture (**1.95**). The story begins in

1.95 Workshop of the Master of Osservanza (Sano di Pietro?), *The Meeting of St. Anthony and St. Paul*, c. 1430–35. Tempera on panel, 18½ × 13¼". National Gallery of Art, Washington, D.C.

Motion: the effect of changing placement in time
Medium (plural **media**): the material on or from which an artist chooses to make a work of art, for example canvas and oil paint, marble, engraving, video, or architecture

the upper left-hand corner, where St. Anthony sets out across the desert to seek the hermit St. Paul. In the upper right, St. Anthony encounters a mythical creature called a centaur: half-man, half-horse, it was associated with the Greek god of wine, Bacchus. This symbol of earthly temptation does not deter St. Anthony. He continues on his lone journey through thick forest until he finally meets and embraces St. Paul: their meeting is the culminating incident in the foreground. The entire painting signifies a pilgrimage on the long and winding road of time, rather than merely a single moment. This linear method is still used by artists, comic-book writers, and designers who want to tell a story or express the passing of time.

The American artist Nancy Holt (b. 1938) examines cycles of time in her works. Many of Holt's sculptures intertwine the passage of time with the motion of the sun. Her *Solar Rotary*, at the University of South Florida, Tampa, is designed to express meaning from shadows cast by the sun throughout the year (**1.96**). The work features an aluminum sculptural "shadow caster" perched on eight poles high above the center of a circular concrete plaza. The shadow caster—a circular ring with eight serpentine arms—is oriented so that shadows cast by its central ring encircle notable dates set into the surrounding concrete plaza. The different angles of the sun at different times of the year make shadows at different locations in the sculpture. For example, on March 27 a circle shadow surrounds a marker that recounts the day in 1513 when the Spanish explorer Juan Ponce de León first sighted Florida. In the center, a concrete circular bench, into which a meteorite has been set, is encircled by the shadow at noon on the summer solstice, the longest day of the year (in the northern hemisphere), when the sun reaches its northernmost point. The meteorite symbolizes the connection between our world and the larger universe.

1.96 Nancy Holt, *Solar Rotary*, 1995. Aluminum, concrete, and meteorite, approx. height 20′, approx. diameter 24′. University of South Florida

The Attributes of Time

Time-based arts, such as film, embody six basic attributes of time: duration, tempo, intensity, scope, setting, and chronology. All these attributes exist in one of the first American movies, *Fred Ott's Sneeze*, made by Thomas Edison and W. K. Dickson in 1894 (**1.97**). The duration, or length, of this film is 5 seconds. The tempo, or speed, is 16 frames per second. The intensity, or level of energy, is high because the activity is sudden and strong. This film has a limited scope, or range of action, because it is confined to a simple activity. The setting, or context, is Thomas Edison's studio. The chronology, or order of events, can be seen in the still frames as Fred Ott appears to be placing some snuff in his nose, recoiling, then jerking forward as he sneezes.

1.97 Thomas Edison and W. K. Dickson, *Fred Ott's Sneeze*, 1894. Still frames from kinetoscope film. Library of Congress, Washington, D.C.

By the end of the nineteenth century, many visual artists had created their own techniques that made time part of the language of visual art.

Motion

The aim of every artist is to arrest motion, which is life, by artificial means and hold it fixed so that a hundred years later, when a stranger looks at it, it moves again since it is life.

(William Faulkner, American novelist)

Faulkner tells us that an artist can make even a still image move and come to life. Motion occurs when an object changes location or position. Because this process occurs as time passes, motion is directly linked to time. To communicate motion without actually making anything move, artists can choose to imply time or, alternatively, create the illusion of it.

Implied Motion

When artists imply motion, they give us clues that a static work of art portrays a scene in which motion is occurring or has just occurred. In the case of implied motion, we do not actually see the motion happening, but visual clues tell us that it is a key aspect of the work.

The seventeenth-century Italian sculptor Gianlorenzo Bernini (1598–1680) emphasizes implied motion in many of his marble sculptures. *Apollo and Daphne* illustrates a story from ancient Greek mythology in which the sun god Apollo falls madly in love with the wood nymph Daphne (**1.98**). Terrified, she runs from him and begs her father, the river god Peneius, to save her. As Apollo reaches Daphne, Peneius transforms his daughter into a bay laurel tree. To convey the action, Bernini uses diagonal lines in the flowing drapery, limbs, and hair. Daphne's fingers sprout leaves as bark encases her legs. At the pivotal moment in the story, the scene is suddenly frozen in time. Thereafter, since she could not be his wife, Daphne became his tree, and Apollo made the laurel wreath his crown.

1.98 Gianlorenzo Bernini, *Apollo and Daphne*, 1622–4. Carrara marble, 8' high. Galleria Borghese, Rome, Italy

1.99 Giacomo Balla, *Dynamism of a Dog on a Leash*, 1912. Oil on canvas, 35⅜ × 43¼". Albright-Knox Art Gallery, Buffalo, New York

The Italian **Futurist** Giacomo Balla (1871–1958) uses a different method of implying motion in his painting *Dynamism of a Dog on a Leash* (**1.99**). Balla paints a series of repeating marks to give the impression that we are seeing motion as it happens, as if we are viewing several separate moments at once. He paints the dog's tail in eight or nine different positions to communicate movement. Its feet are merely indicated by a series of strokes that give a sense of very rapid motion. The leash, a white **implied line**, is also repeated in four different positions. The **composition** gives viewers a sense of ongoing forward motion even though the paint on the canvas is perfectly still.

The Illusion of Motion

In the works by Bernini and Balla, the artists *imply* motion: we do not actually see it occurring, but visual clues tell us that the works, although static, portray motion. Artists can also communicate the idea of motion by creating an illusion of it. Artists create this illusion through visual tricks that deceive our eyes into believing there is motion as time passes, even though no actual motion occurs.

The American artist Jenny Holzer (b. 1950) uses the illusion of motion to enhance her

1.100 Jenny Holzer, *Untitled (Selections from Truisms, Inflammatory Essays, The Living Series, The Survival Series, Under a Rock, Laments, and Child Text)*, 1989. Extended helical tricolor LED, electronic display signboard, site-specific dimensions. Solomon R. Guggenheim Museum, New York

text-based presentations. Her untitled 1989 **installation** (in the Guggenheim Museum, New York, which was designed by Frank Lloyd Wright) displays messages as text (**1.100**). Although the text does not actually move, it appears to spiral up the ramped circular atrium of the museum as the tiny light-emitting diodes (LEDs) are illuminated and then switched off in an automated sequence. Thus the impression is created that the text is moving as time elapses. The intermittent flashing of lights creates a scrolling series of letters and words, like the flashing lights of the casinos on the Las Vegas Strip. Holzer uses this illusion to invigorate her messages and critiques of society.

Another illusion of motion that deceives the eye forms the basis for **Op art** (short for Optical art). During the 1960s, painters in this **style** experimented with discordant **positive–negative** relationships. There is a noticeable sense of movement when we look at *Cataract 3* (**1.101**), by British artist Bridget Riley (b. 1931). If we focus on a single point in the center of the work, it appears there is an overall vibrating motion. This optical illusion grows out of the natural physiological movement of the human eye; we can see it because the artist uses sharp contrast and hard-edged graphics set close enough that the eye cannot compensate for its own movement. Riley understands that the natural oscillation of the eye combined with the passage of time makes us feel a sense of motion.

1.101 (below) Bridget Riley, *Cataract 3*, 1967. PVA on canvas, 7'3¾" × 7'3¾". British Council Collection

1.102 Zoetrope, 19th century. Bill Douglas Centre for the History of Film and Popular Culture, University of Exeter, England

which a series of drawings was placed in a slotted cylinder (**1.102**). A viewer who looked through the slots as the cylinder was spun could see an image appearing to move and repeat, even though the drawings that made up the series were, of course, static. Inventions like the zoetrope were early forms of animation.

Cartoon animation grew out of these early stroboscopic experiments, and today's computer animation follows the same principle. Disney's *Finding Nemo* is compiled from individual frames that were computer-generated using 3-D modeling software (**1.103**). The animator can make changes to the images and then produce all the individual frames in a sequence that the computer plays in rapid succession. This succession of images is combined with other scenes and eventually committed to film—or, increasingly, digital media—for distribution to movie theaters.

"Movie" is an abbreviation of "moving picture," and movies became the dominant mode of artistic expression in motion during the twentieth century. Billy Wilder's *Double Indemnity* was one of the first films that used sharply contrasting modeling, angled shadows, and lighting effects to give a sense of emptiness.

Stroboscopic Motion

When we see two or more repeated images in quick succession they tend visually to fuse together. Many early attempts to show moving images were based on this effect, known as stroboscopic motion. One was the zoetrope, in

1.103 Walt Disney Pictures, frame from *Finding Nemo*, 2003

Installation: an artwork created by the assembling and arrangement of objects in a specific location
Op art: a style of art that exploits the physiology of seeing in order to create illusory optical effects
Style: a characteristic way in which an artist or group of artists uses visual language to give a work an identifiable form of visual expression
Positive–negative: the relationship between contrasting opposites

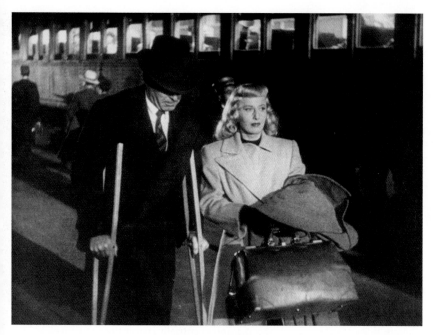

1.104 Still from *Double Indemnity*, Billy Wilder, 1944

the couple's deliberate movements. Wilder uses this kind of strong lighting effect throughout the film to enhance the drama of the plot.

Film relies on individual frames played in quick succession. Similar advanced forms of stroboscopic motion have been developed to stream digital video for the Web. Files with a series of multiple images (and sound files) are electronically transferred to a computer where they are played in rapid succession, much like a film movie. Internet users experience this when they view Flash animations posted on YouTube.

Actual Motion

We perceive actual motion when something really changes over time. We see it in **performance art** and in **kinetic art** when objects physically move and change in real **space** and time. Performance art is theatrical; the artist's intention is to create not an art object, but an experience that can exist only in one place and time in history. Kinetic art plays out the passage of time through an art object, usually a sculpture, that moves.

Performance art emerged as a specific form of visual art during the twentieth century when

The stark contrasts in lighting influenced an entire genre of movies called *film noir* (French for "dark film"). In the still shown in **1.104**, the two main characters walk through a darkened railway station as they prepare to murder the woman's husband. Notice the crisp long shadows behind them: the shadows create a sense of tension and foreboding by getting us to focus on each of

1.105 Blue Man Group perform at the Venetian Hotel, Las Vegas, Nevada, September 17, 2005

Performance art: a work involving the human body, usually including the artist, in front of an audience
Kinetic art: a work that contains moving parts
Space: the distance between identifiable points or planes

such artists as the German Joseph Beuys (1921–86) began performing his works, which he called Actions. Following his traumatic experiences in the German Air Force in World War II, Beuys incorporated everyday objects—such as animals, fat, machinery, and sticks—into his Actions, a series of self-performed situations in which the artist would interact with these things in a defined space and time. By putting common items in new situations Beuys conjured up different ways of thinking about our world so that we might question past practices.

Performance artists need not focus on a social or political issue. For example, from the 1980s the Blue Man Group performed in ways that integrated humor and music for passersby on the streets of New York (**1.105**). They used sound and **mime**, relying on bodily movements to communicate ideas without speech.

Kinetic sculpture has evolved during the twentieth century and is a notable example of art that moves. The earliest kinetic artwork is credited to French artist Marcel Duchamp (1887–1968), who mounted a bicycle wheel on a barstool so that the wheel could be spun. Later, the American sculptor Alexander Calder (1898–1976) invented the **mobile**, taking the name from a suggestion by Duchamp. The mobile relies on air currents to power its movement. Calder's kinetic sculptures were so finely balanced that even the smallest breeze would set them in motion. His final sculpture is the huge aluminum-and-steel mobile suspended in the National Gallery of Art in Washington, D.C. (**1.106**). It resembles its predecessors in being made up of counterbalanced **abstract** elements that move independently of each other. The result is a constantly changing visual **form**.

1.106 Alexander Calder, *Untitled*, 1976. Aluminum and steel, 29'10⅜" × 75'11¾". National Gallery of Art, Washington, D.C.

Mime: a silent performance work; actors use only body movements and facial expressions
Kinetic sculpture: three-dimensional art that moves, impelled by air currents, motors, or people
Mobile: suspended moving sculptures, usually impelled by natural air currents
Abstract: art imagery that departs from recognizable images from the natural world
Form: an object that can be defined in three dimensions (height, width, and depth)

Gateway to Art: Lange, *Migrant Mother*
Time and Motion in Photography

Although photography is a still medium, the work of a photographer is deeply concerned with motion and time. Photographers move around their subject, choosing the right focus for the shot and putting the camera in the best position to capture the image they seek. We can get a sense of how a still photographer captures a moment in time in the sequence of photographs Dorothea Lange took of Florence Thompson and her children (**1.107a–f**). In the span of a few minutes, Lange went from showing the family in the environment in which they lived—a tent—to an intimate portrayal of an individual. The first frame Lange shot includes the barren landscape of the farm and the lean-to in which the family lived. In the second shot, Lange has moved her camera closer to the tent, but the image does not give us much information about the people. In the third through the sixth shots, Lange zooms in on the woman and the children around her.

Still photographers must make decisions about the images they create. If we look at this series, the process of selection becomes clear. Lange chose specific moments to capture, and from those moments she further selected the one she felt most effectively communicated what she thought was most true (**1.107f**). Lange's careful composition of her image of the family did not end with shooting her photographs. Further changes were made to the negative in the dark room. Lange's original shot included the mother's hand holding onto the tent pole; Lange retouched the negative to crop out the hand. Because this photograph was meant to be an objective portrayal, the change was kept secret at the time, and has since been considered controversial.

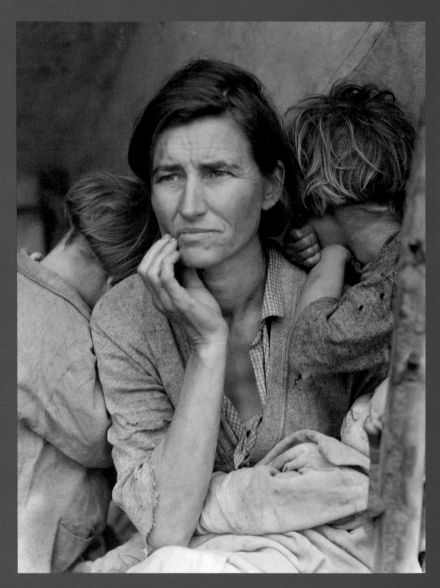

1.107a–e (top of page) Dorothea Lange, *Destitute Pea Pickers in California. Mother of Seven Children. Age Thirty-two. Nipomo, California*, 1936. Images a, c–e: Library of Congress, Washington, D.C. Image b: Oakland Museum of California

1.107f (above) Dorothea Lange, *Migrant Mother*, 1936. Library of Congress, Washington, D.C.

Natural Processes and the Passage of Time

Motion is not the only indicator of the passage of time in art. Some artists use biology and organic materials to create their artwork. Organic materials grow and degrade with the passage of time, so work by "bioartists" is always changing. Adam Zaretsky (b. 1968) has "grown" and performed works, such as *Workhorse Zoo*, that include living things. In this performance piece, he and Julia Reodica (b. 1970) lived for a week in an 8 × 8 ft "clean" room with an assortment of organisms: bacteria, yeast, plants, worms, flies, frogs, fish, and mice (**1.108**). During the week all the organisms were either growing or deteriorating. The artists' intention was to draw attention to the pros and cons of animal research.

Natural processes also dominate the work of American sculptor Ron Lambert (b. 1975), for whom the water cycle illustrates the passage of time. For *Sublimate (Cloud Cover)* he created a large transparent plastic environment in which water endlessly evaporates and condenses (**1.109**). Lambert draws attention to our immediate environment as he shows how the rhythms of nature become a measure of natural time that we gauge by how long we have to wait for the next rain.

1.108 Adam Zaretsky and Julia Reodica, *Workhorse Zoo*, 2002. Performance at the Salina Art Center, Salina, Kansas

1.109 Ron Lambert, *Sublimate (Cloud Cover)*, 2004. Water, vinyl, humidifiers, steel, aluminum, and acrylic, dimensions variable

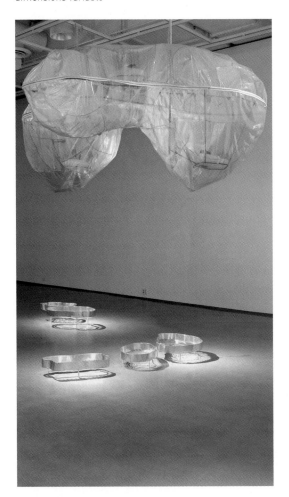

Conclusion

Movement and change are the essence of life and time. The traditional visual arts, although inherently static, have always been inventive and creative in finding ways to try to reflect, distill, and mimic the ceaseless flux of a world in motion. By means of illusion (Op art) or imitation (performance, kinetic, or "bioart"), in the last hundred years or so artists have been able to incorporate the passage of time and movement into their works using a variety of modern media. With the technological advances of the twentieth century, artists acquired new tools to capture time and create works that represent time and motion. Through film and video, we can appreciate the motion of life and have come to experience time in new ways. Television, movies, the Internet, and a multitude of other technologies use movement as an important visual element.

1.6

Unity, Variety, and Balance

Unity: the imposition of order and harmony on a design
Elements: the basic vocabulary of art—line, form, shape, volume, mass, color, texture, space, time and motion, and value (lightness/darkness)
Composition: the overall design or organization of a work
Variety: the diversity of different ideas, media, and elements in a work
Medium (plural **media**): the material on or from which an artist chooses to make a work of art, for example canvas and oil paint, marble, engraving, video, or architecture
Grid: a network of horizontal and vertical lines; in an artwork's composition, the lines are implied
Gestalt: complete order and indivisible unity of all aspects of an artwork's design
Principles: the "grammar" applied to the elements of art—contrast, balance, unity, variety, rhythm, emphasis, pattern, scale, proportion, and focal point

Unity—creating order or wholeness, the opposite of disorder—is central in the creation of a work of art or design. Unity refers to the imposition of order and harmony on a design. It is the sense of visual harmony that separates the work of art from the relative chaos of the surrounding world. Unity refers to the "oneness" or organization of similarities between **elements** that make up a work of art. Artists use the principle of unity to make choices that link visual elements to each other in a **composition**.

By comparison, **variety** is a kind of visual diversity that brings many different ideas, **media**, and elements together in one composition. Sometimes artists will use the discordance of variety to create uneasy relationships between visual elements. Sometimes this lack of similarity between elements can actively create a sense of unity when an artist imposes on the work a **grid** or other visual structure.

Balance refers to the distribution of elements, whether unified or varied, within a work. The number and distribution of different elements influence the composition. Balance in visual art is much like the balance we experience in real life. If we carry a large heavy bucket in one hand it pulls us to one side and we orient our body to

offset its weight. In art, the visual elements in one half of a work are offset by the elements on the opposite side. By making sure that the elements are distributed in an organized way, artists create balance.

Unity

Unity provides an artwork with its cohesiveness and helps communicate its visual idea. Artists face a communication challenge: to find a structure within the chaos of nature and to select and organize materials into a harmonious composition. An artist will identify specific elements in a scene and use them to create unity (see Gateway Box: Hokusai). Artists are concerned with three kinds of unity: compositional, conceptual, and **gestalt**.

Compositional Unity

An artist creates compositional unity by organizing all the visual aspects of a work. This kind of harmony is not easy to achieve. Too much similarity of shape, color, line, or any single element or **principle** of art can be monotonous and make us lose interest. Too much variety can lead to a lack of structure and the absence of a central idea. Experienced artists learn to restrict the range of elements: working within limitations can be liberating. The three similar diagrams in **1.110** illustrate the idea of compositional unity. Although A is unified, it lacks the visual interest of B. While C is a unified work, its visual variety feels incoherent and chaotic.

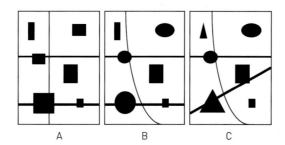

1.110 Three diagrams of compositional unity

A   B   C

Gateway to Art: Hokusai, "The Great Wave off Shore at Kanagawa"
A Masterpiece of Unity and Harmony

1.111 Katsushika Hokusai, "The Great Wave off Shore at Kanagawa," from *Thirty-Six Views of Mount Fuji*, 1826–33 (printed later). Print, color woodcut. Library of Congress, Washington, D.C.

In his print "The Great Wave off Shore at Kanagawa," Japanese artist Katsushika Hokusai created a unified composition by organizing repetitions of shapes, colors, textures, and patterns to create a visual harmony even though the scene is chaotic (**1.111**). These repetitions visually link different parts of the picture. Even Mount Fuji (A), in the middle of the bottom third of the work, almost blends into the ocean: because whitecaps on the waves (B) mimic the snow atop Mount Fuji, the mountain's presence is felt and reiterated throughout the composition. The shape and placement of the boats also creates a pattern among the waves. Because the great wave on the left is not repeated, it has a singular strength

that dominates the scene. Hokusai has also carefully selected the solids and voids in his composition to create opposing but balancing areas of interest. As the solid shape of the great wave curves around the deep trough below it (C), the two areas compete for attention, neither one possible without the other.

The words unity and harmony suggest peaceful positive coexistence in a chaotic world. A skillful artist can depict unity and harmony even in a work that portrays a scene that in reality would be chaotic and threatening. Here, Hokusai has organized a group of visual elements into a structure that makes sense because it has been simplified and ordered.

1.112 (right) Interior design,
I. Michael Interior Design,
Bethesda, Maryland

1.113 (far right) Linear
evaluation of elements in
interior design by I. Michael

The interior designed by I. Michael Winegrad (**1.112**) closely reflects the design in **1.113**. The interior has a balance of curved and straight lines that complement each other. The linear patterns of curved lines repeat (red), as do the other directional lines. Shapes are distributed throughout the scene (green). The composition appears harmonious without being boring.

In the work of Russian artist Marie Marevna (1892–1984), the unifying features are the angular lines and flat areas of color or pattern (**1.114**). Marevna was one of the first female members of the **Cubist** movement; here her Cubist **style** breaks apart a scene and re-creates it from a variety of different angles. In this image she shows us the seltzer bottle

1.114 Marie Marevna (Marie Vorobieff-Stebelska), *Nature morte à la bouteille*, 1917. Oil on canvas with plaster, 19¾ × 24"

Cubism: a twentieth-century art movement that favored a new perspective emphasizing geometric forms
Style: a characteristic way in which an artist or group of artists uses visual language to give a work an identifiable form of visual expression

from the side while we look down at the tabletop from above. The entire work becomes unified, however, because the artist paints a variety of different viewing angles using flat areas of color and pattern throughout, rather than relying on a more realistic representation. Even though we view the **still life** from many different angles, the artist was able to unify the composition by using similar elements. The texture of the paint, the hard diagonal angular lines, and the dominant gray-brown color all work together to counteract the potentially excessive variety that could have come from the many points of view presented.

The great masters of the **Renaissance** understood the importance of unity in their works. They also appreciated the value of putting limits on the number of different elements they introduced into a design, as Piero della Francesca (*c.* 1415–92) does in *The Flagellation* (**1.115**).

He concentrates on two major areas, **foreground** and **background**, where stand two different groups of figures. The organic human shapes in the foreground are balanced against the geometric lines of the background. The two groups complement each other and create an order that is reinforced by the strong horizontal and vertical lines throughout the work. This scene depicts Christ, before his crucifixion, being flogged by his captors. The figures in the foreground—whose identities are not known— seem oblivious to what is going on behind them. Rather than communicating a feeling of tension and violence, the composition is quiet and logical, emphasizing the mood of detachment and contemplation.

Some artists create compositional unity while gathering together bits and pieces of visual information. The African-American artist Romare Bearden (1911–88) captures the unity

1.115 Piero della Francesca, *The Flagellation*, c. 1469. Oil and tempera on panel, 23 × 32". Galleria Nazionale delle Marche, Urbino, Italy

Still life: a scene of inanimate objects, such as fruits, flowers, or motionless animals
Renaissance: a period of cultural and artistic change in Europe from the fourteenth to the seventeenth century
Foreground: the part of a work depicted as nearest to the viewer
Background: the part of a work depicted furthest from the viewer's space, often behind the main subject matter

1.116 Romare Bearden, *The Dove*, 1964. Cut-and-pasted printed papers, gouache, pencil, and colored pencil on board, 13⅜ × 18¾". MOMA, New York

of New York in the bits that make up his **collage** *The Dove* (**1.116**). In this work we see snippets of faces and hands, city textures of brick walls and fire escapes, and other associated images assembled into a scene that, at first glance, seems frenetic and chaotic. We may feel this pace of life when we visit a big city, but if we look beyond our first impressions we often notice the orderly grid of streets and the organization that underpins city life. Bearden reflects this order with an underlying grid of verticals and horizontals in the street below and in the vertical streetposts and buildings in the upper section of the work. The hectic composition is subtly coordinated by an implied triangular shape that runs from the cat in the lower left and the woman's feet in the lower right to the dove (hence the title) at the top center. These three points create a sense of depth while stabilizing the lively image of a hectic street scene.

Conceptual Unity

Conceptual unity refers to the cohesive expression of ideas within a work of art. Ideas can come to us in haphazard and unpredictable ways. Sometimes the expression of these ideas may not look organized, but an artist can still communicate them effectively by selecting images that conjure up a single notion. For example, an artist wishing to communicate the feeling of flight can use such symbols as feathers, kites, or balloons. Each of these has different visual attributes, but they all have an idea in common. That common idea is emphasized when they are placed together in the same work. The artist links images that, although different—perhaps even drastically different—in their appearance, have an idea, symbol, aspect, or association in common. Sometimes, on the other hand, an artist may deliberately break or contradict linkages between ideas to freshen up our tendency to find conventional—even boring—connections between them.

Artists bring their own intentions, experiences, and reactions to their work. These ideas—conscious and unconscious—can also contribute to the conceptual unity of a work and are understood through the artist's style, attitude, and intent. In addition, the conceptual links that artists make between symbols and ideas derive from the collective experiences of

Collage: a work of art assembled by gluing materials, often paper, onto a surface. From the French *coller*, to glue their culture: this too influences both the means that artists use to create unity and the viewer's interpretation of the work.

American **Surrealist** sculptor Joseph Cornell (1903–72) created boxes that contain compositions of **found objects**. His works seem to suggest mysterious ideas and elusive feelings. The disparate shapes, colors, and other characteristics of everyday things come together to form distinctive images. Cornell's works are like a complex game with the viewer, a game that reveals and conceals—just as in a dream or psychoanalysis—the artist's personality. In *Untitled (The Hotel Eden)*, Cornell has collected objects from life and sealed them in a box (**1.117**). Although the interior of the box is a protected place, the bird is caged and unable to get out. A yellow ball sits trapped on two rails that limit its freedom of movement to roll back

and forth. Neither the bird nor the ball is free. Placed together, all the different objects in the box make an idea greater than any one of them could create on its own. The artist has fused (and deliberately confused) his memories, dreams, and visualizations; the resulting artwork is a rich and complex visual expression of Cornell's personality and methods.

Gestalt Unity

Gestalt, a German word for form or shape, refers to something (here a work of art) in which the whole seems greater than the sum of its parts. The composition and ideas that go to make a work of art—as well as our experience of it—combine to create a gestalt. We get a sense of gestalt when we comprehend how compositional unity and conceptual unity work together.

1.117 Joseph Cornell, *Untitled (The Hotel Eden)*, 1945. Assemblage with music box, 15⅛ × 15⅛ × 4¾". National Gallery of Canada, Ottawa

Surrealist: an artist belonging to the Surrealist movement in the 1920s and later, whose art was inspired by dreams and the subconscious
Found object: an object found by an artist and presented, with little or no alteration, as part of a work or as a finished work of art in itself

1.118 *Vishnu Dreaming the Universe, c.* 450–500 CE. Relief panel. Temple of Vishnu, Deogarh, Uttar Pradesh, India

We can discover the many faces of gestalt by examining the ancient Hindu relief *Vishnu Dreaming the Universe* (**1.118**). In this stone carving, an abundance of human figures surrounds a much larger reclining figure; this is Vishnu dreaming. The repetition of the human shapes that attend Vishnu creates compositional unity: these similar shapes link to each other visually.

According to some texts written in the ancient Indian language known as Sanskrit, the existence of the universe, and its creation, are directly dependent on the god Vishnu, who is sheltered by the great serpent Ananta and sleeps on the Cosmic Sea. Through his sleep, the universe is reborn over and over into eternity. Hindu pantheism (the unity of many gods as one) is elegantly illustrated in this work. Brahma is the upper figure seated on a lotus that has sprouted from Vishnu's navel. Here he becomes the active agent of creation. The god Shiva, riding a bull

Value: the lightness or darkness of a plane or area

(Nandi), is at Brahma's left. Lakshmi, Vishnu's wife, attends her sleeping husband. Their unity of male and female creates a partnership that results in the birth of a new universe and many other universes into eternity. The dualities of male/female, life/death, good/evil are illustrated in the complex stories of the gods. Shiva, for example, is both creator and destroyer, destruction being necessary for creation—yet another unifying duality.

As is often the case, a religious idea provides profound conceptual unity. The image, the religious idea that the image illustrates, and the fervent belief of the artist who created the work interconnect through a symbolic representation in carved stone. As we come to appreciate how these aspects combine so completely in an artwork, we experience a sense of gestalt, an awakened understanding of the whole. This is a goal in any artwork.

Variety

If "variety is the spice of life," it is also the spice of the visual world. In art, variety is a collection of ideas, elements, or materials that are fused together into one design. Inasmuch as unity is about repetition and similarity, variety is about uniqueness and diversity. Artists use a multiplicity of values, textures, colors, and so on to intensify the impact of a work. It is unusual to see a good composition that has just one type of **value**, shape, or color. Variety can invigorate a design. The example in **1.119** shows a composition of shapes set into a rectangle on a grid. Even though

1.119 Variety of shapes and values set into a grid

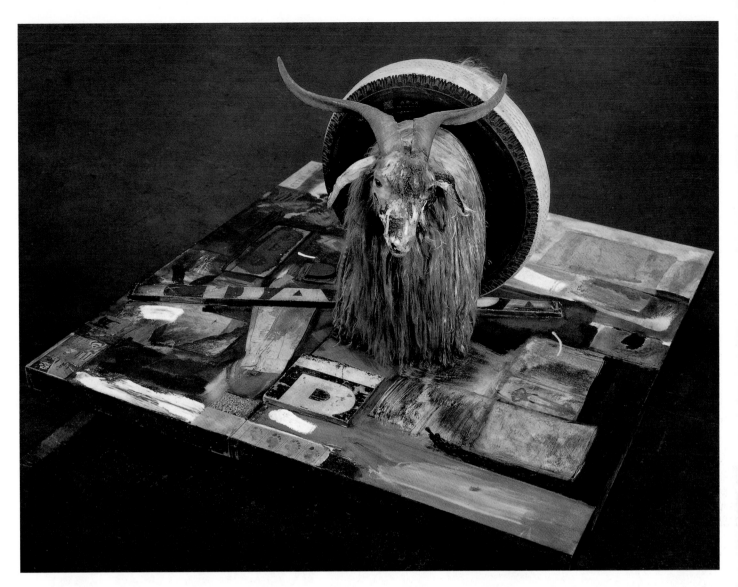

1.120 Robert Rauschenberg, *Monogram*, 1955–9. Mixed media with taxidermy goat, rubber tire, and tennis ball, 42 × 63¼ × 64½". Moderna Museet, Stockholm, Sweden

the grid structure is predictable, the variety of shapes and values counteracts the rigid structure. Many artists use this kind of variety to express an energy that would be lost if there were too much unity. Variety is the artist's way of giving a work of art a jolt.

The American Robert Rauschenberg (1925–2008) used variety to energize his artwork and challenge his viewers. In the work *Monogram*, Rauschenberg has used all kinds of different things to form his composition (**1.120**). The work features a stuffed goat with a tire around its middle standing on a painting. By combining these objects, Rauschenberg creates an outlandish symbol of himself as a rebel and outcast. The goat, an ancient symbol of male lust and a Christian symbol of souls cast out from salvation, becomes the totem of Rauschenberg's own provocative

behaviors and his violation of art-world conventions. The stuffed goat penetrates the tire and stands atop a symbol of the established art world (painting) while defecating a dirty tennis ball on it. For the first time in modern art, too, Rauschenberg breached the divide between painting and sculpture and took painting "off the wall." By using a variety of non-traditional art materials and techniques, the work becomes a transgression against traditional art and morals.

Using Variety to Unify

Although it might seem contradictory, variety can be unifying. Even while using a variety of different shapes, colors, values, or other elements, an artist can create visual harmony. This can be

1.121 Album quilt, probably by Mary Evans, Baltimore, Maryland, 1848. Appliquéd cottons with ink work, 9 × 9'. Private collection

seen in Baltimore album quilts, created by Maryland artists in the nineteenth century (**1.121**). These carefully sewn quilts are named after the scrapbooks kept by Baltimore girls. Rather than being constructed from scraps of leftover material, as many quilts are, these fiber works were made from new pieces of fabric, a reflection of the wealth of this port city. Like a scrapbook, these quilts use a variety of images and fuse them together into a finished work. Because a strong structure is imposed on the many different shapes through the use of a grid,

the work holds together as a unified whole. The quilted surface is an arrangement of shapes that form a unified composition.

Balance

Just as real objects have physical weight, parts of a work of art can have visual weight, or impact; these need to be balanced to achieve a sort of visual equilibrium. We can identify visual balance in a form or composition, the same as we can with weighted objects, by noting differences between the two halves we are looking at. If the amount of visual weight does not have a reasonable counterweight on the opposite side, the work may appear to be unsuccessful or unfinished. If there are reasonable visual counterweights the work seems complete, and balance has been achieved. Even placing a visual weight in the center of a composition can impose a strong balance on a design.

Finding visual weight and counterweight is a challenge for the artist; balance in a work is not always easy to define. But there are some situations that often arise. For example, dark and light, although opposites, can act as counterbalances. Large shapes or forms can be countered by groups of smaller shapes or forms. For many artists this process is intuitive; they make decisions about the work based on what looks right, rather than on a rigid set of rules.

Symmetrical Balance

If a work can be cut in half and each side looks exactly (or nearly exactly) the same, then it is symmetrically balanced. Near-perfect symmetry exists in the human body. For example, each side of our face has half a nose, half a mouth, half a chin, and so on. The same is true for most animals and a number of geometric shapes, such as circles and squares. Because it is a part of our physical body, symmetry can seem very natural and we can make natural connections to it.

Artists of ancient China designed a creature born of symmetry called the *t'ao t'ieh*. The image of the creature in an artwork is not immediately apparent, because its form is "hidden" amongst many separate symmetrical shapes and forms. It is as if a symmetrical collection of elements coalesce to reveal a monster mask. The image of the t'ao t'ieh has been used widely in Chinese art since the Shang Dynasty (1766–1122 BCE), when it appeared on ceremonial bronze objects. The meaning of this **motif** is mysterious, but it may symbolize communication with the gods. According to some accounts, the t'ao t'ieh mask represents a monster that, through its own gluttony, is devouring itself: a warning against overindulgence.

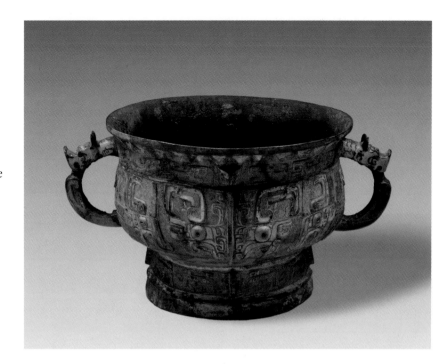

1.122 Ritual container from Gui, China, Shang Dynasty, 1600–1100 BCE. Bronze, 6¼ × 10¾". University of Hong Kong Museum

The t'ao t'ieh can be found on the bronze ritual container in **1.122** by identifying a pair of perfectly round "eyes" on either side of the central vertical ridge. On each side of this central ridge are patterns that mirror each other. Some of these signify horns, claws, fangs, ears, and even smaller images of animals. If you look carefully you may see two rhinoceros heads jutting out at the top of the left and right handles. The "monster" of symmetry lurks amongst the many parts of the image and waits for us to discover its hiding place.

Asymmetrical Balance

On an old-fashioned scale, the kind with a long arm centered on top of a vertical support, a single heavy object on one side can be balanced by several lighter objects on the other side as long as the weight on both sides is the same. Similarly, when artists organize a composition they often use different visual "weights" on each side of the composition. This is asymmetrical balance, also called dynamic balance; it applies when the elements on the left and right sides are not the same, but the combination of elements counters each other.

Chinese artists have used asymmetrical balance to reflect on life and spirituality. The thirteenth-century Zen Buddhist monk

Motif: a design or color repeated as a unit in a pattern

1.123 Muqi, *Six Persimmons*, Southern Song Dynasty, *c*. 1250. Ink on paper, 14¼ × 15". Ryoko-in, Dailoxu-ji, Kyoto, Japan

Axis: an imaginary line showing the center of a shape, volume, or composition
Facade: any side of a building, usually the front or entrance
Mandala: a sacred diagram of the universe, often involving a square and a circle

Muqi expresses balanced asymmetry in his work *Six Persimmons* (**1.123**). In this work, dark, light, and the subtle differences in shape are not distributed evenly between the left and right sides of the work. Muqi creates subtle variations in the placement of the persimmons on each side of the central **axis**. On the right are two large dark shapes with a heavy visual weight, one of which partially overlaps a light shape. On the left there is one light shape and two dark shapes, one of which is placed lower in the picture. Muqi brilliantly counteracts the visual "heaviness" of the right side by placing one shape lower on the left. The lower placement of the smallest persimmon in the picture adds visual weight to the left side and counters the visual weight of the largest fruit just above it. For Muqi, the use of brush and ink was a form of meditation, through simple, thoughtful actions, in search of higher knowledge. Although this work may look simple, the thoughtful arrangement of the shapes cannot be changed without undermining the "perfect" asymmetry.

Radial Balance

Radial balance (or symmetry) is achieved when all elements in a work are equidistant from a central point and repeat in a symmetrical way from side to side and top to bottom. Radial symmetry can imply circular and repeating elements. Artists can employ this kind of balance when it is necessary to depict an element more than twice. It is sometimes used in religious symbols and architecture where repetition plays an important role in the design.

Although the term "radial" symmetry suggests a round shape, in fact any geometric shape can be used to create radial symmetry. Italian architect Andrea Palladio (1508–80) decided to use the same elements on four sides of the Villa Capra (also called the Villa Rotonda) to achieve a perfect radial balance and allow the owner of this villa to take advantage of four views (**1.124**). Palladio referred to this symmetry in this way:

> The place is nicely situated and one of the loveliest and most charming that one could hope to find; for it lies on the slopes of a hill, which is very easy to reach. The loveliest hills are arranged around it, which afford a view into an immense theatre…; because one takes pleasure in the beautiful view on all four sides, loggias were built on all four facades.

Palladio wants people who live in this building to be able to experience four views of the surrounding countryside from a single vantage point. If we were to open all four sets of doors we could look in four separate directions as we turned on the villa's center point. Palladio's plan repeats the loggias, or porch-like entrances, on all four **facades**; they are all equidistant from the center of the building.

The Tibetan sand painting in **1.125** is a diagram of the universe (also known as a **mandala**) from a human perspective. The Tibetan Buddhist monks who created this work have placed a series of symbols equidistant from the center. In this mandala the colors vary

1.124 Andrea Palladio, Plan and part elevation/section of the Villa Rotonda, Vicenza, Italy, begun 1565/6. From the *Quattro Libri*, Book II

1.125 (below) Amitayas mandala created by the monks of Drepung Loseling Monastery, Tibet

but the shapes pointing in four different directions from the center are symmetrical. The creation of one of these sand paintings is an act of meditation that takes many days, after which the work is destroyed.

Conclusion

Unity, variety, and balance are central principles that artists use to create visual impact. Unity gives a work a certain oneness or cohesion. So powerful is the force of cohesive oneness that even a fragment of a work—for example, a broken piece of a ceramic pot—may have aesthetic unity. An artist may unify a work in one or more of three ways: through the arrangement of its elements, such as shape, line, and color; through its subject matter or the ideas it describes; and by drawing us in so that we become intensely aware of what the artist intends to communicate—a perception of wholeness sometimes known as gestalt.

The other two fundamental principles that affect the visual impact of a work are variety and balance. Variety is expressed in contrast and difference, which create visual interest and excitement; artists may use extreme variety quite deliberately to give an artwork a sense of chaos and lack of control. Variety can be created by the use of different kinds of lines, shapes, patterns, colors, or textures, or even by intentionally distinguishing many separate brushstrokes or chisel marks.

Balance is imposed on a work when the artist achieves an appropriate combination of unity and variety. We appreciate balance by "weighing up" the organization of the visual elements in our minds, as we consider and examine an artwork; our comprehension of balance is primarily intuitive, and our intuitions are based on an instinctive ability to discern symmetries and patterns in the world around us. This innate awareness of symmetry is reflected in the abundance of symmetrical artworks, but artists also exploit it when they create artworks that rely for their effect on the disturbing feelings caused by asymmetry.

1.7

Scale and Proportion

The nineteenth-century French poet Charles Baudelaire wrote that "All which is beautiful and noble is the result of reason and calculation." Baudelaire was speaking of cosmetics and makeup, and not referring specifically to works of art, but his statement neatly summarizes the care with which artists determine **scale** and **proportion**. Artists use these key **principles** of design to control how they implement the basic **elements** of art, just as grammar controls how words work in a sentence.

We perceive scale in relation to our own size. Art objects created on a **monumental** scale appear larger than they would be in normal life. This monumentality imposes itself on us. In a work created on a human scale, its size corresponds to the size of things as they actually exist. Work at this scale often surprises us. Small-scale objects appear smaller than our usual experience of them in the real world. Often scale is used to indicate importance. Even so, scale does not always indicate significance; sometimes the smallest thing is the most significant.

Proportion is a core principle in the **unity** of any art object. Usually, an artist ensures that all the parts of an object are in proportion to one another. Alternatively, an artist can create a contradiction by portraying objects or figures out of proportion. For example, a cartoonist may portray a figure with disproportionately large nose or ears to exaggerate the prominent facial features distinctive to a famous personality. Careful proportion is a sign of technical mastery; discordant proportions can express a wide range of meanings.

Scale: the size of an object or artwork relative to another object or artwork, or to a system of measurement
Proportion: the relationship in size between a work's individual parts and the whole
Principles: the "grammar" applied to the elements of art—contrast, balance, unity, variety, rhythm, emphasis, pattern, scale, proportion, and focal point
Elements: the basic vocabulary of art—line, form, shape, volume, mass, color, texture, space, time and motion, and value (lightness/darkness)
Monumental: having massive or impressive scale
Unity: the imposition of order and harmony on a design

Scale

The scale of a work of art communicates ideas. A small work of art communicates something very different than a larger work. Small-scale pieces force viewers to come in close to experience the artwork. A small-scale work implies intimacy, like whispering in someone's ear or admiring a ring on their finger. Large-scale works can be experienced by groups of viewers and usually communicate big ideas directed at a large audience. Artists and designers make conscious choices about the scale of a work when they consider the message they want to put across.

Artists may also consider scale as they make more practical choices about a work. Considerations of cost, the time it will take to execute the piece, and the demands that a specific location may place on the work: all come into play in decisions about scale.

Scale and Meaning

Usually a monumental scale indicates heroism or other epic virtues. War monuments, for example, often feature figures much larger than life-size in order to convey the bravery of the warriors. However, the Swedish-born artist Claes Oldenburg (b. 1929) uses monumental scale to poke fun while expressing admiration for the little things of everyday life. Oldenburg believes that the items of mass culture, no matter how insignificant they might seem, express a truth about modern life. So he restyles small, often

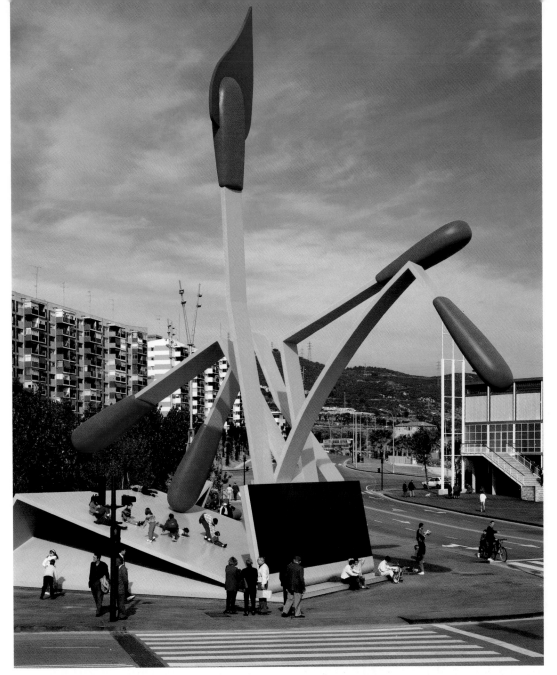

1.126 Claes Oldenburg and Coosje van Bruggen, *Mistos (Match Cover)*, 1992. Steel, aluminum, and fiber-reinforced plastic, painted with polyurethane enamel, 68′ × 33′ × 43′4″. Collection La Vall d'Hebron, Barcelona, Spain

overlooked objects on a monumental scale, giving clothes-pins and ice-cream cones a grandeur and significance they do not usually have. In the process, Oldenburg transforms the essence of these everyday things as he magnifies their sculptural form. Look at, for example, the enormous book of matches in **1.126**, a collaboration between Oldenburg and his wife, the Dutch-born sculptor Coosje van Bruggen (1942–2009).

The American Robert Lostutter (b. 1939) uses small scale to enhance the character of his work. Lostutter likes to create his works on the scale not of a human but of a bird. He paints the plumage of exotic birds in great detail onto human faces, while the tiny size evokes the bird from which the plumage was copied (**1.127**). The small scale of Lostutter's work—only one person at a time can see it properly—forces us to come closer; looking at it becomes an intimate experience.

1.127 Robert Lostutter, *The Hummingbirds*, 1981. Watercolor on paper, 1¾ × 5⅝″. Collection of Anne and Warren Weisberg

Hierarchical Scale

Artists can use size to indicate the relative importance of figures or objects in a composition: almost always, larger means more important, and smaller means less important. Hierarchical scale refers to the deliberate use of relative size in a work in order to communicate differences in importance. **1.128** shows the use of hierarchical scale in a **relief** sculpture from ancient Egypt. In the art of ancient Egypt, the king, or pharaoh, was usually the largest figure depicted because he had the highest status in the social order. Here, the largest symbol (A) represents the pharaoh; the figure is visually

1.128 Hierarchical scale: Relief from the northern wall of the hypostyle hall at the great temple of Amun, 19th Dynasty, *c.* 1295–1186 BCE. Karnak, Egypt

1.129 Jan van Eyck, *Madonna in a Church*, 1437–8. Oil on wood panel, 12⅝ × 5½". Gemäldegalerie, Staatliche Museen, Berlin, Germany

more dominant than the others. This scene depicts the military campaign of Seti I against the Hittites and Libyans.

The Flemish artist Jan van Eyck (*c.* 1395–1441) uses hierarchical scale to communicate spiritual importance. In his painting *Madonna in a Church*, van Eyck enlarges the scale so that the enormous mother and child fill the massive space of a **Gothic** church (**1.129**). In his effort to glorify the spiritual importance of Mary and the Christ child, van Eyck also separates them from normal human existence. Their gigantic appearance, relative to the interior, makes these figures appear to be larger than normal human beings. Van Eyck has scaled them to symbolize their central importance in the Christian religion.

Distorted Scale

An artist may deliberately distort scale to create an abnormal or supernatural effect. In the twentieth century, artists known as **Surrealists** created works that use dreamlike images to subvert our conscious experiences. The American Surrealist artist Dorothea Tanning (1910–2012), in *Eine Kleine Nachtmusik*, paints a sunflower at a scale that contradicts its surroundings (**1.130**). The sunflower seems huge in relation to the interior architecture and the two female figures standing on the left. By contradicting our ordinary experience of scale, Tanning invites us into a world unlike the one we know. This is a world of childhood dreams and nightmares where odd things happen, like the strangely alive sunflower and the unexplained wind that lifts the hair of one figure. The title, *Eine Kleine Nachtmusik* ("A Little Night Music"), is borrowed from a lighthearted piece of music by the eighteenth-century Austrian composer Wolfgang Amadeus Mozart, but ironically Tanning's scene exhibits a strange sense of dread.

Proportion

The relationships between the sizes of different parts of a work make up its proportions. By controlling these size relationships an artist can enhance the expressive and descriptive characteristics of the work.

As size relationships change, proportions change. For example, **1.131** shows the profile of a Greek vase. If we change the width (B) or the height (C) the overall proportions change. Each of these vase profiles communicates a different

1.130 Dorothea Tanning, *Eine Kleine Nachtmusik*, 1943. Oil on canvas, 16⅛ × 24˝. Tate, London

Surrealist: an artist belonging to the Surrealist movement in the 1920s and later, whose art was inspired by dreams and the subconscious

1.131 Examples of how proportion changes on vertical and horizontal axes

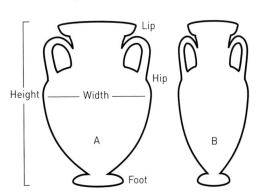

feeling simply because the ratio of height to width is different. When the width is reduced the vase seems elegant and light. Reducing the height makes the opposite true: the vase seems clumsier and weightier than the original profile (A).

For a two-dimensional work the artist chooses an area, or **format**, on which to make a drawing, painting, print, or design. The format's dimensions—its height and width— dictate a great deal about what kind of image can be created. For example, a format that is only 2 inches tall and 10 inches across will require that the artist create an image that is short and wide. Artists must plan ahead and choose the format that best fits their intended image.

Human Proportion

As we saw when discussing **1.131**, carefully chosen proportion can make an art object seem pleasing to the eye. As it happens, the parts of a vase are given names based on the human body: the lip, body, and foot. Just as the body of a vase can have agreeable or disagreeable proportions, the same is true of the human body.

In ancient Egypt the palm of the hand was a unit of measurement (**1.132**). Six palm widths equaled a unit of measurement called a cubit. The height of an average man was estimated at 4 cubits or 24 palms: the proportion of the man's palm to the height of his body was therefore 24:1.

The ancient Greeks were especially interested in proportion. Greek mathematicians investigated, in the visual arts and in other forms of art, such as music, the mathematical basis of beauty and of ideal proportions. The Greek sculptor Polykleitos wrote a treatise describing how to create a statue of a human being with ideal or perfect proportions. In the first century BCE the Roman writer Vitruvius wrote his book *On Architecture*, in which he claimed to set out the rules that Greeks and Romans applied to the design of architecture.

The Greeks sought an ideal of beauty in the principle of proportion. Figures made during the **Classical period** of Greek sculpture share similar proportions. To the Greeks, these proportions embodied the perfection of the gods. In contrast, fifteenth-century African sculptors preferred to

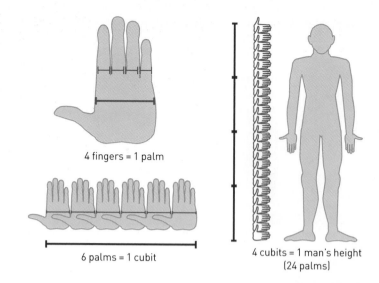

4 fingers = 1 palm

6 palms = 1 cubit

4 cubits = 1 man's height
(24 palms)

1.132 Ancient Egyptian system using the human hand as a standard unit of measurement

show status and individuality. Pictured in **1.133** is a sculpture of the Oni of Ife in **cast** brass. The Oni, or Monarch, of the Ife dynasty of the Yoruba people is shown standing in full regalia (ceremonial clothing and adornments). The Oni is the most powerful and important figure in this culture, yet his proportions here are neither realistic nor idealized. The head—about a quarter of the entire figure—is large; the Yoruba believe that the head is the seat of a divine power from whence a life source emanates to control personality and destiny. This figure, like Ife kings, represents a direct descendant of Oduduwa, the heroic leader whose children became the great leaders of the Yoruba. The facial features are idealized, suggesting that a personal heritage shapes one's destiny as a great leader. Many African sculptures exaggerate the head and face as a way to communicate status, destiny, and a connection to the spiritual. Both the Yoruba and the Greeks were concerned with creating a connection to the spiritual world, but African artists celebrated the importance of history (inheritance) and one's unique affiliation or office, while the Greeks sought an impersonal, ideal model.

The models used by the Greeks for calculating human proportion were later adopted by artists of ancient Rome and then by the artists of the **Renaissance**. Raphael used them in *The School of Athens* (see Gateway Box: Raphael) to ensure that the figures in his composition had the ideal human proportion used in the ancient world.

Format: the shape of the area an artist uses for making a two-dimensional artwork
Classical period: a period in the history of Greek art, c. 480–323 BCE
Cast: a sculpture or artwork made by pouring a liquid (for example molten metal or plaster) into a mold
Renaissance: a period of cultural and artistic change in Europe from the fourteenth to the seventeenth century

1.133 Nigerian Ife artist, Figure of Oni, early 14th–15th century. Brass with lead, 18⅜" high. National Museum, Ife, Nigeria

Gateway to Art: Raphael, *The School of Athens*
Scale and Proportion in a Renaissance Masterpiece

1.134 Raphael, *The School of Athens*, 1510–11. Fresco, 16'8" × 25'. Stanza della Segnatura, Vatican City

The Italian painter Raphael's sensitivity to proportion reflects his pursuit of perfection, an ideal of Renaissance artists. Raphael indicated the importance of his masterpiece by creating it on a magnificent scale: it measures 17 × 25 ft (**1.134**). The figures inhabit a well-proportioned interior that makes them seem human despite the large size of the work.

The figures in this work are particularly important because Raphael is showing us a gathering of great scholars from Classical antiquity. Raphael composed the individual figures so that the parts of each figure are harmonious in relation to each other and portray an idealized form. We notice two of these ideal human figures immediately

because Raphael has positioned them in the center of the work to draw our attention to them. In addition, Raphael has oriented the perspective, used to give the architectural elements a sense of depth, so that our eyes are drawn to the center of the work. This double emphasis on the center brings our attention to the opposing gestures of two famous Greek philosophers (Plato points to the heavens while Aristotle holds the palm of his hand down to the earth, a reference to their differing philosophical positions). Raphael's deft use of proportion and emphasis ensures that he is able to communicate his admiration for the ideas of the great minds of antiquity and the Renaissance.

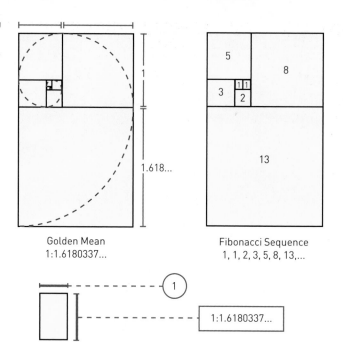

Golden Mean
1:1.6180337...

Fibonacci Sequence
1, 1, 2, 3, 5, 8, 13,...

Root 5 Rectangle

1:1.6180337...

1.135 The Golden Section

The Golden Section

The Greeks' interest in the use of mathematical formulas to determine perfect proportions has fascinated artists ever since. One of the best-known formulas is what has become known since the Renaissance as the **Golden Section (1.135)**, a proportional ratio of 1:1.618, which occurs in many natural objects. It turns out that real human bodies do not have exactly these proportions, but when the ratio 1:1.618 is applied to making statues, it gives naturalistic results. It is likely that Greek sculptors used much simpler methods than the Golden Section to calculate the proportions of their sculptures, but the resulting proportions are often very close to the Golden Section. The sculpture of Poseidon (some art historians say it is Zeus) is a famous example (**1.136**). Poseidon, a Greek god, had to have perfect proportions. The Greek sculptor applied a conveniently simple ratio, using the head as a standard measurement. In **1.136** and **1.137** you can see that the body is three heads wide by seven heads high.

Proportional Ratios

Artists have learned other ways to apply proportional formulas to organize their compositions and ensure that their work is visually interesting. One such technique is known as "Golden Rectangles," because it is based on nesting inside each other a succession of rectangles based on the 1:1.618 proportions of the Golden Section. The shorter side of the outer rectangle becomes the longer side of the smaller rectangle inside it, and so on. The result is an elegant spiral shape. In 1858 the English photographer Henry Peach Robinson (1830–1901), one of the great innovators of the photographic arts, used this idea to compose a photograph titled *Fading Away* (**1.138a** and **1.138b**). Robinson was well known for his work in fusing many different negatives to create a new image. This image shows his attention to the coordinated ratios in artistic composition. Notice how the right-hand drape divides the photograph

1.136 *Poseidon* (or *Zeus*), *c.* 460–450 BCE. Bronze, 6′10½″ high. National Archaeological Museum, Athens, Greece

1.137 (below, right) Diagram of proportional formulas used in the statue

1.138a (above left) and **1.138b** (above right) Proportional analysis: Henry Peach Robinson, *Fading Away*, 1858. Combination albumen print. George Eastman House, Rochester, New York

into two Golden Rectangles and how the spiral draws our eye to the dying young woman.

The Greeks applied their proportional systems to architecture as well as to sculpture. By applying the idealized rules of proportion for the human body to the design of the Parthenon, a temple of the goddess Athena, the Greeks created a harmonious design. As it happens, the proportions correspond quite closely to the Golden Section (**1.139**). The vertical and horizontal measurements work together to create proportional harmony (**1.140**).

Conclusion

Scale—whether monumental, human, small, hierarchical, or distorted—carries meaning and communicates a part of an artwork's message. It also sets the tone for proportion, the size relationships between the various parts of a work. When proportion conforms to scale, all the parts of the work look the way we expect them to; they seem proper and harmonious. In other times and places, the proportions of the representations of human figures have reflected the values of the societies that produced them. Scale and proportion are basic to most works; size choices influence all the other elements and principles in the design. Because scale and proportion have such an impact on the whole artwork, they are essences of the artwork's unity.

1.139 Iktinos and Kallikrates, Parthenon, 447–432 BCE, Athens, Greece

1.140 The use of the Golden Section in the design of the Parthenon

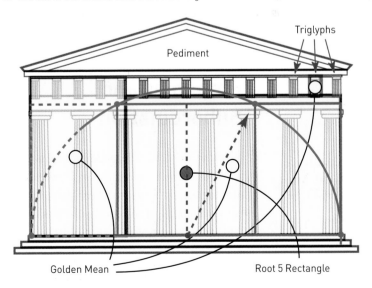

1.8

Emphasis and Focal Point

Emphasis and **focal point** are **principles** of art that draw attention to specific locations in a work. Emphasis is the principle by which an artist draws attention to particular content. A focal point is a specific place of visual emphasis in a work of art or design.

Most works of art have at least one area of emphasis and multiple focal points. Those few artworks that do not have areas of emphasis or focal points usually have little or no variation. An artist can emphasize focal points through the use of line, implied line, value, color—in fact, any of the **elements** of art can help focus our interest on specific areas. Like the bull's-eye on a target, focal points concentrate our attention. Even though our field of vision is fairly wide, at any given moment we can only focus our vision on a small area. The physiology of vision underlies the principle of focal point.

Emphasis and focal point usually accentuate concepts, themes, or ideas the artist wants to express: they signal what the artwork is about.

Emphasis and Subordination

When an artist emphasizes different elements in a work of art, he or she creates visual relationships and connections between them. The artist activates our visual and conceptual linkages and connects up new thoughts for us; he or she expands the scope of the work and highlights its main ideas. This is the essence of emphasis.

The opposite of emphasis is **subordination**: subordination draws our attention away from certain areas of a work. Artists choose carefully—in both two- and three-dimensional works—which areas to emphasize or subordinate.

We can see how emphasis works in **1.141**: a double-chambered vessel with mouse, by an ancient Peruvian artist. The mouse on the top left side of the work attracts our attention because it is so detailed, both in its three-dimensional modeling and its painted pattern. (Its eyes are a particularly strong focal point; in fact, eyes are primal focal points that fascinate us from early infancy.) The spout of the vessel also stands out, not only because of its color but also because of its geometric simplicity, which contrasts with the organic modeling and painting of the mouse. We find third and fourth areas of emphasis in the

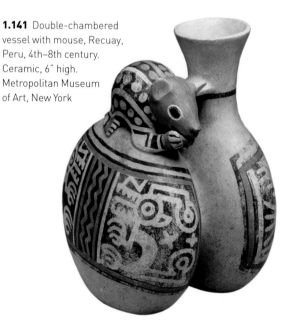

1.141 Double-chambered vessel with mouse, Recuay, Peru, 4th–8th century. Ceramic, 6" high. Metropolitan Museum of Art, New York

with the optical effects of **color**. In his work *Tin Lizzie Green*, Olitski frames our attention on the color field in the center of the work with three colored dots on the right, red horizontal strokes on the top and bottom, and a tan-colored stroke on the left (**1.142**). These color shapes support the real focus of this work, which is the blue-green color in the center. Olitski surrounds this with other colors so that we repeatedly alternate our view from the edges to the center and back again. The artist emphasizes the central area and subordinates the edges through the use of contrast between the **positive shapes** on the edges and the **negative space** of the center.

When a work does not have areas of emphasis, that changes the way we respond. For example, the painting *Blue Interior* by Mark Tobey (1890–1976) has an overall **implied texture** so uniform that we are hard-pressed to find places where our eye can rest (**1.143**). Tobey, who grew up in the Pacific Northwest, was inspired by the landscape near his native Seattle. He wishes to provide us with a sense of the Puget Sound area, with (as the artist says) its "virginal winds, air currents, and intermingled seasons." He is especially interested

1.142 Jules Olitski, *Tin Lizzie Green*, 1964. Acrylic and oil/wax crayon on canvas, 10'10" × 6'10". Museum of Fine Arts, Boston, Massachusetts

decorations on the two chambers of the vessel. Although these areas have a great deal of variety, they connect because they share common shapes, coloration, and texture that draw our attention away from the undecorated—subordinated—areas of the vessel. The playful variations of emphasis create a sense of humor and imagination.

Because **abstract** works can never directly evoke our memories of things or people, they frequently rely on compositional principles, such as emphasis. The American **color field** painter Jules Olitski (1922–2007) was primarily concerned

1.143 (right) Mark Tobey, *Blue Interior*, 1959. Tempera on card, 44 × 28"

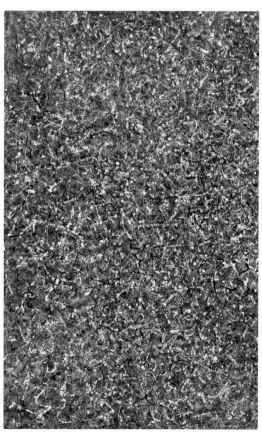

in creating a meditative response to the landscape. Because Tobey does not use areas of emphasis, we are free to roam visually in his painting, without encumbrance. We can immerse ourselves in the work, as if it were an ocean.

Focal Point

In any **composition**, a focal point is that specific part of an area of emphasis to which the artist draws our eye. He or she can do so by using line, implied line, or contrast. These techniques focus our gaze on that point in the work (see Gateway Box: Gentileschi).

In the painting *Landscape with the Fall of Icarus* the artist diverts our attention so that we barely notice Icarus plunging to his doom (**1.144**): a fine example of subordination. Flemish artist Pieter Bruegel the Elder (*c.* 1525–69) illustrates a story from Greek mythology. Icarus and his father Daedalus had been imprisoned on the island of Crete by its ruler, Minos. In order to escape,

Daedalus fashioned two sets of wings from feathers and wax. As father and son flew away from their prison, Icarus became overly exuberant. Although his father had warned him not to, Icarus, recklessly enjoying his new wings, flew too high and close to the sun. The wax in his wings melted, and he fell to his death in the sea below. In Bruegel's version of this story our attention is drawn to the figure in the foreground, plowing his field, unaware of the tragedy. Several other areas of emphasis—the tree on the left, the sunset, the town in the distance, the fanciful ships—also capture our interest. We hardly notice poor Icarus, whose legs are disappearing into the sea just in front of the large ship on the right. Because Bruegel has gone to such lengths to draw attention away from the plight of his subject, art historians think he is illustrating the Flemish proverb, "No plough stands still because a man dies." Or, as we might say, "Life goes on." Either way, it is a brilliant example of using emphasis to divert the viewer's attention away from a particular point in the work.

1.144 Pieter Bruegel the Elder, *Landscape with the Fall of Icarus, c.* 1555–8. Oil on canvas, mounted on wood, 29 × 44⅛". Musées Royaux des Beaux-Arts de Belgique, Brussels, Belgium

Gateway to Art: Gentileschi, *Judith Decapitating Holofernes*
Emphasis Used to Create Drama

1.145 Artemisia Gentileschi, *Judith Decapitating Holofernes*, c. 1620. Oil on canvas, 6'6⅜" × 5'3¾". Uffizi Gallery, Florence, Italy

Artists often take advantage of the strength of a single focal point to force us to give our attention to the crux or pivot of the work. Although a composition can have several focal points, the Italian Baroque painter Artemisia Gentileschi uses just one in her *Judith Decapitating Holofernes* (1.145). Through Gentileschi's use of directional line and contrasting values we are drawn irresistibly to the point where the climax of the story is unfolding. Bright light emphasizes Judith's arms and those of her maidservant (visually connected to the sword itself) as they stretch toward the dark values of their victim's head. The light values of the five bare arms create strong directional lines that lead to the focal point where blood spurts from the violent attack on Holofernes' neck. This double emphasis (contrast of values and directional line) freezes our stare upon the fatal blow, even as it obscures it in darkness.

Emphasis and Focal Point in Action

Artists can use direction, dramatic contrasts, and placement relationships to organize the elements in a work and draw our attention to areas of emphasis and focal points.

Line

1.146 *The Emperor Babur Overseeing his Gardeners*, India, Mughal period, *c.* 1590. Tempera and gouache on paper, 8¾ × 5⅝". Victoria and Albert Museum, London, England

Line is an effective way to focus our attention in an artwork. In Mughal India (the period from 1526 until the mid-nineteenth century), a garden was considered a work of art, one that symbolized the promise of paradise. Zahir ud-Din

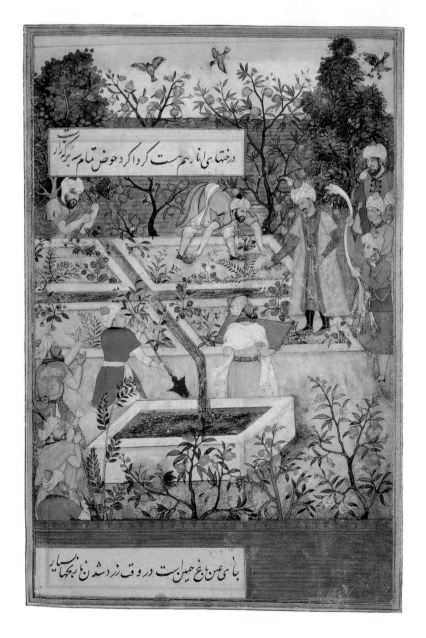

Muhammad bin Omar Sheikh, nicknamed Babur, founded the Mughal Empire in India when he conquered most of Central Asia and northern India. In **1.146**, the gardener/artist Babur is pointing to a feature that channels water in four directions. The life-giving properties of water and the four cardinal directions were important symbols of life and eternity. Because the garden was based on the perfect geometry of a square, it could be expanded an infinite number of times without disturbing the original plantings. In this image of the garden, water is the focal point both conceptually and visually.

We tend to notice diagonal lines because they appear to be more visually active than either horizontal or vertical lines. The strong diagonal of the channel draws our attention to the water as it runs toward us. The central cross-shaped confluence of the waters in the middle of the garden becomes the focal point of the composition.

Contrast

Artists look to create effects of contrast by positioning elements next to one another that are very different, for example areas of different value, color, or size. Value is an effective and frequently used means of creating emphasis and focal point. It also has the advantage that it can be used in subtle ways. In *The Funeral of St. Bonaventure*, a painting by Spanish artist Francisco de Zurbarán (1598–1664), most of the lightest values are reserved for the clothing adorning the dead body of St. Bonaventure (**1.147**). They create a central focal point that stands out in contrast to the surrounding dark values. We are drawn to the whiteness (symbolic of Bonaventure's chaste and spotless reputation) before we look at the surrounding characters. Enough light value is distributed to the other figures to allow our eyes to be drawn away from Bonaventure's body, making the composition more interesting.

Placement

The placement of elements within a composition controls **rhythm** and creates multiple focal points.

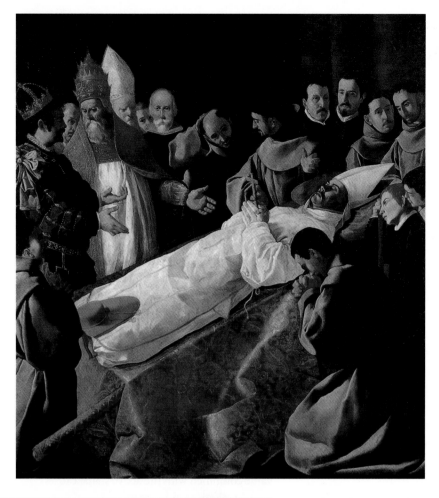

In the print "Riverside Bamboo Market, Kyōbashi," the Japanese artist Ando Hiroshige (1797–1858) has oriented three shapes; all of them are visually independent of each other (**1.148**). The positions of the moon, the bridge, and the figure in a boat form three separate focal points. Each shape commands our attention and draws more of our focus to the right side of the work. Even though the bridge is the largest shape, and so naturally catches our attention, the light value and hard geometry of the moon divert our gaze, and the moon becomes a secondary focal point. We look at the figure under the bridge because of its careful placement under the moon, and because it has a definite **outline** that contrasts strongly with the flat color of the water. The varying distances between the placements of the three focal points also create rhythm that adds visual interest. Hiroshige, a master of **woodcut** printing, uses placement to emphasize specific points in the work and enliven the composition.

Conclusion

Emphasis and focal point give a work of art punch. They announce important content in an artwork and call attention to the concepts the artist wishes to communicate. Artists rely on emphasis and focal point to give their work visual and conceptual impact.

All the elements and principles of art can serve to create emphasis. Both **actual** and **implied lines** shape our examination of a work of art by directing the movement of our gaze. Contrasts between different values, colors, or textures can sometimes be so dramatic and distinct that we cannot help but feel drawn to that area of a work. Our vision keeps coming back to these focal points; they are places where our thoughts linger for a while. During the process of artistic design, artists are constantly adjusting the elements of composition, calculating how they are going to influence the focus and duration of these pauses. The placement of these "centers of attention" generates rhythmic sequences while emphasizing the core significance of the artwork: its ideas, feelings, and images.

1.147 (above) Francisco de Zurbarán, *The Funeral of St. Bonaventure*, 1629. Oil on canvas, 8'2" × 7'4". Musée du Louvre, Paris, France

1.148 (left) Ando Hiroshige, "Riverside Bamboo Market, Kyōbashi," from *One Hundred Famous Views of Edo*, 1857. 15 × 10⅜". James A. Michener Collection, Honolulu Academy of Arts, Hawaii

Outline: the outermost line of an object or figure, by which it is defined or bounded
Woodcut: a print created from an incised piece of wood
Actual and **Implied lines:** actual lines are solid lines. Implied lines are impressions of lines created from a series of points that orient our gaze along a visual path

1.9

Pattern and Rhythm

Space: the distance between identifiable points or planes
Pattern: an arrangement of predictably repeated elements
Elements: the basic vocabulary of art—line, form, shape, volume, mass, color, texture, space, time and motion, and value (lightness/darkness)
Unity: the imposition of order and harmony on a design
Rhythm: the regular or ordered repetition of elements in the work
Composition: the overall design or organization of a work
Shape: the two-dimensional area the boundaries of which are defined by lines or suggested by changes in color or value
Value: the lightness or darkness of a plane or area
Color: the optical effect caused when reflected white light of the spectrum is divided into a separate wavelength
Contrast: a drastic difference between such elements as color or value (lightness/darkness)

Each day the sun rises and sets; we believe it will do so again tomorrow. Patterns and rhythms in nature help us make sense of the world. They express the order and predictability of our lives. Artists use pattern and rhythm to bring order to **space** and to create a dynamic experience of time.

When events recur, this creates a **pattern**. But other patterns are more regular, more predictable. In art, we can see patterns as the recurrence of an art **element**. In a work of art the repetition of such patterns gives a sense of **unity**.

Rhythm arises through the repetition of pattern. It adds cohesiveness in artistic **composition** because it links elements together. Rhythm affects our vision as we study a work of art. The rhythm of a series of linked elements guides the movement of our eyes across and through a design. The artist can also use rhythm to add variety.

Pattern

The use of repetition in a work of art usually results in the creation of a pattern. These patterns are sometimes based on occurrences in nature, such as the regular repetition of fish scales or the pattern created by the cracks that open as mud dries in the desert. Other patterns may be derived from the repeated shapes of mass-produced human-made objects, such as stacked tin cans or the warp and weft of woven cloth. Artists often create unity in works of art by repeatedly using a similar **shape**, **value**, or **color**, for example.

An artist can use repetition of a pattern to impose order on a work. But simple repetition can become more complex and make a work even more interesting when the pattern changes. Sometimes artists use alternating patterns to make a work more lively. The area covered by pattern is called the field; changes in the field can invigorate visual forms. The pattern in **1.149** shows a series of star shapes set on alternating black and white backgrounds on a rectangular field. The drastic difference in value combined with the active shape causes a visual vibration.

A variety of different colors and patterns enlivens work by the French painter Suzanne Valadon (1865–1938). In *The Blue Room*, Valadon includes three **contrasting** patterns (**1.150**). In the blue bed covering, in the lower portion of the painting, Valadon has used

1.149 Horizontal alternating pattern

1.150 Suzanne Valadon, *The Blue Room*, 1923. Oil on canvas, 35½ × 45⅝". Musée National d'Art Moderne, Centre Georges Pompidou, Paris, France

1.151 Huqqa base, India, Deccan, last quarter of 17th century. Bidri ware (zinc alloy inlaid with brass), 6⅞ × 6½". Metropolitan Museum of Art, New York

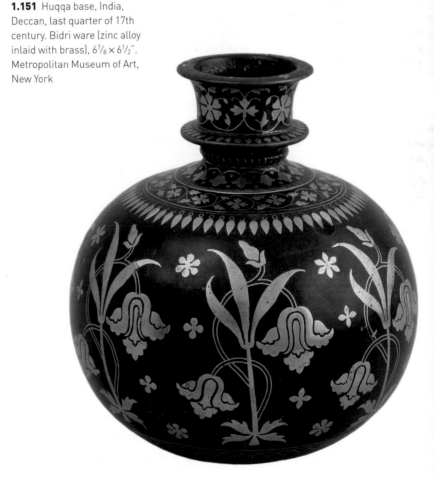

an organic pattern of leaves and stems. The green-and-white striped pattern in the woman's pajama bottoms dominates in direct contrast to the blue bed covering. Above the figure is a mottled pattern that again contrasts with the other two. The differences in these patterns energize the work.

Motif

A design repeated as a unit in a pattern is called a motif. Motifs can represent ideas, images, and themes that can be brought together through the use of pattern. An artist can create a strong unified design by repeating a motif.

A single motif can be interlaced with others to create complex designs. Many Islamic works use complex interlaced motifs, as two objects created in seventeenth-century India demonstrate. The huqqa base (a huqqa is a water pipe used for smoking) in **1.151** may at first glance appear

Abstract: art imagery that departs from recognizable images from the natural world

1.152 Pashmina carpet with millefleur pattern, northern India, Kashmir or Lahore, second half of 17th century. Ashmolean Museum, Oxford

to use little repetition. Nevertheless, as we study the overall design we discover that elements, such as the flowers and leaves of the plants, recur at intervals. Similarly, in the detail of a carpet (**1.152**), repeated flower-like motifs are arranged in a pattern in the center. Islamic artists delighted in the detail of pattern, as these two works show.

The American artist Chuck Close (b. 1940) uses motif to unify his paintings. Close uses a repeated pattern of organic concentric rings set into a diamond shape as the basic building blocks for his large compositions. These motifs, which appear as **abstract** patterns when viewed closely, visually solidify into realistic portraits of the model. In his *Self Portrait*, there is a distinct

1.153a Chuck Close, *Self Portrait*, 1997. Oil on canvas, 8'6" × 7'. MOMA, New York

1.153b Chuck Close, *Self Portrait*, detail

1.153c Chuck Close, *Self Portrait*, detail

difference between a close-up view of the painting and the overall effect when we stand back from this enormous canvas (**1.153a**–**1.153c**). The motif unifies the work and allows Close the freedom to control the color, **texture**, and value. In this case, the motif that Close uses is the result of a technical process. When applied to the larger image, however, it almost disappears because of each unit's tiny size. A grid that subdivides the entire image organizes the placement of each cell.

Randomness

Although nearly all artists have used pattern in their work, some have consciously tried to eliminate it. If pattern imposes order, then the introduction of chance metaphorically symbolizes anti-order. Artists who introduce randomness to a work try to avoid predictable repetition. Works made in this way purposely contradict widely used traditional methods. Some artists consciously fight against order, while others have relied on their subconscious and a kind of **automatic** reaction to the art materials.

Dada reveled in absurdity, irrationality, the flamboyantly bizarre, and the shocking. Nearly all the Dada artists had moved to neutral Switzerland by 1916 to avoid the draft. They vehemently opposed the so-called "rationality" of treaties and alliances that led to the horrific slaughter in the trenches of World War I. They also detested art and art movements—Dada was "anti-art": "Use a Rembrandt as an ironing board," said Marcel Duchamp. Dada design, writing, and theater were also expressly "irrational." Hans Arp (1886–1966), a German-

1.154 Hans Arp, *Trousse d'un Da*, 1920–21. Assemblage of driftwood nailed onto wood with painting remains, 15 × 10½ × 1¾". Musée National d'Art Moderne, Centre Georges Pompidou, Paris, France

French Dada sculptor and artist in Zürich, worked on creating "chance" arrangements. The shapes were derived from nature, but Arp made a point not to copy directly. Arp claimed that the arrangement of the shapes happened by random placement, as he dropped shaped wooden pieces onto the **picture plane** and glued them where they landed (**1.154**).

Rhythm

Rhythm is something you either have or don't have, but when you have it, you have it all over.

(Elvis Presley)

Rock and roll icon Elvis Presley might as well have been speaking about visual art when he was talking about musical rhythm. Rhythm is something that visual art has "all over." Rhythm gives structure to the experience of looking, just as it guides our eyes from one point to another in a work of art. There is rhythm when there are at least two points of reference in an artwork. For example, the horizontal distance from one side of a canvas to the other is one rhythm, and the vertical distance from top to bottom another. So, even the simplest works have an implicit rhythm. But most works of art have shapes, colors, values, lines, and other elements too; the intervals between them provide points of reference for more complex rhythms.

In Flemish painter Pieter Bruegel's work we see not only large rhythmic progressions that take our eye all around the canvas, but also refined micro-rhythms in the repetition of such details as the trees, houses, birds, and colors (**1.155**). All these repetitive elements create a variety of rhythms "all over."

In *Hunters in the Snow*, the party of hunters on the left side first draws our attention into the work. Their dark shapes contrast with the light value of the snow. The group is trudging over the crest of a hill that leads to the right; our attention follows them in the same direction, creating the first part of a rhythmic progression. Our gaze now traverses from the left **foreground** to the **middle ground** on the right, where figures

1.155 Pieter Bruegel, *Hunters in the Snow*, 1565. Oil on panel, 46 × 63¾". Kunsthistorisches Museum, Vienna, Austria

---

Background: the part of a work depicted furthest from the viewer's space, often behind the main subject matter

Focal point: the center of interest or activity in a work of art, often drawing the viewer's attention to the most important element

appear to be skating on a large frozen pond. Thereafter, the color of the sky, which is reflected in the skaters' pond, draws our attention deeper into the space, to the horizon. We then look at the **background** of the work, where the recession of the ridgeline pulls the eye to the left and into the far background. As a result of following this rhythmic progression our eye has circled round and now returns to re-examine the original **focal point**. We now naturally inspect details, such as the group of figures at the far left making a fire outside a building. As our eye repeats this cycle, we also notice subsidiary rhythms, like the receding line of trees. Bruegel masterfully orchestrates the winter activities of townspeople in sixteenth-century Flanders (a country that is now Belgium, the Netherlands, and part of northern France) in a pulsating composition that is both powerful and subtle at the same time.

Simple Repetitive Rhythm

Artists create repetition by using the same shape, color, size, value, line, or texture over and over again. A repeating "pulse" of similar elements sets up a visual rhythm that a viewer can anticipate. Such regularity communicates reassurance.

The design of buildings is often intended to reassure us about the stability and durability of the structure. Stability was so important to the ancient Romans that when the builders finally removed the temporary support structures for archways, the architects who had designed them were made to stand underneath. If the arch failed, the architect would be crushed. Like Roman architects, we want reassurance that our structures will endure. For this reason, architectural designs often incorporate simple repetition.

The main hall of the Great Mosque of Córdoba in Spain is full of seemingly endless rows of identical columns and arches made from alternating red and white voussoirs (stone wedges that make up the arch) (**1.156**). Each of these repeating elements—columns, arches, and voussoirs—creates its own simple rhythm. The accumulation of these simple repetitions also enhances the function of the space and becomes a part of the activity of worship, like prayer beads, reciting the Shahada (profession of faith), or the five-times-a-day call to prayer. Our trust in the permanence of architecture is combined with the timelessness of prayer in the repetitions of the Great Mosque of Córdoba.

Progressive Rhythm

Repetition that regularly increases or decreases in frequency creates a progressive rhythm as the eye moves faster or slower across the surface of the work. In the photograph *Artichoke Halved*, by American Edward Weston (1886–1958), the

1.156 Great Mosque of Córdoba, prayer hall of Abd al-Rahman I, 784–6, Córdoba, Spain

1.157 Edward Weston, *Artichoke Halved*, 1930. Silver gelatin print, 7⅜ × 9⅜". Collection Center for Creative Photography, University of Arizona, Tucson outer layers (bracts) of the artichoke bud are closer together nearer the center (**1.157**). Then, as they form the triangular center of the bud, a second progressive rhythm begins and the small bracts below the triangle form a third rhythm. The highly focused close-up view and strong photographic contrasts of black and white accentuate the sense of speeding up.

Alternating Rhythm

Artists can intertwine multiple rhythms until they become quite complex. The addition and alternation of rhythms can add unpredictability and visual excitement. On the island of Belau in the western Pacific, a traditional men's long house, called the *bai*, serves as a place for meeting and ritual (**1.158**). The imagery above the entry of this bai begins, at the bottom, with the regular rhythms of horizontal lines of fish, but the images above become increasingly irregular as they change to other kinds of shapes. The edges of the roof display a regular series of symbolic icons that, together with the building's horizontal beams, frame the composition and give the building **facade** a dynamic feel.

An alternating rhythm can also communicate chaos and make viewers feel uncomfortable.

1.158 Bai-ra-Irrai, originally built *c.* 1700 and periodically restored, Airai village, Airai State, Republic of Palau

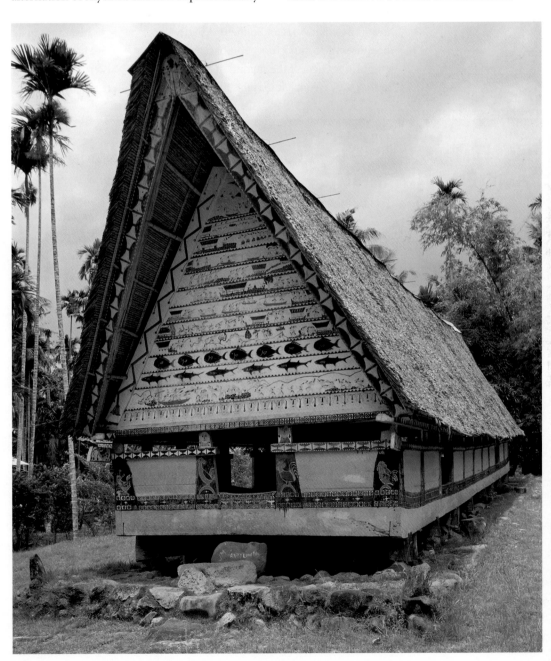

Facade: any side of a building, usually the front or entrance

Emphasis: the principle of drawing attention to particular content in a work

In Spanish painter Francisco Goya's *Third of May, 1808*, the alternating rhythms help define our ideas about humanity and inhumanity (see Gateway Box: Goya).

Rhythmic Design Structure

The idea of rhythmic structure helps us understand how artists divide visual space into different kinds of sections to achieve different kinds of effects. In her painting of 1849 *Plowing in the Nivernais: The Dressing of the Vines*, the French artist Rosa Bonheur (1822–99) creates a horizontal structure that leads our eye in sequence from one group of shapes to the next (**1.160a** and **1.160b**). Bonheur expertly organizes the composition, emphasizing the cumulative effect of the rhythm of the groupings as they move from left to right. Because the composition is so horizontal, the design **emphasis** directs our gaze sideways using a linear direction and rhythm. By changing the width of the gaps between the animals, Bonheur suggests their irregular movement as they plod forward, drawing the heavy plow. Each group also has a different relative size and occupies a different amount of space, creating a visual rhythm and energy that pulls our attention from left to right.

The careful composition and rhythmic structure in such paintings give an air of respectability and nobility to laborers of the field. Bonheur may have been sympathetic toward those who worked outside of the stuffy social order of the time, since her gender may have been a disadvantage in a traditionally male profession. Her effort to bring respectability to hard work also reminds us of the slow physical rhythms created by the brute strength of these beasts and

Gateway to Art: Goya, *The Third of May, 1808*
Visual Rhythm in the Composition

Spanish painter Francisco Goya's *Third of May, 1808*, shows an image of Napoleon's troops executing Spanish citizens during the French occupation of Madrid in 1808 (**1.159**). It can be divided up into two distinct rhythmic groups. Each side of the work has almost the same number of victims as executioners. Goya does not allow the "good" victims to overpower the "bad" occupiers in number, but keeps a visual balance to steady the work. Although the number of figures in each group is the same, they are distributed very differently. The group of French soldiers on the right stands in a pattern so regulated it is almost mechanical. Each of the soldiers adopts the same stance, and the strong horizontal barrels of the guns repeat uniformly. On the left side, the rhythms are much more irregular and unpredictable. The figures are not organized so rigidly: some figures are lying on the ground, some are standing, and some are kneeling. The pose (with arms held high) of the standing figure in white is repeated in the dead figure on the ground. The alternating rhythm in this painting leads our eye from the figure in white through a group of figures downward to the victims on the ground.

1.159 Francisco Goya, *The Third of May, 1808*, 1814. Oil on canvas, 8'4⅜" × 11'3⅞". Museo Nacional del Prado, Madrid

1.160a Rosa Bonheur, *Plowing in the Nivernais: The Dressing of the Vines*, 1849. Oil on canvas, 4'4¾" × 8'6⅜". Musée d'Orsay, Paris, France

1.160b Rhythmic structural diagram of **1.160a**

the irregularity of the plowman's steps as both of them work together to turn the weighty soil.

Conclusion

Artists frequently rely on rhythms and patterns to ground their work. Just like a great theater production, a blockbuster movie, a brilliant ballet, or a catchy tune, a well-composed work of art with visually exciting patterns and rhythms can thrill an audience. In works of art, good composition articulates patterns and rhythms in a way that grabs our attention.

Because the visual rhythm of pattern is predictable, it often tends to unify a work of art. By alternating the rhythm, the artist can reinforce the visual emphases of a work and make its composition visually stronger. The repetition of motifs such as those found in certain pottery and carpets can add the richness we associate with the finer things in life. But some artists try to contradict pattern by imposing randomness and chance to free a work from what they see as suffocating orderliness.

Good works of art, like Elvis as he gyrated on stage, have rhythm "all over." That rhythm dictates how elements visually relate to one another. These relationships make up a work's composition. Rhythm is a core part of any visual composition.

Simple repetitions can give a work a welcoming predictability that makes us comfortable. Progressive rhythm builds like a musical crescendo or diminishes like a fading echo, and can suggest growth or ebbing power. Alternating rhythm can create a dynamic sense of energy and add visual interest, because we may not be able to predict what the rhythm will do next. Irregular rhythm can make a work seem unpredictable or make us feel uneasy. If the elements of art are its life's blood, rhythm is like the beating of its heart.

1.10

Content and Analysis

Elements: the basic vocabulary of art—line, form, shape, volume, mass, color, texture, space, time and motion, and value (lightness/darkness)

Principles: the "grammar" applied to the elements of art—contrast, balance, unity, variety, rhythm, emphasis, pattern, scale, proportion, and focal point

Artworks communicate visual ideas, just as speaking and writing communicate verbal ideas. For the transfer of thought to take place through art, we must interpret the visual language of the artist. Making a formal analysis—a visual study—of a work of art is one way to understand more clearly the language used by an artist in a particular artwork. Artists have many tools at their disposal, which we call the **elements** and **principles** of art. The process of analyzing the elements and principles used by the artist is called formal analysis. The elements include line, shape, form, mass, volume, color, texture, space, time and motion, and value. Artists combine the elements in inventive ways to emphasize certain design principles, such as contrast, balance, unity, variety, rhythm, emphasis, pattern, proportion, scale, and focal point. A work of art is therefore a product of the dynamic interrelationships between the various art elements and principles. These same elements and principles are found in all aspects of visual culture.

Content

The content, or meaning, of a work of art varies greatly between artworks. Both artists and viewers play roles in providing this meaning. An artwork may convey a particular message to those who view it in the context in which it was made, but the same artwork may convey a different meaning to someone living in another time and place. Sometimes an artist intentionally creates an artwork without a specific meaning, and expects the viewer to interpret it. Interpretation is subjective, meaning that each individual can understand art differently.

Works of art may be **representational** (depicting objects or people so that we can recognize them) or **non-objective** (depicting subject matter that is unrecognizable). It is important to understand the concepts of representational and non-objective art. They help us to analyze what the artist had in mind or wished to communicate to us when creating the work.

For example, the statue of the Roman emperor Marcus Aurelius in **1.161** shows him seated on a horse, gesturing in a very lifelike way. This is a representational artwork, because anyone looking at it would agree that the sculpture is of a man on a horse. The proportions of the figures,

1.161 (left) Equestrian statue of Marcus Aurelius, *c.* 175 CE. Bronze, 11′6″ high. Musei Capitolini, Rome, Italy

the sense of movement, and the details in the emperor's face were all made by the artist to represent reality as closely as possible.

Non-objective works of art are deliberately not recognizable as something we might see in the world around us. José de Rivera's *Infinity* is an example of a non-objective work (**1.162**). As it rotates one full cycle every six minutes, the ribbon-like form continually changes. Made of polished steel, the sculpture literally reflects aspects of the world around it, such as the sunlight and the buildings. Non-objective art is also, by definition, subjective: we each determine our own interpretations of what the artwork means or communicates—or whether it means anything at all.

We need to ask ourselves when we study an artwork to what extent the artist has used **abstraction** to communicate visually with us. "To abstract" means to extract something or to

1.162 José de Rivera, *Infinity*, 1967. Stainless steel sculpture in front of National Museum of American History, Smithsonian Institution, Washington, D.C.

Representational: art that depicts figures and objects so that we recognize what is represented
Non-objective: art that does not depict a recognizable subject
Abstraction: the degree to which an image is altered from an easily recognizable subject

1.163 Allan Houser, *Reverie*, 1981. Bronze, 25 × 23 × 13″, edition of 10. Allan Houser Archives

Form: an object that can be defined in three dimensions (height, width, and depth)

emphasize it. Abstraction in art refers to the ways artists can emphasize, distort, simplify or arrange the formal (visual) elements of an artwork. An artwork may be representational or non-objective, or something in between; this can be described as its degree of abstraction.

Allan Houser's *Reverie* is representational because we can recognize two faces, one larger and one smaller (**1.163**). We also interpret the swoop of the **form** downward from the larger face to be a back, and that the smaller face probably represents a baby being held in its mother's arms. The mother's entire body (her back, arms, and knees) is, however, abstracted to be one smooth form in which to cradle the baby. The baby's body is just a bump on the lap of the mother, as if it is swaddled tightly. We can interpret the subject and form of the sculpture because the detailed representation of the figures' faces enables us to see a mother holding her baby. *Reverie* is a

representational work with a considerable degree of abstraction.

Modes of Analysis

There is no single right way to analyze a work of art, and different methods can be combined to develop a more complete interpretation. Let us consider some important interpretive methods.

Iconographic analysis
interprets objects and figures in the artwork as signs or symbols, often based on religious or historical contexts that would have been understood at the time when it was made.

Biographical analysis
considers whether the artist's personal experiences and opinions may have affected the making or meaning of the artwork in some way.

Feminist analysis
considers the role of women in an artwork as its subjects, creators, patrons, and viewers; it explores ways in which the work reflects the experience of women.

Contextual analysis
looks at the making and viewing of the work in its context (historical, religious, political, economic, social, and so on); it studies the context that the artwork itself represents.

Psychological analysis
investigates an artwork through interpretation of the mental state of the artist.

Formal analysis (formalism or visual analysis)
analyzes the artwork's use of the elements and principles of art.

Let us consider these six methods one by one:

Iconographic Analysis

The enormous painting *Marilyn*, by American artist Audrey Flack (b. 1931), is representational: all of the shapes appear as they might in the real world (**1.164**). Even so, the artwork has a dreamlike quality as well: a paintbrush floats in the air, objects rest on the table unnaturally, and the mirror on the left has a slightly inaccurate reflection. The artist has emphasized each object individually, and iconographical analysis demonstrates how each of these objects is symbolic for her.

This painting was made fifteen years after the American film actress Marilyn Monroe died of a drug overdose in 1962. A photograph shows Monroe's public persona as a blonde beauty and is then reflected in the mirror on the left; another mirror is in the compact below. Mirrors, a reference to vanity, are often used to symbolize the transience of youth, beauty, and life. The mirrored compact, makeup, and pearls refer to Marilyn Monroe's mask to the world.

The calendar, clock, and hourglass are symbols of the passing of time. As such they

1.164 Audrey Flack, *Marilyn Monroe*, 1977. Oil over acrylic on canvas, 8 × 8'. Collection of the University of Arizona Museum of Art, Tucson too are reminders of mortality and the brevity of life—as are the burning candle and the flower and fruit, all of which live only a short time. An artwork that serves to remind us of death is known as a **vanitas**. In **1.164** the floating objects create an otherworldly quality, a dramatic contrast to the objects that symbolize time. Using iconographic analysis, we have interpreted this painting to be both an homage to Marilyn and a reflection on the mortality of us all. By including a childhood portrait of herself with her brother, the artist further wishes to remind herself that

the pleasures of her life are as fleeting as those of the movie idol.

Biographical Analysis

At first glance, the minimalist sculpture *Hang-Up* by Eva Hesse (1936–70) seems absurdly empty of content (**1.165**). The artwork consists of a wood frame wrapped in painted cloth, and a thin steel tube wrapped in painted cord, which dangles exaggeratedly out onto the floor. The frame is empty, an open hole,

1.165 Eva Hesse, *Hang-Up*, 1966. Acrylic, cloth, wood, cord, and steel, 72 × 84 × 78". Art Institute of Chicago

Vanitas: an artwork in which the objects remind the viewer of the transience of life a blank wall. The cord goes nowhere special, looping out nonsensically from opposite corners, as if to emphasize the absence of any purpose in the work.

A biographical analysis might go something like this: "Hesse faced many challenges in her life. She was born a Jew in Germany in 1936. While her parents fled the Nazis, she was placed in an orphanage in the Netherlands for two months. After she was reunited with her parents, Hesse and her family moved to New York City in 1939. Her parents divorced when she was ten, and shortly thereafter her mother committed suicide by jumping out of a window. Later Hesse was married briefly to the sculptor Tom Doyle, from whom she separated during the making of *Hang-Up*. Dealing with the breakup might have been part of the motivation for this artwork. Some viewers have also interpreted Hesse's frame in *Hang-Up* as a window that leads to nothingness, and associate the imagery with her mother's death. The phrase 'hang-up' might refer to putting up a picture frame, but it is also slang for a problem one is unable to let go of."

Often using only one method of analysis runs the risk of limiting our understanding of what an artwork is truly about. For example, while Hesse's biography is interesting, and likely relates to much of her work, we do not have enough evidence to say for sure that the sculpture had these meanings for Hesse. On the contrary, her few comments on the artwork suggest a more subtle meaning, perhaps one that would be different for different viewers. She described this sculpture as "the most ridiculous structure that I ever made and that is why it is really good. It has a kind of depth I don't always achieve and that is the kind of depth or soul or absurdity or life or meaning or feeling or intellect that I want to get."

Feminist Analysis

Biographical analysis usually takes gender, race, and societal position into account. Feminist analysis is a subset of biographical analysis when it studies the work of women artists, but feminist analysis also considers both the perspective toward gender of viewers and the role of women at the time the artwork was made.

Grande Odalisque by the French artist Jean-Auguste-Dominique Ingres (1780–1867) was made in 1814 for a male French audience (**1.166**). Feminist analysis might compare this

1.166 Jean-Auguste-Dominique Ingres, *Grande Odalisque*, 1814. Oil on canvas, 35⅞ × 63¾". Musée du Louvre, Paris, France artwork to others made at the time and find that female nudes were often depicted as objects of desire and beauty. The woman is dressed as an odalisque (a woman in a harem), and so a feminist analysis might study the French view of women in Near Eastern society, who were considered fascinating for their exotic sensuality. Feminist analysis could seek an explanation for the interest in harem women in art during this period, and might find that women in France were demanding equal rights, causing men to pine for docile females.

A feminist might also study this subject's demure gaze, whereby she accepts her status as an object of beauty. At the time when the picture was painted, critics complained that the figure's body parts were disproportionate: her back was too long, and her hips too wide. A feminist analysis would point out that Ingres believed that the back was a very sensual part of a woman's body, and claimed he could not stop himself, when painting, from adding what appear to be extra vertebrae.

Contextual Analysis

Art is shaped by the historical context in which it is made. In 1934, German dictator Adolf Hitler commissioned filmmaker Leni Riefenstahl (1902–2003) to film a four-day Nazi Party rally in Nuremberg. Riefenstahl created a propaganda film, *Triumph of the Will* (**1.167**), designed to promote the Nazi ideology and create an impression that Hitler was wholeheartedly supported by the entire German nation.

This film cannot be understood without recognizing its historical context. Riefenstahl's concluding scenes, of a speech by Hitler, are filmed from below, visually emphasizing his importance. At several points in the film the crowd is seen to be cheering wildly, but instead of the cheers we hear dramatic music by the German composer Richard Wagner. In the scenes that film Hitler speaking we can see that the crowd is noisily excited, but there is no sound other than Hitler's voice—an effect that gives his words greater authority. In the film still shown

1.167 Leni Riefenstahl, still from *Triumph of the Will*, 1934

1.168 Edward Hopper, *Nighthawks*, 1942. Oil on canvas, 33⅛ × 60". Art Institute of Chicago

here, three large banners carrying the Nazi symbol are given **emphasis**, and are echoed in the three groups of followers shown underneath. The platform on which Hitler will speak is front and center. *Triumph of the Will*, while considered a pioneering work of modern filmmaking, is also political propaganda; as such it must be viewed as part of the Nazi Party's attempts to consolidate its power and to promote its ideology of German superiority over those it considered inferior, such as Jews, homosexuals, the mentally ill, and other groups (including many modern artists) that the Nazis defined as outside of their "Aryan" norm.

Psychological Analysis

Psychological analysis considers the artist's state of mind when creating an artwork. *Nighthawks*, by the American artist Edward Hopper (1882–1967), reflects the solemn mood many felt in the United States at the beginning of America's entry into World War II (**1.168**). Hopper began this painting immediately after the attack on Pearl Harbor, which had left many Americans shocked and distraught. The artist captured this feeling in his painting. The scene shows a café, which

Emphasis: the principle of drawing attention to particular content in a work

Hopper based on a restaurant in New York's Greenwich Village. Hopper himself was a model for the man seated at the counter whose face can be seen; he used his wife for the figure next to him. Even though the scene takes place in the middle of New York City, the streets are devoid of people, activity, even light. The people seated inside are still and quiet, and the decor is reduced to essentials. The café is the only lit place; no light emanates from windows on the other side of the street. The artist remarked later, "Unconsciously, probably, I was painting the loneliness of a large city."

Despite gathering together in the all-night diner, these individuals appear to be alone in their own thoughts; little interaction takes place between them. A large glass window separating the viewer from the figures leaves the viewer alone as well.

Formal Analysis

Formal analysis considers the way in which the elements and principles of art are applied in an artwork. The famous painting *Las Meninas* (*The Maids of Honor*) by Diego de Silva y Velázquez

1.169 Diego de Silva y Velázquez, *Las Meninas*, c. 1656. Oil on canvas, 10'5¼" × 9'¾". Museo Nacional del Prado, Madrid, Spain

Implied line: a line not actually drawn but suggested by elements in the work

Vanishing point: the point in a work of art at which imaginary sight lines appear to converge, suggesting depth

Linear perspective: a system using converging imaginary sight lines to create the illusion of depth

Depth: the degree of recession in perspective

Volume: the space filled or enclosed by a three-dimensional figure or object

Color: the optical effect caused when reflected white light of the spectrum is divided into a separate wavelength

Neutral tones: colors (such as blacks, whites, grays, and dull gray-browns) made by mixing complementary hues

Palette: the range of colors used by an artist

(1599–1660) shows members of the court of Spanish King Philip IV gathering in a room in the Alcázar Palace (**1.169**). The painter depicts himself on the left, painting a large canvas. The Princess Margarita is posed in the center, with her ladies-in-waiting ("las meninas") surrounding her. Court workers, including dwarfs, are present as well.

The **implied lines** suggested by the black frames on the right wall and the ceiling fixtures converge on the chest of the man standing in the doorway. This is the **vanishing point** required in **linear perspective** to create an illusion of **depth**,

as if the viewer is looking into a real room. All the figures in the painting have a realistic sense of **volume** and are arranged to emphasize further the illusion of looking into a real space. Notice how they overlap one another, and that those toward the back of the room are smaller than those at the front. The painting is more than 10 feet tall, which allows Velázquez to make the figures life-size, further reinforcing the illusion of three-dimensional space. Finally, most of the **colors** in the painting are **neutral**. The color **palette** of brown, grey, beige, and black creates

1.170 Detail of Diego de Silva y Velázquez, *Las Meninas*

the impression of a dark space the depth of which is emphasized by the light coming in from a window on the right and the door at the back.

Velázquez highlights several areas he wants to emphasize. The young princess is in the central **foreground**, the part of the painting nearest to us, well lit, and shown attended by her maids. In the **background**, the mysterious male figure is emphasized because his black form contrasts with the light coming through the doorway. The painter himself stands proudly at his work. And we notice the mirror on the back wall because of its blurry shiny surface: whom does it reflect? (**1.170**). Touches of red lead our eye around the painting to significant points of interest: from Margarita's flowers, to the cross on Velázquez's chest, to the red curtain in the mirror on the back wall.

The painting is **balanced** in various ways. All of the figures are placed in the bottom half of the canvas, balanced by the sparseness of the wall and ceiling that take up the top half. While the figures at first appear to be arranged chaotically, they are actually placed in several stable pyramidal arrangements. One triangle highlights three of the composition's **focal points**: the mirror, Margarita, and the man in the doorway. The frames on the back and side walls form a framework of rectangles that stabilize the space of the room. The figures are of different heights and arranged so that our eye is led from Velázquez on

the left to the right of the painting in a rhythmic line: if you trace the heads of the figures in the foreground with your finger you will sense the visual **rhythm**.

Combined Analysis of *Las Meninas*

A *formal* analysis tells us how the artist has communicated using a visual language. The use of other approaches, however, often enhances our understanding of a work of art. While it is rare to be able to use every method discussed in this chapter on every artwork, we can often consider one artwork in many ways. Using three more of the modes of analysis discussed earlier, we can arrive at a better and more rounded understanding of the painting *Las Meninas*.

A *contextual* analysis gives us a better understanding of the time in which this work was made. The young girl is the Spanish princess Margarita Hapsburg; the couple in the mirror are her parents, King Philip IV and Marianna of Austria. The mysterious man in the doorway is Nieto, the queen's chamberlain. Through the use of the mirror and his portrayal of an essential aide to the queen, Velázquez has subtly indicated the presence of the royal couple without violating etiquette by showing the king and queen in a portrait with lesser court members.

A *biographical* analysis suggests why Velázquez placed himself in a painting that subtly shows the presence of the king. One reason was that he was the king's favorite painter and assistant. It was extremely bold of him to paint himself into a scene with the royal family; by doing so, he wished to show his closeness with the king, and to raise his own status.

An *iconographic* analysis tells us that the cross on Velázquez in *Las Meninas* is the cross of the Order of Santiago. Velázquez had a lifelong ambition to become a knight of the order, but the order challenged his membership for decades. Their bylaws stated that: (1) only those from families of nobility could join, (2) members may have no Moorish (Muslim) ancestry, and (3) a craftsman could not become a member. The members saw painting as simply a manual craft rather than a liberal (or highminded) art.

Foreground: the part of a work depicted as nearest to the viewer
Background: the part of a work depicted furthest from the viewer's space, often behind the main subject matter
Balance: a principle of art in which elements are used to create a symmetrical or asymmetrical sense of visual weight in an artwork
Focal point: the center of interest or activity in a work of art, often drawing the viewer's attention to the most important element
Rhythm: the regular or ordered repetition of elements in the work

In truth, Velázquez did not meet any of these criteria, but after hundreds of supportive interviews, and with the support of both the king and the pope, Velázquez was finally knighted in 1659, three years after he painted *Las Meninas*.

Why, then, is the cross painted here when Velázquez was not knighted until after this painting was completed? Historians have found evidence that the king ordered the cross painted on after Velázquez's death, to honor the artist for having achieved his lifelong goal.

What Is the Meaning of *Las Meninas*?

After considering the various methods of analysis discussed above, scholars have arrived at a hypothesis as to what Velázquez wanted to say. They suggest that the artist was defending the nobility of painting itself. In order to be accepted as a knight, he needed to prove that his skill was not mere craft, but an intellectual endeavor. Therefore Velázquez created a brilliant illusion of **space** through his mastery of atmosphere and perspective. Even more boldly, he included the king in a painting that also included a self-portrait of the artist, demonstrating the king's clear support for the painter. Velázquez's painting is an intentional effort to raise the status of painters, and to raise his own status in Spanish society.

Imitation and Individual Style

Artists often study and copy the work of artists they admire, and may use such studies to create works in their own individual **style**. The Spanish painter Pablo Picasso (1881–1973) did not come to admire Velázquez until late in his own career, when he began to set his skills against the great artists of the past. At the age of seventy-six, Picasso locked himself in a room with a poster of *Las Meninas* and created forty-five paintings in response to Velázquez's masterpiece.

In the first painting in the series, Picasso alters the size of the canvas (**1.171**). While mimicking Velázquez, he uses the elements and principles differently. For example, although Picasso does not use linear perspective, he does create a sense

1.171 Picasso, *Las Meninas*, first in a series, 1957. Oil on canvas, 6′4⅜″ × 8′6⅜″. Museo Picasso, Barcelona, Spain

Space: the distance between identifiable points or planes
Style: a characteristic way in which an artist or group of artists uses visual language to give a work an identifiable form of visual expression

1.172 Thomas Struth, *Museo del Prado 7*, 2005. Chromogenic print, 5'7⅞" × 7'2".

of depth by making Nieto small in **scale** and placing his dark figure in the bright doorway. Velázquez now appears to be stretched or floating up to the ceiling, leaving his paintbrushes and palette below. Is Picasso removing the old master to make room for himself?

Other figures are mere suggestions of the forms they had been in the original painting. Picasso has broken them down into **abstract** parts. Margarita is outlined with no sense of volume, and the heads of the figures on the right are just black lines on white circles. The play of light on the figures is similar to the original, but Picasso's approach is more abstract: on the right, he lines up a row of windows that shine a bright white on the figure there (which correlates to the child dwarf in the original). Margarita, highlighted in Velázquez's painting, is of a much lighter value than the other figures in Picasso's painting, emphasizing that she is the most important person in the group. The majority of the rest of the series, in fact, are studies of Margarita specifically. This may relate to Picasso's own life. The first time he saw *Las Meninas* as a boy was just after his younger sister had died; she had been about the same age as the young Margarita here. Picasso has totally reinterpreted this artwork to make it his own; he has even replaced the large mastiff in Velázquez's painting with his own dog.

German photographer Thomas Struth (b. 1954) used photography to create his own view of *Las Meninas*. In **1.172**, he shows a group admiring the painting at the Prado Museum in Madrid, Spain. There are multiple ways to interpret Struth's artwork. We might study his use of lighting and composition. We might consider which image is the "true" artwork, the photograph of the visitors to the Prado or the painting *Las Meninas*. We might take notice of the boy sketching on the right, creating his own work of art. Finally, we might pay more attention to the multiple layers of looking and reflecting in Struth's photograph. The photograph portrays people looking at art—which is exactly what we are doing when we look at the photograph. In this way, the artwork can be seen as a portrait of art appreciation. In 2007, Struth exhibited this photograph at the Prado, hanging it right next to *Las Meninas*.

Conclusion

The tools of formal analysis are the starting point for understanding any work of art; this will help you realize how it was made. When you see a work of art, take a long look and use the elements and principles of art as your guide. But the other methods of analysis discussed in this chapter can help you to understand why an artwork was made, and what its message is.

You have been introduced to several approaches for doing this. Consider the artist's life when the artwork was created. Delve into the time and place in which he or she lived. What symbols did the artist use, and what was his or her state of mind? Recognize that some artworks are meant to convey distinct messages, which were clear to their contemporary audiences. Many artworks convey more subtle messages, filled with layers of meaning. Some artworks are intentionally subjective, which means that artists expect us to infuse meaning into the work from our own experiences; subjective artworks are often mirrors of the person who looks at them.

Using a variety of methods of analysis, you can endlessly explore both the minds of great artists and the furthest reaches of your own!

Artworks reveal the concerns of humanity. Throughout the world, similar issues, or themes, are explored by artists. By comparing artworks in terms of their meaning, we come closer to understanding the uniqueness of different cultures and artists. Exploring topics commonly addressed by artists throughout space and time, and through a variety of methods and materials, also makes us more aware of shared concerns. Artworks deal with belief systems, survival, the natural world, and technology; and with issues related to status, power, identity, and creative expression. By studying art in this way we can better understand various cultures and ourselves.

PART 4

THEMES

In this part you will study:

Art and Community

Spirituality and Art

Art and the Cycle of Life

Art and Science

Art and Illusion

Art and Rulers

Art and War

Art of Social Conscience

The Body in Art

Art and Gender

Expression

4.1

Art and Community

The community mural process makes art more accessible; it brings art into the lives of people who didn't have it.

(Susan Cervantes, San Francisco muralist)

This is a way of getting your art on the street. Lots of people stop to look at it. It's not like being famous, but it's a way of getting your art looked at. You have an audience.

(Aliseo Purpura-Pontoniere, urban youth arts student)

We tend to think of art as the work of a single individual. However, art often involves large numbers of people, even whole communities. As the statements above by professional artist Susan Cervantes and a student who worked with her demonstrate, artists can create art for the enjoyment and benefit not just of a single **patron**, or for a larger audience in an art gallery, but also for an entire community. Community art may require numerous people to become involved in its construction. Other times, artworks play important roles for performers in ceremonies and group events. Still other community art, situated in public places, is contemplated by countless viewers. A community—whether a small rural town, an apartment complex, a neighborhood, a college campus, an Internet discussion group—shares a common interest, if not a physical space. Studying the art made by and for communities throughout history tells us a great deal about the interaction between artists and their environments.

In this chapter we will examine the many ways in which art has been used to pursue community objectives. Because buildings have such a direct impact on shaping a community, often becoming symbols of a particular place, we will look at several examples of architecture as well as at paintings and ritual performances.

Civic and Ceremonial Places

Structures have been designed to house ceremonies, civic events, and entertainments in times and places as varied as ancient Greece, medieval France, and present-day New York City (see Box: Art in Public Spaces, p. 456). Whether they serve as gathering sites, indicate concerns that are important to a group, or come to symbolize a particular place, buildings (and their appearance) reflect the concerns and practices of the communities that use them.

The Parthenon in Athens, Greece, was the grandest building on the Acropolis, the fortified district located at the highest point of the city. It was an important religious center dedicated to the maiden goddess Athena, the protector of Athens. The masses did not enter the sacred interior space of the Parthenon, but congregated outside the temple to worship at the altar to Athena in front of the building's western end. Relief sculptures on the Parthenon indicate the significance of the celebrations that occurred on this site (**4.1**). Ordinary Athenians are shown participating in the Panathenaic Festival, an annual ritual procession to honor Athena.

Patron: an organization or individual who sponsors the creation of works of art
Gothic: western European architectural style of the twelfth to sixteenth centuries, characterized by the use of pointed arches and ornate decoration
Passion: the arrest, trial, and execution of Jesus Christ, and his sufferings during them
Arches: structures, usually curved, that span an opening
Stained glass: colored glass used for windows and decorative applications
Vaulted: covered with an arch-shaped ceiling or roof
Nave: the central space of a cathedral or basilica

4.1 Detail of *The Procession*, from the Ionic frieze on the east side of the Parthenon, *c.* 445–438 BCE. Marble, 43" high. Musée du Louvre, Paris, France

All of Athens's inhabitants were allowed to take part in the festival, although only citizens could enter the Acropolis.

While the Parthenon was designed for worship at an outside altar, **Gothic** cathedrals were intended, with their magnificent interior spaces, to inspire worshipers to religious devotion. These spectacular churches, built using the resources of the entire community, were a source of great civic pride. Pilgrims traveled to Notre Dame Cathedral (**4.2**) in Paris, France, to worship, both because the building was so impressive and because it held relics Christians considered sacred, such as a piece of the True Cross on which Jesus Christ was crucified, a fragment of the Holy Lance used to pierce his side, and the Crown of Thorns that the Romans made to mock Christ as King of the Jews. Pilgrims curious to see these items from Christ's **Passion** also hoped to benefit from their mystical power. Notre Dame's grand interior combines all of the characteristic elements of Gothic architecture, including pointed **arches** and **stained-glass** windows. The **vaulted** ceiling is 102 feet above the floor and the **nave** is more than 39 feet wide, surrounding receptive visitors with soaring height and spiritual light to transport them beyond the cares and concerns of the ordinary world.

4.2 Notre Dame Cathedral, interior, 1163–1250, Île de la Cité, Paris, France

Art in Public Spaces

Two famous works of art, made more than 4,000 years apart, occupied public spaces used by large numbers of people. Both structures were created by the efforts of masses of laborers. Considering these enormous works together can help us understand how a work of art can change a public place and how people interact with such works.

Very little is known about the makers of Stonehenge (4.3), but the creators of *The Gates* (4.4), Christo (b. 1935) and Jeanne-Claude (1935–2009), explained themselves in countless statements and interviews. We know about the construction methods of Christo and Jeanne-Claude from descriptions and from video documentation, but the techniques used to erect Stonehenge, and the intentions of its builders, remain shrouded in mystery. Stonehenge is still standing after thousands of years, while *The Gates* was designed to last a little more than two weeks. Despite their differences, both works share a common aim: to focus the attention and movements of crowds of people in directions calculated by the artists who designed them.

The oldest parts of Stonehenge, on Salisbury Plain in England, are the circular embankment and ditch that surround the monument. This site was used for hundreds of years before the stones were imported from as far as 23 miles away. The massive stones in the **sarsen** circle weigh up to 50 tons apiece, each one equaling the weight of 500 people or five buses. We will probably never know how the builders moved those stones. Most scholars believe Stonehenge, 106 feet in diameter and up to 20 feet tall in places, served as a giant observatory or calendar. People who gathered at Stonehenge on the longest day of the year (known as the summer solstice) would have seen the sun rise precisely over the great stone known as the Heelstone, which stands outside

4.3 Stonehenge, c. 3200–1500 BCE, Salisbury Plain, Wiltshire, England

4.4 Christo and Jeanne-Claude, *The Gates*, Central Park, New York City, 1979–2005. Steel, vinyl tubing, and nylon fabric, c. 16' high

the circle. For a farming community, such as the one that built Stonehenge, the precise date of the summer solstice was important: it signaled the time to prepare for the fall harvest.

The Gates, installed in 2005, meandered through the 23 miles of walkways in New York's Central Park for just sixteen days. The installation was intended for public enjoyment, and an estimated four million people visited Central Park during the exhibition. The piece required community support garnered through petitions and meetings between the artists and New York City officials. Discussions about *The Gates* began in 1979 and the project was finally approved in 2003. The negotiation process was integral to the production of Christo's and Jeanne-Claude's installations, emphasizing the important role that the community plays in the conception and creation of their artworks.

Facts and figures provided on the artists' website indicate the mind-boggling amounts of material and labor involved in the making of *The Gates*. A total of 60 miles of saffron-colored nylon fabric hung from 7,503 gates. Each gate was 16 feet tall with fabric coming down to approximately 7 feet above the ground. The gates ranged from about 5 feet to 18 feet

across, depending on the width of the walkway. The artists employed engineers; project directors; fabricators for the materials in the U.S. and Germany; 600 paid workers to install, monitor, and remove the pieces; and security guards to protect the work at night. After *The Gates* was taken down the materials were recycled, reflecting the artists' environmentally sustainable practices.

Although these two works were made at different times on different continents, they have in common the fact that their construction required the efforts of significant numbers of people and that they were used or viewed by an entire community. While it is uncertain how or why Stonehenge was built, it is clear that a highly organized social structure must have been in place to see such a venture through. *The Gates* similarly required teams of experts and construction crews to carry out the artists' vision. Keen on involving the community and having their work enliven public spaces, but interested in maintaining creative freedom, Christo and Jeanne-Claude did not accept any government or public funding and themselves paid for the creation, installation, and maintenance of the work.

Sarsen: a type of hard, gray sandstone

While worship is a common function of many community buildings, others have been built for public entertainment. Amongst the most famous arenas of the ancient world was the Colosseum, one of Imperial Rome's largest public buildings and an extraordinary feat of architecture and engineering (**4.5**). Measuring 615 feet long by 510 feet across and standing 159 feet tall, the Colosseum could hold between 45,000 and 55,000 people. The Romans were the first to exploit fully the structural possibilities of **concrete**, which they used to construct the Colosseum's massive foundations and parts of its vaulted ceilings. The exterior was covered with travertine limestone and marble and decorated with columns and with **pilasters** made of another type of local limestone. There were 76 entrance doors, called *vomitoria*, a word that offers a vivid mental image of the crowds spilling from the doors after an event. Roman citizens flocked to the Colosseum to see mock sea battles and gladiatorial fights with both man and beast.

The Colosseum was designed almost 2,000 years ago for the entertainment of enormous crowds. Today, in addition to stadiums and amphitheaters, we have museums to attract the public for entertainment, cultural instruction, and reflection. Museums also serve as sources of local distinction, much as cathedrals did centuries ago. The design of the Guggenheim Museum in New York City employs strong geometric shapes, which is characteristic of many modern buildings. This white circular building, though, is distinctive among the city's rectangular blocks and glass skyscrapers. For large numbers of visitors its design is as much of an attraction as the art collected inside. Architect Frank Lloyd Wright (1867–1959) sought to provide what the

4.6 Frank Lloyd Wright, Solomon R. Guggenheim Museum, 1956–9, New York

Concrete: a hard, strong, and versatile construction material made up of powdered lime, sand, and rubble

Pilaster: a vertical element, square in shape, that provides architectural support for crossing horizontal elements in post-and-lintel construction; also used for decoration

Atrium: a central, normally public, interior space, first used in Roman houses

Pyramid: ancient structure, usually massive in scale, consisting of a square base with four sides that meet at a point or apex with each side forming a triangular shape

Ziggurat: Mesopotamian stepped tower, roughly pyramid-shaped, that diminishes in size toward a platform summit

director of the museum had asked for, "a temple of spirit, a monument." The interior is open, with a continuous spiral ramp around the central **atrium** connecting each successive floor. The space is filled with light from the domed skylight above.

Manmade Mountains

Buildings and other constructions intended to shape and dominate the environment—as Wright surely intended with his design for the Guggenheim—have been made since ancient times. Earthen mounds and **pyramids** are amongst the most intriguing kinds of architecture. Mysteries surround their creation, function, and symbolic significance. Why were such substantial human and material resources devoted to these manmade mountains? Whether they were built as memorials for the dead, for administrative purposes, or for religious worship and rituals, these structures had a dramatic and lasting impact on the geography of their locations (see Gateway Box: The Great Pyramid of Khufu, **4.8**, p. 460).

While they resemble the Egyptian pyramids in their form, the **ziggurats** of the ancient Near East, such as the one in the city-state of Ur in Sumer (now part of Iraq), were built to be used by the living rather than to bury the dead (**4.7**). The ziggurat was part of a temple complex with civic and ceremonial purposes. The mud-brick structures are made up of at least three stepped levels, accessed by stairways or ramps. The lowest level is about 50 feet high and about 210 by 150 feet in area, with the others decreasing in size as they get closer to the heavens. The topmost platform served as an elevated stage for the priest. The priest, one of the few people allowed access to the ziggurat, served both as the principal human intermediary to the god who protected the city and the chief administrator of the ziggurat. The ziggurat at Ur was dedicated to the moon god Nanna, one of the three important sky deities in Sumerian religion, whose sacred city it was. Festivals were organized around the phases of the moon, especially when it appeared as a crescent, and offerings were left on the high platform to please Nanna and ensure the abundance of such sacred liquids as water, milk, and blood.

4.7 Ziggurat, Ur (near Nasiriyah, Iraq), originally built *c.* 2100 BCE and heavily restored

Gateway to Art: The Great Pyramid of Khufu
Community Art: The Building of the Pyramids

4.8 Great Pyramids at Giza, left to right: Menkaure, Khafre, and Khufu, *c.* 2560 BCE, Giza, Egypt

There are many theories as to how the ancient Egyptians managed to build pyramids of such enormous size and precision. Renowned archaeologist Mark Lehner wrote about assembling a team to test methods that may have been used to construct the Great Pyramids (4.8). This experiment showed that an enormous communal effort over many years was required to make these great structures. The exact method employed to build the pyramids remains a mystery, however.

I teamed up with Roger Hopkins, a stonemason from Sudbury, Massachusetts, and a team of Egyptian masons, quarrymen, and laborers to build a small pyramid near the Giza plateau. Working in the shadow of the Great Pyramids, pressures of a film schedule allowed us only three weeks for quarrying and three for building, so we were forced to use tools and technology not available to the ancient Egyptians. Our masons used iron hammers, chisels, and levers—their ancestors had only wood, stone, and copper. And Roger brought in a front-end loader for shifting and setting the stones of lower **courses** so that we would have time to test different methods at the top, where restricted space created special difficulties.

We knew that to fully replicate pyramid building would require nothing less than replicating ancient Egyptian society. Although

we failed to match the best efforts of the ancient builders, it was abundantly clear that their expertise was the result not of some mysterious technology or secret sophistication, but of generations of practice and experience.

We found that stones weighing as much as 2.5 tons could be moved simply by **tumbling**. Just four or five men were able to lever up and flip over blocks of less than 1 ton. To shift heavier blocks, a rope was looped around the top and it was then pulled by up to twenty men, with a couple more on levers behind. But it is most unlikely that sufficient stones could have been tumbled up a ramp to build a whole pyramid within a king's lifetime. Faster methods were needed.

Wooden sledges on rollers offered a much quicker way of moving stones, even though, as we soon discovered, simply loading a block on to a wooden sledge is an operation requiring considerable skill. Next, on soft sand we built an artificial trackway of planed lumber, though ancient tracks were wider, with a surface of hardened **gypsum** or packed clay. Then we used rollers consisting of small, cylindrical pieces of wood. The lynchpin of the entire operation was the man who received the rollers from the back of the sledge and put them down in front, creating a continually rolling roadway. With twelve to twenty men pulling the load at a swift pace, his was a very skilled task. A huge number of rollers would have been needed to move the stones up on to the pyramid. With neither abundant supplies of wood, nor the mechanical lathe, this method must have had only restricted application.

Artificial slideways proved a much more efficient method. In our experiment we built two parallel retaining walls which were then filled with debris to create an inclined ramp. On top we built a roadbed with wooden crosspieces, following the approximate specifications of those at Lisht [another site]. We found that a 2-ton stone on a sledge could be pulled by twenty men or fewer. This success, in conjunction with

4.9a (right) First course of pyramid is leveled
4.9b (right below) Raising heavy blocks by levering
4.9c (far right) Raising topmost blocks by levering
4.9d (far right below) Masons trim casing from the top downward

evidence of tomb representations and remains of ancient embankments and trackways at Lisht, convinced us that this was the most likely means the Egyptians used to bring in the bulk of the core stones.

While it is widely agreed that ramps were used to raise blocks, several theorists have proposed that it was achieved by **levering**. When we put levering to the test, unforeseen difficulties emerged. A set of levers is needed on two sides to lift a block: one side is raised and supported, then the other side is levered up to bring it level. As the stone is rocked upward it is supported on a stack of wood. This required two deep notches in each side of a block, which are not found on pyramid core stones. More critically, the wooden supports were precarious and unwieldy, in spite of our using planed lumber. Similar difficulties arose with the fulcrum, which had to rise with the load. It seemed to us, therefore, that some system involving a ramp or ramps was the most likely method used.

Many pyramid theorists resort to levering to explain how the **capstone** and the topmost courses were set, since by that level there was simply no longer room for ramps. However, to climb the pyramids of Khufu and Khafre and look down their steep slopes and narrow steps is to realize that the great bulk of the pyramid could not have been raised in this way.

Course: a single row of stones or bricks forming a horizontal layer of a structure
Tumbling: the use of levers to roll heavy objects over short distances
Gypsum: fine-grained, powdery mineral often used to make a smooth plaster
Levering: to move or raise an object using a leverlike action
Capstone: a final stone forming the top of a structure; on a pyramid, it is pyramid-shaped

4.10 Tomb mound and complex of Emperor Qin Shi Huangdi, *c.* 210 BCE. Lintong, Shaanxi Province, China (CGI reconstruction)

4.11 Soldiers from mausoleum of Emperor Qin Shi Huangdi, *c.* 210 BCE. Terracotta and pigment, figures approximately lifesize. Lintong, Shaanxi Province, China

Rather like the Egyptian pharaohs, the emperors of ancient China also tried to take their riches with them to the afterlife. Ancient historians described how the first Emperor of China, Qin Shi Huangdi, prepared for his death by constructing a burial mound with a vast underground city palace that matched the one he occupied in life. These accounts were believed to be sheer legend until 1974 when excavations of a tomb mound revealed evidence that the ancient stories were true (**4.10**). Soon after he came to the throne at the age of thirteen, Qin Shi Huangdi began overseeing the elaborate preparations for his own resting place, which continued for thirty-six years until his death in 210 BCE. Artisans filled the complex surrounding Qin Shi Huangdi's tomb with all the treasures he would need in the afterlife, including an army of terracotta soldiers and horses (**4.11**). The 8,000 figures were intended to guard the body of the Emperor. They have similar rigid and upright poses, indicating that a mold might have been used for the general shape, but each one has unique clothing, weaponry, and facial features.

More than one thousand years after the death of Qin Shi Huangdi, builders made the largest earthen mound ever discovered in North America (**4.12**). Cahokia, located in what is now southern Illinois near St. Louis, covered 6 square miles and had an estimated population of

10,000–20,000. As with other communities that built such impressive structures, there is evidence of a highly organized society, advanced engineering knowledge, and a productive work force at this site.

The focal point of the settlement at Cahokia was Monks Mound, which was originally surrounded by about 120 smaller mounds. The base of Monks Mound measures 1,080 by 710 feet and is topped by two smaller platforms. Though its exact purpose is uncertain, Monks Mound likely served as an elite residence, a temple, a burial structure, or perhaps all three. Monks Mound is aligned with the sun at the equinoxes, the two times of the year (in spring and fall) when day and night are exactly the same length. These alignments suggest that it may have functioned as a calendar and also served a ceremonial purpose. The site was abandoned around 600 years ago due to climate changes and the depletion of natural resources. Because Monks Mound has suffered from slumping and erosion, the huge earthen mound's appearance is much less dramatic and impressive than it must have been at the height of Cahokia's occupation.

Unlike Monks Mound, we know that the Aztec stepped pyramid called the Templo Mayor, or Great Temple, was designed for a specific purpose: as a platform for performing ritual sacrifices (**4.13**). Our information about the Great Temple comes from Aztec manuscripts, Spanish accounts, and archaeological excavations of the temple's remains underneath present-day Mexico City. On top of the Great Temple were two shrines. The North Temple, dedicated to Tlaloc, the rain god, was painted white and blue and adorned with symbols of rain and water, including water plants. To the south was the temple of Huitzilopochtli, the god of war, painted white and red and decorated with symbols of war and sacrifice. The construction of the 200-foot-tall Great Temple must have required the labor of hundreds of people and vast quantities of construction materials, but clearly the Aztecs considered it a price worth paying. The hearts of war captives were cut out on a sacrificial stone on top of the pyramid, a sacrifice presented to the rain god in the hope that the crops would be renewed and life would continue to flourish.

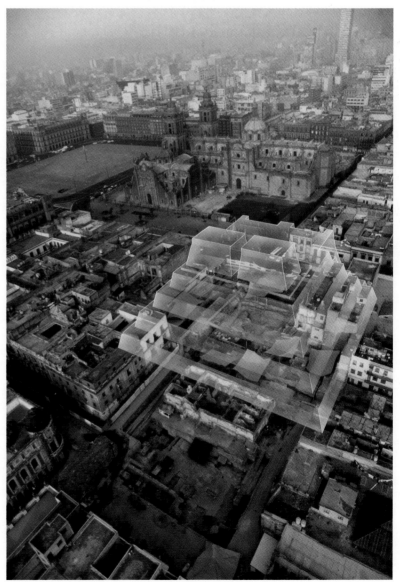

Ritual: Performance, Balance, and Healing

The production of art is often deeply connected to philosophical, religious, and ideological beliefs. Artworks made to be used in a ritual context often have symbolic meanings in addition to their appearance and visual impact. With such objects as musical instruments, temporary constructions, and masks, it is important to keep in mind that the way they were experienced in their original context would have been very different from the way we now see them in the pages of a book or inside glass cases in museums. The objects themselves are suggestive of the sights, sounds, and even smells to which we no longer have access.

Three **lyres**, stringed instruments similar to a harp, were found amongst the magnificent objects in the Royal Cemetery of Ur. Lyres were popular musical instruments in ancient Sumer, but the example in **4.14** is more elaborate than most. As it was found in a grave, it seems to have been intended as a suitable burial offering for a powerful person. Although the body of the instrument disintegrated long ago, the wooden section of the lyre has been reconstructed to give an idea of its appearance. The original panels on the sound box of another of the lyres, made of **lapis lazuli** and shell, have survived (**4.15**). They reveal that the lyre, which played music we can no

4.14 Sumerian bull lyre, c. 2550–2450 BCE. Wood, lapis lazuli, gold, silver, shell, bitumen, in modern wood support, 46 × 55". From the King's Grave, Royal Cemetery, Ur, Iraq. University of Pennsylvania Museum of Archaeology and Anthropology, Philadelphia

4.15 Inlaid panel from a Sumerian lyre's sound box, showing mythological figures, c. 2550–2400 BCE. Gold, silver, lapis lazuli, shell, bitumen, and wood, 13" high. From the King's Grave, Royal Cemetery, Ur, Iraq longer hear, was also covered in symbols that we now do not entirely understand. The panels show animals engaged in such human activities as dancing, walking on two legs, and bringing instruments and refreshments to a ceremony, probably much like the ones in which this lyre was used. The fusion of humans and beasts, such as the scorpion man below and the human-headed bulls above, suggests a sacred event, perhaps a marriage or a funeral procession. Some scholars, however, suggest that the scenes decorating the lyre show activities in the supernatural realm of the dead.

Although the details of some cultures' ritual performances, like the music of the Sumerians, can no longer be recovered, other groups recorded their rites in rock art that has survived for thousands of years. Still other ancient people, such as the Navajo of New Mexico, intentionally chose an impermanent **medium** for their important ceremonies. Navajo **sand paintings** are temporary works of art, constructed as part of a prayer or ceremony (**4.16**). The paintings are closely connected to nature, both in materials used (such as corn, pollen, charcoal, sand, and powdered stones) and imagery. The subject matter comes from Navajo creation mythology

4.16 Navajo medicine man in healing ceremony

4.17 Pair of Gèlèdé masqueraders wearing appliquéd cloth panels, Ketu area, town of Idahin, Benin. Photo by Henry John Drewal, 1971

and includes logs, holy plants, animals, and deities. After an image has been meticulously created over the course of days or weeks, a healing ceremony takes place, overseen by a **shaman** or medicine man (rarely a woman). The person to be healed sits in the painting's center in order to absorb power from Navajo ancestors and from the gods, whose images are depicted in the painting. The shaman acts as an intermediary between the natural, physical world and the supernatural, spiritual realm.

Masks and **masquerades** serve a similar function of mediating between the human and spiritual realms. Masquerades enable humans to communicate with the spirit world, allowing the masker's personality to be replaced temporarily with that of the spirit being evoked. At the same time, the ritual performance of masquerades is often designed to reinforce the cultural beliefs of a community. While the mask is generally the focal point of the performance, it must be combined with costumes, music, and dance in order to invoke a particular spirit. **Gèlèdé rituals** performed by the Yoruba in Nigeria celebrate female power, honor women as mothers, and commemorate the woman's role in producing children in order to help sustain the community (**4.17**). These ceremonies acknowledge the important part played by female ancestors in Yoruba society and also promote spiritual well-being and social harmony.

Lyre: a stringed instrument that is played by being plucked; the strings hang from a crossbar that is supported by two arms connected to a hollow box, which amplifies the sound

Lapis lazuli: bright blue semiprecious stone containing sodium aluminum silicate and sulphur

Medium (plural **media**): the material on or from which an artist chooses to make a work of art

Sand painting: also known as dry painting, a labor-intensive method of painting using grains of sand as the medium

Shaman: a priest or priestess regarded as having the ability to communicate directly with the spiritual world

Masquerade: performance in which participants wear masks and costumes for a ritual or cultural purpose

Gèlèdé ritual: ritual performed in Nigeria's Yoruba society to celebrate and honor women

Art in the Public Sphere

Not all art exists in galleries and museums. Public art generally appears in plazas and parks, or on the exterior walls of buildings. Public artworks are therefore accessible to a wide audience, and they are often much beloved by the community. But they can also cause problems. Sometimes public art can be taken out of context or misunderstood. Sometimes people can have different views about what should be seen in public or is appropriate in a particular environment. Public artworks can excite strong emotions, both positive and negative, and can sometimes spark fierce controversies.

Tilted Arc, by the American **Minimalist** sculptor Richard Serra (b. 1939), was

Perspectives on Art: Richard Serra
A Sculptor Defends His Work

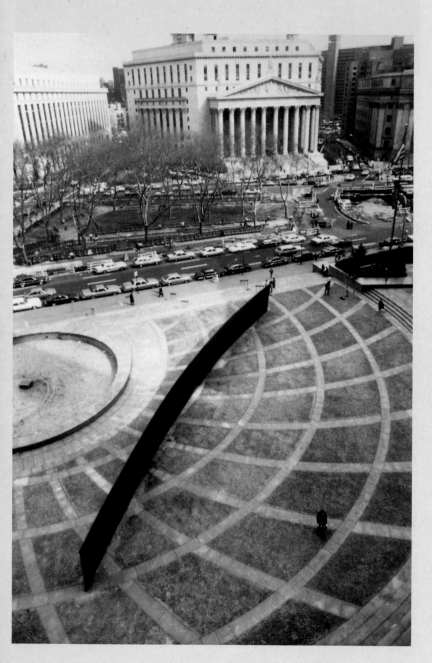

In 1979 the General Services Administration (GSA) contracted the American sculptor Richard Serra to install a work on Federal Plaza in New York City. The sculpture, Tilted Arc, *was erected in 1981. The work proved controversial and in 1985 Serra had to defend his sculpture at a public hearing.*

My name is Richard Serra and I am an American sculptor.

I don't make portable objects. I don't make works that can be relocated or site adjusted. I make works that deal with the environmental components of given places. The scale, size, and location of my site-specific works are determined by the topography of the site, whether it be urban, landscape, or an architectural enclosure. My works become part of and are built into the structure of the site, and they often restructure, both conceptually and perceptually, the organization of the site.

My sculptures are not objects for the viewer to stop and stare at. The historical purpose of placing sculpture on a pedestal was to establish a separation between the sculpture and the viewer. I am interested in creating a behavioral space in which the viewer interacts with the sculpture in its context.

4.18 Richard Serra, *Tilted Arc*, 1981 (destroyed March 15, 1989). Weatherproof steel, 12′ × 120′ × 2½″. Collection General Services Administration, Washington, D.C. Installed at Federal Plaza, New York commissioned by the federal General Services Administration (GSA) and installed on Federal Plaza in downtown New York City in 1981 (**4.18**). It became the subject of controversy shortly after it was installed. The 12 foot by 120 foot sculpture, a curving wall of **Cor-ten steel**, cut across the plaza. Some of the people who worked in the GSA building complained that it interfered with their use of the plaza and caused a safety hazard as well,

One's identity as a person is closely connected with one's experience of space and place. When a known space is changed through the inclusion of a site-specific sculpture, one is called upon to relate to the space differently. This is a condition that can be engendered only by sculpture. This experience of space may startle some people.

When the government invited me to propose a sculpture for the plaza it asked for a permanent, site-specific sculpture. As the phrase implies, a site-specific sculpture is one that is conceived and created in relation to the particular conditions of a specific site, and only to those conditions.

To remove *Tilted Arc*, therefore, would be to destroy it...

It has been suggested that the public did not choose to install the work in the first place. In fact, the choice of the artist and the decision to install the sculpture permanently in the plaza were made by a public entity: the GSA. Its determination was made on the basis of national standards and carefully formulated procedures, and a jury system ensured impartiality and the selection of art of lasting value.

The selection of this sculpture was, therefore, made by, and on behalf of, the public.

The agency made its commitments and signed a contract. If its decision is reversed in response to pressure from outside sources, the integrity of governmental programs related to the arts will be compromised, and artists of integrity will not participate. If the government can destroy works of art when confronted with such pressure, its capacity to foster artistic diversity and its power to safeguard freedom of creative expression will be in jeopardy.

attracting graffiti artists, rats, criminals, and potentially even terrorists. Although the majority of testimonies at a public hearing to decide whether or not to leave the sculpture in place were in favor of keeping the work, it was ordered to be removed. The artist's lawsuit against the GSA failed to reverse the decision and the sculpture was dismantled in 1989. Serra had argued that *Tilted Arc* was designed specifically for Federal Plaza and that relocating it was the equivalent of destroying it, so the metal was sent to a scrap yard (see Perspectives on Art Box: Richard Serra: A Sculptor Defends His Work). Even though the sculpture was demolished, the artist's hope of making people aware of their environment, pay attention to the path they follow on the way to work, and think about their surroundings was in some ways achieved by the attention generated by the controversy.

The dispute over Serra's *Tilted Arc* raises many questions that have a bearing on the form and functions of all public art. What is the desired impact of public art? Does it need to please its audience, or can it be used as a tool to challenge their beliefs and experiences? How much weight should be given to the artist's freedom of expression? Should consideration be given to whether the artwork is in keeping with the kind of work an artist is known to produce? How much power should public voices be given, whether they belong to specialists in the art world or members of the general community? What bearing does the issue of funding—which may come from the government through special programs aimed at promoting public art or from individual patrons—have on how one answers such questions?

The subject matter of public art, especially when it has political implications, has also been a source of debate. One of the most infamous scandals surrounding a public art project occurred in 1932 when the Mexican artist Diego Rivera (1886–1957) was commissioned by American businessman and millionaire Nelson Rockefeller to paint a **mural** in the Radio Corporation Arts (RCA) Building at Rockefeller Center in Manhattan. Rivera was inspired by Mexico's tradition of adorning walls with paintings and sculptures, which originated long

Minimalist: a mid-twentieth-century artistic style characterized by its simple, unified, and impersonal look, and often employing geometrical or massive forms
Cor-ten steel: a type of steel that forms a coating of rust that protects it from the weather and further corrosion
Mural: a painting executed directly on to a wall

4.19 Diego Rivera, *Man, Controller of the Universe, or Man in the Time Machine*, 1934. Fresco, 15'11" × 37'6⅞". Full composite view of the fresco. Palacio de Bellas Artes, Mexico City, Mexico

before European contact. Such murals create an environment rich with stories related to all aspects of life. Rivera's written plan for *Man at the Crossroads Looking with Hope and High Vision to the Choosing of a New and Better Future*, which Rockefeller approved, included depictions of forces of nature as well as technology, and looked forward to "the liquidation of Tyranny" and a more perfect society. In the course of painting, however, Rivera made some changes inspired by his communist inclinations. The most notable was on the right side of the mural, where he included a portrait of the Russian revolutionary Vladimir Lenin leading a demonstration of workers in a May Day parade.

When he was asked to remove Lenin's portrait, Rivera refused, and offered instead to balance it with a depiction of Abraham Lincoln. Rockefeller rejected this proposal, paid Rivera his full fee, and banned him from the building. Rockefeller then made plans to remove the mural. An outpouring of public support for the project followed: picket lines were formed, newspaper editorials were published, and Rivera made a speech at a rally outside City Hall. Despite suggestions that the mural be moved a few blocks away to the Museum of Modern Art, it was ultimately demolished with pickaxes in February 1934. That same year Rivera re-created the mural, with the new title *Man, Controller of the Universe*, in Mexico City (**4.19**). Rivera rather bluntly described the conflict that can arise between the vision of artists with strong opinions and their audiences: "[The artist] must try to raise the level of taste of the masses, not debase himself to the level of unformed and impoverished taste."

Rivera's public art projects have influenced artists since the 1930s, though by no means do all public murals generate such controversy. The hundreds of murals that now adorn the walls of buildings in San Francisco are part of a rich tradition that began with the three murals Rivera painted at the Pacific Stock Exchange, the San Francisco Art Institute, and the 1939 World's Fair (now at San Francisco City College). Contemporary muralist Susan Cervantes (b. 1944) founded the Precita Eyes Mural Arts Center in San Francisco to focus on issues of Hispanic heritage, to promote community-based art projects, and to make art accessible to inner-city residents. The community aspects of all these initiatives are crucial. Local residents help decide the subjects of the murals and they also collaborate on their creation. Cervantes served as lead artist for an award-winning mural called *Precita Valley Vision* on the facade of the Precita Valley Community Center (**4.20**). In addition to showing activities promoted by the center, the mural commemorates a tragic event in nearby Precita Park, where two teenagers had been murdered while on a picnic. Their faces are included among the depictions of cultural performances, athletic displays, and welcoming scenes of community. As this mural project reveals, art displayed in public places often reflects issues that resonate for the community, by commemorating people who were once part of it and by raising issues—such as violent crime— that need to be addressed.

4.20 *Precita Valley Vision*, 1996. Lead muralist Susan Cervantes. Mural, 30 × 28'. Precita Valley Community Center, San Francisco, California

Discussion Questions

1. In this chapter you have studied artworks that in different ways reflect the importance of community. What does community mean to you? Think of an artwork in your community (a building, painting, or sculpture for example). Discuss the ways in which it conveys (or perhaps contradicts) your own ideas of the importance of community.

2. Research a public artwork that interests you. Consider art in public buildings, parks, schools and colleges, churches, etc. Do you consider the work controversial? Explain your reasons. Was the artwork publicly funded? Are you in favor of such works receiving public funding? Compare the artwork to a controversial artwork discussed in this chapter.

3. Choose a work in this chapter that was the result of the combined efforts of a number of people. Then find three other collaborative works elsewhere in this book (**1.1**, **1.125**, **2.120**) or by searching the Internet. Compare the ways in which collaboration affected the works and how the results were innovative or inspiring.

4.2

Spirituality and Art

For as long as art has been made, there have been artworks inspired by beliefs in ancient deities, spirit beings, and the sacred figures of the world's religions. Through these works artists have sought to express things that cannot be seen and are little understood. In this chapter we use the term spirituality to examine the ways in which beliefs have generally inspired artists for thousands of years. Spirituality encompasses our sense of being connected to others, our awareness of both mind and body, and our wish to understand life's meaning and the world in which we find ourselves. Spirituality serves as a source of inspiration and a way for us to share our beliefs. This chapter investigates four broad categories of artworks with a spiritual context: artworks that incorporate specific gods or deities; artworks that refer to the spirits of the natural world or ancestors; artworks that reflect communication with the spirit world; and places that have a sacred resonance.

Deities

Artists communicate the stories of specific religious figures or deities to help explain their importance. Depictions of individuals considered divine in Greek mythology, the Christian Bible, and Buddhist scripture can make those individuals more accessible and memorable.

The ancient Greeks often made artworks to honor their gods and deities. The sculptures in **4.21** are from the **pediment** of the temple dedicated to the god Zeus at Olympia, Greece,

4.21 Apollo, Centaur, and Lapith, fragments of relief sculptures from West Pediment of Temple of Zeus, Olympia, Greece, *c.* 460 BCE. Marble, 8'8" × 10'10". Archaeological Museum, Olympia, Greece

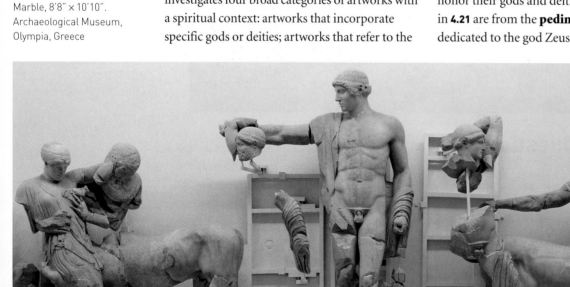

Pediment: the triangular space, situated above the row of columns, at the end of a building in the Classical style
Idealized: represented as perfect in form or character, corresponding to an ideal

where the Olympic Games were born. The scene depicts the legendary battle between the Lapiths of Thessaly and the Centaurs—half-human and half-horse creatures, which, according to Greek mythology, lived in the nearby mountains. During the wedding feast of the Lapith king, the Centaurs, who were amongst the guests, drank too much wine and tried to abduct the bride and the other women. The civilized Lapiths are depicted as **idealized**, rigid, and without emotion. The barbarian Centaurs, on the other hand, are shown with more dramatic gestures and ferocious expressions. Apollo, the god of the sun, who was also associated with the poetic arts and medicine, stands at the center of the event and brings order to the violent struggle. He is the appropriate deity for this scene because he represents reason, order, and male beauty. The Centaurs, who are associated, by their drinking, with Dionysus the god of wine, represent the opposite attributes of change, chaos, and even madness.

In Christian Europe in the eleventh century, visual artists often illustrated themes and events from the Bible. Bishop Bernward, who directed the building of the Church of St. Michael's at Hildesheim, Germany, commissioned a set of doors that depict scenes from the book of Genesis on the left side and scenes from the life of Christ on the right. In chronological order the doors are read counterclockwise, beginning at the top of the left door. But the panels are also arranged so that events from the Old Testament are paired with related episodes from the New Testament (**4.22 a–c**).

For example, the third panel from the top matches the Tree of Knowledge on the left with the Tree of Life on the right. In the left scene the original sin is committed. Because Eve accepted the forbidden fruit from the Tree of Knowledge, she and Adam were expelled from the Garden of Eden into the world of suffering and death. On the right, the cross on which Jesus was crucified, understood as the Tree of Life, offers eternal life to believers who ask for forgiveness of their sins and accept Christ as their savior. The elongated

4.22a (above) Detail of Hildesheim Doors: Expulsion from the Garden of Eden

4.22b (right) Doors depicting scenes from Genesis and the Life of Christ, commissioned by Bishop Bernward for the Abbey Church of St. Michael's, Hildesheim, 1015. Bronze, 16'6" high. Dom-Museum, Hildesheim, Germany

4.22c (far right) Diagram with identification of panels on Hildesheim Doors

	Old Testament	New Testament	
Paradise Lost	Formation of Eve	Noli Me Tangere	Paradise Gained
Salutations	Eve Presented to Adam	The Three Marys at the Tomb	Salutations
Tree of Knowledge (sin)	Temptation and Fall	The Crucifixion	Tree of Life, The Cross, Salvation
Judgment	Accusation and Judgment of Adam and Eve	Judgment of Jesus by Pilate	Judgment
Separation from God	Expulsion from Paradise	Presentation of Jesus in Temple	Reunion with God
Firstborn Son of Eve (Cain) and Poverty	Adam and Eve Working	Adoration of the Magi	Firstborn Son of Mary (Jesus) and Wealth
Abel's Sacrificial Lamb	Offerings by Cain (grain) and Abel (lamb)	The Nativity	Jesus, Lamb of God
Despair, Sin, Murder	Cain Slaying Abel	The Annunciation	Hope and Everlasting Life

4.23 *Life of Buddha*, stela, Gupta period, *c.* 475 CE. Sandstone, 41" high. India Museum, Calcutta, India

behind him. At the top of the sculpture he is shown reclining as he achieves tranquillity, called nirvana. The smaller carvings along the sides of the stela show noteworthy moments after he decided to leave his princely life at the age of thirty to become a holy man.

Spiritual Beings and Ancestors

In African cultures, artworks often reflect beliefs in the spirits of gods and ancestors. According to these cultures' traditional beliefs, objects are infused with a spiritual presence. They help to continue and preserve cultural practices, beliefs, and family ties. Contemporary artists who examine black history often refer to traditional African art, customs, and rituals in their artwork.

The religion of the Senufo people of West Africa is centered on a creator deity, nature spirits, and ancestors, including a female ancestral spirit called "ancient mother" or "ancient woman." These spirits can be beneficial or harmful. They are often depicted as beings with an anatomy very different from that of humans. The head, legs, and detailed features of the Senufo sculpture in **4.24** are relatively small while the arms and breasts are exaggerated. The inclusion of a nursing baby suggests that this is one of the female ancestral spirits. Such an "ancient woman" would serve as a guiding spirit for adult males in the community, who were responsible for maintaining Senufo religious and historical traditions.

In traditional African cultures, functional objects were often esteemed as status symbols. These objects, which could include staffs, masks, and even wooden stools, acquired their power through use, and only people of a certain rank could own them. This chair from the Democratic Republic of

4.24 Mother-and-child figure, late 19th–mid-20th century. Wood, 25" high. Cleveland Museum of Art, Ohio

and frail appearance of the figures and the unnaturalistic settings reflect the Christian emphasis on internal, spiritual matters and themes instead of the exterior, physical world.

The subject matter of Buddhist art is the life of Buddha and his teachings and beliefs, which are considered pathways to achieving spiritual perfection. Buddha, or the Awakened One, was a Hindu prince named Siddhartha Gautama who lived in Nepal and northern India from about 563 to 483 BCE. The larger panels of the **stela** in **4.23** show the cycle of Buddha's life. In the bottom section we see his miraculous birth as he emerges from his mother's right side. The second section, above the birth scene, is the moment of his enlightenment as he touches the earth with a symbolic gesture of strength and renewal. In the third section he is shown giving his first sermon, seated with his legs crossed and his hands posed in prayer, with the wheel of law

4.25 Chair, early 20th century. Wood, brass, and iron tacks, 23⅝ × 13¼ × 23¾". National Museum of African Art, Smithsonian Institution, Washington, D.C.

Congo is believed to have belonged to a chief of the Ngombe people (**4.25**). It was carved from a single block of wood (with the exception of the crossbeams) and decorated with brass and iron tacks imported from Europe. This stool, by itself a symbol of dignity and authority, contains a triangular **chevron** motif at the top and bottom of the seat, which suggests masculinity and royalty. Such a stool, used throughout a person's life, acquired additional significance after the user died by serving as the resting place for the soul. Family ties and the continuation of practices established by ancestors were especially important in the case of the chief, who was considered divine or semidivine. This stool was a tangible reminder of its owner's status and values even after he died. As it was passed down or prepared to accompany the ruler in the afterlife, such an object served as a tangible reminder of the owner's life and carried his legacy for later generations.

The contemporary African American artist Betye Saar (b. 1926) has adopted some of the influences that were important to traditional African groups as she explores themes of personal and communal identity. Saar examines the survival of African traditions in black culture and often challenges **stereotypes**, such as those represented by figures like "Aunt Jemima." Saar has an ongoing interest in religious beliefs and revered objects, finding imagery and ideas in the traditions of **voodoo** and spirit worship. The title of her sculpture *Ancestral Spirit Chair* conveys the power an object can have for later generations (**4.26**). Like the Ngombe chair in **4.25**, which incorporates European tacks and construction techniques, Saar's chair combines contrasting materials and methods. The European-style legs, seat, and back are made of unrefined twigs that have been embellished with paint, bone, glass, and metal. Saar has stated:

> I am not about imitating African art or primitive art, but I am interested in the power it has and that kind of power being transferred to the work I do. And by power, I mean some kind of communication between me and my materials on one level and then the final product, communicating with the viewer.

4.26 Betye Saar, *Ancestral Spirit Chair*, 1992. Painted wood, glass, plastic, metal, and vine, 60 × 46 × 32". Smith College Museum of Art, Northampton, Massachusetts

Connecting with the Gods

Communication with the gods has been an important subject matter for art in many cultures. Sometimes special individuals serve as intermediaries between people and a deity. Christian saints and mythological figures interact with gods to provide role models or to help educate viewers about religious practices.

4.27 Stela of Naram-Sin, c. 2254–2218 BCE. Pink sandstone, 6'7" × 3'5". Musée du Louvre, Paris, France

In other cases, rulers have been depicted interacting directly with divine beings or travelling into supernatural realms. Artworks that show these kinds of interaction reinforce the power of rulers by convincing their people that they are blessed, even aided by the gods, and worthy of their exalted position.

Human interaction with a deity is the focal point of the Stela of Naram-Sin (**4.27**). Naram-Sin, an Akkadian king who ruled central Mesopotamia (part of modern Iraq) around 2254–2218 BCE, was both a religious figure and a military leader. His stela commemorates the Akkadian victory over the Lullubi people. The lower portions of the scene show signs of the battle that has taken place on a mountain. Above, Naram-Sin stands victorious near the summit, his horned helmet and larger size emphasizing his importance. The sun god is not depicted in human form but appears symbolically as a sunburst. Naram-Sin's location as close as possible to the sun god illustrates his own supreme, divine status in society and, especially considering the recent victory, suggests that he was looked upon with approval by the gods. In the ancient Near East there was a close relationship between people and the gods. Because humans were imperfect and in need of assistance from a higher being, prayers were offered, and rituals and sacrifices performed, to keep the gods happy. As the deified representative of his community, a ruler like Naram-Sin needed to maintain a favorable connection with the supernatural realm in order to ensure continued prosperity for his kingdom.

During the Middle Ages, Christians in the Eastern Orthodox Church used **icons** depicting holy figures as a focus of devotion and a source of inspiration. Icons were believed to be able to communicate with God and were even sometimes considered to have other miraculous powers. Many were painted on wood panels, which meant they could be carried around, although some were attached to chapel screens in churches. The portable icons, however, were more accessible for ordinary people. They could also be transported from Byzantium to distant places, such as Russia, in order to help spread Christian beliefs. Although icons themselves were not been in Moscow almost continuously since 1395). Only the faces are original; the rest of the panel, probably damaged by people touching it, has been repainted.

The Ecstasy of St. Teresa by Gianlorenzo Bernini (1598–1680) is another Christian artwork that is meant to inspire devotion and reverence (**4.29**). It was made between 1647 and 1652 to decorate a funerary chapel for the

Icon: a small, often portable, religious image venerated by Christian believers; first used by the Eastern Orthodox Church
Linear outline: a line that clearly separates a figure from its surroundings
Stylized: art that represents objects in an exaggerated way to emphasize certain aspects of the object

4.28 *Virgin of Vladimir*, 12th century (before 1132). Tempera on panel, 30¾ x 21½". Tretyakov Gallery, Moscow, Russia

worshiped as divine, they became the subjects of intense veneration because they depicted individuals whose saintliness meant they were close to God, and therefore able to spread goodness.

The Orthodox Church required the form and content of icons to follow traditional rules. As a result, although each painting is unique, it has a family resemblance to other icons: gold backgrounds, **linear outlines**, and **stylized** but believable poses. It was important that the figures in the icons could be recognized by anyone who saw them. Thus the Madonna and Child were always shown with haloes to represent their holiness. The *Virgin of Vladimir* portrays Mary as the "Virgin of Loving Kindness," with her face touching Jesus to emphasize her virtue (**4.28**). This icon, probably made in Constantinople, was intended to bless and protect the city in which it was housed (it has

4.29 Gianlorenzo Bernini, *The Ecstasy of St. Teresa*, 1647–52. Polychromed marble, gilt, bronze, yellow glass, fresco, and stucco, 4'11" high (figures only). Cornaro Chapel, Santa Maria della Vittoria, Rome, Italy

Cornaro family in the Church of Santa Maria della Vittoria in Rome, Italy. This massive marble sculpture (more than 11 feet tall) depicts one of St. Teresa of Ávila's mystical visions: she is about to be pierced by an angel's arrow that will infuse her with divine love. The theatrical staging and the emphasis on dramatic light—created by the use of gilt bronze rays behind the figures and by the light falling from a hidden window above the sculpture—are typical of the **Baroque** style. Bernini's sculpture is executed with great attention to detail. The whole scene seems to take place in the clouds and the angel almost hovers above St. Teresa. Marble is made to suggest several different textures including smooth skin, gauzy fabric, clinging draperies, and the heavy wool of the nun's habit worn by the saint. The combination of accurate and believable details with an exaggerated picture of devotion reflects the Catholic Church's new emphasis at that time on believers establishing a strongly personal relationship with Christ. In Bernini's sculpture Christ's **Passion** is relived in the intensity of

St. Teresa's piety, which serves as an example to be followed by the devout.

In Bernini's Christian artwork, it is the angel who has had to descend from heaven to visit St. Teresa on earth. But in Mesoamerica it was the human rulers who possessed the ability to cross the threshold from one world to another. Olmec leaders sat on "altars," or thrones, during public ceremonies. The altar from the Olmec site of La Venta, Mexico, in **4.30** shows a ruler emerging from a cave opening. He holds a rope that stretches around the back of the monument and wraps around the carved necks of several seated prisoners. All of the elements in the altar reflect important motifs in the creation mythology and belief systems of the Olmec. The cave is a point of access to the here and now from a previous world or an underworld. The carvings over the man's head indicate that the cave is a living being with eyes, nose, and teeth. This opening is like the jaws of the earth monster. The cave was considered the place of creation, like a womb, so when it is combined with the

4.30 Altar 4, La Venta, c. 800 BCE. Basalt, 59¼" high. Parque Museo La Venta, Villahermosa, Tabasco, Mexico

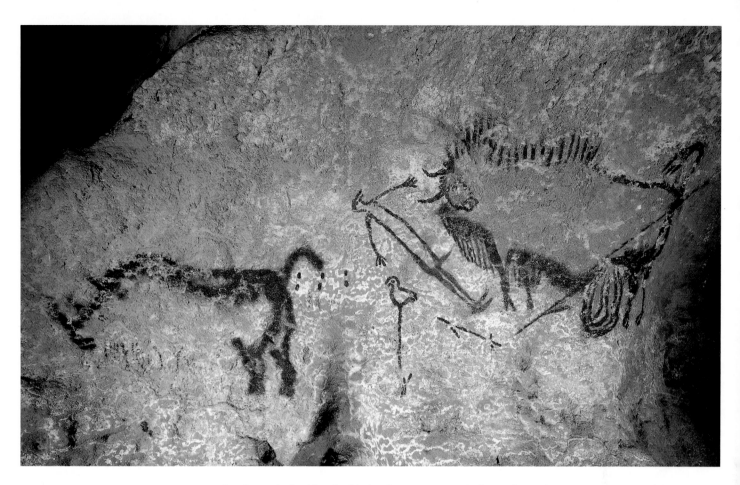

Baroque: European artistic and architectural style of the late sixteenth to early eighteenth centuries, characterized by extravagance and emotional intensity
Passion: the arrest, trial, and execution of Jesus Christ, and his sufferings during them
Paleolithic: prehistoric period, extending from 2.5 million to 12,000 years ago
Shaman: a priest or priestess regarded as having the ability to communicate directly with the spiritual world

emerging figure it signifies the birth of man, as if all life originates from the ruler. The rope in his hand reveals that he also possesses the power to capture and control the prisoners who will be sacrificed in order to appease the gods and ensure continued prosperity for the entire community.

The spirit world and its impact on people have been conceived of in numerous ways even before written history began. The bird-headed man painted on a cave wall at Lascaux in southern France is a rare example of a human depicted during **Paleolithic** times (**4.31**). In this case, it may have been important to show a person in order to tell a specific story about the interaction between a man, a rhinoceros, and a bison. The figure seems to be lying down, suggesting that he has been killed by one of the beasts. Because the human has the head of a bird, he may represent a **shaman**, who acts as an intermediary between the invisible spirit world and the physical realm of humans. A shaman uses magic for healing or to control events. Wearing an animal or bird mask can

indicate that a shaman is in a trance-like state, when he or she becomes another being and brings divine properties to the community. In this painting, therefore, the human figure may be depicted with a bird's head to show that he is becoming a bird or a bird deity. Thus, this painting probably served a ritual or ceremonial function.

Sacred Places

We all have places that restore our souls. Whether it is the mountains, the beach, or the family dinner table, there are places that allow us to feel connected and at peace. Certain artworks represent places of personal retreat or communal worship as sites of reverence, renewal, and contemplation. By marking these sites and communicating these experiences, artists and architects give us a sense of their connectedness to nature, religion, or community (see Box: What Makes a Place Sacred?, pp. 478–9; and Gateway Box: Matisse, **4.37**, pp. 482–3).

What Makes a Place Sacred?

Places that people returned to again and again, like the **prehistoric** caves of Lascaux and the **catacombs** of Rome, were clearly important for their users. When such places, which had been created for memorial or religious purposes, were adorned with artworks, their sacred nature took on a new dimension.

The walls of the Lascaux Caves in southern France (**4.32a**) were painted sometime between 15000 and 13000 BCE. One section is densely packed with paintings of animals (**4.32b**). The effort required to adorn the walls of the caves with so many images suggests that these depictions of animals that were encountered on a daily basis were incredibly important. Some of the most magnificent paintings are contained in the Hall of the Bulls (**4.32b**) in the main cave, which is 66 feet wide and 16 feet high. The hall is located near the entrance to the system of caves, unlike the painting in **4.31** (see p. 477), which is in a remote part of the complex. The hall, as its name suggests, is decorated with outlines and **realistic** details of numerous bulls—one of them more than 15 feet long. The paintings in this area overlap, indicating that the site was visited repeatedly, that it was decorated over a period of time, and that making these paintings in this particular place was significant. They mark it as a location that was sacred in some way to the people who used it.

Because the makers of the paintings at Lascaux had no system of writing, we must deduce the stories of these images from the pictures themselves. In addition to telling a story, which was one likely purpose of the images, prehistoric cave paintings may also have been used to teach hunting and to represent shamanic or ritual practices (as suggested by the bird-headed man). Paintings similar to those at Lascaux have been found in other places in France and also in Spain, indicating that these paintings were part of a widespread cultural practice by people who either moved from place to place or shared ideas with others.

The human desire to paint important or sacred places is equally evident in the catacombs constructed outside the city of Rome, Italy, between the second and fourth centuries CE. An underground system of tunnels measuring between 60 and 90 miles in length and containing the ancient remains of 4 million people, the catacombs were sacred spaces for Romans, who held different religious beliefs and went there to visit their ancestors' burial places. While pagan Romans practiced both cremation and burial of the dead, burial was especially important for Jews and Christians. The catacombs were also used as temples for religious observances, a space where Christians could gather, and hiding places for fugitives.

4.32a Hall of the Bulls. Plan of Lascaux Caves, Dordogne, France

4.32b Hall of the Bulls. Pigment on limestone rock. Lascaux Caves

Catacomb of Priscilla

Cubicle of
the Velata

N
E
W
S

Entrance

Prehistoric: dating from the period of human existence before the invention of writing
Catacombs: an underground system of tunnels used for burying and commemorating the dead
Realistic: artistic style that aims to represent appearances as accurately as possible
Fresco: a technique where the artist paints onto freshly applied plaster. From the Italian *fresco*, fresh

4.33a Plan and section (through main gallery of oldest region) of catacomb of Callixtus, 2nd century CE, Rome, Italy

4.33b Catacombs of Priscilla, 2nd and 3rd centuries CE, Via Salaria, Rome, Italy

Like Lascaux, the catacombs contain paintings in different types of areas. In the catacombs, **frescoes** ornament both the places used for burial and the rooms in which people could congregate. The paintings consist of pagan, Jewish, and Christian scenes. Although the same imagery was seen by Romans of all three faiths, particular subjects, such as banquet scenes or shepherds, would be interpreted differently, according to the viewer's religion. For example, the central figure in the Christian fresco from the catacombs of Priscilla is shown standing in a praying position (**4.33b**). Such a pose appears in pagan art, but it has a distinct meaning for Christians, who understand the figure to be praying to their god. Using imagery, such as this prayerful person, that was familiar to practitioners of other religions probably helped win potential converts to Christianity while also conveying a clear message to existing believers.

A mosque is a building where Muslims gather to pray to Allah. Because mosques are often the largest structures in a city, they have also played a significant role in community activities when used as schools or hospitals. The Mosque of the Imam in Isfahan (present-day Iran) has four iwans, or vaulted entrances between the courtyard and the mosque's interior. Large towers (minarets) rise above the city to call citizens to prayer. Pointed arches, a characteristic feature of Islamic architecture, crown the mihrab, iwans, and decorative walkways throughout the mosque. In its central courtyard there is a large pool for cleansing before prayer. Muslims must pray five times a day facing the direction of the city of Mecca. A special prayer niche (mihrab), placed on the wall oriented toward Mecca (qibla wall) indicates the correct direction for worshipers' prayers.

The walls of the Mosque are decorated with the intricate blue tilework, calligraphic texts, and foliage designs commonly found in Islamic architecture. A fine example of complex Islamic geometric patterning can be seen in the honeycomb design of the muqarnas in one iwan entrance to the Mosque (**4.34**). The muqarnas (or stalactite vaults) are decorative elements originally used to cover the tombs of holy men. The shape of the muqarnas in the pointed vault resembles a series of small domes lined up in rows and stacked on top of one another. One description suggests that the muquarnas sanctify the space by symbolizing "the rotating dome of heaven."

Marking a site as sacred is a common practice in the long-standing Japanese religion called Shinto, which emphasizes the ways such natural elements as the sun, mountains, water, and trees are connected to well-being. Unlike Christianity and Islam, Shinto focuses on the here and now and reveres nature itself as a deity. For example, Shinto recognizes a mountain as a sacred object because it is the source of water for rice cultivation. Such a mountain was once worshiped directly, but over time shrines were built as places to worship a god, known as a *Kami,* that was important to a particular area or community. These sites, like the Grand Shrine of Ise, or Ise Jingu, started with small piles of stones in an area surrounded by stone enclosures, which have gradually evolved to include buildings, fences, and gates.

Ise Jingu is one of thousands of shrines throughout Japan dedicated to the sun goddess Amataerasu Omikami. Local residents visit the shrine to revere the goddess and seek her assistance. The site is now marked by a stately **A-framed** wooden building that is simple in design and made with natural materials (**4.35**). Because nature is cyclical, the shrine must also be renewed and refreshed. Since 690 CE, Ise Jingu has been rebuilt every twenty years with a special ceremony in which meals are shared with the *Kami,* infusing the everyday act of eating with ritual significance.

4.34 Main entrance portal (iwan), Masjid-i-Shah, early 17th century, Isfahan, Iran

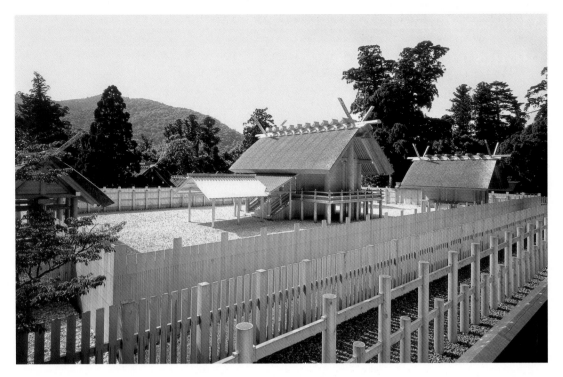

A-frame: an ancient form of structural support, made out of beams arranged so that the shape of the building resembles a capital letter A
Octagonal: eight-sided
Abstract Expressionism: a mid-twentieth-century artistic style characterized by its capacity to convey intense emotions using non-representational images

4.35 Ise Jingu, site dates from 4th century CE, rebuilt 1993, Mie Prefecture, Japan

The Rothko Chapel in Houston, Texas, is a place of worship open to people of all beliefs (**4.36**). The chapel's **octagonal** interior walls hold fourteen paintings by the Russian-born American **Abstract Expressionist** painter Mark Rothko (1903–70). Rothko worked closely with the architects on the designs for the chapel. He wanted his paintings to be hung a certain distance from the floor, presented in low lighting, and shown together in a group in order to create an environment that enveloped and transported viewers beyond their everyday experience. The canvases at the Rothko Chapel employ a restricted, dark palette of colors ranging from

4.36 Rothko Chapel, 1966–71, Menil Collection, Houston, Texas

Gateway to Art: Matisse, *Icarus*
Designs with Cutouts

The French artist Henri Matisse (1869–1954) employed paper cutouts to create finished works of art, but he also used cutouts to plan works in other **media**. *Icarus* was designed as a cutout and produced as a **stencil** print in a book (**4.38**). Late in his career Matisse used cutouts to design the entire interior of a building.

In 1941, while recovering from surgery for intestinal cancer, Matisse was cared for by a nurse named Monique Bourgeois. Bourgeois later became a nun and she asked Matisse to build a chapel for her convent in Vence, near the Mediterranean coast of France. Matisse agreed and worked on the Chapel of the Rosary from 1948 to 1951.

Matisse considered the Chapel of the Rosary to be his masterpiece (**4.37**). It combined the interests in form and color that had been developing throughout his entire career, and it

4.37 Chapel of the Rosary, Vence, Côte d'Azur, France. Plan devised by Henri Matisse, 1948–51

4.38 Henri Matisse, *Icarus*, from *Jazz*, 1943–7. Page size 16⅞ × 12⅞". MOMA, New York

incorporated elements derived from his method of working with cutouts in order to emphasize graphic shapes and bold patterns. He designed all aspects of the project: the architecture of the building; its stained-glass windows; its interior decoration, including painted wall tiles; and its furniture. The interior of the space is bright, white, and serene. The Mediterranean light enters the chapel through three sets of stained-glass windows, which transform it into washes of bright color. Matisse designed these stunning windows to look like fluid drawings. Their appearance was inspired by his many years of emphasizing an economical use of color, as seen in his cutouts. Like *Icarus*, the chapel windows employ a limited color **palette**. While *Icarus* uses bold blue, yellow, red, and black, the stained glass has bright yellow and an intense blue (representing the sun and the sea) with a slightly more subdued green for tree and leaf forms.

Black contour drawings are printed on the otherwise pure white ceramic tiles that cover the walls. Designs include such natural forms as clouds, life studies of figures representing scenes from the Bible, and symbols related to the Christian faith. The furniture, designed to have clean lines and geometric shapes, includes an altar with a crucifix and candlesticks. The chapel brings together many of the essential aspects of Matisse's art: his selective use of light and color, his emphasis on bold shapes from the cutouts, and his love of drawing and sculpture.

maroon and plum to black. The fields of color are intense and powerful, creating a tranquil and contemplative atmosphere. The chapel marks a culmination in the artist's search for the simplest means to express universal truths that are spiritual in nature but unconnected to any particular religious experience or doctrine. The Rothko Chapel has become a sacred place for worship and religious services, a site for performances and scholarly lectures, and a space for visitors to contemplate while immersed in an experience that integrates Rothko's paintings with architecture.

Discussion Questions

1   Find three works of art that deal with spirituality (in other chapters in this book, in your community, or any other examples that you know about). Into which category of works in this chapter do they fit? If they do not seem to fit any of these sections, how would you categorize them?

2   Review the sacred places covered in this chapter and then think of a building, public space, or sculpture that is important to you. Choose a place or artwork that you are comfortable discussing with others and that is personally significant and connected in deep ways to your sense of self. Describe it as fully as possible (the function of the space, what you do there, what it looks like, how you feel when you are there, whether other people have similar experiences there, and so on). Be sure to consider how your experience could best be shared with someone unfamiliar with your personal sacred space.

3   In this chapter you have encountered some spaces that have been sacred to a large community and even to a global body of followers. Alone or in groups describe a sacred space with universal appeal, or invent and design one. Sacred spaces often harmonize with nature or feature geometric forms, and include sacred symbols. Will your space include any of these elements? Try to make your chosen space reflect feelings and/or physical attributes that are important to you.

Medium (plural **media**): the material on or from which an artist chooses to make a work of art
Stencil: a perforated template allowing ink or paint to pass through to print a design
Palette: the range of colors used by an artist

4.3

Art and the Cycle of Life

> How strange is the lot of us mortals! Each of us is here for a brief sojourn; for what purpose he knows not, though he senses it. But without deeper reflection one knows from daily life that one exists for other people.
>
> (Albert Einstein, physicist and Nobel Prize winner)

Human cultures from the earliest times to the twenty-first century have been deeply concerned with fundamental questions of existence: where do we come from? What happens when we die? What lies beyond death? These persistent concerns, not surprisingly, have also been a frequent subject of works of art.

In this chapter, we look at the ways in which artists have examined the cycle of life. Visual artists have dealt with topics as unfathomable as the beginning of human existence, as miraculous as the birth of a child, as enduring as natural forces or the passage of time, and as overwhelming as the finality of death. The artworks in this chapter suggest the enormous variety of ways in which artists have addressed these themes. The examination of life's mysteries takes the form of mythical visions, narrative accounts, and direct portrayals of life's beginnings, its endings, and what happens in between.

Life's Beginnings and Family Ties

Stories about the beginning of civilization and the creation of humankind are found

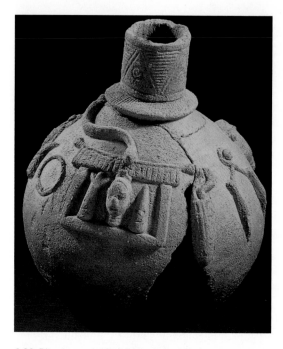

4.39 Ritual vessel, 13th–14th century. Terracotta, 9⅞" high. University Art Museum, Obafemi Awolowo University, Ife, Nigeria

throughout history in cultures across the globe. Creation myths can help us come to grips with concepts that we may not understand intellectually, such as the fact of life itself. Equally important are stories that tell about the process of childbirth and emphasize how we are connected to our family members. Artworks with such subjects often reflect the beliefs of an entire community.

Many creation myths tell of separate realms inhabited by gods and people. A ritual vessel made by the Yoruba of West Africa displays many literal and metaphorical references to their culture's ideas

4.40 Tlazolteotl giving birth to the maize god, *c.* 1500. Aztec granite carving, 8 × 4¾ × 5⅞". Dumbarton Oaks Museum, Washington, D.C.

about creation and the origins and authority of their kings (**4.39**). The vessel was made in Ife (now in Nigeria), a city sacred in Yoruba mythology. Ife was the "navel of the world," because it was believed to be the place where humans were created and kingship began. Yoruba kings still trace their ancestry to the first ruler of Ife. The top of the vessel in **4.39** refers to the navel as the central point of the body as well as an opening that connects the exterior to the interior. The vessel's round shape, which resembles a piece of fruit, a pregnant female, or perhaps the earth itself, further reinforces the biological connection with human birth. The snake-like form on the side of the vessel resembles an umbilical cord. The snake, which is associated with the earth, regeneration, and rebirth, is joined to the human figure shown in a rectangular house. Vessels like this one were ceremonially broken, allowing the offerings contained within them to flow into the earth and play a key role in the cycle of birth and rebirth.

For some cultures, such as the Aztecs of central Mexico, it was important to mark the physical, if still mystical, beginnings of human life. For the Aztecs, a woman giving birth was seen as a female warrior going to battle on behalf of the state. Women who died in childbirth were afforded the same respect as men who died on the battlefield; they resided in the same final resting place as heroes, accompanying the sun on its daily

journey through the sky. The goddess Tlazolteotl, an earth mother and patron of childbirth, was known as the "filth eater" because she visited people at the end of their lives and absolved, or ate, their sins. She was responsible for bringing disease as well as curing it. A stone sculpture of Tlazolteotl shows her in the act of giving birth (**4.40**). The grimace on her face resembles a skull, and a tiny figure, a miniature adult, emerges from her body. Female deities worshiped by the Aztecs, like Tlazlteotl, often had dual personalities. Not only were they acknowledged as life-givers, but they were also feared as powerful and terrifying.

While the Tlazolteotl sculpture shows a symbolic representation of childbirth, the Dutch artist Rineke Dijkstra (b. 1959) highlights some of the stark realities of birth in her *Mothers* series. *Julie* (**4.41**) captures a mother and her newborn baby just one hour after delivery, at a time and in a

4.41 Rineke Dijkstra, *Julie, Den Haag, The Netherlands, February 29, 1994.* C-print, 60¼ × 50¾"

4.42 Tierney Gearon, *Untitled*, 2004. From the series *The Mother Project*. C-print

way that defies most expectations of mother-and-child imagery. They are standing against a cold, anonymous wall. Their position starkly exposes the vulnerability, even shock, that both mother and baby probably feel. Dijkstra makes public a time in a woman's life that is now generally considered private and personal. Inspired by watching the birth of a friend's baby, Dijkstra's photographs capture the awkwardness and enduring strength of the early moments of a new life.

Photographs taken by the American artist Tierney Gearon (b. 1963) of her own close relations also show unexpected views of family interactions. For this reason they have sometimes been controversial. Indeed, Gearon gained notoriety for a series of images showing her children nude and wearing masks. In the *Mother Project* series she shows her aging mother—sometimes nude and sometimes dressed in what look like costumes—either alone, or with Gearon and her children (**4.42**). According to the artist, this project was important because:

My mom is mentally ill, and a big part of it is how I celebrated my mom instead of being embarrassed or trying to hide from her. Instead, I celebrate the beauty in her and a lot of people—especially older people—are moved because it is something they can relate to.

Through these pictures Gearon portrays both her own experiences with her mother and the reality of her mother's life altered by age and illness.

The Asmat people live on the island of New Guinea in the southern Pacific Ocean. They trace their origins to the mythical figure called Fumeripits, who carved the first humans from wood and brought them to life by playing a drum. Woodcarving is thus an esteemed tradition amongst the Asmat, and sculptures are often made to represent and honor people who have recently died and the ancestors they are joining in the afterlife.

Ancestor poles known as bis (**4.43**) represent both stories about the cyclical nature of human

4.43 Bis poles, late 1950s. Wood, paint, and fiber, 18' × 3'6" × 5'3". Metropolitan Museum of Art, New York

ancestors. Once a sculpture has served its ritual function it is returned to the groves of sago palms to decay and strengthen future harvests of the trees.

Inlay: substance embedded in another, contrasting material

Sacrifice, Death, and Rebirth

Art and ritual often mark different stages of life. Artists have recorded images of birth and death as ways to consider the fleeting existence of the life force that ultimately defies comprehension. While some artifacts refer to the ceremonies undertaken to ask ancestors or supernatural beings to ensure continued prosperity, others present the lifeless body itself. There are many questions, often unanswerable, that artists confront. What happens after we die? Do we leave the world of the living? Is it important for the body to stay intact? Is there a place to which the soul is believed to go? These concerns about life, death, and the afterlife have inspired artists for millennia.

For the Kongo people of the Democratic Republic of Congo (in Central Africa) an important connection between past and present exists in the reverence they show for their ancestors and the nature spirits that influence their lives. The rituals they perform are as crucial to their livelihood as the chores and tasks of daily life. A painted wooden sculpture made by the Kongo people shows a woman kneeling as she holds a bowl in one hand and supports a child with the other (**4.44**). This sculpture could be a simple representation of a routine daily event—a woman goes to collect water and takes her child with her—but the artist has given us clues that it has further significance. Her hairstyle and pose, as well as the objects she possesses, suggest the woman is performing a ceremonial function. She is kneeling to show respect to a person of higher social status, an ancestor or deity. The shiny **inlay** used for her eyes indicates that she is in some sort of trance, perhaps

4.44 Kneeling female figure with bowl and child, late 19th/ early 20th century. Wood, pigment, and glass, 21½ × 10 × 9½". Dallas Museum of Art, Texas

life and the social and family ties that connect the community. The bis is carved with imagery associated with power, virility, and fertility, including strong bodies, horns used in headhunting, and trees where the spirits dwelled. At the top, a root from the tree has been retained, creating a wing-like projection. In the main section of the sculpture, there are representations both of the dead individual for whom the bis was made and also of other ancestors. The lower part of the sculpture, called the "canoe," is believed to carry the deceased into the afterlife.

Ancestor poles like this one were once made in connection with headhunting and warfare but now serve a ritual function for male initiation and memorial feasts. A profound bond exists between the figures the Asmat carve and the trees they come from, which are as important as the relationships between generations of

4.45 *Shiva Nataraja* (*Lord of the Dance*), Chola Period, 11th century. Bronze, 43⅞" high. Cleveland Museum of Art, Ohio

in contact with a god. The bowl and the child may be gifts bestowed by the god, or they may represent sacrifices the woman is prepared to make. For the Kongo people, white paint (as has been used on this sculpture) identifies nature spirits, who are associated with the ancestors. This woman thus provides a role model for the living members of the community: they are to honor their ancestors with gifts of sustenance and with children who will continue the traditions they have worked so hard to establish.

In India, connections between the present life and those before and after it are central to the Hindu belief system. One of the principal Hindu deities, Shiva, embodies a balancing of contradictory qualities: half-male and half-female, benevolent and fearsome, giver and taker of life. As Nataraja, or "Lord of the Dance" (**4.45**), Shiva is responsible for dancing the world into existence and bringing to life the endless cycle of death and rebirth, known as *samsara*, in which Hindus believe. The flames surrounding Shiva's agile form represent the periodic chaos and

destruction that happen when the dance ceases. During these periods of inactivity, the fire cleanses the physical world by providing a release from *samsara*. Shiva dances while poised on top of a dwarf who represents the evil and ignorance that are stamped out during the dances. Shiva's dance creates a balance between creation and destruction that, over the course of time, manifests itself in the cycle of life.

For the Inca of South America, the deceased were believed to continue to exist in a separate reality that was parallel with the living human world. As a result, spirits could inform the life of the living and ancestors could be consulted after death. The Inca sacrificed human beings to ensure prosperity for the community, to appease the gods, and to achieve balance among natural forces. For them, sacrifice was a sacred act in which something precious was given up in order to gain something else. A number of mummified children have been found on high mountain peaks throughout the Inca territory. These children, who usually came from wealthy or noble families, were adorned with fine tapestries, jewelry, and feather work, and were accompanied

4.46 Mummy of a boy, *c.* 1500. Museo Nacional de Historia Natural, Santiago, Chile by several specific objects. One mummy, a boy of about nine years old found at Cerro el Plomo in Chile, appears still to be sleeping (**4.46**).

Children were selected for these sacrifices because they were innocent and considered near perfection. It was a great honor to be one of these sacrificial victims. The Cerro el Plomo mummy was preserved along with a feather bag containing coca leaves, a silver figurine with an elaborate featherwork headdress wrapped in textiles, and several llama figurines. After a prolonged series of rituals, the child would have been given a strong drink called *chicha* (corn beer), fallen into an intoxicated slumber, and passed on into the afterlife. As a result of the mummifying effects of the freezing temperatures and dry climate, this child's body has been preserved, achieving a kind of immortality that matches the Inca conception of the spirit living on.

Another way in which artists have pondered what happens after a person dies is by creating images of the deceased. Christian artists during the **Renaissance** often made pictures of the body of Christ after his crucifixion. Such images were important because Christ was thought to live on after the demise of his physical body, and the concept of eternal life after death is at the core of Christianity. The artist Andrea Mantegna (*c.* 1431–1506), who was born near Padua in northern Italy, created a direct and intimate view of the body in *Dead Christ* (**4.47**). Because Mantegna has **foreshortened** the scene, we are first confronted by the stigmata (the wounds from the nails with which Christ was hung on the cross) in his feet and, further into the picture, in his hands. His body, covered in carefully depicted drapery, extends away from us on a marble slab. Beyond the muscular torso, we see his lifeless face. By Christ's side are the Virgin Mother and Mary Magdalene, who are mostly cropped out of the picture. While their grief adds to the atmosphere of the scene, the artist focuses our attention on the immediacy of Christ's body and the fact that he is no longer alive.

Perhaps because we are somewhat detached from death, or perhaps out of a sense of propriety, contemporary images of the deceased are not as common as they were during the Renaissance. Photographs of the dead can be especially shocking because today we no longer have such a

direct relationship with the dead as people did in the past. Then, loved ones died at home, not in hospitals; bodies were laid out for burial by family members, not by funeral homes. The American artist Andres Serrano (b. 1950) made a series of photographs in a morgue in which the subjects are identified only by the manner of their deaths. The composition of *The Morgue (Gun Murder)* (**4.48**), with the feet pointing away from the

4.47 Andrea Mantegna, *Dead Christ, c.* 1500. Tempera on canvas, 26¾ × 31⅞". Pinoteca di Brera, Milan, Italy

4.48 Andres Serrano, *The Morgue (Gun Murder)*, 1992. Cibachrome print, 50 × 60"

viewer, is the opposite of Mantegna's *Dead Christ*. The dark background, the white bandages and body bag, and the strong lighting create a sense of drama and contrast. The formal beauty of the image itself contradicts the shocking reality that this person, whose identity we will never know, was murdered. As Serrano's photograph demonstrates, art can often challenge us intellectually. Even if we do not find the imagery pleasant, it can convey a powerful message and provide us with a deeper understanding of difficult subjects.

4.49 Sarcophagus lid, tomb of Lord Pacal (Shield 2), Temple of the Inscriptions, Palenque, Mexico, *c.* 680

Life, death, and the afterlife are inseparably connected in many religions and belief systems. A tomb lid made for Pacal, the seventh-century ruler of the Maya city-state of Palenque in southern Mexico, illustrates the king's integral role in the cycle of life (**4.49**). The elaborate scene, carved in **low relief**, shows Pacal reclining on a slab that marks the intersection of the earthly realm and the underworld. Just beneath Pacal is the face of the setting sun, representing death. From Pacal's navel sprouts the world tree, which connects the three cosmic realms: its roots are in the underworld, its trunk is in the earthly world, and its branches are in the sky. The ruler himself serves a similar purpose. By carrying on the lineage of his ancestors, he ensures sustenance and productivity for his people and provides a connection with the gods.

The Power of Nature

Artists have long been fascinated by the power of nature to benefit or harm humankind. Many cultures believe that natural events are caused by gods. The authority that the gods possess can explain everything from the movements of the sun and moon to the absence or presence of life-giving rain. Personifying natural forces, as artists often do in stories and images, makes them more accessible and memorable.

For the Hopi of the southwestern United States, kachinas are supernatural spirits that personify events and natural elements. The phenomena represented by kachinas include the solstices (the longest and the shortest days of the year, which marked the beginning of a new stage in the seasonal ritual cycle), patterns of stars (constellations), plants, and animals. During the planting season, masked dancers embody the kachinas in annual festivals dedicated to rain, fertility, and good hunting. Dolls associated with these spirits are also made. Originally they were intended to teach the Hopi about the nature deities; over time, they were also sold to tourists. The kachina doll shown in **4.50** represents the Jemez kachina, which appears near the end of the season when the kachinas are about to leave the steep-sided, elevated plateaus known as

4.50 Hopi kachina doll, *c.* 1925. Wood, feathers, and pigment, 25¼" high. Gustav Heye Center, New York (National Museum of the American Indian)

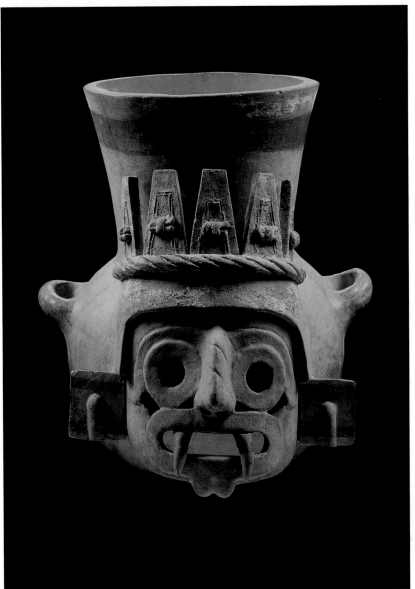

4.51 Vessel with mask of Tlaloc, *c.* 1440–69. Fired clay and paint, 13¾ × 14 × 12⅜". Museo del Templo Mayor, Mexico City, Mexico

mesas, where the Hopi lived, for six months. The elaborate headdress on the Jemez kachina contains cloud symbols, denoting its effectiveness in bringing rain, and it carries a rattle in one hand and a sprig of Douglas fir (here represented by a feather) in the other. As the first kachina to bring mature corn to the Hopi, this figure helps ensure a successful corn crop.

Because rain is essential to sustain life, rain gods were important to the ancient Mexicans. For many groups in central Mexico, such as the Aztecs, their rain god is known as Tlaloc. Also associated with the earth's fertility, Tlaloc is represented by the colors blue and white and by the symbols for raindrops and water plants. A large ceramic vessel representing Tlaloc, which was found at the Templo Mayor in the Aztec city of Tenochtitlan (under present-day Mexico City), exhibits the god's most prominent characteristics: goggle-like circles around his eyes as well as snake-like fangs (**4.51**). In Mexico's dry climate, the crops depend on seasonal rains. If there

Low relief: carving in which the design stands out only slightly from the background surface

4.52 Gustave Courbet, *Fox in the Snow*, 1860. Oil on canvas, 33½ × 50". Dallas Museum of Art, Texas

was no rain, people went hungry, so the Aztecs were careful to keep Tlaloc happy. It is likely that offerings were made during ceremonies in which this vessel was used in order to prevent droughts and ensure that rain would nourish the Aztec crops.

The French artist Gustave Courbet (1819–77) painted a very different representation of the violent forces of nature (**4.52**). Courbet shows an ordinary moment in the wilderness when one life is given for the sake of another. A red fox is devouring a rat that it caught on a snowy day. Courbet was renowned for his ability to render realistic details: he depicts the fluff of the fox's coat, the coarseness of the rocks, the delicacy of the snow on the grasses, and the intensity of the rat's blood. By choosing this subject, Courbet has captured a moment that emphasizes the fleeting quality of life, in which tomorrow the fox could very well be the hunted instead of the hunter.

Pyramid: ancient structure, usually massive in scale, consisting of a square base with four sides that meet at a point or apex with each side forming a triangular shape

Judgment

As we live our lives, our choices determine the impact we will have and how we will be perceived. In many belief systems, the moral implications of our decisions have lasting consequences. As a result, the act of judging a life before the deceased is allowed to pass into the afterlife has been the theme of numerous artworks.

In ancient Egypt, the deceased were buried with a set of belongings that reflected their position in life (see Gateway Box: The Great Pyramid of Khufu). One of the most important of these possessions was a book of the dead, a scroll with spells and incantations designed to help the deceased navigate the passage into the afterlife. As we can see in the book of the dead that belonged to a scribe named Hunefer, who lived over 3,000 years ago, a successful journey required proof that one had lived an honorable life and that proper respect had been paid to the gods (**4.53**).

At the top of the scroll, Hunefer pleads his case to the forty-two judges of the dead, represented here by just fourteen mummified deities because the artist did not have room to show them all. In the bottom panel, Hunefer is escorted by Anubis (the jackal-headed god associated with mummification and the afterlife) to the scales where his soul will be weighed.

4.53 *Book of the Dead*: Last Judgment before Osiris, *c.* 1275 BCE. Painted papyrus, 15⅜" high. British Museum, London, England

Gateway to Art: The Great Pyramid of Khufu
Mathematical and Astronomical Alignments of the Pyramids

The ancient Egyptians' beliefs about the cycles of life and death grew out of their daily experiences. For example, their work habits were controlled by the cycles of the Nile. Its annual flooding followed the harvesting of the crops, which were able to grow because of the previous year's inundation by the river. The Egyptians, believing that people lived forever after death, spent much of their time on earth preparing for the afterlife. They saw the building of the Great Pyramids, which were tombs for pharaohs, as integral to the cycle of life.

The **pyramids** built by the ancient Egyptians on the Giza plateau around 2500 BCE are among the most impressive structures in the world (4.54). Although the geometric shape of the pyramid appears simple, complicated mathematical calculations and astronomical knowledge went into the making of the complex at Giza. The base of each pyramid is oriented so that the four triangular sides align with the four cardinal directions. Alignments with such celestial bodies as planets and stars have also been noted. Perhaps the most interesting proposition is that the location and size of the three pyramids exactly mimicked the arrangement of the stars in the "belt" of the constellation Orion (4.55). After their deaths, the Pharaohs Khafre, Khufu, and Menkaure, who were buried in the pyramids, were believed to take their places as immortal beings in the star that corresponded with each tomb. It seems that the ancient Egyptians believed in a profound connection between life on earth, a resting place for the deceased, and an afterlife in the night sky.

4.54 (top right) Great Pyramid of Khufu, *c.* 2560 BCE, Giza, Egypt

4.55 (right) Diagram illustrating the proposition that the location and size of the three pyramids exactly mimicked the arrangement of the stars in the "belt" of the constellation Orion

As Ammit ("Eater of the Dead," with the head of a crocodile, mane and forequarters of a lion, and hindquarters of a hippopotamus) anxiously looks on, Anubis determines that Hunefer's soul, in the form of his heart in a **canopic jar**, is lighter than the ostrich feather it is weighed against. Having been proven worthy, Hunefer is presented by Horus (falcon-headed god of the sun, sky, and war) to Osiris (god of goodness, vegetation, and death), who is seated on his throne. This book of the dead was placed in Hunefer's coffin with the hope that its script would be followed and he would successfully gain immortality in the afterlife.

In twelfth-century Europe, depictions of the Last Judgment took on an ominous tone in scenes showing the fate of the blessed and the damned side by side. In **4.57**, the **lintel**

4.56 (right) Detail from Gislebertus, *Last Judgment*

4.57 (below) Gislebertus, *Last Judgment*, c. 1120–35. Tympanum from West Portal, Cathedral of Saint-Lazare, Autun, France

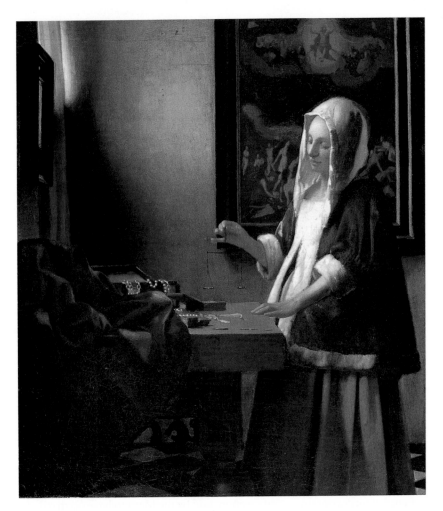

4.58 Johannes Vermeer, *Woman Holding a Balance*, c. 1664. Oil on canvas, 16¾ × 16". National Gallery of Art, Washington, D.C.

Canopic jar: a jar used by ancient Egyptians to hold the embalmed internal organs removed from the body during mummification
Lintel: the horizontal beam over the doorway of a portal
Tympanum: an arched recess above a doorway, often decorated with carvings
Baroque: European artistic and architectural style of the late sixteenth to early eighteenth centuries, characterized by extravagance and emotional intensity

underneath the main panel contains a row of figures awaiting judgment. A pair of hands comes down from above to gather the sixth figure from the right for his weighing. In the center of the carved **tympanum** Christ is shown as larger than all the rest of the figures, indicating his key role in the judgment of humankind. On his right (our left) are the angels and the souls of the blessed who will go on to live out eternity in heaven. Their bodies are smooth, elegant, and peaceful. On Christ's left are the scales in which souls are weighed, and the ravaged bodies of the damned. Their horrid, grotesque appearance was meant to send a strong message to churchgoers about the consequences of living a sinful life and give them a glimpse of the misery that an afterlife in hell would hold.

The Dutch **Baroque**-era painter Johannes Vermeer (1632–75) subtly includes religion in a scene from everyday life in his *Woman Holding a Balance* (**4.58**). As was common at the time,

Vermeer focuses on an ordinary moment, in which the woman is standing at a table by a window near her open jewelry boxes. The painting on the wall behind her provides a symbolic backdrop for her actions. It shows the Last Judgment, with Christ in the sky above and the souls to be judged below, and serves as a reminder that life is short and that it is important to be honest and decent. The scales the woman holds are empty, but perfectly balanced, suggesting that one's actions rather than one's possessions are the true indication of a person's worth.

Discussion Questions

1   Choose two artworks from this chapter that fit one of the following criteria: (1) one that depicts a human and one that depicts a mythical being; (2) one personal and one communal; (3) one about birth and one about death. Compare and contrast what the artworks look like and what they are communicating and note at least three points of comparison and contrast. What does this comparison reveal to you about the artworks that you had not considered before?

2   Find several artworks in this chapter or elsewhere in this book (for example, **2.2**, **2.218**, **3.76**, **3.93**, **4.47**, **4.49**, **4.52**) from the same cultural tradition that deal with the theme of the cycle of life. What do your chosen artworks have in common? In what ways are they similar? What do they tell you about your chosen culture's attitudes to life and death?

3   Many artworks that deal with the cycle of life are full of symbolic meanings, chosen to make the work memorable. Find two works in this chapter that use symbols in this way and discuss what they hope to communicate to their audience. Then think of an event in your life that could be represented by symbols. What things (colors, scents, feelings) stand out most in your mind? Finally, translate your own personal myth into a picture that can visually communicate the event's importance to others.

4.4

Art and Science

Customarily, we consider science and art to be separate disciplines, even complete opposites. We tend to think of art as intuitive and emotional, and science as rational and objective. But this has not always been the case. In fact, numerous artists in history actively engaged in the scientific questions of their day. The great **Renaissance** artist Leonardo da Vinci (1452–1519), for example, was not only a painter, but an engineer, anatomist, botanist, and mapmaker. Art and science interact more often than we might suppose.

Like scientists, artists are keen observers of phenomena and events. Often, artworks contain scientific knowledge and ideas. Sometimes, artworks openly celebrate scientific advancements, and some artists have even used scientific methods to make art. The appreciation of art relies, of course, on the human senses, and artists have always been particularly keen on manipulating the perception of the viewer of artworks. This has involved some artists in the science of **psychology** and the **physiology** of perception as well.

Astronomical Knowledge in Art

For millennia, the regular yet ever-changing night sky was a source of endless fascination and study. We know, for example, that in the Middle East, navigation guides called astrolabes, which tracked the skies and the planets, were in use by 500 CE. In another part of the world, in ancient Mexico, amongst the Maya and Aztecs, the planets were

regarded as gods, and their movements were closely monitored. Some of the most fascinating artworks of the Maya and Aztecs reflect this interest in astronomy. Careful astronomical observation enabled these people to create remarkably precise calendars.

The **flint** in **4.59** incorporates elements of the cosmology (beliefs about the origin of the world) and astronomical knowledge of the Maya. The delicate carving of this very hard stone reveals a high level of craftsmanship. Light enough to be held in one hand, the flint depicts the story of creation, said by the Maya to have occurred precisely on August 13, 3114 BCE, when the First Father was sacrificed after losing a ball game against the Lords of Death. The First Father's soul is seen riding a crocodile to the Maya underworld (called the Place of Creation, ruled by a water-monster god) accompanied by other Maya lords. The **profiles** of the First Father and two of the lords appear on top of the crocodile, leaning back to suggest the speed of the journey. Two additional figures are shown facing downward toward the underside of the crocodile. The serrated edge on the bottom of the flint represents the forceful waves encountered on the journey. The moment shown here is the transformation of the crocodile into a sacred canoe just before it dives into the rough waters, signifying the death of the First Father. Soon thereafter, the First Father will rise from the waters, transform into the maize god, and become the creator of humans.

The flint, however, is more than a depiction of a Maya story; it is also an instrument for

Renaissance: a period of cultural and artistic change in Europe from the fourteenth to the seventeenth century
Psychology: a science that studies the nature, development, and operation of the human mind
Physiology: a science that studies the workings of the body and its organs
Flint: an object or tool made from the very hard, sharp-edged stone of the same name
Profile: the outline of an object, especially a face or head, represented from the side

4.59 Flint depicting a crocodile canoe with passengers, 600–900 CE. 9¾ × 16¼ × ¾″. Dallas Museum of Art, Texas

astronomical observations. When held up to the sky on August 13 each year, the five heads on this flint align with the brightest stars of the Milky Way galaxy. For the Maya, the stars reenact the story of man's creation when, at midnight, the stars of the Milky Way align horizontally east to west. In the next several hours, the galaxy appears to pivot and fall out of the sky, resembling a canoe diving into water. Then, immediately before the sunrise, the three stars of Orion's belt appear, symbolizing for the Maya the three hearthstones at the site of the First Father's rebirth.

Like the Maya, the Aztecs were skillful observers of the skies. The Aztec Sun Stone in **4.60** is a store of astronomical and mathematical knowledge. Originally painted in shades of brown, red, white, blue, and green, the heavy Sun Stone (weighing 24 tons) stood atop the main temple at Tenochtitlan, the capital of the Aztec empire. Later it was buried, to be uncovered again only in 1790 in what is now downtown Mexico City.

The Sun Stone, also known as a calendar stone, reveals how the Aztecs counted time, and illustrates their belief that the earth endures recurring cycles of destruction and creation. The center of the stone shows the face of Tonatiuh, the sun god to whom Aztecs offered frequent human and animal sacrifices. Each of the four squares emanating from Tonatiuh's face frames a symbol representing the ways in which the earth previously came to an end: by wind, by fire, by floods, and by wild beasts. The Aztecs

4.60 Calendar stone (Sun Stone), late postclassic. Basalt, 12′ diameter. National Museum of Anthropology, Mexico City, Mexico

4.61 Muhammad Mahdi al-Yazdi, Astrolabe, 1659–60. Gilt brass, silvered brass, brass, and glass, 7⅜" diameter. National Maritime Museum, London, England

Latitude: a point on the earth's circumference measured to the east or west
Tracery: a complex but delicate pattern of interwoven lines
Enlightenment: an intellectual movement in eighteenth-century Europe that argued for science, reason, and individualism, and against tradition
Tenebrism: dramatic use of intense darkness and light to heighten the impact of a painting
Realism: nineteenth-century artistic style that aimed to depict nature and everyday subjects in an unidealized manner

believed that the earth would be destroyed again by an earthquake. In the ring surrounding these symbols are twenty animals, each framed by a rectangle. These represent the days of the Aztec month. Priests used the calendar stone to determine sacrificial periods.

Used as guides for navigation, astrolabes were made as early as the fifth century CE in the Middle East, and by 800 they had become extremely common in the Islamic world. During the early twelfth century, the technology spread to Europe via Muslims living in Spain. The astrolabe was especially useful to Muslims, who were required to pray while facing toward the city of Mecca five times a day; the astrolabe could find the direction of Mecca as well as calculate the time of day.

An astrolabe is made up of layers of disks or plates that fit into a larger brass dial called a mater. Each of the five plates in the example in **4.61** is aligned to a different **latitude**. On the very top is a smaller disk called a rete, which has been cut out almost completely and on which the positions of heavenly bodies are indicated.

The brass astrolabe shown here is an example of fine metalwork. It was made during the seventeenth century in the Safavid Empire, in what is now Iran. Floral decorations serve as the pointers on the rete. The astrolabe is covered with Persian and Arabic inscriptions. For example, on the outside edge, there are verses about fourteen important Islamic figures. On the rete, there is a series of verses that describe the parts of the astrolabe metaphorically. The **tracery** around the mater contains a dedication inscribed to a Safavid leader. And on the back of the instrument, there is an inscription by the astrolabe's maker dedicating himself to God.

Art Celebrating Science

While art can be used to decorate scientific instruments, many artists have also observed science in action and recorded their studies in works of art.

The English painter Joseph Wright of Derby (1734–97) was friendly with members of the Lunar Society, an informal club of scientists, intellectuals, and manufacturers who met monthly to discuss developments in science and technology. Wright lived during the period known as the **Enlightenment**, a time of intense interest in science and reason. He often painted scientific and industrial subjects, employing a notably dramatic use of light and dark, called **tenebrism**.

His painting *An Experiment on a Bird in the Air Pump* shows a traveling scientist demonstrating the creation of a vacuum before an audience (**4.62**). If the scientist removes all the air from the glass container in which a bird is imprisoned, the bird will suffocate and die a dreadful death. The artist has chosen to depict the climactic moment of truth. He has increased the drama by his use of shadows and light, which highlights reactions of concern and indifference, contempt and resignation, pity and fear. Strong light from behind the glass (which contains a skull) in the center of the table shines on the faces of the observers. While light is a symbol of knowledge, the scientist's outward gaze involves us, the viewers of the painting, in the moment's moral dilemma as well. We feel a strong desire to stop the experiment and prevent the bird from suffocating.

4.62 Joseph Wright of Derby, *An Experiment on a Bird in the Air Pump*, 1768. Oil on canvas, 6 × 8′. National Gallery, London, England

4.63 Thomas Eakins, *Portrait of Dr. Samuel D. Gross* (*The Gross Clinic*), 1875. Oil on canvas, 8′ × 6′6″. Philadelphia Museum of Art and Pennsylvania Academy of Fine Arts

Artists study anatomy to learn how to depict figures, and many artists have become interested in dissection and medical procedures. The American painter Thomas Eakins (1844–1916) depicted a demonstration he witnessed by a famous surgeon, Dr. Samuel Gross, in Philadelphia (**4.63**). Assistants surround the body while the white-haired doctor lectures to medical students, dimly lit in the seating in the background. Eakins's detailed observation of the procedure created such a brutally **realist** depiction that a critic for the *New York Daily Tribune* commented,

> It is a picture that even strong men find it difficult to look at long, if they can look at it at all.

Eakins's meticulous detail makes his painting a useful historical document of early surgical procedure. For instance, he shows us the use of anesthesia (the anesthetist holds a white cloth over the patient's face), a recent invention that had made such surgery as this possible. The artist was not however satisfied with mere accuracy; he also wanted to give his painting emotional impact. The lighting is not typical of an operating room, but instead is highly theatrical. Eakins also includes the patient's distraught mother, seen on the left, who in reality was probably not present at the surgery.

Using Science to Create Art

Advancements in science enable artists to create new kinds of art. The advent of the microscope, for example, has enabled one artist to create minuscule artworks, while medical studies have enabled a scientist to preserve bodies and exhibit them as art.

The British artist Willard Wigan (b. 1957) has created the smallest sculptures in the world. His artwork is only possible because he uses a microscope: his creations can barely be seen by the naked eye. He carves individual pieces of sand or grains of rice and places them on equally tiny bases, such as the head of a pin or a strand of human hair. The Statue of Liberty in **4.64** was re-created inside the eye of a needle. Wigan then paints his artworks using an eyelash for a brush. To create one of these microscopic works, Wigan puts himself into a very calm state of mind, which slows his heartbeat and decreases hand tremors: "I need to work between heartbeats, or else the pulse in my finger will cause a mistake," he says. He works through the night so that daylight activity, such as cars frequently driving by, will not disturb his steady hand. Wigan found that the intense concentration required for this sculpting helped him come to terms with his difficulties as a dyslexic child. As he recalled:

> I became obsessed with making more and more tiny things. I think I was trying to find a way of compensating for my embarrassment at having learning difficulties: people had made me feel small so I wanted to show them how significant small could be.

A German medical scientist, Gunther von Hagens (b. 1945), used his knowledge of anatomy and science to develop a technique, called plastination, that preserves bodies after death and allows them to be arranged in poses. His popular traveling exhibition, *Body Worlds*, has been seen by millions of people, many of whom consider it to be art. The exhibition, however, has been controversial. Although all the bodies featured in it are those of willing donors, many people consider the display irreverent, and complain about the overly theatrical poses of the bodies as well as the fact

4.65 *Basketball Player*, 2002. Gunther von Hagens's *Body Worlds* exhibition, www.bodyworlds.com

4.64 (left) Willard Wigan, *Statue of Liberty*

that the shows are often promoted as art, rather than science.

One specimen, *Basketball Player*, is posed as if dribbling a ball down the court (**4.65**). The skull has been split so that we can see the brain. This dramatic presentation allows us to see the tension of the inner body and to understand better how we ourselves move. The *Body Worlds* exhibition also includes a body with the damaged lungs of a smoker, and a pregnant woman with her deceased fetus still in her body.

The Science of Perception and the Senses

Since art is a visual medium, artists expect viewers to respond to the artwork through their sense of sight. It is not surprising, therefore, that artists have often been keenly aware of scientific studies of visual perception. Some artists,

however, have also experimented with ways to use their images to trigger responses from the other senses, such as hearing or smell.

Sunday on La Grande Jatte (**4.66**) is a picture of people engaged in the activities of everyday life. But its artist, the Frenchman Georges Seurat (1859–91), also applied to this artwork recent scientific studies on the way that the human eye perceives color. Seurat developed a process called **pointillism**, a meticulous way of applying **color theory** in his paintings. He relied on two optical effects (**optical mixture** and **afterimage effect**) to create scenes in which the figures are very distinct, almost like cutouts, because of the precise way in which he applied tiny dots of color to the canvas. The colors we see when we view *Sunday on La Grande Jatte* from several feet away are quite different from the colors we see up close. For example, the green grass is made up of dots not only of various shades of green but also of oranges and purples. Seurat took three years to paint this work, meticulously applying dots while

Pointillism: a late nineteenth-century painting style using short strokes or points of differing colors that optically combine to form new perceived colors
Color theory: the understanding of how colors relate to each other, especially when mixed or placed near one another
Optical mixture: when the eye blends two colors that are placed near each other, creating a new color
Afterimage effect: when the eye sees the complementary color of something that the viewer has spent an extended time viewing (also known as successive contrasts)

4.66 Georges Seurat, *Sunday on La Grande Jatte*, 1884–6. Oil on canvas, 6'9¾" × 10'1¼". Art Institute of Chicago considering the effects of color theory on his **palette** choices. To ensure that the optical arrangement would not be disrupted when the painting was framed, Seurat also painted a border using the same pointillist technique.

The American artist Jasper Johns (b. 1930) makes us take a second look at familiar subjects, objects the artist says are "seen but not looked at." He uses iconic images such as numbers, letters, targets, and, perhaps most famously, the American flag, of which he painted several versions. In the version of *Flag* reproduced here, Johns uses his knowledge of color theory to create an optical illusion that forces a viewer to stare intently at an image of the flag (**4.67**). The top flag is made up of black and green stripes, while black stars are placed on a background of orange; these colors are **complementary** to the white, red, and blue colors of the American flag. Johns's optical effect depends on the use of these complementary colors. The rectangle on the bottom half of the painting is just a faded ghost of a flag. For the optical illusion to work, stare at the top flag for a full minute. Focus your attention on the white dot in the center. After a minute has passed, blink and look at the black dot in the center of the lower flag. The red, white, and blue of the American flag will appear. Johns is utilizing the science behind afterimage effect. While looking at the top flag, your eyes became fatigued from the colors. Therefore, when you blinked your eyes and looked at the lower flag, your eyes produced the complementary colors of each aspect of the upper flag.

4.67 Jasper Johns, *Flag*, 1965. Private collection

4.68 Marcia Smilack, *Cello Music*, 1992. Photograph, 12¾ × 24". Collection of the artist

At times, artists often try to trigger other senses in addition to sight. The process whereby stimulation in one sense causes experiences in a different sense—such as visualizing color when we hear music—is called **synesthesia**. The artist Marcia Smilack (b. 1949) experiences life as a synesthete, and creates artworks that reflect this correspondence between the senses. She describes her experience:

> The way I taught myself photography is to shoot when I hear a chord of color… I hear with my eyes and see with my ears.

Of the photograph *Cello Music* (**4.68**), Smilack says:

> I walked by the water and heard cello… I couldn't resist the sound so I gave in and aimed my camera at what had elicited it. As soon as I let go of my thoughts, the texture of the water washed over me in synch with the sound and turned to satin on my skin. When I felt myself climb into the shadows between the folds, I snapped the shutter. I hear cello every time I look at it today, though I discovered that if I turn it upside down, it becomes violin.

Science of the Mind

While some artists have introduced the science of perception and color theory into their works, others have explored different aspects of the science of the mind. Some artists have tried to understand and mimic the workings of the minds of children or the mentally ill. Others have studied psychology and dream theories and tried to represent the subconscious world in their work.

Many artists speak of trying to recapture the creativity we all have as children. The French artist Jean Dubuffet (1901–85) was influenced by the art of children as well as by art made by the mentally ill. He coined the term **Art Brut** to mean art that is raw, inspired by very basic instincts, or, as Dubuffet said, "works produced by persons unscathed by artistic culture." Dubuffet's artwork often has heavy **impasto** and a childlike quality. In *Cow with the Subtle Nose* a bold outline separates the cow from its green background (**4.69**). The brushstrokes are not smooth, but spontaneous. The cow's eyes are simply round circles; the horns, udder, and tail are simple scratches, like those of a child.

In the 1940s, Dubuffet began to collect art made by the insane. Dubuffet's collection marked

Palette: the range of colors used by an artist
Complementary colors: colors opposite one another on the color wheel
Synesthesia: when one of the five senses perceives something that was stimulated by a trigger from one of the other senses
Art Brut: "raw art," artworks made by untrained artists, and having a primitive or childlike quality
Impasto: paint applied in thick layers

4.69 Jean Dubuffet, *Cow with the Subtle Nose*, 1954. Oil and enamel on canvas, 35 × 45¾". MOMA, New York

4.70 Salvador Dalí, *Persistence of Memory*, 1931. Oil on canvas, 9½ × 13". MOMA, New York

the beginning of increased public interest in artworks by the mentally ill (see Perspectives on Art Box: Art Inspired by Insanity). His collection is now housed at the Musée de l'Art Brut in Lausanne, Switzerland.

Salvador Dalí (1904–89) was one of a group of artists known as the **Surrealists**, who were inspired by psychology and dream studies, and most particularly by the theories of the father of **psychoanalysis**, Sigmund Freud. Themes of sexual desire and fear are common in Dalí's paintings, which he associated with Freud's studies on sexual desire and behavior.

In *Persistence of Memory* (**4.70**), the stretched form in the center (a nose with long eyelashes and a tongue hanging out) is a self-portrait, and the cliffs in the background resemble the Catalan coast in Spain, where Dalí lived. After a late night with some friends, Dalí was inspired to paint *Persistence of Memory* while playing with some melted cheese left over from dinner. He said the painting was "nothing more than the soft,

extravagant, solitary, paranoiac-critical Camembert cheese of space and time." Dalí invented the term paranoiac-critical, which he defined as the

spontaneous method of irrational knowledge based on the critical and systematic objectivity of the associations and interpretations of delirious phenomena.

The consistency of the cheese inspired the three warped, dangling watch faces. The limp watches may be interpreted as symbols of both impotence and recent sexual satisfaction.

Scholars have remarked on a link between this work and the physicist Albert Einstein's theory of relativity, which addresses the complexities of time. In Dalí's painting, the clocks each read a different time, conveying a distorted sense of time and space. Dalí also painted a fly on the drooping watch on the ledge, a visual metaphor for the phrase "time flies."

Perspectives on Art: Martín Ramírez
Art Inspired by Insanity

Painful experiences and disabling illness can be sources of extraordinary art, as works produced by psychiatric patients demonstrate. Here, the art historian Professor Colin Rhodes, an expert on this subject, discusses the work of the Mexican schizophrenic artist Martín Ramírez (1895–1963), who spent thirty-three years in Californian mental hospitals where he produced hundreds of artworks, many now in major museums.

For a long time, the images created by Mexican artist Martín Ramírez were thought to be the more or less unconscious outpourings of a mind liberated from daily reality by mental illness. His practice was markedly obsessive, characterized by repetition of a few motifs, which nonetheless were combined in powerful and subtle variations. There is a visionary feel to his work, born of his use of stylized, large forms loosely anchored on an indistinct background. His store of **motifs** is closely connected to his cultural background. Ramírez was a native of Jalisco, Mexico, who left for California in 1925 to support his wife and children. The Great Depression left him unemployed and homeless. He became a patient in Californian asylums from 1931 until his death. Ramírez's diagnosis was first manic depression and subsequently schizophrenia.

Many of Ramírez's works include iconic images of the Madonna, particularly in the form of Our Lady of the Immaculate Conception, standing on a globe, with a serpent at her feet, symbols he would have seen in his home parish. Though it is always dangerous to attribute specific pictorial qualities to illness, there can be little doubt that Ramírez's condition and experience of incarceration were a source of artistic creativity. Artistic production can fix memory in the face of separation from loved ones and of boredom. And since his illness made it impossible to communicate in the usual sense, Ramírez created an alternative world in his imagination. In this work Ramírez replays his life in Mexico before incarceration (**4.71**). The two Mexican Madonnas float above a shallow landscape of shell-like mountains. Their gaze is contemplative and their faces expressive. Their dress, though, is as much landscape as clothing. In the background another, more worldly, woman half imitates their pose. Like most of Ramírez's works, the large drawing is made from a number of smaller sheets pasted together—the only materials available to him, but also indicative of his compulsive need to expand the universe of his drawing to accommodate the developing image, as opposed to fitting the image into a single sheet. The result, in the case of Ramírez, whose illness caused a withdrawal from physical and verbal interaction with the world, was an outpouring of some of the most powerful visual art of its time.

4.71 Martín Ramírez, *Untitled (La Inmaculada)*, 1950s. Crayon, pencil, watercolor, and collaged papers, 7'8" × 3'9". High Museum of Art, Atlanta, Georgia

The Scientific Restoration of Artworks

Scientific advancements in chemistry have helped improve the techniques used in the restoration of artworks. The most momentous restorations in recent times have been the cleaning of the **frescoes** at the Vatican in Rome, Italy. The restoration of Michelangelo's Sistine Chapel ceiling, which began in 1980, took nine years to complete, twice as long as it took Michelangelo to paint the ceiling originally (**4.72**).

In order to decide on the best way to clean the frescoes, restorers first had to determine what was original and what was due to the effects of time, such as candle smoke, the interventions of previous restorers, rain damage, the settling of building foundations, and even bacteria introduced by the visits of millions of tourists.

4.72 Cleaning of Sistine Chapel ceiling, Vatican City, 1980–9

Fresco: a technique where the artist paints onto freshly applied plaster. From the Italian *fresco*, fresh

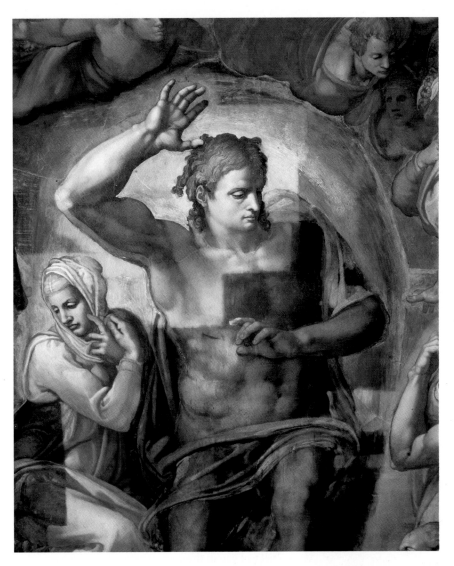

4.73 Detail of Christ from Michelangelo, *The Last Judgment*. Photo taken during restoration of Sistine Chapel, Vatican City, 1990–4

of the restorers' research, methods, and handiwork, the panel unanimously declared that the team had been thorough and painstaking, and that their approach was accurate and correct: the original paintings had indeed been this bright.

The cleaning of the Sistine Chapel ceiling paved the way for further restorations at the Vatican, including Michelangelo's *Last Judgment* (**4.73**) on the altar wall of the Sistine Chapel (restored 1990–4) and, down the hall, four rooms of paintings by Raphael, including *The School of Athens* (restored 1995–6).

Discussion Questions

1 Many artists study synesthesia, are synesthetic themselves, or try to trigger synesthetic responses in the viewer. Study the work of an artist who is known for trying to evoke music in his or her artworks, for example Georgia O'Keeffe (**1.24**), James McNeill Whistler (**4.170**), Vasily Kandinsky (**3.189**), or Paul Klee. Choose a single painting and, through formal analysis, determine how the artist is trying to inspire sensations that are similar to those stimulated by the playing of music.

2 Elsewhere in this book we have looked at examples of the artwork of the great Italian Renaissance artist Leonardo da Vinci (see for example **08** and **3.121**). Find three scientific studies by Leonardo (**2.1** and **2.2**, for example) and discuss how they might have contributed to his paintings and other artworks. Would you categorize Leonardo's drawings as art or science, or both? Why? How do you think his scientific studies may have contributed to the making of his paintings?

3 In this chapter we discussed the art of Willard Wigan and Gunther von Hagens. Many contemporary artists create computer-generated artwork or reflect subjects (such as outer space or DNA) influenced by discoveries in science. Can you find any examples of contemporary art that were influenced by such recent technological advancements?

They analyzed the chemical composition of numerous minuscule samples of the paint, glue, wax, and varnish taken from the many layers they found on the ceiling. This analysis, plus their ability to examine the entire ceiling at close range, caused them to believe that Michelangelo had painted the ceiling almost entirely in *buon fresco* (when the plaster was still wet) with only slight corrections executed *a secco* (after the plaster had dried), and that all other layers were later additions.

The most shocking discovery, revealed after centuries of dirt were removed, was the bright colors that Michelangelo had used. Critics denounced the cleaning as a disaster, accusing the restorers of removing Michelangelo's original varnish. However, an international committee of the world's leading art conservators was convened to review the approach taken by the restoration team, and after a lengthy inspection

4.5

Art and Illusion

Zeuxis painted a boy carrying grapes, and when the birds flew down to settle on them, he was vexed with his own work, and came forward saying…I have painted the grapes better than the boy, for had I been perfectly successful with the latter the bird must have been afraid.

(Pliny the Elder, *Natural History*)

The ancient Roman author Pliny the Elder tells a story that reveals the centuries-old efforts by artists to create convincing illusions. Pliny describes a contest between two great Greek painters, Zeuxis and Parrhasius, to see who could paint the most realistic picture. As Pliny tells it, Zeuxis's painting of grapes was so realistic that birds flew down to peck at them. Parrhasius in turn painted such a convincing curtain that Zeuxis reached for the drapery, hoping to see the painting on which his rival was working. After being fooled, Zeuxis conceded that Parrhasius had won the competition.

Many artists since have striven to continue and even surpass these achievements, developing techniques that fool us into thinking we are looking at real spaces and objects rather than artworks. *Trompe l'oeil* ("fool the eye") is the French term for **two-dimensional** artworks that convincingly appear to be **three-dimensional** objects. Even in three-dimensional art, such as architecture, artists have employed visual tricks to "fool the eye."

Art as an Illusionistic Window

Although the paintings of Zeuxis and Parrhasius do not survive, other examples of illusionism exist from the ancient world in paintings found in cities that were covered by the eruption of Mount Vesuvius in southern Italy in 79 CE. **Frescoes** from a villa owned by a wealthy Roman family create the illusion of architectural features that are in fact

4.74 Cubiculum from the Villa of Publius Fannius Synistor, Boscoreale, Italy, *c.* 50–40 BCE. Fresco, room size 8'8½" × 10'11" × 19'7⅛" . Metropolitan Museum of Art, New York

only painted, not part of the structure, and of a distant landscape beyond (**4.74**). Similarly illusionistic scenes in other Roman wall paintings show fruit, birds, greenery, and stage-like settings, all recalling the story of Zeuxis and Parrhasius.

Artists of the Italian **Renaissance** revived the ideals of the ancient Greeks and Romans, including the desire to impress others with artworks that imitate the real world. The architect and thinker Leon Battista Alberti (1404–72) wrote in his treatise *On Painting* that artists should design their paintings as illusionary windows through which viewers would be able to perceive a new reality (see Gateway Box: Raphael).

Humanism: the study of such subjects as history, philosophy, languages, and literature, particularly in relation to those of ancient Greece and Rome

Gateway to Art: Raphael, *The School of Athens*
Architectural Illusion

4.75 Raphael, Stanza della Segnatura, Vatican City, 1509–11

The Italian artist Raphael (1483–1520) painted *The School of Athens* on one of the walls of the library of Pope Julius II in the Vatican, in Rome, to create the illusion of an architectural space that was separate from the actual room and filled with life-sized figures linking the Classical world with the **humanist** Renaissance (**4.75**). This painting was designed as part of a larger program including three other paintings, an intricately tiled floor, and a painted ceiling, all choreographed thematically as a backdrop for Pope Julius II's library. The pope's hundreds of books were laid on shelves built directly under the paintings on each of the four walls (these shelves have since been removed).

The School of Athens highlights the development of learning in the ancient world, focusing particularly on the great philosophers Plato and Aristotle, who are the two central figures in the painting. The other large paintings, turning counterclockwise around the room, are: *Parnassus*, a mythological story of Apollo, representing poetry (seen on the left wall in **4.75**); *Disputa*, a work that unites Classical ideas with Renaissance Christian theology; and *Jurisprudence*, which emphasizes law and justice. The thematic decorative scheme reflects the purpose of the room: the subjects of Julius's books were arranged to correspond with the Classical topic addressed in the wall painting above them. Beneath *The School of Athens* were books on philosophy and mathematics; beneath *Parnassus*, poetry; and so on. The ceiling further unites the themes of the walls through the depiction on it of four female figures, who personify Philosophy, Poetry, Theology, and Justice. To one standing in the room, the illusion of depth created in *The School of Athens* is even more successful because the paintings on all four walls appear to be separate rooms.

4.76 Andrea Mantegna, Detail of central oculus, ceiling of the Camera degli Sposi. Fresco, 8'9" diameter. Ducal Palace, Mantua, Italy

During the Renaissance, the Italian artist Andrea Mantegna (*c.* 1431–1506) created a *trompe l'oeil* for an entire room of the palace of Ludovico Gonzaga, the Duke of Mantua. The chamber, known as the Camera degli Sposi (Room of the Newlyweds), was used both to greet government officials and as a bedroom for the duke and his wife (**4.76**). Mantegna painted the walls with scenes of the royal family and of historical victories of the Gonzagas.

In the vaulted ceiling the artist painted the illusion of what seems to be an **oculus** opening onto a blue sky, and surrounded it with figures looking down at the people below. There are **putti** with their chubby baby bodies, some hanging on to the painted **balustrade**, others looking down through the painted oculus.

Several young girls peer over the balustrade, as does an enigmatic turbaned figure. One light-skinned girl wears a white veil, referring to the title of the room and to the duke's recent marriage to his wife. Similarly, the prominent peacock symbolizes Juno, the Roman goddess of marriage. All of this activity surprises the viewer below, who may feel particularly nervous about the potted plant precariously held in place with a pole by two smirking young girls.

The Italian artist Francesco Mazzola (1503–40), known as Parmigianino ("the little one from Parma"), gave a self-portrait to Pope Clement VII in order to attract commissions (**4.77**). The painting is on a **convex** piece of wood; holding it, one seems to be looking into a convex mirror—except that one does not see one's own

Oculus: a round opening at the center of a dome
Putto (plural **putti**): a representation of a nude or scantily clad infant angel or boy, common in Renaissance and Baroque art
Balustrade: a railing supported by short pillars
Convex: curved inward, like the exterior of a sphere

4.77 Parmigianino, *Self-portrait in a Convex Mirror*, *c.* 1524. Oil on wood, 9½" diameter. Kunsthistorisches Museum, Vienna, Austria

reflection in the artwork, but the portrait of Parmigianino, who studied himself in an actual convex mirror to create this painting. Parmigianino, however, made one change from what he saw when he studied his reflection. The artist accurately depicted himself as right-handed, but in order to do so he would presumably have had to study his left hand when he actually painted. Parmigianino also featured a portion of the frame of the painting he was creating (visible on the right side of the artwork) in order to heighten the illusion of it being a handheld mirror.

In the nineteenth century, the American painter William M. Harnett (1848–92) was so skillful at tricking his audiences with *trompe l'oeil* that, when he created a truly convincing dollar bill in one of his paintings, he was investigated for counterfeiting by the U.S. Treasury Department. In *The Old Violin*, Harnett painted a violin and sheet music so that they appear to be hanging from a real wooden door (**4.78**). The only part of the painting that is in fact real is a blue envelope signed by the artist, which he attached to the lower left corner of the painting. The artist teases viewers, leading us to question what is reality and what is illusion. If we were to read the small piece of torn newspaper so

skillfully painted slightly to the left of the bottom of the violin, we would find that the text is gibberish: it is not a newspaper, but another superb illusion. When this painting was first exhibited, guards had to be posted around the painting constantly to prevent viewers from reaching out to test if the objects were real.

The contemporary Japanese artist Shigeo Fukuda (1932–2009) is known for his optical tricks. In fact, he filled his own home in Tokyo with deceptions. What appeared to be the front

4.78 William M. Harnett, *The Old Violin*, 1886. Oil on canvas, 38 × 23⅝". National Gallery of Art, Washington, D.C.

4.79 Shigeo Fukuda, *Encore*, 1976. Wood, 19½ × 19½ × 11¾". Private collection

Illusionism as Trickery

> With wonderful skill, he carved a figure, brilliantly, out of snow-white ivory…and fell in love with his own creation.
>
> (The ancient Roman poet Ovid on Pygmalion's carving of Galatea)

In Classical mythology, the sculptor Pygmalion created a statue of a woman so fine and beautiful that he fell in love with her. He dressed and pampered her, believing her more perfect than any human woman. He begged the gods to grant him a wife as perfect as his statue, and the goddess of love, Venus, granted his wish by bringing the statue to life. The myth suggests that an artist's love for his work, and his skill at re-creating the natural world, will reap great rewards.

Like Pygmalion, sculptors can use their skill to create works that appear to be convincingly real. With painstaking attention to every minute detail, the Australian artist Ron Mueck (b. 1958) infuses his sculptures with life. He patiently re-creates each hair, wrinkle, and pore on his human figures through a lengthy process that would be tedious for most of us. The remarkable realism of his works—one is tempted to reach out to touch the figures—catches us by surprise. A sculpture of Mueck's own sleeping face, even though it is a disembodied head, is so believable that we

Form: objects that can be defined in three dimensions (height, width, and depth)
Silhouette: a portrait or figure represented in outline and solidly colored in
Stylobate: the uppermost platform on a Classical temple, on which the columns stand
Entasis: the slight swelling or bulge at the midpoint of a column

4.80 Ron Mueck, *Mask II*, 2001–2. Mixed media, 30⅜ × 46½ × 33½". Private collection

door opened onto a blank wall; his real front door blended into the exterior wall, which created a secret passageway. Utilizing **form**, light, and shadows, Fukuda created numerous artworks in two and three dimensions, many of musicians, in which the subject changes depending on the beholder's point of view. In *Encore*, a **silhouette** of a piano and pianist transforms into a violinist when the carved wooden sculpture is viewed from a different angle (**4.79**). The title of the work (audiences traditionally call out "encore!" at the end of musical performances, to encourage the musician to play "again!") expresses the way the work is experienced, as if more than one performance is being seen.

anxiously wait for the mask to open its eyes (**4.80**). Each feature, no matter how small, is precisely reconstructed. And the lips and cheeks droop slightly, as if subject to the effects of gravity, just as they would on a human face. At the same time, Mueck subverts his own illusion by making his figure extremely oversized.

In ancient Greece, the designers of the Parthenon understood that the human eye could play tricks on the beholder. They used their knowledge of mathematics to ensure that the building would appear just as they wished it to (**4.81a**). Because of the great size of the temple, the base and columns would appear warped unless the architects could adjust their design to counteract these naturally occurring optical illusions. For example, the **stylobate**, or platform on which the columns stand, would appear to sag if it were constructed as a precisely straight horizontal structure. To account for this, the architects created a slight upward swelling in the center of the stylobate, which makes the base of the temple seem perfectly horizontal when we look at it.

Several other visual manipulations were utilized in the design of the columns. For example, the columns of the Parthenon actually swell at about mid-height (**4.81d**). This optical trick prevents them from appearing, when looked at from a distance, to be hourglass-shaped, which would happen if the columns were flawlessly straight sided. This swelling at the midpoint of such columns is called **entasis**. In addition, the columns are not perfectly vertical but actually slightly tilted. If they were extended into the air, the implied lines created by the four corner columns would eventually intersect about a mile and a half into the sky. Finally, the columns are not all spaced equidistantly, as they appear to be; those closer to the corners have less space between them. This is another visual trick used to compensate for the optical illusion that makes columns near the end of a row appear further apart than ones near the middle.

4.81a (top right) Kallikrates and Iktinos, Parthenon, 447–432 BCE, Acropolis, Athens, Greece

4.81b–d (right) Diagram showing the optical illusions utilized in the Parthenon

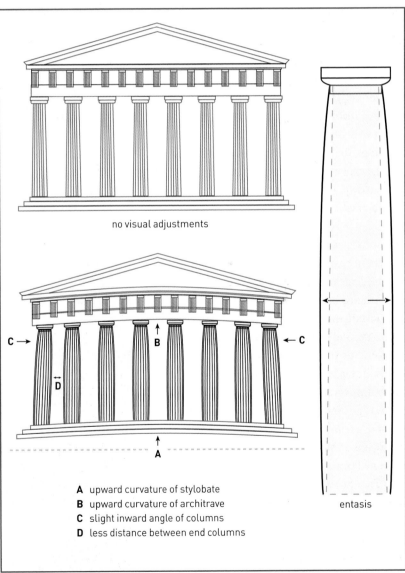

no visual adjustments

A upward curvature of stylobate
B upward curvature of architrave
C slight inward angle of columns
D less distance between end columns

entasis

Architectural and two-dimensional illusory techniques were both utilized by the Italian artist and architect Giulio Romano (*c.* 1499–1546) designed a villa for the same Gonzaga family that had commissioned the decoration of the Camera degli Sposi from Mantegna (see **4.76**). As both architect and interior painter for the Palazzo del Tè in Mantua (**4.82**), Giulio Romano designed a building that subtly broke many of the rules of Classical architecture, with the result that, when looked at closely, the villa appears to be unstable. Romano achieved this playful illusion by taking Classical architectural elements used in such buildings as the Parthenon, and arranging them to create the impression of instability rather than the solidity normally expected of architecture. The **architraves** that rest on the columns are narrower than would normally be the case; but, even stranger, they seem to break in the middle rather than reaching from one column to the next, as they should. As a result, some of the **triglyphs** in the **frieze** above the columns appear to be slipping down, as if they might even fall to the ground. The material of the structure itself is also an illusion; rather than marble or stone, which were normally used for luxurious buildings, the exterior is **stucco**-covered brick.

The explanation for the odd design of the Palazzo del Tè's exterior becomes apparent when one enters the building (**4.83**). A painted scene of the *Fall of the Giants* playfully suggests why the exterior appears to be falling apart. The painting depicts an episode from Greek mythology, when the gods defeated the giants in battle. Having been trained by Raphael, and having worked as his assistant on his paintings for the Vatican (see p. 509), Giulio Romano built on the techniques of his master for this powerful painted illusion. The building in Giulio's painting appears to be tumbling down, crushing the struggling giants below. The powerful wind, shown in the corner blowing a trumpet, is controlled by the gods in the clouds of Mount Olympus, and therefore protected from the turmoil below.

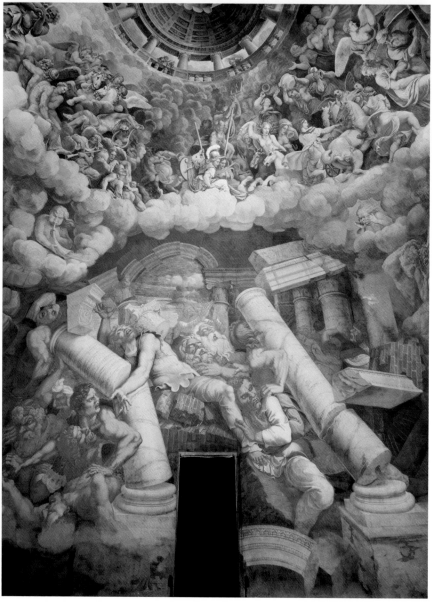

4.82 Giulio Romano, Palazzo del Tè, exterior, 1527–34, Mantua, Italy

4.83 Giulio Romano, *Fall of the Giants*, 1526–35. Fresco, Sale dei Giganti, Palazzo del Tè, Mantua, Italy

The British artist Julian Beever (b. 1960) applies a special form of *trompe l'oeil* known as **anamorphosis** to his sidewalk art. An anamorphic image is one that is stretched and distorted, but becomes clear and realistic when viewed from a single, oblique angle. Beever's chalk drawings confront passersby with what appear to be convincing scenes taking place in three-dimensional space. When his *Woman in Pool* is viewed from the right vantage point, it appears that a woman is lying back in a swimming pool, drink in hand, kicking her leg in the air (**4.84a**). But when it is viewed from the opposite direction, the illusion is destroyed and one can see that Beever used extreme **foreshortening** to represent the woman's leg (**4.84b**). The only

4.84a (top right) Julian Beever, *Woman in Pool*, drawn in Brussels, Belgium, 1992. Colored chalks, 14'9¼" × 13'1½" (correct viewing point)

4.84b (below right) Julian Beever, *Woman in Pool*, drawn in Glasgow, Scotland, 1994. Colored chalks, 14'9¼" × 13'1½" (incorrect viewing point)

Architrave: a beam that rests on the top of a row of columns
Triglyph: a projecting block carved with three raised bands, which alternates with figurative reliefs in a frieze
Frieze: the strip that goes around the top of a building, often filled with sculptural ornamentation
Stucco: a coarse plaster designed to give the appearance of stone
Anamorphosis: the distorted representation of an object so that it appears correctly proportioned only when viewed from one particular position
Foreshortening: a perspective technique that depicts a form at a very oblique (often dramatic) angle to the viewer

genuinely three-dimensional element in the photograph of the illusionistic drawing (**4.84a**) is the artist himself, who is holding a drink and has his foot placed flat on the pavement.

Illusion and the Transformation of Ideas

The American artist Chuck Close (b. 1940) creates artworks that inspire us to question what we see. As a child, one of Close's favorite pastimes was to entertain neighbors and schoolmates by doing magic tricks. As an adult artist, he has become known for manipulating portraits of friends and family. He begins his creative process by taking photographs of them, which he then transforms into artworks in another **medium**. For example, although *Fanny/Fingerpainting* looks like a photograph, Close actually hand-painted an image of his wife's grandmother using only his thumb- and fingerprints (**4.85**). As with most of his artworks, Close laid a grid over the original photograph of the subject, and then carefully enlarged and copied each block so that the entire image fills an 8 foot 6 in. by 7 foot canvas. Through this process, the

4.85 Chuck Close, *Fanny/Fingerpainting*, 1985. Oil on canvas, 8'6" × 7'. National Gallery of Art, Washington, D.C.

original photograph is transformed into a much bigger image that appears to be a photographic enlargement produced by technology. Close's process, while still quite mechanical, remains personal because of the use of the artist's own hands in the act of creation.

The painting *A Bar at the Folies-Bergère*, by French artist Édouard Manet (1832–83), similarly asks the viewer to consider the relationship between truthfulness and illusionism in a work of art (**4.86**). The Folies-Bergère was one of the most popular bars and entertainment houses in Paris in the nineteenth century; the club offered entertainment by dancers, singers, and even trapeze artists (a pair of feet can be seen hanging in the upper left of Manet's painting), all dressed in revealing and provocative clothes. The blurry background behind the barmaid suggests she is standing

in front of a mirror, which reflects the Parisian club scene she is facing. Discrepancies in the reflection, however, make one question the accuracy of what one sees. For example, the bottles next to the barmaid on the left of the canvas appear to be placed in a different order and in a different place in the reflection behind her. In addition, some viewers question whether the posture of the barmaid on the far right is an accurate reflection of the barmaid looking out at us. Manet certainly had the skill to depict **perspective** precisely, so one must consider why he chose to create such an ambiguous reflection.

Several interpretations of *A Bar at the Folies-Bergère* have been suggested. If we assume that the figure on the right is indeed a reflection of the barmaid, then we viewers are standing in the place of the man in the top hat to whom she is

4.86 Édouard Manet, *A Bar at the Folies-Bergère*, 1882. Oil on canvas, 37⅞ × 51¼". Courtauld Gallery, London

talking. He is presumably a client. It was common for the female entertainers and barmaids at the Folies-Bergère to be hired by the clientele for sexual favors. Perhaps that is the nature of the interchange taking place between them. The

ambiguities in the reflection may be a way for the artist to suggest different emotional states in the barmaid, contrasting her personal experience or feelings with her external appearance. Some have argued that she appears to be much more

Satirizing Illusionism: Hogarth's *False Perspective*

In this work, William Hogarth (1697–1764), an eighteenth-century British artist, satirizes the traditional training of painters who were taught to use the rules of perspective to create believable spaces (**4.87**). Here, Hogarth applies these rules in order to break them. He thus creates the illusion of a space that is, in fact, impossible. On the bottom of the print, he wrote:

> Whoever makes a Design without the Knowledge of Perspective will be liable to such Absurdities as are shown in this Frontispiece.

See if you can find these spatial impossibilities:

- The woman in the window of her building is lighting the pipe of the man standing on top of the hill. Lower in the image, we can see a tree, and horses pulling a wagon, between the building and the base of the hill. How can the woman reach the man?
- The man in the right foreground must have quite an extraordinarily long fishing line in order to reach beyond the rod of the man in the distance.
- In the lower left, the sheep closest to us are smaller than those further away.
- Similarly, the trees at the bottom of the hill get larger as they recede into the distance, suggesting that the bird on the furthest tree is improbably big.
- The church in the distance appears to be both grounded on land and floating on water.
- The man in the boat in the center of the scene appears to aim his gun at a swan, but instead shoots the underside of the bridge.
- The sign on the building in the foreground

seems to be hanging behind the trees on the hill in the background.
- The barrel behind the large man in the foreground shows both the top and bottom of the container.
- The **vanishing point** of the grid upon which the man in the foreground stands is projecting into the viewer's space, rather than receding into the pictorial space, making it seem as if the man should be falling forward out of the picture.

4.87 William Hogarth, *False Perspective*. Engraving from *Dr. Brook Taylor's Method of Perspective Made Easy, Both in Theory and Practice*, 1754

engaged in the reflected image than she is as she stands before us in the center of the painting. Her gaze leaves us questioning her state of mind: is she sad, distracted, or bored? Another interpretation suggests that the artist is depicting a fantasy.

Some artists employ **satire** to question or play with the tradition of using perspective and other illusionary tools to create artworks that imitate reality (see Box: Satirizing Illusionism). The Belgian artist René Magritte (1898–1967) asks the viewer to question what appears to be a painting of a landscape on an easel, which has been placed before a window that looks out onto the same landscape (**4.88**). However, we realize that the scene outside the window is also an invention; the window and drapes and the painting on the easel are both part of the painted canvas that we behold. The artist explains,

> [The tree] exists for the spectator, both inside the room in the painting, and outside in the real landscape, in thought. Which is how we see the world: we see it as being outside ourselves even though it is only a mental representation of it that we experience inside ourselves.

Magritte confronts us with issues of representation and truth and refers directly to the achievements in **linear perspective** made by the artists of the Renaissance. What at first seems an extension of the desire to create a convincing view through a window is shattered when Magritte forces us to consider what is real, and what is only of the mind. Magritte showed that the "illusionistic window" of the Renaissance is indeed only a canvas. By so doing, he opened the door for artists to make paintings with purposes other than the representation of perfect three-dimensional illusions of subjects as if they were real life. As Magritte demonstrated, painting can be a powerful mode for expressing complex ideas, rather than solely re-creating what we see with our eyes.

Discussion Questions

1. Look at artworks by René Magritte (for example, *The Human Condition* in this chapter (**4.88**) and *The Treachery of Images* on p. 76 (**1.47**)). Write a short essay of two or three paragraphs explaining what Magritte was saying about the Renaissance idea of the "illusionistic window."

2. Select one of the artists in this chapter and study other works by them. Does the artist use illusionism frequently? What do you think is the artist's motivation for doing so?

3. Study Hogarth's *False Perspective*. Now draw a scene from your imagination and include in it at least three examples of altered visual reality like those included in Hogarth's print.

Vanishing point: the point in a work of art at which imaginary sight lines appear to converge, suggesting depth

Satire: work of art that exposes the weaknesses and mistakes of its subjects to ridicule

Linear perspective: a system using converging imaginary sight lines to create the illusion of depth

4.6

Art and Rulers

Rulers have always made use of works of art to help define and assert their political power and to influence their people. Seeking to demonstrate supreme control, leaders have used artworks to highlight their right to rule, sometimes even to claim that their authority has been granted by the gods. Regal portraits are often idealized, emphasizing rulers' importance by portraying them in elaborate clothing, or showing them seated on a throne, placed centrally in the composition, or depicted larger than other figures. Leaders have frequently commissioned artworks to reinforce their reputations as skillful commanders and to project an image of military strength. Thus artworks can be a potent propaganda tool for sustaining a ruler's power. This chapter explores how rulers have seen themselves and how they wished to be viewed by both friend and foe.

Regal Portraits

What image comes to mind when you think of a great leader? Artists have endeavored for centuries to develop ways to show rulers as figures of grace and authority, deserving the trust of the people whom they govern. **Byzantine** artists created glorious tile **mosaics**, and the Chinese used rich silks as the base for luxuriously colorful royal portraits. The ancient Olmec conveyed their leaders' power in the massiveness of the stone images they carved (see Gateway Box: Colossal Olmec Heads, **4.91a** and **4.91b**, p. 522). Portraits vary in the degree to which they accurately depict the physical characteristics of the sitter. Rulers are sometimes identified by their attire and placement rather than their facial features.

The Byzantine emperor Justinian is remembered as a remarkable military and civil leader, as well as a great **patron** of the arts who funded the building of hundreds of churches. Portraits of Justinian, who ruled in the sixth century, were often placed in these churches to demonstrate his patronage as well as his power, which was believed to have been granted by God. In the Church of San Vitale, in Ravenna, Italy, there is a glorious coloured glass mosaic of the Emperor, which he probably never saw (**4.89**).

Justinian stands in the center of the mosaic, wearing the imperial color purple. On either side of him are clergy in white robes. To his far right are soldiers, who display a large shield that bears the Greek letters for Christ (*chi-rho*), emphasizing Justinian's role as a Christian military leader. There are other Christian symbols in the mosaic: the men to the left of the emperor hold a cross, a copy of the Gospels (the first four books of the New Testament), and a censer used to burn incense in church services. Justinian holds the bread used to represent the body of Christ in the communion service, and the mosaic itself is displayed near the altar where the service would take place. Interestingly, one other figure in this mosaic is given special recognition: the local bishop, Maximianus, who arranged the commission, organized the composition so that his figure was the only one identified in writing on the image

Byzantine: relating to the East Roman Empire, centered on Constantinople (modern-day Istanbul) from the fifth century CE to 1453
Mosaic: a picture or pattern created by fixing together small pieces of stone, glass, tile, etc.
Patron: an organization or individual who sponsors the creation of works of art

4.89 Justinian mosaic,
c. 547 CE. Glass. San Vitale,
Ravenna, Italy

(his name is written above his portrait), and so
that his feet should be placed slightly in front of
the emperor. One wonders what Justinian would
have thought, had he seen the mosaic. Justinian
himself needed no such label: the imperial robe,
in addition to his crown and halo, were enough
to identify the ruler.

Unlike the depiction of Justinian, which
shows the ruler surrounded by followers, the
portrait of the Yongzheng Emperor (who
reigned between 1722 and 1735) in **4.90** shows
the Emperor of China by himself and enthroned.
Many aspects of the portrait—the ruler's
expression and pose, his yellow robe, and the
rich colors on the silk scroll—follow the
traditions of royal portraiture used for centuries
in China. The accurate depiction of the facial
features, however, makes each portrait unique.
The gilded throne and richly colored textiles
of his robe, seat cushion, and carpet emphasize
the wealth and authority of the ruler. Dragons
intricately stitched all over the robe, and the
monstrous carving on the throne, symbolize
the emperor's fearsome power. Imperial portraits
like these were often made upon the death of

4.90 Portrait of the
Yongzheng Emperor in
court dress, Yongzheng
period, 1723–35. Hanging
scroll, colour on silk,
9'1" × 4'8½". Palace Museum,
Beijing, China

Gateway to Art: Colossal Olmec Heads
Portraits of Powerful Rulers

The distinctive facial features and individual headdresses of the seventeen Colossal Olmec Heads suggest that each one represented a real person (**4.91a**). Scholars think they probably depict specific Olmec rulers. The effort it must have taken to create each sculpture is evidence of the power of the ruler. The material used to make the colossal heads is a hard volcanic stone known as basalt. In San Lorenzo, Mexico, where ten colossal heads have been found, the stone would have been transported more than fifty miles over rivers and marshy terrain, suggesting that the ruler had a wealth of resources at his disposal. Many Olmec heads have been discovered underground, indicating that they were buried as part of a ritual. In addition, many of the heads have been mutilated or carved from the stone of Olmec "altar-throne" sculptures, leading some scholars to conclude that old sculptures were damaged, buried, or recycled as new sculptures when a new ruler took power. Scholars cannot say with certainty why this was done, but it seems likely that the burial and mutilation of Olmec monuments occurred when the ruler died. Although there is much we will never know about why these heads were made, it seems clear that they express the power of mighty rulers.

4.91a Colossal Head, Olmec, 1200–600 BCE. Museo Nacional de Antropología, Mexico City, Mexico

4.91b Colossal Head, Olmec, 1500–1300 BCE. Basalt. Museo de Antropología, Veracruz, Mexico

the ruler and hung in family shrines. The ruler's descendants would burn incense and bow before their ancestor's portrait, asking for protection and guidance. Such images were themselves safeguarded by an ancestral power. In fact, it was considered blasphemous and even dangerous to possess the portrait of someone who was not your own ancestor.

Art to Demonstrate Absolute Power

A ruler with absolute power is one who has the freedom to govern as he or she pleases. How is such unlimited power achieved? Often such leaders are believed to have been given their authority by divine powers. Even when rulers seem unjust or extreme, their subjects are less likely to rebel if their authority is believed to have derived from God. Absolute rulers control the wealth of their country, and may choose to spend it on personal luxuries, rather than for the benefit of all (see Box: The Extravagance of the French Monarchy, pp. 524–5). Leaders with such total power may determine the religion of their people and how that religion is practiced.

In ancient Maya culture, a ruler's power was reinforced through prayers and sacrifices to the gods. An intricately carved **lintel** from a temple in Yaxchilán in southern Mexico shows Lady Xoc, wife of the ruler Shield Jaguar, kneeling before her husband and pulling a rope covered with thorns through a hole in her tongue in a bloodletting ritual (**4.92**). The writing around the edges of the scene tells us the names of the figures and describes what is taking place. According to the symbols above the king's head, this ritual took place on October 28, 709 CE.

Bloodletting led to what is called a hallucinogenic state, in which the individual concerned imagines that he or she is seeing things. The Maya may have enhanced such states by fasting and taking drugs; they believed that such rituals caused spiritual visions. Shield Jaguar and Lady Xoc prayed to the sun god; they both wear his image on their **pectorals**. This ritual

may be related to a specific battle, as Shield Jaguar, dressed as a warrior, wears an elaborate headdress that includes the shrunken head of a victim sacrificed to the gods. He holds a large burning torch to light the evening ritual.

This lintel is one of three that depict specific bloodletting ceremonies undergone by Lady Xoc (each with different dates); they were placed together over a doorway in a temple dedicated to her. Although Lady Xoc is shown as clearly subordinate to Shield Jaguar, her

Lintel: the horizontal beam over the doorway of a portal
Pectoral: a large ornament worn on the chest

4.92 Shield Jaguar and Lady Xoc, *c.* 725 CE. Limestone, 43 × 30". British Museum, London, England

The Extravagance of the French Monarchy

Louis XIV (1638–1715) ruled France as an absolute monarch and his power was thought to be based on the divine will of God. He proclaimed himself the Sun King, believing that he was the center of all things, and that the world revolved around his whims. The regal portrait by Hyacinthe Rigaud (1659–1743) is meant to demonstrate the king's absolute power (4.93). Louis is dressed in royal attire, the gold fleur-de-lis (or "lily-flower," the symbol of the French monarchy) embroidered on a rich blue velvet gown, lined in expensive white fur known as ermine. Insisting on the finest of everything, Louis XIV dressed himself in the most opulent textiles from around the world. He invented the high heels shown here, which he used to increase his height (5 ft. 4 in.) and to show off his healthy legs. This painting was done when the monarch was in his sixties.

The Sun King stands at the entrance to the famed Hall of Mirrors, an opulent chamber filled with mirrors (an expensive commodity at the time) in his grand new palace of Versailles, near Paris. This enormous edifice had hundreds of rooms, each ornately decorated by the finest artists in Europe. Vast gardens covering almost 2,000 acres were designed to surround the palace. They were filled with 200,000 trees and 210,000 flowers, which were replanted frequently, and with 2,100 sculptures, many of them placed on spectacular fountains. Versailles has more than fifty fountains. There was not enough water to run them all at once, though, and servants used a system of whistles to alert one another to turn on the fountains whenever the Sun King was within viewing range.

By the late eighteenth century, the wasteful spending of the monarchy had

4.93 (below left) Hyacinthe Rigaud, *Louis XIV*, 1701. Oil on canvas, 9'1" × 6'4⅜". Musée du Louvre, Paris, France

4.94 (below right) Élisabeth-Louise Vigée-Lebrun, *Marie Antoinette and Her Children*, 1787. Oil on canvas, 9'½" × 7'⅝". Musée National du Château de Versailles, France caused such popular opposition that the monarchy itself took notice. Marie Antoinette, the wife of King Louis XVI (1754–93), had become the symbol of the royal family's extravagance. While the French state suffered financial strain and the people went hungry, the queen decorated herself with expensive clothes and jewels and was given her own chateau, or palace, which she decorated extravagantly. The French directed much of their anger at the queen; many considered her promiscuous, even incestuous, although historians find that some of the accusations against her were greatly exaggerated.

The portrait of *Marie Antoinette and Her Children* (4.94) was painted to improve the queen's reputation. She is shown seated in Versailles with the Hall of Mirrors behind her right shoulder, just as Louis XIV had been portrayed. While her rich velvet dress shows her status as Queen of France, her wardrobe is neither overly revealing nor lacking in French style and taste, which had been a criticism of previous portraits. In dramatic opposition to her growing reputation as promiscuous and unavailable to the king, she is shown as a loving mother adored by her children, who cling to her. Her somber expression suggests sorrow over the recent loss of her youngest daughter, for whom the empty cradle was intended. In fact, Élisabeth-Louise Vigée-Lebrun (1755–1842), who painted this and many other portraits of Marie Antoinette, wrote in her diary of the kind nature of the queen, and of the queen's sympathy for the painter when she herself was pregnant and when she faced challenges as a female artist in the Royal Academy of Painting and Sculpture. The portrait did not, however, assuage the growing anger of the French people. It was removed from public display shortly after being exhibited in 1788, for fear that it would be attacked. The following year, the French Revolution began. Three years later, in 1792, the monarchy was overthrown, and in 1793 Louis XVI and Marie Antoinette were beheaded.

4.95 Akhenaten, Nefertiti, and three daughters, *c.* 1353–1335 BCE. Limestone, 12¼" high. Ägyptisches Museum, Staatliche Museen zu Berlin, Germany

Sunken relief: a carved panel where the figures are cut deeper into the stone than the background

elaborate costume, her role in the ritual, and the fact that this bloodletting scene was imitated in artworks of later generations highlights that she too was a person of importance.

The ancient Egyptians believed their kings, known as pharaohs, were descended from the gods. The pharaoh Akhenaten, like Shield Jaguar, ruled under the authority of a sun god. Although previous pharaohs had worshiped many gods, Akhenaten, who ruled in the fourteenth century BCE, used his supreme power to recognize only the sun god Aten. Akhenaten's beliefs are clearly stated in a **sunken relief**, originally painted, that depicts the pharaoh on the left, his wife and trusted adviser Nefertiti opposite him, and their three daughters cradled on their laps (4.95). The sun is carved deeper than anything else in the relief, which signifies visually its importance as a god, and its rays emanate toward the family, suggesting the sun god's support of the royal family. The flames at the end of the rays are small hands, some holding an *ankh*, the character that symbolizes life in ancient Egyptian writing. The depiction of Nefertiti as almost the same size as her husband indicates her importance. Some historians believe she ruled the kingdom with Akhenaten.

The Power to Command

The power to command a nation's army is one of a leader's most important duties. Rulers are expected to protect their people, to defeat their enemies in battle, and bring peace. Countless artworks have been made to record successful military campaigns. Many rulers themselves have commissioned artworks they hope will lead to eternal recognition of their military prowess, or that will persuade their people to consider them as gods. Such objects are meant to show the ruler as protector of and peacemaker for his people.

The Palette of Narmer, one of the earliest surviving ancient Egyptian artworks, records the unification of Egypt by the first pharaoh, Narmer (**4.96a** and **4.96b**). Before the reign of Narmer, Egypt was divided into Lower Egypt (near the mouth of the Nile River, to the north) and Upper Egypt (higher terrain, to the south). **Palettes** were used to grind **pigment** that both men and women painted around their eyes to protect them from the sun. The round area on the front of the Palette of Narmer, in which the necks of two creatures intertwine, would have been used for the mixing of the paint. The detailing and expense of this object, however, suggest that it may not have been used; or if it was, that it was used only for a very important ceremony.

The front of the palette is divided into four **registers**. The top register shows a pair of horned bull heads, which represent the aggressive strength of the king. Between them is a symbol for the name of the king. In the next register the king is shown larger than the other figures to indicate his importance, a convention known as **hierarchical scale**. Narmer's unification of Egypt is recorded by a number of symbols. He wears the Red Crown of Lower Egypt, denoting his rule over that region. (The palette was painted, originally, so the red of the crown would have been clearly visible.) The figures lined up in a procession in front of him hold standards with markings that probably signify regions now under Narmer's control. On the far right of this register are ten bodies with severed heads between their legs, indicating the scores of enemies Narmer has killed. The intertwining of the fantastical long-necked creatures in the next register embodies the unification of Upper and Lower Egypt. In the bottom register, Narmer is again represented as a bull, who bows his head toward a fortified city and tramples on an enemy.

The back of the palette features a large scene in which the pharaoh, wearing the White Crown that symbolizes Upper Egypt, prepares to club an enemy who kneels before him. The falcon represents the god Horus, suggesting that Narmer was supported by the gods. Horus stands on papyrus plants, symbols of Lower Egypt, where the plants grew. The smaller figure standing behind Narmer is a servant, who carries the pharaoh's

4.96a (front) and **4.96b** (back) Palette of Narmer, Early Dynastic Period, c. 2950–2775 BCE. Green schist, 25¼ × 16⅝". Egyptian Museum, Cairo, Egypt shoes. (Another servant appears behind the ruler on the other side of the palette.) At the very bottom of the reverse side of the palette is a scene of two fallen enemies, viewed as if from above. Much of the picture writing on the palette has not yet been interpreted, but it seems to record the names of places conquered by Narmer. Taken as a whole, the palette shows this pharaoh's military might as he unifies all of Egypt under his rule.

Just as the Palette of Narmer focused on the military successes of Egypt's first pharaoh, Augustus, the first Emperor of Rome, used art as propaganda to demonstrate his military prowess and to claim descent from the gods. Augustus wished to present himself as an exceptional military leader, and in fact he defeated the rival Roman general Mark Antony and Cleopatra, Queen of Egypt, in 31 BCE, and thus expanded the Roman Empire. The *Augustus of Primaporta* portrays him in military garb and with his arm upraised, ready both to lead his troops into battle and to deliver an inspiring speech (**4.97**). Cupid, son of Venus, the Roman goddess of love, is shown at Augustus's feet. He represents the divine lineage of Augustus, who claimed to be the descendant of Aeneas (also a son of Venus), the mythical founder of Rome. The pose and proportions were copied from Greek art, which the Romans admired, and were believed to represent an ideal youthful physical form, although Augustus was actually in his forties when the statue was made.

Originally much of the sculpture was painted with bright red and blue, making the scenes on Augustus's armor easier to read. In the center of his chest plate is a scene showing the return of one of the Roman military standards captured by the army of the Parthian Empire, a reference to Augustus's superb diplomatic skills. Both Mark Antony and the talented general and politician Julius Caesar had failed to retrieve the standards, so Augustus's success shows him as more powerful than his predecessors.

A plaque from the palace of an African king suggests, as did the statue of Augustus, that military strength is often needed to bring peace to a kingdom (**4.98**). The kings, or obas, of Benin, were both military and spiritual leaders of a West African state that was at its height between 1450 and 1700. The obas commissioned hundreds of brass artworks to reflect their power, including plaques to cover the royal palace, many of which depict warriors who followed the orders of the oba. The central warrior in this plaque is larger than the two beside him, signifying his importance; he is in **higher relief** than the others, making him seem closer to us. The ceremonial sword he carries in his left hand and his elaborate helmet tell us that he is a high-ranking chief. His spear and the shields of those beside him are imposing, emphasizing their physical power and that of their ruler, the oba. The chief wears a leopard tooth necklace and has dotted markings on his stomach and arms resembling the spots of a leopard. Leopards, known for their power and speed, were a symbol of the oba.

4.97 *Augustus of Primaporta*, early 1st-century CE copy, after original bronze from 20 BCE. Marble, 6'8" high. Vatican Museums, Vatican City

4.98 Plaque with warrior and attendants, 16th–17th century. Brass, 18¾" high. Metropolitan Museum of Art, New York

Art and Societal Control

4.99 Stela of Hammurabi, *c.* 1792–1750 BCE. Diorite, 88⅝ × 25⅝". Musée du Louvre, Paris, France

Leaders have the authority to try to influence the course of history, and they frequently use art to announce their intentions. Strong leaders also understand the power of art as a tool for propaganda, both to convey their messages and to influence the people to adhere to their laws. The ancient Babylonian king Hammurabi used an image to emphasize his divine connection to the gods in order to persuade his people to follow his decrees. Both the Roman emperor Constantine and the Chinese communist leader Mao Zedong utilized their own portraits on a grand scale to symbolize their political strength.

King Hammurabi of Babylon (now part of Iraq) is best known today for the code of law that he established around 1790 BCE. It was innovative for being a set of written statutes, as opposed to unwritten or arbitrary rules, which might vary by region or local authority. His code was carved into a **stela** for public viewing (**4.99**). King Hammurabi's code has often been summarized as "an eye for an eye," because it often called for a person to be punished for wrong-doing by suffering in the same way as the person who had been wronged. Yet Hammurabi's laws were often more complex and less even-handed when they pertained to people with low status, such as slaves, freedmen, and women. For example, the law did

not punish a husband for adultery, although it did consider the wife's financial well-being if her husband decided to leave her. In contrast, a woman caught in an adulterous affair was thrown into a river, with her hands tied, along with her lover. If her husband only suspected her of adultery, but had no proof, she was required to jump into the river. If she survived, she was deemed innocent.

The scene at the top of the stela shows that Hammurabi's power has been given to him by the gods. The sun god Shamash, seen with flames radiating from his shoulders, is seated upon a throne that is in the mountains, signified by the three steps below the god's feet. The sun god reaches toward Hammurabi as he dictates to the king the laws he will implement. Written below this scene is a long description of the gods' support for Hammurabi and the king's law code.

Constantine the Great ruled part of the Roman Empire from 306 CE and was sole emperor from 324 until his death in 337. Constantine was successful in numerous military campaigns, and he is notable for having been the first Christian Roman emperor. A colossal marble and bronze statue of the emperor seated on a throne was made in 325 to be placed in a **basilica** in the center of Rome. Only parts of the statue survive (**4.100**), but the head alone, which is more than 8 feet tall, gives an idea of the imposing force one must have felt standing in the presence of this

4.100 Remnants of colossal statue of Constantine the Great, 325–6 CE. Marble, head 8′6″ high. Palazzo dei Conservatori, Rome, Italy

statue, which was made to remind the people of Constantine's power even when he was away.

In its youthful features and ideal athletic body, the statue was modeled after portraits of earlier emperors. The emperor was enthroned in a manner similar to seated statues of the Roman god Jupiter, but he held in his hand an orb on which a Christian cross was placed. This statue is one of the earliest examples of how pagan art was often reinterpreted to incorporate Christian symbolism and meaning. Constantine's far-off gaze toward the heavens is also distinct from earlier portraits of Roman emperors and signifies his close connection to, and therefore power derived from, God.

Mao Zedong led the Communist Party to power in the Chinese civil war that ended in 1949. Mao, who ruled the most populous country in the world for twenty-seven years, understood the power of imagery and, like leaders for centuries before him, used artwork to promote his political and social agenda amongst his thousands of subjects. Mao installed a huge portrait of himself at Tiananmen (the Gate of Heavenly Peace), in Beijing, the capital of China, when he declared the country to be the People's Republic of China (**4.101**). Tiananmen, the site of many important political and cultural events in China's history, was built in the fifteenth century as a gateway to the Forbidden City, the home of the Chinese emperors for centuries. The portrait has been replaced over the years by replicas with only slight

variations. Originally Mao wore the collared white suit seen in the portrait today, but his head was slightly turned. In the mid-1960s the portrait was altered to show both of Mao's ears, symbolizing that he listened intently to the people. The total number of portraits of Mao made for this location is unknown; however, the Chinese appear to have copies in storage in case of damage to the one currently hanging.

Mao's colossal image is considered a national symbol in China. Portraits of Mao, in the form of posters, paintings, sculptures, badges, and postage stamps, were disseminated more than any other image throughout China in the 1960s and 1970s. When Mao died in 1976, the large oil painting at Tiananmen was replaced temporarily with a black-and-white photograph to signify China's mourning. The portrait is a powerful symbol both for supporters of the Chinese government as well as for its opponents. It was splattered with red paint during the pro-democracy student protests of 1989, and in 2007 an unemployed man set fire to it. In both cases, the portrait was replaced immediately and the vandals arrested.

Discussion Questions

1   In this chapter we have examined portrayals of rulers from many cultures and eras. Find another artwork in which a ruler is represented. Considering the elements and principles of art discussed in Part 1 of this book, perform a visual analysis of your selected artwork. How does the artist convey the power of the ruler?

2   Rulers are often shown as powerful warriors. Select one such work from this chapter and then find another in another chapter in this book (for example, **1.133**, **3.12**, **4.27**): make sure the two are from different cultures or eras. Compare the two representations. In what ways are they similar and in what ways different?

3   Do royal portraits tell us what a ruler really looked like? Choose four examples from this chapter and for each make a list of aspects of the artwork that seem individual and realistic and those aspects that may exaggerate or idealize the ruler's appearance. Discuss your findings in a short essay.

4.101 Mao Zedong's portrait. The Gate of Heavenly Peace, Tiananmen (south entrance to the old Forbidden City), Beijing, China

4.7

Art and War

War has been a theme of artworks for centuries. Artists re-create the terror of battle, the tragedy of death, the joy of victory, and the sorrow of defeat. Artists choose war as a theme for a variety of reasons: to educate us about the realities of conflict, to inspire us through the depiction of heroism, or to shock us into opposing violence. Artworks about historical events can be rich sources of information, skillfully documenting the kinds of weapons used in a particular battle or the uniforms the soldiers wore; but artists may also manipulate scenes in order, for example, to inspire support for one side over another. Art about war should therefore be treated with caution, for just as we bring our own biases when we engage with an artwork, so artists may also be promoting their own point of view.

Documenting War: Unbiased Facts or Biased Judgments?

As a viewer, do you question certain visual documents of history more than others? Do you assume that visual images (such as photographs and video) that show current events are accurate, or do you sometimes think they might have been manipulated?

When artists document actual events, they may try to record exactly what they have seen. More frequently, however, artists tend to infuse their images with the emotions aroused by the sight of death, destruction, and tragedy. An image of battle,

therefore, can have a profound impact on the people who see the artwork, even as the artist's emotions sometimes distort the facts of history. Art that seems to be documentary evidence may not be entirely factual. It is important to assess the art of war with great care and attention as to the context in which the work was created. (For two contrasting views of the same battle, see Gateway Box: Goya, **4.104** and **4.105**, p. 532.)

American Timothy O'Sullivan (1840–82) took the famous Civil War photograph *Harvest of Death* after a day at Gettysburg, the battle that caused the most casualties of the entire conflict (**4.102**). His photograph shows a field covered with bodies, highlighting the tragic loss of life. The clothes of some of the soldiers have been partly removed, suggesting that thieves have been searching their bodies. O'Sullivan has focused the composition on the face of the soldier in the foreground, his arms flung out from his sides. By concentrating on this individual, whose features we can see, O'Sullivan reduces to a human level the great loss of life at Gettysburg.

One often assumes that a photograph can be trusted as an accurate documentation of an event. Yet photographers, like other artists, can manipulate their scenes through lighting and **composition**. O'Sullivan was known to rearrange bodies and otherwise alter the setting before taking his photos. We do not know if he arranged the corpses or their clothing in order to heighten the emotional impact of this powerful image. If we knew he had staged the scene in some way, would we doubt the truth of the tragedy he represents?

Composition: the overall design or organization of a work

We tend to assume that photography is "real" in a way that painting is not. In contrast to a photographer, who makes an image of a subject that already exists, a painter begins with a blank canvas. The French painter Ernest Meissonier (1815–91), however, depicted a scene that eyewitnesses to the event described as remarkably accurate, as truthful and "real" as one would assume an eyewitness video to be today (**4.103**).

Meissonier was serving in the French National Guard during the insurrection of 1848, when Parisians fought their fellow Parisians, and rebels overthrew the monarchy and established the Second Republic. More than 1,500 people died in the short civil war, many of them innocent bystanders. Meissonier recorded the carnage:

I saw the defenders shot down, hurled out of windows, the ground strewn with corpses, the earth red with blood.

In his painting, bodies are piled one upon another amongst the rocks of a collapsed barricade in the middle of Paris. The painting,

admired at the time as a true representation of what had happened, was removed by the French government from the important public art exhibition, the Salon of 1850, because it provided too powerful a reminder of the recent past.

4.103 Ernest Meissonier, *Remembrance of Civil War*, 1848 (*The Barricade, rue de la Mortellerie, June 1848*), exhibited 1850. Oil on canvas, 11½ × 8¾". Musée du Louvre, Paris, France

Gateway to Art: Goya, *The Third of May, 1808*
Two Views of a Battle

Sometimes, we can look at a painting on its own and reach one conclusion; but when we look at it next to another work, our opinion of both paintings changes. If we look at Francisco Goya's painting *The Third of May, 1808* on its own, for example, we might conclude that it is a powerful condemnation of the French Emperor Napoleon and his troops (**4.104**). But what happens if we view the work beside another that Goya painted in the same year, *The Second of May, 1808* (**4.105**)? Can both paintings be understood better as a condemnation, not of Napoleon in particular, but of war in general?

The Spanish War of Independence (1808–14), the beginnings of which are depicted in *The Second of May, 1808*, was known for its guerrilla fighting and for the heroism of the civilian population. Goya's *Third of May* shows the punishment of civilians who had brutally attacked the invading French soldiers on the previous day (the subject of *The Second of May, 1808*).

Unlike *The Third of May*, *The Second of May* does not show sympathy for the Spanish rebels. While the figures in *The Third of May* seem to be still, as if frozen by the horror of the moment, *The Second of May* is full of movement and chaotic action. In fact, when the two paintings are viewed together, we may view the executions on May 3 to be inevitable following the violent slaughter of French soldiers the day before. The French general Joachim Murat, angered by the riots, proclaimed, "French blood has flowed. It demands vengeance." At least 400 Spaniards were executed in Madrid, more than forty on the hill of Príncipe Pío, the location depicted in Goya's *Third of May*.

4.104 Francisco Goya, *The Third of May, 1808*, 1814. Oil on canvas, 8'4⅜" × 11'3⅞". Museo Nacional del Prado, Madrid, Spain

4.105 Francisco Goya, *The Second of May, 1808*, 1814. Oil on canvas, 8'9" × 11'4⅛". Museo Nacional del Prado, Madrid, Spain

Historians consider O'Sullivan's and Meissonier's artworks to be amongst the most truthful records of the aftermath of battle, yet the emotional impact created by each scene suggests that they may have been somewhat manipulated. The photograph by the Vietnamese Nick Ut (b. 1951) of children running from their village in Vietnam after a napalm attack was so shocking that some, including the U.S. president Richard Nixon, questioned its authenticity when it appeared in newspapers on June 12, 1972 (**4.106**). The image also moved many Americans to question their nation's involvement in the Vietnam War. The photographer defended its authenticity for years:

> The picture for me and unquestionably for many others could not have been more real. The photo was as authentic as the Vietnam War itself. The horror of the Vietnam War recorded by me did not have to be fixed. That terrified little girl is still alive today and has become an eloquent testimony to the authenticity of that photo.

Although the photograph records an actual event, Ut's disapproval of the war and his concern for its victims influenced the way his shot was composed. He focused on the little girl, Kim Phuc, screaming in terror, running naked, her clothes having been burned off her body. Her two brothers are running on the left side of the image, while her two cousins hold hands behind her on the right. The soldiers in the background appear strangely calm, a dramatic contrast to the horrified expressions of the running children.

The story of the people in the photograph did not end with that moment. The nine-year-old girl kept screaming; the photographer gave her his water and rushed her to a hospital. Physicians predicted Phuc would die. But because of the fame of the photograph, money poured in to save her. She underwent seventeen surgical operations and later emigrated to Canada. Nick Ut became "Uncle Nick" to the little girl and the two have remained in close contact throughout their lives. Although this photograph shows the suffering of a small group of people, it symbolizes for many the tragedy of the entire Vietnam War.

4.106 Nick Ut, *Vietnamese Girl Kim Phuc Running after Napalm Attack*, June 8, 1972. Photograph

In contrast to Nick Ut, who stated plainly that he opposed the Vietnam War and wanted to influence opinion with his images of the conflict, the American artist Chris Burden (b. 1946) has said that his 1987 work *All the Submarines of the United States of America* was meant to be unbiased: it simply documented the total number of submarines there had ever been in the United States Navy up until the year this artwork was made (**4.107**). His **installation** comprises 625 cardboard models of submarines hung at

Installation: an artwork created by the assembling and arrangement of objects in a specific location

4.107 Chris Burden, *All the Submarines of the United States of America*, 1987. 625 cardboard submarines, 80 × 20 × 12'. Installation at the 1989 Whitney Biennial different heights from the ceiling of a large room. The name of each submarine is listed in black on a wall of the gallery.

It is left to the viewer to interpret the artwork, as the piece embodies opposing forces: individualism versus unity, war versus peace. Individualism is represented by each crafted submarine; at the same time, the submarines work as a whole unit, appearing in the room like a school of fish. One viewer might naturally see U.S. Navy submarines as weapons of war because submarines are stealthy by nature, traveling secretly under water. Another viewer, conversely, might interpret a submarine as a tool for keeping the peace.

Warriors and Scenes of Battle

Artists have often recorded and celebrated the bravery of warriors, both their successes and defeats, in great detail. Although at times, as we have seen, an artist's interpretation of historical events is skewed and presented through an emotional lens, artworks can be valuable records of critical historical moments. They can teach us the significance of certain battles, and provide accurate studies of the kinds of weapons used and the uniforms worn by those who took part in them.

4.108 Tula warrior columns, 900–1000 CE. Basalt, 15–20' high. Tula, Hidalgo, Mexico

4.109 *Alexander Mosaic* (*Battle of Issus*), c. 200 BCE. Mosaic, 8'10" × 16'9". National Archaeological Museum, Naples, Italy

Four large warrior columns, standing between 15 and 20 feet tall, are some of the few remaining artworks of the ancient Toltec people of Mexico (**4.108**). Little is known about this militaristic society except what can be learnt from the legends of later cultures, such as the Aztecs, who often sought to demonstrate an ancestral link with the Toltec. These legends suggest that the Toltec ruled a substantial empire. It is believed that around 1000 CE the Toltec capital of Tula was the largest city in Mexico at that time, with a population of more than 50,000.

The warriors in **4.108** stood high above the city, painted in bright colors. The imposing figures once supported the roof of a temple that stood on a pyramid and was reached by a steep stairway. The carving of the columns gives us some sense of how a Toltec warrior would have looked. The figures are identical, each wearing a feathered headdress, a butterfly-shaped **pectoral**, sandals decorated with symbols of the gods, and a belt supporting a large mirror or shield on their lower back. Each warrior holds spears or arrows in his left hand and a spearthrowing device in his right. Similar warriors—ranging from the small scale to the large, and occurring both as freestanding figures and as columns in temples—comprise the majority of the few Toltec sculptures that survive. This suggests that the Toltec probably lived in a time of frequent warfare, and that they revered their warrior rulers.

The Tula warriors are not shown fighting in the heat of battle but are standing still, acting as guards. By contrast, the so-called *Alexander Mosaic* in **4.109** glorifies the military prowess of Alexander the Great (shown on the far left) and his victory over King Darius III of Persia (to the right of center) in the Battle of Issus in 333 BCE.

This **mosaic**, a copy of a well-known Greek painting that does not survive, was made around 200 BCE for a private home in the city of Pompeii in southern Italy. Its dynamic composition gives us an idea of the beauty of Greek **fresco** painting, complete examples of which no longer exist. It also displays the skill of ancient mosaicists, who pieced together more than one million **tesserae** in numerous subtly different shades to create a battle scene with layers of depth and figures with three-dimensionality.

The composition of the *Alexander Mosaic* is designed to convey action and emotion. The men and horses are crowded together in the lower two-thirds of the scene, while the lengthy spears pointing in various directions evoke the chaos that takes place on the battlefield. Darius is shown rising above the rest, eyes wide open with fear. The horses communicate the urgency of the movement with their expressive faces and their bodies turning in every direction, including away from the viewer. Under Darius's left arm, and lying on the ground, one man witnesses in horror his own demise through the reflection in his shield. Alexander (on the left) is depicted as a fearless warrior, ready to face Darius's entire army as he stabs an enemy soldier with his long spear.

Pectoral: a large ornament worn on the chest
Mosaic: a picture or pattern created by fixing together small pieces of stone, glass, tile, etc.
Fresco: a technique where the artist paints onto freshly applied plaster. From the Italian *fresco*, fresh
Tesserae: small pieces of stone or glass or other materials used to make a mosaic

DERVN · SIMVL · ANGLI ET FRA NCI · INPRELIO ·

Other artists have conveyed the sounds and sensations of war using completely different **media**. Both the *Bayeux Tapestry* and the *Tale of the Heiji Rebellion* (*Heiji Monogatari*) portray rousing battle scenes (**4.110** and **4.111**). We can almost hear the clanking of weapons and smell the odor of burning flesh. And while a few figures illustrate the courage of the enemy, both artworks are skewed toward celebrating the overwhelming prowess of the victors. Both artworks, too, consist of multiple scenes and are meant to be viewed slowly, unravelling their historical stories one incident at a time. Their very long horizontal formats take the viewer on a visual journey through history.

The 275-foot-long *Bayeux Tapestry* records the events surrounding the Battle of Hastings (1066), in which the Normans, led by William the Conqueror, seized control of England from the Anglo-Saxons. It was probably commissioned by William's brother Odo, the Bishop of Bayeux in France, shortly after the Norman victory. The so-called **tapestry** was actually embroidered by women (legend says William's wife was one of the embroiderers), and took more than ten years

to complete. It shows the events that led to the battle, the preparations of the Norman fleet, the Battle of Hastings itself, and finally the coronation of William the Conqueror as King of England. More than six hundred men, but only three women, are shown in the fifty scenes on the tapestry. The embroiderers were highly skilled. To establish a sense of depth, each figure is given a border, which is filled in with stitches running in the opposite direction to the rest of the embroidery, and then outlined in boldly contrasting colors. The process creates clearly delineated figures, a flat sense of space (to guide the viewer in a horizontal direction), and, through repeated patterns, a sense of overall **rhythm**.

The *Night Attack on the Sanjo Palace* (**4.111**) is one scene from one of five long painted scrolls that depict battles from the *Tale of the Heiji Rebellion*, a Japanese war epic about the short-lived Heiji era (1159–60). In this period several clans fought for control of Kyoto, the historical capital of Japan. This scene shows the burning of the palace by samurai warriors of the Fujiwara and Minamoto clans during the raid in which

4.110 Detail of Battle of Hastings, *Bayeux Tapestry*, c. 1066–82. Linen with wool, 275′ long. Bayeux Tapestry Museum, Bayeux, France

4.111 *Night Attack on the Sanjo Palace*, from *Heiji Monogatari*, Kamakura period, late 13th century. Hand scroll, ink and color on paper, 16⅛" × 22'11¼" (whole scroll). Museum of Fine Arts, Boston

they captured the Emperor Nijo. Soon afterward, another clan, the Taira, rescued the emperor and regained control of Kyoto.

Like the *Bayeux Tapestry*, the *Night Attack on the Sanjo Palace* is representative of the visual style of its period. The 23-foot-long Japanese scroll employs **isometric perspective** from a bird's-eye view: the diagonal lines of the buildings and the layering of the figures function as a kind of guide to direct the viewer (reading from right to left) from one scene to the next. The horses and warriors are carefully delineated and detailed. The precise lines and limited use of blurry brushwork (as in the horses' tails and the billowing smoke) demonstrate the artist's intense skill.

As with the sculptures of the Toltec warriors, the attention to detail in both the Japanese scroll and the Norman tapestry gives us a strong sense of the equipment and weapons used by the warriors of these peoples. The Japanese samurai

are shown covered in intricately detailed armor atop their fine and powerful horses. Lengthy bows and arching swords are their weapons of choice. The soldiers of the Bayeux tapestry wear patterned armor and conical helmets, and carry broadswords, kite-shaped shields, and spears.

The Artist's Response to War

Artists have often created artworks that attempt to convey their personal experience of war. This is sometimes a cathartic exercise, releasing emotion, and it is sometimes meant to inspire awareness of the realities of war. But by no means all powerful responses to war have been created by artists who actually witnessed the events they portray. Artists can produce powerful visual statements about the horrors of war from both their experiences and their own imagination. (See the Perspectives on Art Boxes: Michael Fay, *Storm and Stone*: An Artist at War, pp. 538–9, and Wafaa Bilal, *Domestic Tension*: An Artist's Protest against War, p. 540.)

Medium (plural **media**): the material on or from which an artist chooses to make a work of art
Tapestry: hand-woven fabric—usually silk or wool—with a non-repeating, usually figurative, design woven into it
Rhythm: the regular or ordered repetition of elements in the work
Isometric perspective: a system using diagonal parallel lines to communicate depth

Perspectives on Art: Michael Fay
Storm and Stone: An Artist at War

Michael Fay was a combat artist in the United States Marine Corps. He is now retired from the Marines. As he says, "I am a combat artist. My job is simple, go to war, do art." Here he explains how he created one of his works and why, even in war, fine art has value.

I am often asked why, in our era of instant digital satellite imagery, the traditional practice of fine art is still valid in capturing images of war. Perhaps the answer lies in the "slowed" vision of the images. With a painting or sculpture the artist can take many personal impressions, images, and memories and through the creative process distill them into a single composite creation. War is often seen as one of the most potentially dehumanizing and destructive experiences and perhaps it is also reassuring that artists are still willing to witness and create from it.

My painting, *Storm and Stone*, is a composite of personal experiences while deployed to Afghanistan during the spring

4.112 Michael Fay, *Storm and Stone*

of 2005 (**4.112**). I participated in a long-range patrol into the foothills of the Tora Bora Mountains to a place called Wazir Pass. The ride there was a bone-jarring journey crisscrossing rivers swollen with the spring melt, and along rocky trails lined with mulberry trees, and whitewashed stone cairns warning of minefields.

The German painter Otto Dix (1891–1969), who fought in World War I, recorded the horrors he witnessed in the painted **triptych** *The War* (**4.113**). The central panel shows death and destruction. A soldier wearing a gas mask, representing Dix himself, witnesses the devastation first hand. Bloody bodies are piled on top of one another, one with legs in the air. Chaos fills the scene. Arched pieces of metal stretch out across the sky and support a skeletal figure, whose outstretched finger points toward the bullet-ridden body on the right. The arching forms enclose the scene, leaving us feeling smothered by the horror that is shown. Our anxiety is increased with nothing to calm us or to rest our eyes upon.

The left wing of the triptych shows heavily equipped soldiers, united in their duty and prepared for battle. The scene precedes the horror that will take place in the central panel. The right-hand wing shows a man, a self-portrait of Dix, carrying a wounded soldier. The sky in the triptych symbolizes the increasing danger of the situation, beginning on the left with pale sunlight, moving toward foreboding clouds, and ending with a stormy and destructive sky on the right. Underneath the central panel, in a section called the **predella**, Dix has painted a sleeping or dead soldier, lying in a trench.

The triptych format is traditionally used for religious scenes, with Christ's crucifixion portrayed in the center and his entombment in the predella below. By using this format, Dix elevates the importance of his subject matter. And in associating an ordinary soldier with the soon-to-be-resurrected Christ, he endows him with the status of a martyr.

Everywhere you looked there was the intense beauty of earth and sky framed by snow-capped peaks. At the same time this beauty was juxtaposed with the imminent threat of a violent death.

Our first night out was marked by the most violent thunderstorm I've ever witnessed. In the lightning flashes through thick curtains of torrential rain I could see fellow Marines being rolled about in uprooted tents. Later, in the damp inky blackness, I could hear them stumbling about righting gear and nursing bruised bodies. With the next day's dawn the phrase *storm and stone* was deeply etched in my mind.

Storm and Stone is essentially figures in a landscape. I wanted to express several key elements: an expanse of space, groups of figures, and the approach of a storm. But I also wanted to get something of the feeling of being far off the beaten path in the most violent and dangerous place on Earth. From field sketches and photos I created two distinct groups of figures. To the far left are four Marines, the basic "fire team," and at the right is a lieutenant pointing into the distance while conferring with his sergeant. I deliberately left a void, a source of visual tension, in the middle. I was not after a well-balanced soothing pastoral effect, but rather something unsettling that went to the core of my own personal experience on that particular patrol.

My own artistic impulse is *naturalistic*, to render as closely as possible the reality of what is before me in the context of my own experience. It is also my hope that this personal experience, though grounded in realism, is more poetry than prose, and more art than journalism. I have been to war; in the heat, watchful and tense at the beginning of a dawn raid; surrounded by children at the edge of a soccer field littered with unexploded mortar rounds; confronted by the slack and ashen gray faces of friends killed in battle. I have been discomfited by the horrors and boredom of war, and at the same time filled with the mystery of people and places in times of conflict. It is from this internal chemistry, steeped in genuine experience and rooted more in art than science, that I've tried to create an exterior reality, a body of authentic artwork flowing from the most controversial and demanding of human experiences... war.

Triptych: an artwork comprising three painted or carved panels, normally joined together and sharing a common theme
Predella: an artwork designed as a companion piece to a more important work

4.113 Otto Dix, *The War*, 1929–32. Oil and tempera on wood, 6'8⅜" × 13'4¾". Staatliche Kunstsammlungen, Gemäldegalerie Neue Meister, Dresden, Germany

Perspectives on Art: Wafaa Bilal
Domestic Tension: An Artist's Protest against War

4.114 Wafaa Bilal, *Domestic Tension*

Iraqi-born Wafaa Bilal teaches photography and art and technology at the School of the Art Institute of Chicago. His art reflects his concerns with the injustices committed in Iraq under the dictatorial regime of Saddam Hussein and, since then, during American military operations in the country.

As an Iraqi artist living in the U.S. since 1992, I have created many provocative works to raise awareness and create dialog about U.S.–Iraq conflicts. But when my brother Haji was killed by an American bomb at a checkpoint in our hometown of Kufa, Iraq, in 2004, the war became deeply personal.

I had to find an unconventional new approach to translate this tragic event into a work of art that empowered its audience. Not something that lectured the audience, nor something dogmatic, but a dynamic encounter between me and my audience.

A TV news segment about a soldier in Colorado remotely dropping bombs on Iraq highlighted the anonymous and detached nature of this current war, and the complete disconnect between the comfort zone here in the U.S. and the conflict zone in my home country. I needed to create a platform for people to be nudged out of their comfort zone.

The result was an interactive performance entitled *Domestic Tension* (**4.114**). I stayed in a Chicago gallery for a month with a paintball gun aimed at me. People could control the paintball gun, and command it to shoot at me, over the Internet.

I wanted to create a virtual and physical platform, turning the virtual to physical and vice versa, and, by putting my body on the line, create a physical impact in viewers by enabling them to identify with the physical effect on my body.

The project generated worldwide attention, with more than 60,000 shots taken and 80 million hits to the website from 137 countries.

I never anticipated how many people would be drawn to the project and how it would become a truly dynamic artwork in which the viewers had control over the **narrative**. It achieved an unexpected goal of democratizing the process of the viewing and the making of the artwork, by enabling the audience to participate.

As evidenced by dialog on the website's chat room, the experience had a profound impact on many people from all sides of the political spectrum. At the conclusion of the project, I felt fulfilled in my mantra that, "Today we silenced one gun; hopefully one day we will silence all guns."

4.115 Anselm Kiefer, *Breaking of the Vessels*, 1990. Lead, iron, glass, copper wire, charcoal, and Aquatec, 12′5″ × 27′5½″ × 17′. St. Louis Art Museum, Missouri

Narrative: an artwork that tells a story

During World War II, Otto Dix's work was censored by the Nazis for its negative presentation of war. The contemporary German artist Anselm Kiefer (b. 1945) addresses such censorship in his work. Kiefer was born in Germany just months before World War II ended. He grew up in a society ashamed of its past. His artworks force viewers to acknowledge the horrors of the Nazi regime that ruled Germany from 1933 until 1945. His attempts to confront this past have often shocked and angered Germans. For example, he photographed himself making the Nazi salute—a gesture that has been illegal in Germany since 1945.

Kiefer's *Breaking of the Vessels* conveys the loss of life and the destruction of knowledge caused by the extermination of millions of Jews during the Holocaust (**4.115**). The imposing 27-foot-tall artwork is made of lead and glass. The heavy lead books appear to be scorched, just like the human beings (also holders of knowledge) who were incinerated in concentration camps. The shattered glass also recalls *Kristallnacht* (Night of the Broken Glass), when the Nazis destroyed hundreds of Jewish stores and synagogues in 1938. The splintered glass on the ground makes any access to these books of knowledge a dangerous and frightening proposition. Symbolically, Kiefer has conveyed the fear and pain one must face to confront the past.

In *Breaking of the Vessels*, Kiefer draws upon the Jewish religion and more specifically the Kabbalah, a collection of Jewish mystical writings. The words "Ain-Sof," which mean the infinite presence of God, are written on the arched piece of glass above the bookshelf. Ten lead labels are placed around and on the bookshelf; these represent the ten vessels containing the essence of God as described in the Kabbalah. In this way, the books represent the presence of God even in the midst of human destruction.

Discussion Questions

1. Find an artwork that depicts a battle. Perhaps choose one from the Revolutionary War, Civil War, or a famous battle from European history. Study the history of the battle and then ask yourself whether the artist recorded the event accurately. Did he or she try to persuade the viewer to support one side in the battle? How?

2. Find a photograph that documents a scene from the Civil War, World War II, or the Vietnam War. Considering the elements and principles of art discussed in Part 1 of this book, perform a visual analysis of the photograph. What does this tell you about the way the artist used the medium of photography to convey a message?

3. Study images of the entirety of the *Bayeux Tapestry* and of the *Heiji Monogatari* scroll. Bearing in mind the format of these works, how do they use their format to convey a narrative? Stylistically, how does each artwork show scenes of battle?

4.8

Art of Social Conscience

The visual language of art can be an extremely effective medium for communicating a point of view on social issues. While words can describe an event, art can demonstrate it visually with raw power. Art often reflects historical, social, and political concerns. It can even provoke change. Artists can spur people to become involved in a social issue, and can call for the punishment of those responsible for a wrong. Art is able to arouse such strong emotions that artworks themselves can become the focus of protest, sometimes suffering damage or destruction as a result. Art can commemorate with enormous power the sacrifices made by individuals or an entire nation.

It can also inspire us toward a better and more just world. This chapter is concerned with the ways that artists have expressed their convictions through artworks that have, at times, caused powerful, even violent, reactions.

Art as Social Protest

By creating potent artworks that activate emotional responses, artists can instigate social change. Here we examine artworks that have sought to combat cruelty and slavery, and protested against the barbarities of war. And, closer to

4.116 Théodore Géricault, *Raft of the Medusa*, 1819. Oil on canvas, 12′1³⁄₈″ × 17′9⁷⁄₈″. Musée du Louvre, Paris, France

Perspectives on Art: Dan Tague
Art Made from Dollar Bills

4.117 Dan Tague, *Unite NOLA*, 2008. Archival inkjet print on rag paper, 42 × 34". Collection New Orleans Museum of Art

*The American artist Dan Tague (b. 1974) lives and works in New Orleans. He was displaced for a year after Hurricane Katrina, in 2005. When he returned to the city he created a series of works made from folded dollar bills to protest at the lack of resources to rebuild New Orleans (**4.117**). Here he explains why and how he made these artworks.*

The appeal and power of money are the issues at the core of this series. In a capitalist society cash rules everything. Society teaches us that you can buy love, happiness, and status through possessions. You can even right wrongs by taking away a bit of someone's happiness through fines and lawsuits. Politicians buy votes through claims of lowering taxes.

Lack of money was the reason that the rebuilding of New Orleans was slow and for most of the city non-existent for well over a year after Katrina devastated the city. Displaced, confused, and feeling neglected, I decided to use the design qualities of dollar bills, which contain detailed decorative engravings, masterful portraits and architectural renderings, and elegant type. I folded and twisted the bills to create **abstract** imagery. The precise and calculated folds of the bills combined to make political messages from the letters on the bills in such works as *Unite NOLA* (New Orleans, LA) as a battle cry for the community and the nation to take action; *Home Is a Tent*, inspired by people living in a tent city; and *The End Is Near*, referring to the failing economy and failure to rebuild the city.

I scanned the folded bills at very high resolution and made ink-jet prints on archival rag paper. I made fifteen prints and showed them at the Jonathan Ferrara Gallery, in New Orleans, and later at galleries in New York, North Carolina, and Florida.

home, we look at a project that focused attention on the plight of the people of New Orleans after Hurricane Katrina in 2005 (see Perspectives on Art Box: Dan Tague: Art Made from Dollar Bills). While considering this section's protest artworks from past and present, also think about your own response. Does the artist inspire you to agree with his or her point of view?

The painting *Raft of the Medusa* (**4.116**), by the French artist Théodore Géricault (1791–1824), memorializes on a grand scale a scandalous event in history. On July 2, 1816, the French naval vessel *Medusa* ran aground off the coast of West Africa. While the captain and approximately 250 crew boarded the lifeboats, the rest of the passengers—146 men and one woman, some of them slaves—got onto a makeshift raft that had been built from the wreckage. Although the raft was pulled by the lifeboats initially, the captain soon abandoned it. Left to battle starvation, sunburn, disease, and dehydration, only fifteen men survived the horrors of the sea; some cannibalized their shipmates. Géricault's painting shows with emotional intensity the moment when the raft's survivors are about to be rescued.

Géricault interviewed the survivors, studied corpses, and even had a replica of the raft built in his studio in preparation for this project. The

Abstract: an artwork the form of which is simplified, distorted, or exaggerated in appearance. It may represent a recognizable form that has been slightly altered, or it may be a completely non-representational depiction

survivors told him of their despair and madness
when they saw a ship on the horizon on the
thirteenth day. They had seen ships in the distance
before but the ships' crews had not seen them, and
many feared this ship, too, would disappear. But
the survivors, all close to death, were rescued, and
they told the world the story of their abandonment.

In *Raft of the Medusa*, Géricault depicts the
emotions of the survivors. Several men, their
arms reaching out toward the tiny ship in the
distance, convey desperate hope. Another is
shown still slouched in despair, and surrounded
by corpses; he even holds one on his lap. The
artist painted the skin of the men with a green
pallor to indicate that they are near to death.
Yet the musculature of their bodies gives them
nobility. Standing at the painting's apex, atop
a pyramid of bodies, a black man waves a piece of
his clothing to get the attention of the ship in the
distance. The dramatic intensity is heightened by
the use of diagonal lines that compose the figures
into a large X. From the bottom left corner of the
composition the bodies of the men are arranged
in a line that leads the viewer's eye to the black
man in the upper right. An opposing diagonal is

made from the mast in the upper left to the nude
male body on the lower right, which appears to be
falling from the raft.

Géricault's picture criticizes not only the
Medusa disaster but also colonization and slavery.
Although only one African survived the wreck,
Géricault includes three in this painting,
including the powerful figure trying to attract
the attention of the distant ship.

A couple of decades later, the British painter
J. M. W. Turner (1775–1851) created a painting
that also condemned the slave trade (**4.118**).
Although slavery was illegal by this time
throughout Britain, Turner was highlighting the
injustice of the slave trade and protesting against
any consideration of its renewal. His dramatic
canvas portrays an infamous incident aboard the
slave ship *Zong* in 1781. It was common practice
for slave-ship captains to fill their vessels with
more slaves than they would need, knowing that
disease might spread amongst them. The captain
of the *Zong* knew that he would be paid for any
slaves lost at sea, but not for those who were sick
when they arrived. He therefore had sick slaves
thrown overboard while still far from land.

4.118 Joseph Mallord
William Turner, *Slave Ship
(Slavers Throwing Overboard
the Dead and Dying, Typhoon
Coming On)*, 1840. Oil on
canvas, 35¾ × 48¼". Museum
of Fine Arts, Boston

Turner's chaotic canvas shows a fierce storm. Body parts, still shackled and being attacked by sharp-teethed fish, can be seen in the central and right foreground. Turner uses intense colors and turbulent brushstrokes to convey the heightened emotion of the event. Man versus nature was a common theme in art during the nineteenth century, and here the immense power of nature overpowers the slaves. Turner's canvas has an abstract quality, making its subject matter difficult to understand. Turner placed beside his painting a quotation from the book that had inspired it, in order to help viewers understand his artwork's meaning.

The Spanish artist Pablo Picasso (1881–1973) painted *Guernica* as a passionate response to the aerial attack carried out on April 26, 1937, on a small town of that name in northern Spain (**4.119**). During the Spanish Civil War, the Nationalist general Francisco Franco, who would later become the country's ruler, allowed German and Italian planes to test their bombing tactics on Guernica and learn about the psychological effects of air warfare. More than 1,000 civilians were killed in three hours of bombing. News of the attack quickly spread to Paris, where Picasso read stories and saw photographs of the devastation.

While the general meaning of *Guernica* is clearly outrage against the violence directed at the citizens of the small Spanish town, Picasso never explained the specific symbolism of the figures in the painting, nor elaborated on his political motivations for the work. Picasso would have accepted all interpretations because he believed in viewers making their own reading of an artwork. He stated:

> A picture is not thought out and settled beforehand. While it is being done it changes as one's thoughts change. And when it is finished, it still goes on changing, according to the state of mind of whoever is looking at it.

The painting is black, gray, and white, perhaps because Picasso associated the attack with black-and-white newspaper photographs. The small dashes on the body of the horse also seem to recall the print from a newspaper. Expressive faces with distorted necks scream and cry in despair. On the right, a figure reaches to the sky as it escapes from a burning building; flames appear like scales on the back of a dragon. The tortured figure on the left experiences the horror of her child's murder.

The bull, often associated with the violence of Spanish bullfighting, is seen by many as a symbol of Franco. The terrified horse, as it tramples upon a man lying on the ground, may represent the chaos inflicted upon the people by the attack.

4.119 Pablo Picasso, *Guernica*, 1937. Oil on canvas, 11′5½″ × 25′5¾″. Museo Nacional Centro de Arte Reina Sofía, Madrid, Spain

The lightbulb shining powerfully at the top of the canvas may symbolize awareness and knowledge, as if illuminating the situation.

Picasso exhibited this large protest statement at the Spanish Pavilion during the 1937 World's Fair in Paris, France, and declared that neither he nor the painting would go to Spain as long as Franco ruled. The artwork travelled the world before coming to rest in New York's Museum of Modern Art. Franco died in 1975, two years after Picasso. In 1981, *Guernica* was finally sent to Madrid, Spain, to be exhibited permanently.

Many artists use the plight of a single person to address larger social problems (see Gateway Box: Lange). The movie *Hotel Rwanda* (2004) increased the American public's awareness of the 1994 genocide of 800,000 Tutsi people by Hutu militias in the small Central African country of Rwanda (**4.120**). The killings resulted in the deaths of approximately one out of every seven Rwandans. The film, which tells the true story of one man's personal sacrifice during the atrocities, is also a protest against the world's failure to intervene. The Irish director Terry George (b. 1952) focuses the story on a single individual to reveal the impact one person can have, even on a monumental problem.

Paul Rusesabagina, manager of the Hôtel des Milles Collines, protected more than 1,000 hotel guests, mostly vulnerable Tutsi, when the violence broke out. The film depicts the atrocities he witnessed, and shows him risking his own life to get supplies for the people hiding in his hotel. The film also highlights the role played by the Americans and the Europeans in allowing the war to continue. The weapons possessed by the Hutu, we learn, were obtained from France and Belgium. The local presence of the United Nations is depicted as ineffective and helpless. Through the medium of film, Terry makes the unimaginable vividly real, and condemns the violence in Rwanda and the lack of intervention by the world community. The film's goal is to inspire more activism against contemporary genocides.

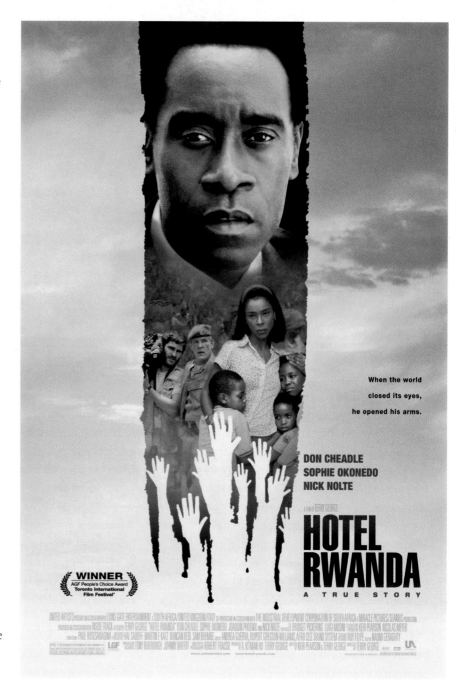

Art as the Object of Protest

Art can inspire a forceful response. Sometimes the power of a work of art is such that viewers wish to destroy it, along with the message or attitude they see represented in it. The following two artworks were not made in protest at a social issue. They were, in fact, not intended to be offensive to anyone. Each, however, came to represent something offensive or even dangerous to somebody.

Medium (plural **media**): the material on or from which an artist chooses to make a work of art

Gateway to Art: Lange, *Migrant Mother*
The Impact and Ethics of Documentary Photography

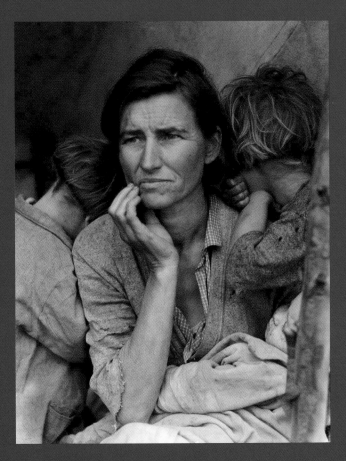

4.121 Dorothea Lange, *Migrant Mother*, 1936. Library of Congress, Washington, D.C.

Dorothea Lange's famous photograph of Florence Thompson, known as the *Migrant Mother*, was used to demonstrate the plight of the poor and remains a powerful symbol of the struggle against poverty (**4.121**). The picture was taken in 1936 when Florence and her children were living in the remains of a Californian pea-picker's camp. Lange's image had an immediate impact. The photograph was published in several newspapers and *Time* magazine. The federal government sent 20,000 pounds of food to the camp. Unfortunately, the Thompson family had migrated elsewhere before the supplies arrived.

While the photograph had an incalculable affect on people's understanding of the devastation of the Great Depression, Thompson herself was always ashamed and irritated by the portrait. To her mind, it never had a positive effect on her life. When the photograph was taken she was recently widowed, had six children, and worked wherever she could to support her family. She eventually had eleven children, and lived in fear that if the government knew of her financial difficulties they might take her children away. The identity of Thompson was not discovered until 1978, and she was quoted as saying, "I wish she hadn't taken my picture," and complained about never being compensated.

After Thompson's death, her children spoke of the frustration the photograph caused them as well. When they first saw their mother's photograph in a newspaper in 1936, with an ink mark across her forehead, they assumed she had been shot and ran home, relieved to find her there alive and well. Additionally, Lange's notes seem to have mixed up the details of the Thompsons with another family. The newspapers never mentioned that Thompson was a native American who became a migrant when she was displaced from her tribal land at a young age. It was not until 1983, when Florence lay on her deathbed, and letters of sympathy poured in, that the children changed their outlook:

> None of us really understood how deeply Mama's photo affected people...it gave us a sense of pride.

The experience of the Thompson family raises questions of the role of an artist when depicting an actual event. To what extent should the subject's privacy be protected, and to what extent should they be compensated, if at all, when their image has demonstrable effects on the social conscience? Because photography is a **medium** that can be reproduced and manipulated, an image like *Migrant Mother* also raises the ethical question of how such an image should be used later. Lange's photograph continues to be a symbol of people struggling against poverty and deprivation. Since 1936 it has been published many times in books and newspapers and has twice featured on U.S. postage stamps.

4.122b (above) Photograph of damage to the *Rokeby Venus* caused by Mary Richardson, 1914

4.122a Diego Velázquez, *The Toilet of Venus (Rokeby Venus)*, 1647–51. Oil on canvas 48¼ × 69¾". National Gallery, London, England

The *Rokeby Venus* (or *The Toilet of Venus*) by the Spanish artist Diego Velázquez (1599–1660) (**4.122a**) may seem inoffensive to the modern viewer, but in 1914 it was the target of a violent protest. A woman called Mary Richardson, armed with a meat cleaver she had hidden inside her coat, slashed the *Rokeby Venus* seven times (**4.122b**). Richardson was a member of the Suffragette movement, which campaigned to give women the right to vote. For her, the painting represented a sexist definition of ideal beauty, showing a woman solely as an object of male desire. Richardson was motivated more specifically to protest against the imprisonment of the Suffragette leader Emmeline Pankhurst. Richardson later explained that she believed justice to be more valuable than art:

> I have tried to destroy the picture of the most beautiful woman in mythological history as a protest against the Government for destroying Mrs. Pankhurst, who is the most beautiful character in modern history.

Richardson's attack on the painting did not have its intended effect on perceptions of the *Rokeby Venus*. The seven slashes were soon completely repaired, and many still consider the painting to be a defining representation of female sensuality and beauty. Richardson was imprisoned briefly after the attack; the incident did not seem to help the Suffragette movement either (although some women did gain the right to vote in Britain in 1918). For a while after the incident, in fact, women were forbidden to enter the National Gallery, unless they were accompanied by a male chaperone.

While Velázquez's Venus was the subject of protest centuries after its creation, the American artist Eric Fischl's (b. 1948) *Falling Woman* provoked an instantaneous reaction (**4.123**). When the bronze sculpture, intended as a tribute to the victims of the terror attacks of September 11, 2001, was unveiled in New York City, it was

4.123 Eric Fischl, *Falling Woman*, 2001–2. Bronze, 38 × 72 × 48". Private collection considered so offensive that it was covered over almost immediately. It shows a woman in freefall, with her legs above her head and her arms flailing. Fischl placed a poem next to his artwork:

> We watched,
> Disbelieving and helpless,
> On that savage day.
> People we love
> Began falling,
> Helpless and in disbelief.

Many New Yorkers had witnessed firsthand the tragedy of desperate victims, trapped in the World Trade Center towers, jumping to their deaths to escape the fire. Perhaps because of this, Fischl's sculpture, displayed only a year after the terrorist attack, was seen as too potent and heart-wrenching. The artwork and the response to it reflect one of the challenges artists face when they address contemporary issues. Would Fischl's sculpture have been accepted if it had been unveiled many years later, when the event was no longer fresh in the minds of so many? Or was it simply too graphic, depicting a moment too shocking and too unbelievable for people ever to want to remember?

Some viewers, however, were upset that the sculpture was covered up, considering it a powerful reminder and a valid, even cathartic (emotionally releasing) response to what happened. "The sculpture was not meant to hurt anybody," said the artist:

> It was a sincere expression of the deepest sympathy for the vulnerability of the human condition. Both specifically towards the victims of Sept. 11 and towards humanity in general.

In 1996 a movement known as the Taliban took control of the government of Afghanistan. The Taliban forbade the practice of all religions other than Islam, including the representation of figures from those religions. In the Bamiyan valley in Afghanistan, more than 800 caves are carved into the cliffs, which were used as Buddhist temples and monasteries between the fifth and the ninth centuries CE. Within most of these caves were small sculptures and wall paintings of Buddhas and other religious figures. The cliff face also held two colossal sculptures of Buddha, one of them the tallest in the world at 175 feet (**4.124a**).

Ignoring appeals from the international community, the Taliban dynamited the colossal Bamiyan sculptures in 2001 (**4.124b**). They also destroyed hundreds of artworks in the caves, and

4.124a and **4.124b** Colossal Buddha from Bamiyan, Afghanistan, 6th or 7th century CE, destroyed by Taliban, 2001. Before and after destruction

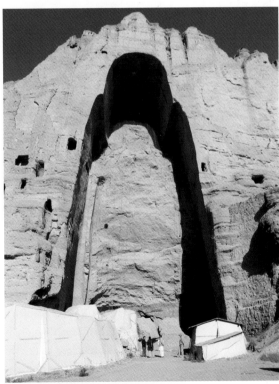

Iconoclasm: Destruction of Religious Images

4.125 *Virgin and Child Surrounded by Saints*, 6th century. Encaustic, 27 × 19⅝". Monastery of St. Catherine, Sinai, Egypt

Icons, or religious images, are designed to create a state of meditation, in which the artworks are studied for long periods, inspiring worship. Iconoclasm, or the destruction of religious images, shows the power art can have, and the fear its power can generate. The Byzantine Empire's iconoclastic controversy in the eighth and ninth centuries was provoked by divisions among Christians over the interpretation of the Bible's Second Commandment: "You shall not make for yourself an idol in the form of anything in heaven above or on the earth beneath or in the waters below. You shall not bow down to them or worship them." Some Christians took this commandment to mean that icons, which might inspire too much worship, should be prohibited.

A study of the icon *Virgin and Child Surrounded by Saints* (**4.125**) can help us understand why the **iconoclasts** were so concerned that Christians might confuse worship of an image with worship of the holy figures themselves. In the icon, Mary initially attracts our attention because she sits in the center, wearing a dark purple gown (the imperial color), and presents Christ, who sits on her lap. The bearded St. Theodore and the beardless St. George stand slightly in front of the Virgin's throne. The saints are closest to us because they are human and therefore most like us. A hierarchy is thus created as we "enter" the picture through them and become closer to Mary, who is herself an intercessor for Christ. The two figures behind the enthroned Mary are angels looking up at heaven. Their gaze reminds Christian believers that the figures in the icon will bring them closer to the heavens above.

Iconoclasts believed that the faithful were worshiping icons of religious figures rather than worshiping Mary and Jesus directly. This fundamental disagreement led to the destruction of thousands of Byzantine icons, including almost all portrayals of Christ and Mary. Most of the surviving icons from before the ninth century are in St. Catherine's Monastery at the foot of Mount Sinai, where they were protected by their location in the Egyptian desert. Iconoclasm has occurred many times in the history of humankind, whenever people passionately believe that certain art has gained too much influence and power.

when paintings could not be completely removed from the walls, they scraped out the eyes of the faces. That such destruction happened at Bamiyan is particularly disheartening: located on the Silk Road, a centuries-old trade route running from China to the Mediterranean, it was historically a place where cultures from East and West had met and exchanged ideas. The sculptures reflected this blending of cultures, fusing two very different styles. The body forms and facial features followed Asian traditions, while the figures wore drapery represented in a manner derived from the artistic style of the ancient Greeks.

The Taliban said that they destroyed the Buddhas because they considered them to be false idols (see Box: Iconoclasm: Destruction of Religious Images). They later argued, however, that they had destroyed the artworks to protest that so many countries wanted to give money to preserve the statues but did not think to make donations to help feed the people of Afghanistan. Many people believed that the Taliban would use any donations for weapons instead of helping the people. Today the Bamiyan area is still a refuge for the poor, and the enormous cliffs and niches that were made for the now destroyed sculptures can be seen from miles away, an ever-present reminder of their violent destruction.

Memorials and Remembrance

Art can serve as a way to acknowledge a historical tragedy, mistreatment, or suffering, often in the hope that similar events will not be repeated. Memorials may address the history of a single individual or of many people. While memorials are often designed to promote healing and comfort the grieving, they can also be statements of tragedy, and can fuel uprisings. They can also express hope for a better world in the future.

The French artist Jacques-Louis David (1748–1825) memorialized the French revolutionary leader Jean-Paul Marat in a painting completed a few months after his murder (**4.126**). Marat, who suffered from a skin disease that required him to spend much of his time in a medicinal bath, worked and even received visitors while in his tub. A young woman named Charlotte Corday, who claimed to have the names of conspirators working against the French revolutionaries, in fact supported a political party opposed to Marat; she stabbed him in his bathtub on July 13, 1793. Corday was executed by guillotine for the murder.

David, a close friend of Marat, was a master of propaganda. In order to fuel the revolutionaries' anger, he organized a spectacle two days after Marat's death, which included a public viewing of Marat's corpse. The body was nude from the waist up to display the wound. The dead man's bathtub, the wooden crate on which he wrote, and his inkpot and pen were also carried in procession behind him. Later, David organized a ceremonial viewing of his

Icon: a small, often portable, religious image venerated by Christian believers; first used by the Eastern Orthodox Church

Iconoclast: someone who destroys imagery, often out of religious belief

4.126 Jacques-Louis David, *Death of Marat*, 1793. Oil on canvas, 5'3" × 4'1". Musée Royale des Beaux-Arts, Brussels, Belgium

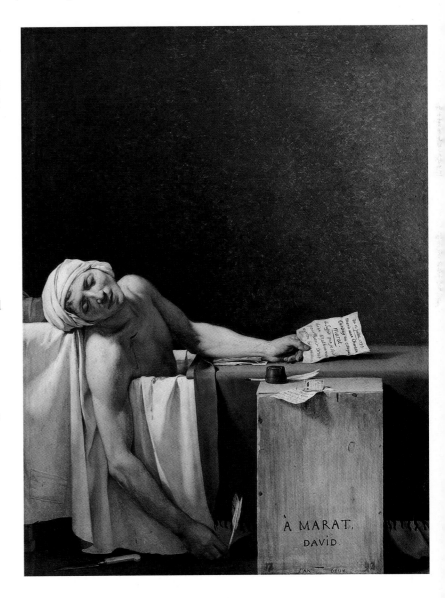

painting, on the same day that the queen, Marie Antoinette, the symbol of the selfish waste of the French monarchy, was guillotined.

In this painting, David portrays Marat as if in a tomb. The bathtub resembles a rectangular box, like a coffin, covered by green cloth. The box placed next to the bathtub represents a tombstone, with a dedication to the fallen leader: "To Marat, [from] David." It is dated from the beginning of the revolutionaries' new regime: "Year Two." In the painting, Marat's left hand holds the note from Charlotte Corday that allowed her to visit him. The letter on the crate is an offer of money to a widowed mother of five, suggesting that Marat was a generous man. The stab wound and knife on the ground highlight the violence of his death. Marat's pose is that of a martyr.

The Vietnam Veterans Memorial was built in Washington, D.C., to pay tribute to many fallen men and women and in the hope of laying to rest some of the lingering controversy over the war (**4.127**). The design itself was immediately controversial, however. The competition to design the monument—which drew more than 1,400 submissions—was won by a 21-year-old American of Chinese descent studying architecture at Yale University. Maya Lin (b. 1959) envisaged her monument as a place for mourning and healing. A black-granite, V-shaped wall descends into the earth, and then ascends, giving one a sense of coming into the light. The wall also becomes taller as one descends, creating a

4.127 Maya Lin, Vietnam Veterans Memorial, Washington, D.C., 1981–3. Granite, each wing 246' long, 10'1" high at highest point

powerful visual expression for the enormous loss of life during the war. It symbolizes the eternal wound in America caused by the conflict, but also the healing that Lin hoped would take place as those who experienced the monument would physically rise again.

The names of the dead are carved into the wall and organized by the date of death. The surface is polished because, the artist explained, "the point is to see yourself reflected in the names." The walls are aligned toward two other monuments, the Washington Monument and the Lincoln Memorial. The integration of the Vietnam Veterans Memorial with these important structures acknowledges the significance of the Vietnam War to American history.

Lin intended the memorial as a tribute, and most visitors are moved upon experiencing it. Some veterans, however, saw it as part of a continued condemnation of the war. Rather than uplifting and instilling pride in the soldiers who fought, they said, the monument's descent into the ground symbolized a moral criticism both of the war and its soldiers. They also perceived the choice of black granite, as opposed to the more conventional pure white marble, as a criticism. In response to these protests, a bronze sculpture of three soldiers, more traditional in style, was later placed a short distance from the wall.

The Chinese artist Wenda Gu (b. 1956) says that he makes his so-called "hair monuments" in an effort to unite the people of the world through a chain of artworks. The monuments are made of walls or screens woven from human hair that has been donated by people from countries around the globe. Gu then paints what appear to be **ideograms** (symbols that convey the meaning of words) with a brush that is itself made from human strands of hair. The signs he paints are simply suggestive of particular cultures rather than literal transcriptions. *China Monument: Temple of Heaven* (**4.128**) is reminiscent of a Buddhist temple in which one partakes of a tea ceremony, and includes ancient-looking Chinese tables and chairs. Video monitors in each chair seat show clouds, so that the people experiencing this artwork are given the sense that they are sitting in the heavens. The artist's words are also seen in the video. When translated, they read:

4.128 Wenda Gu, *United Nations—China Monument: Temple of Heaven*, 1998. Mixed media, 52 × 20 × 13'. Hong Kong Museum of Art

Ideogram: a symbol that expresses an idea or a thing without representing the sounds in its name (for example, "8")

Ancient wisdom says that life is as fleeting as clouds…

you shall sit…
you shall listen…
you shall be silent…
you shall meditate…
you shall be free from gender, nationalities, races, politics, cultures, religions…
you shall fantasize while you ride on running clouds…
you shall have moments of transcending…

The space also unites a variety of cultures by including symbols that imitate Arabic, Hindi, and Chinese, as well as the Latin alphabet used by western languages. Gu's *United Nations* series of hair monuments has been made in more than twenty countries on five continents. More than a million people have contributed their hair to this series. Humans around the world are thus physically connected, through their common biology, in Gu's work. The artist hopes someday to create monuments in every country in the world, linking all the different cultures of humanity.

Discussion Questions

1 In this chapter we have studied many ways in which artists have made a powerful case about an issue that concerned them. Now ask yourself what issue you feel most passionately about, and create an artwork that communicates your ideas. Be persuasive and try to convey the reasons you believe as you do.

2 Study artworks in this chapter that have been censored or in some other way withheld from public view. Are there any other works you have read about that the public has been prevented from seeing? Do you believe that artworks should never be censored, or do you think that there are some subjects that should be banned? Write half a page defending your belief in the limits or freedom of expression in art, using at least two specific artworks as examples to make your point.

3 Which of the artworks in this chapter do you find to be the most moving or persuasive? Considering the elements and principles of art discussed in Part 1 of this book, perform a visual analysis of the artwork and consider what the artist did (in your opinion) so successfully.

4.9

The Body in Art

The human form is one of the most common subjects in art. Some of the earliest sculptures made during **prehistoric** times depict human figures. Since then, artists have continued to portray the body, both clothed and unclothed, in motion and in repose. The body is not always portrayed as it "actually looks," and it may even be altered so much that it does not resemble a real human body at all. The reality of the body can be distorted to suggest great beauty, or to emphasize such qualities as power, status, wisdom, even god-like perfection. Personal and cultural preferences often determine the way an artist chooses to portray a body. Of course, the body itself can also participate in art: through performances, dances, rituals, and so on. The body as a subject offers endless expressive possibilities.

Archetypal Images of the Body

The Dutch-born American artist Willem de Kooning (1904–97) made a series of paintings of women that incorporate bold, apparently aggressive, even violent, marks and slashing strokes. De Kooning famously said that his *Woman* series referred to "the female painted through all the ages, all those idols." The types of ancient figures to which de Kooning alluded, for example the *Woman from Willendorf* (**4.129**), serve as **iconic** artistic models for the idea and image of woman.

The *Woman from Willendorf* is one of the earliest known artworks, dating to about 26,000

years ago. Female figurines have been discovered all over the world. In fact, such sculptures as this are commonly among the oldest created objects in a number of societies. The small size of this figurine, just over 4 inches tall, made it easily portable, a benefit for nomadic people. Because of the maker's emphasis on female anatomy (breasts, buttocks, and rotund belly), the *Woman*

4.129 *Woman from Willendorf*, c. 24,000–22,000 BCE. Oolitic limestone, 4⅜" high. Naturhistorisches Museum, Vienna, Austria

Prehistoric: dating from the period of human existence before the invention of writing
Iconic: a sign, the form of which directly suggests its meaning

4.130 Willem de Kooning, *Woman I*, 1950–52. Oil on canvas, 6'3⅞" × 4'10". MOMA, New York

from Willendorf is believed to be a fertility figure. Perhaps it was used as a charm to encourage pregnancy, or as a teaching tool. It almost certainly celebrates the woman as a mother and bringer of life.

The exaggerated form and emphasis on characteristically female elements of human anatomy visually connect the *Woman from Willendorf* with de Kooning's *Woman I* (**4.130**). This large painting, made thousands of years after the tiny sculpture was created, features the glaring eyes and grinning mouth of a woman's face at the top of the composition. By contrast, the *Woman from Willendorf* does not include facial features at all. In *Woman I* the most prominent parts of the body are the breasts, while the arms and legs are minimized in a manner similar to the *Woman from Willendorf*. Although both artworks convey the inherent power of women as givers and protectors of life, they do so very differently. De Kooning's woman seems strong to the point of being ferocious. The painting is physically big, over lifesized, making literal the larger-than-life feeling conveyed by the small sculpture. Both figures have an **abstracted** form, visible in the rough shapes of the *Woman from Willendorf* and the jagged brushstrokes of *Woman I*. Their appearance makes them less representations of individual people and more reflections of a universal idea of powerful women. As de Kooning's statement suggests, *Woman I* embodies "the female…through all the ages."

Ideal Proportion

Long before de Kooning's search to find something universal about the female figure, the ancient Egyptians applied formal mathematical systems in consistent ways to depict their ideal of the human form. They developed a standardized method for depicting men and women and used it for thousands of years. The Egyptian system of proportion was later adopted by the Greeks for their **figurative** sculpture and influenced

European artists during the **Renaissance**. These **idealized** proportions, clearly visible in figurative paintings, reliefs, and three-dimensional sculpture, were applied to architectural construction as well. The **canon of proportions** was developed to make the depicted body match ancient Egyptian notions of perfection.

The Egyptian canon of proportions is calculated in the form of a grid that provides consistent measurements of the parts of the body (**4.131a**). Each square of the grid represents a standard small measurement, or a unit, based on the width of the palm of the hand. Sometimes other ratios are used to make the grid, resulting in a slightly different but still standardized appearance.

Thus, in ancient Egyptian art, the portrayal of the body followed **conventions**, or prescribed methods, that produced consistent results. Egyptian depictions of the human body, as a result, look very similar even when they have been produced thousands of years apart. In sculpture,

4.131a (below left) Canon of proportions: *Menkaure and His Wife, Queen Khamerernebty*

4.131b (below right) *Menkaure and His Wife, Queen Khamerernebty*, 4th Dynasty, *c.* 2520 BCE. Greywacke, 54¾ × 22½ × 21¼". Museum of Fine Arts, Boston

2 palms

12 palms

6 palms

18 palms

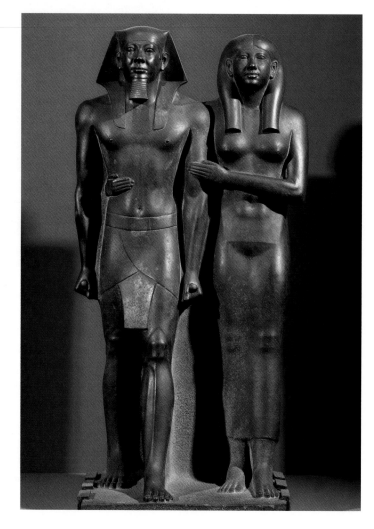

royal figures are shown either seated or standing, firmly connected to the stone from which they are carved, with their arms and hands close to their sides. In standing poses, the feet are firmly planted on the ground with the legs slightly apart and one foot in front of the other, as if the figure is about to take a step. Any suggestion of movement is potential, however, as if the figure is frozen; if it were in motion, its weight would shift to one side or the other. In the Egyptian figure, the feet are flat, the hips are even and immobile, and the shoulders are entirely square.

The use of the canon gives the sculpture of *Menkaure and His Wife, Queen Khamerernebty* an austere strength (**4.131b**). Their poses make the figures look rigid, calm, and enduring. They stand close together, as a single unit, his hands close to his sides and hers embracing his arm and torso. Their bodies do not twist and the features are bilaterally symmetrical (meaning that the left side matches the right). The strong, frontal pose suggests that the power of the pharaoh is changeless, unwavering, and eternal. This representation is idealized: the couple's appearance is based on abstract concepts rather than direct observation.

Notions of Beauty

Ideal proportions inform many cultural notions of preferred body type. Our notions of beauty are formed by our personal experiences and by the society in which we live. If we look at the ways in which artists have depicted the human form, we soon realize that in different times and places beauty can mean very different things (see Box: Reclining Nudes, pp. 560–61). In some cultures small feet or long necks are admired. Some groups may favor plump, even voluptuous, bodies, while others prefer slender, very thin and angular physiques. Our bodies can also express many things about our personalities: we can appear calm or agitated, elegant or unkempt, smart or stupid, sensuous or intellectual. The complex relationship between internal characteristics and outward appearance has led artists to explore these aspects of beauty through the human **form**.

The notions of beauty held by the ancient Greeks were based upon the combination of an underlying canon of mathematical proportions with the finely honed physiques possessed by male athletes. It was far more common to see a Greek male than a Greek female figure sculpted in the nude. Depicting the body without clothes allowed artists to study musculature and reflect observations and knowledge of the anatomy in a way that a clothed body does not show. Because the Greeks hoped to model themselves after gods, they aimed for perfect balance between mind and body in both their lives and their art. Such sculptures as the *Discus Thrower* demonstrate the ideal musculature of the athletic body (**4.132**). Greek athletes competed in the nude, and sculptures of male sportsmen celebrated the strength and virility inherent in the masculine form. The *Discus Thrower* also shows the competitor immersed in concentration, his mind in complete harmony with his physique.

Abstract: art imagery that departs from recognizable images from the natural world

Figurative: art that portrays items perceived in the visible world, especially human or animal forms

Renaissance: a period of cultural and artistic change in Europe from the fourteenth to the seventeenth century

Idealized: represented as perfect in form or character, corresponding to an ideal

Canon of proportions: a set of ideal mathematical ratios in art, used to measure the various parts of the human body in relation to one another

Convention: a widely accepted way of doing something; using a particular style, following a certain method, or representing something in a specific way

Form: an object that can be defined in three dimensions (height, width, and depth)

4.132 Myron, *Discus Thrower* (*Discobolos*), Roman copy of bronze original from *c.* 450 BCE. Marble, 5'1" high. British Museum, London, England

4.133 Sandro Botticelli, *The Birth of Venus*, c. 1482–6. Tempera on canvas, 5′8″ × 9′1⅝″. Uffizi Gallery, Florence, Italy

In ancient Greece, although the male **nude** was certainly more common, the female nude eventually began to gain respectability in the late fourth century BCE. Years later, during the Renaissance, such Italian artists as Sandro Botticelli (*c.* 1445–1510) revived the appearance of the female nude as it had been depicted in antiquity. In Botticelli's day the female nude became an acceptable subject as long as it appeared in a historical or mythological context. According to Classical mythology, Venus, the goddess of love and beauty, first emerged from the sea as a fully formed adult on a shell. In his painting *The Birth of Venus* (**4.133**), Botticelli focuses on the moment when Venus has been blown to shore. She is wafted toward the land by Zephyr, the god of the west wind, who is accompanied by the earth nymph Chloris. Awaiting her is a goddess or nymph who will wrap her in a blanket of flowers. Venus has smooth ivory-colored skin, long flowing hair, and an elegant pose. She discreetly covers her nudity,

indicating that chastity is part of her appeal. The graceful shape and the flawless quality of her body reflect the purity of the newborn goddess and create a harmonious and pleasing composition. Botticelli has modeled his figure on an ancient sculpture, thus basing his conception of beauty on Classical Greek standards.

In African societies, notions of beauty are often closely tied to the community's core values of composure, wisdom, and power. In other words, beauty is about more than external appearance. It is also about internal and societal principles. Being calm, wise, and composed were important attributes for the kings of Ife in West Africa. The elegant lines, delicate features, and elaborate headdress of the terracotta head in **4.134** indicate that it probably represents an Ife king, or *oni*. As the head was considered the seat of intelligence and the source of power, this sculpture's exquisite features draw our attention there. The lifelike details—the folds of the ears, and her *gei*, or art. After three years of apprenticeship, a geisha adopts less elaborate kimonos tied with simpler knots, lighter makeup, and a subdued hairstyle, like the one seen in Kaigetsudo Dohan's *Beautiful Woman* (**4.135**). Like other Japanese artists, Kaigetsudô Dohan (working 1710–16) celebrated beautiful women, here emphasizing the experienced geisha's impressive attire and relatively natural appearance. In addition to her musical skills and gift for intelligent conversation, this mature geisha would have been appreciated for her inner beauty.

4.134 Head, possibly a king, 12th–14th century. Terracotta with residue of red pigment and traces of mica, 10½ × 5¾ × 7⅜". Kimbell Art Museum, Fort Worth, Texas

the contours of the nose, and the plumpness of the lips—are extremely naturalistic, but also graceful and refined. The fine lines on the face resemble scarification patterns, or scars created by cutting or branding the skin. Beauty in this case is a balance of invisible internal characteristics and an idealized visible outward appearance.

Many cultures determine beauty by a person's ability to conform to expectations, whether through clothes, cosmetics, or body shape. In Japan, traditional female performers called *geisha* are known for their social skills and artistic talents, such as singing, dancing, and serving tea. Geisha, not to be confused with courtesans or prostitutes, have a professional relationship with their clients and are strongly discouraged from becoming too intimate with them. A geisha's appearance changes over the course of her career. Early on she wears dramatic hairstyles, heavy makeup, dark eyeliner, and red lip pencil applied to make her lips look small. As an apprentice, the source of her beauty lies in her appearance, but later it is seen to derive from her maturity

4.135 Kaigetsudo Dohan, *Beautiful Woman*, Edo Period, 18th century. Hanging scroll, ink and color on paper, 64⅜ × 20⅛". Metropolitan Museum of Art, New York

Nude: an artistic representation of the naked human figure

Reclining Nudes

While nudes have long been a subject in the history of art, the tradition of depicting the nude female figure lying down or reclining was established during the Renaissance. These types of picture recall the ancient Greek emphasis on the beauty and honesty conveyed by the nude human form. In some cases they also suggest the sensuality of the nude.

The Venetian painter known as Titian (c. 1488–1576) was influenced by the Classical tradition when he painted a female nude for the duke of the Italian town of Urbino (**4.136**). The roses in the woman's right hand hint at her identity: they are a symbol of Venus, the Classical goddess of beauty (hence the name by which the painting is commonly known, the *Venus of Urbino*). She looks out from her couch with a coy expression and casually covers her pubic area, at once modest and inviting, as if she exists simply to be looked at. The presence of the maids in the background preparing her clothes, however, connects her to the concerns of a real woman. But by suggesting that his painting depicted a mythological figure,

Titian was able to explore in depth such secular themes as the nature of love and desire.

It is clear that the French artist Édouard Manet (1832–83) was familiar with the *Venus of Urbino* when he painted his *Olympia* (**4.137**). The composition of the paintings and the posture of the women within them are almost identical. Manet, however, has replaced the sleeping dog at the foot of the bed with a hissing black cat. And instead of the maids in the background, there is a black servant who brings Olympia flowers. In this painting, as in others, Manet took a Classical subject and updated it for his own time. In modernizing the reclining nude, Manet considered the reality of the situation. Why would a woman be naked and on display? One obvious answer: because she is a prostitute. Not only was Olympia a common name for a prostitute, but Manet depicted her as a real woman, thin (at least by the standards of the time) and probably poor. Olympia's pose would have seemed confrontational because she stares out at

4.136 Titian, *Venus of Urbino*, 1538. Oil on canvas, 3'10⅞" × 5'5". Uffizi Gallery, Florence, Italy

the viewer in an assertive way, while people at that time were used to seeing more passive women with voluptuous bodies and docile expressions similar to the *Venus of Urbino*'s.

In the late twentieth century, the Japanese artist Yasumasa Morimura (b. 1951) revisited the theme of the reclining nude (**4.138**). The meaning of this piece, like that of Manet's *Olympia*, gains depth if one knows about the earlier artworks to which it alludes. Morimura employs digital processes, which allow him to play the roles of both Olympia and the servant. The resulting photograph is part of a series that the artist made in which he impersonates famous female icons from western culture, transcending race, gender, and ethnicity. Here, the act of covering the genitalia with the left hand takes on entirely new significance in disguising the truth of his masculinity. The robes of the earlier pieces are replaced with a kimono and the cat at the foot of the bed is a porcelain Lucky

Cat, commonly found in Japanese restaurants and shops as a talisman of good fortune. Morimura's reclining nude updates the theme with current technology and raises pertinent questions about identity, suggesting that appearances can be deceptive, that race and gender are artificial constructions, that we should not make assumptions about identity, and that our understanding of who we are is influenced by the past.

4.138 Yasumasa Morimura, *Portrait (Futago)*, 1988–90. Color photograph, printed in 2 editions at varying sizes

Performance Art: The Body Becomes the Artwork

Geisha are considered living works of art. Similarly, in **performance art**, and in some **installations**, the body and its actions become the artwork (see pp. 564–5, Perspectives on Art Box: Spencer Tunick: Human Bodies as Installations.) A performance by definition involves the human form in action, but by engaging all of a viewer's senses through movement, expression, sound, smell, and so on, it also activates the space itself. The performers share a space with the audience, and the art becomes part of the viewer's lived experience. Because performances are not permanent or static, once they are finished they can only be re-experienced indirectly, through documentation. Written accounts, photographs, and videos taken at the time later remind us of the performances themselves.

Perhaps inspired by his deep interest in the martial art of judo, the French artist Yves Klein (1928–62) began experimenting with "living brushes," or women using their bodies as the vehicle for applying paint to canvas. In the late 1950s he had been one of the first artists to make **monochromatic**, or one-color, paintings. He used a bright, dense, ultramarine blue, a color that he eventually patented as "International Klein Blue" (IKB). Klein integrated performance in an innovative way to make the blue paintings for which he was known. The first paintings made by the "living brushes" were monochromes that looked like the ones Klein himself had produced. Later, the women left imprints of their bodies on the canvas or paper (**4.139 b**).

Klein devised the pieces, directed the women, and hired an orchestra for the first public performance of the "living brushes," called *Anthropométries de l'époque bleue* (or *Anthropometries of the Blue Period*) (**4.139 a**). In order to create a musical accompaniment that was suitable for monochromatic paintings, Klein had the musicians play a single chord for twenty minutes and then sit in silence for twenty minutes. In an art gallery, works of art are usually inert, still objects and it is the viewers who move around (often in silence). In the case of Klein's performances, the artwork itself moved and made sounds while the audience sat still, giving the work a very physical presence in the usually quiet and austere gallery. At the same time, attention was brought to the odd circumstance of living nude figures as "art," now active in the gallery space instead of represented in artworks, and surrounded by a fully clothed audience.

Performance art: a work involving the human body, usually including the artist, in front of an audience
Installation: an artwork created by the assembling and arrangement of objects within a specific location
Monochromatic: having one or more values of one color

4.139a Yves Klein, *Anthropométries de l'époque bleue*, March 9, 1960. Galerie Internationale d'Art Contemporain, Paris, France

4.139b Yves Klein, *Anthropométrie sans titre*, 1960. Pure pigment and synthetic resin on paper mounted on canvas, 50⁷⁄₈ × 14⁵⁄₈". Private collection covered with gestural marks, viewers were pushed out of the gallery space. The artwork comments on several typically "feminine" actions, including the domesticity of mopping and the messiness of using cosmetics for beautification. Antoni takes the dynamic creative role here, bringing attention to the actions she is performing as well as to the status of women in the art world and in society.

The Italian artist Vanessa Beecroft (b. 1969) also brings the female figure out of the frame and into the gallery space. She takes the idea of the confrontation between the model and the viewer to a new extreme. Her performance pieces consist of groups of women standing in the gallery space with instructions not to speak or move. They create a sense of discomfort because the models are occupying the same space as the viewers, and actively returning their stares.

In pieces like *VB35* ("VB" stands for Vanessa Beecroft and "35" is an identifying number, given sequentially to her performances), the women's appearance at once embodies and challenges the expectations of ideal beauty established by contemporary media (**4.141**). The women are all model thin and posed like mannequins, reinforcing the idea that women, in order to be beautiful, must all look the same. Closer

4.140 Janine Antoni, *Loving Care*, 1993. Performance with Loving Care hair dye Natural Black, dimensions variable. Photographed by Prudence Cuming Associates at Anthony D'Offay Gallery, London, 1993

Unlike Klein, who directed rather than participated in his artworks, artist Janine Antoni (b. 1964 in the Bahamas) uses her own body and her own actions as the basis for most of her performances. In *Loving Care*, named for a brand of hair-care products, Antoni dipped her head in a bucket of hair color and proceeded to mop the floor with it, using her hair as a paintbrush (**4.140**). As more and more of the floor became

4.141 Vanessa Beecroft, *VB35*, 1998. Performance at Solomon R. Guggenheim Museum, New York

Perspectives on Art: Spencer Tunick
Human Bodies as Installations

The American photographer Spencer Tunick (b. 1967) is famous for his installations involving large numbers of nude people (4.142a). Here he explains how he came to make work that sometimes involves thousands of nudes, and how complicated it can be to organize them.

I didn't start out photographing hundreds or thousands of nude people. From 1992 to 1994 I worked on individual portraits of nudes on the streets of New York. I gained confidence in my ability to work on a public street, to deal with traffic, traffic light intervals, and the police. I switched to multiples when I had so many people to work with. I would carry the photographs round in my wallet and show them to people. By 1994 I had phone numbers for twenty-eight people and I decided to photograph them all at once outside the UN building in New York. Then in 1997 I gathered 1,000 people on an air-force base in Maine at a music concert.

I travel with a team of eight. In each city a contemporary art museum commissions my work and I can work wherever in the city I like. The museum provides team leaders and volunteers. Mexico City took three years to organize and one day to make the art. There were 250 team leaders and volunteers and 250 police officers. In Caracas, Venezuela, there were almost 1,000 police and military.

I know 75 percent of what I am going to do before we start but I like to keep an element of mystery. I have control of thousands of people, but in a way I don't like that control. I like to keep the event loose, personal, and intimate. Participants are not involving themselves in a spectacle but in a work of art. After ten minutes, once they get used to being nude, they get excited and start raising their hands in the air and so on, and then they calm down and we get organized.

I consider my works to be installations, not performances or photographs. I document the installations with photos and videos. I have two videographers and could have people take the photographs also, but I like to frame the photos and tweak them on location.

I still do individual portraits in streets. I am interested in the body and its relationship to the background. Instead of the body creating a meaning for the background, the background creates a new meaning for the body.

inspection reveals the women's individuality. Some have darker skin, others lighter. They have different hair color and different hairstyles. Their black bathing suits—like their bodies, poses, and posture—are not identical, but individual to each woman. In fact, some women in the performance were nude and did not wear a bathing suit at all. Beecroft's performances broach the subject of body image for a world of women, young and old, trying to live up to impossible standards.

The Body in Pieces

Artists have used exaggeration, stylization, and innovation to create abstract representations of the human body. Approaches from outside the western European tradition, such as African masks and Pre-Columbian sculptures from the Americas, influenced some modern European artists to make works that suggest forms that are altered but recognizable. Others have taken certain elements of the anatomy out of their usual context by distorting or fragmenting the body. We do not have to see a whole body to read it as a human figure (see Gateway Box: Matisse, **4.145**, p. 566). Recognizing this fact, artists have focused attention away from identifying a particular individual or illustrating a coherent story in order to emphasize ways in which the body can be broken down and presented as a product of the human imagination.

The French artist Auguste Rodin (1840–1917) altered the appearance of the human body, which is one of the reasons he is known as a pioneer in the field of modern sculpture. His innovations influenced many twentieth-century sculptors, including Henry Moore and Alberto Giacometti (see **4.146** and **4.147**). Although he had been formally trained, Rodin chose not to make his sculptures in the traditional way. Instead of idealizing figures to look like perfected versions of actual people, Rodin intentionally left his surfaces rough, as seen in his sculpture *Walking Man* (**4.143**). The scrapes and gouges on the figure's chest, torso, and hips stand as evidence of the material the artist touched and manipulated to make the sculpture. Rodin also considered fragmentary representations, such as this one, which has no

4.143 Auguste Rodin, *Walking Man*, c. 1890–95. Bronze, 33¾ × 22 × 11". MOMA, New York

Gateway to Art: Matisse, *Icarus*
The Blue Nude: Cutouts and the Essence of Form

Experimental artists like the Frenchman Henri Matisse (1869–1954) have consistently used the female nude as a subject for creative innovation. Throughout his career, Matisse was moving toward a more economical use of artistic elements. Early on, he made very detailed recordings of the world he observed around him. After the 1940s, he chose to isolate forms and reduce the range of his palette, emphasizing the elements he thought to be the most important for a particular subject, because, as he wrote, "exactitude is not truth." Even his sketches for individual artworks went from complex recordings of very detailed observations to pictures with selected details and limited colors. This approach suited the technique of making cutouts. In his cutouts, as seen in both *Icarus* (**4.144**) and *Blue Nude II* (**4.145**), Matisse gives us enough information to know that we are looking at a human body. Their shapes are rough, but energetic. The palette in *Blue Nude II* is restricted to blue only. The color blue is not used to shade the female figure or to make her look as if she is bathed in blue light. Instead, her form is made entirely of flat planes of color.

An essay of 1947 by Matisse, describing a series of self-portraits made using a mirror, helps explain how he arrived at this technique and what he hoped to communicate by making art the way he did:

These drawings sum up, in my opinion, observations that I have made for many years about the character of drawing, a

4.145 Henri Matisse, *Blue Nude II*, 1952. Gouache on paper, cut and pasted on white paper, 45³⁄₄ × 32¹⁄₄". Musée National d'Art Moderne, Centre Georges Pompidou, Paris, France

character that does not depend on forms being copied exactly as they are in nature, or on the patient assembling of exact details, but on the profound feeling of the artist before the objects that he has chosen, on which his attention is focused, and whose spirit he has penetrated.

My conviction about these things crystallized when I realized for example that in the leaves of a fig tree—of a fig tree particularly—the great difference of forms that exists among them does not keep them from sharing a common quality. Fig leaves, whatever their fantastic variations of form, always remain unmistakably fig leaves. I have made the same observation about other growing things: fruits, vegetables, etc.

Thus there exists an essential truth that must be disengaged from the outward appearance of the objects to be represented. This is the only truth that matters...

Exactitude is not truth.

4.144 Henri Matisse, *Icarus*, from *Jazz*, 1943–7. Page size 16⁷⁄₈ × 12⁷⁄₈". MOMA, New York

4.146 Henry Moore, *Recumbent Figure*, 1938. Green Hornton stone, 35 × 52¼ × 29″. Tate, London

Contours: the outlines that define a form
Avant-garde: early twentieth-century emphasis on artistic innovation, which challenged accepted values, traditions, and techniques

4.147 Alberto Giacometti, *Man Pointing*, 1947. Bronze, 70½ × 40¾ × 16⅜″. MOMA, New York

head or arms, to be completed sculptures rather than preparatory sketches. At the time, Rodin's pieces, which looked so different from the smooth, idealized figures people had come to expect, were harshly criticized. Since then, his approach has been praised for allowing the figures to be more expressive, emotional, and individual.

Like Rodin, the British sculptor Henry Moore (1898–1986) created figures that did not match the way the human body actually looks. Instead Moore made connections with natural forms in the shapes of bodies and their parts, which often resemble mountains, hills, cliffs, and valleys. The organic lines in his sculptures mimic the organic **contours** of the materials he used, usually wood and stone. In addition to nature, Moore was inspired by other works of art. He studied a range of artistic traditions outside the West, as well as Classical and **avant-garde** European approaches. As a result of these influences, he departed from visible reality for the sake of making a strong artistic statement. A consistent characteristic of his sculptures is his use of the void, an empty space that opens up the figure and creates visual interest. In *Recumbent Figure* the large hole in the center of the piece is surrounded by the masses that make up the body (**4.146**). The legs look like peaks while the abdomen is in the place of a valley. The breasts help to identify the shape as a female figure.

The Swiss artist Alberto Giacometti (1901–66) also stretched the

boundaries of the recognizable form: first through Surrealist examinations of the human body, and then, after World War II, through the existential views represented in such sculptures as *Man Pointing* (**4.147**). Giacometti's obsessive nature at times caused him to reduce figures to the point where they were almost nonexistent. Eventually he began to accept his own artistic vision, in which the bodies look as if they are being seen from an extreme distance. The figures seem to have stepped out of the artist's dreams and into reality, carrying with them an air of mystery. *Man Pointing* is an imposing figure, despite its apparent fragility. At almost six feet tall, it is hard to believe that it can support its own weight. Giacometti struck a delicate balance between the figure and its surroundings in this sculpture, which he first made in clay and then cast in bronze. Nothing indicates why the man is pointing, but the space around him seems almost heavy. The sculpture looks like a trace of the shadow the man casts rather than the man himself, emphasizing the figure's loneliness and isolation.

Discussion Questions

1 Thinking of artworks you have studied in this chapter, compare and contrast a work that contains static representations of the human form with a performance. How would making these two types of artwork have been different for their creators? What role does the person represented in the artwork play? How do the results compare visually?

2 What have the artists in this chapter discovered through their exploration of the human body? Find an example in the chapter that was especially interesting to you. What did learning about that artist's exploration reveal to you?

3 In this chapter we have looked at several ways in which artists have explored the body as an artistic theme. Identify three of those approaches. Now think of other works you have seen in this book and select three examples from outside this chapter that take a different approach to the body. List the ways in which your chosen works differ from those discussed in this chapter.

4.10

Art and Gender

Gender affects all people, including artists, whether they are male, female, or someone who does not fit neatly into either of those categories. Unlike sex, which indicates whether a person is biologically male or female, gender refers to a person's inner identity. It is one of the most significant aspects of a person's sense of self. But it is not clear whether common assumptions about gender roles are natural or imposed by society: should pink and dolls always be associated with females and blue and airplanes with males?

While gender affects everyone on some level, it often becomes an issue for discussion in relation to groups that have been disenfranchised by the mainstream and male-dominated culture, perhaps because they are female, or homosexual, or transsexual. At several points in the twentieth century, feminism encouraged us to consider the role of women as both creators and subjects of important artworks. Contemporary feminist and lesbian, gay, bisexual, transgender (LGBT) movements have inspired a great deal of debate about and exploration of the ways gender affects personality, relationships, and preferences.

The artworks in this chapter illustrate some of the ways in which artists have explored, reinforced, and challenged traditional gender distinctions. By presenting their own personal experiences of daily life, their interpretations of historical events, and their commitment to social or political agendas, artists encourage us to question common assumptions about gender and the possibilities beyond the binaries of male and female.

Gendered Roles

Our assumptions about gendered roles are often based on cultural stereotypes. For example, the ancient Egyptians and Greeks developed formal methods for representing the ideal human figure in art, with males being presented as strong and athletic, while females appear demure. Similarly, in our modern society we construct our own ideas about what men and women should look like and how they should behave. Artworks depicting men have historically referred to their powerful bodies or leadership roles. In contrast, women have tended to be shown in artworks either as passive, eroticized subjects who exist solely for the viewer's pleasure, or, alternately, in the role of nurturers in domestic scenarios. There are, however, numerous examples of artworks that consciously counter these stereotypical representations and show images of men as vulnerable and women in positions of power.

In many cultures, heroes manifest the desirable attributes of the society in a larger-than-life way. The sculpture *Chibinda Ilunga*, made by the Chokwe people of Central Africa, depicts a legendary leader who was a masterful hunter, a successful king, and a descendant of a deity (**4.148**). The figure carries a staff, a symbol of prestige that stands for the passage of power from an ancestor to a chief or from one chief to another. His flaring nostrils and the antelope horn he carries identify him as a hunter. The horn was a trophy of his successes

4.148 *Chibinda Ilunga*, mid-19th century. Wood, hair, and hide, 16 × 6 × 6". Kimbell Museum of Art, Fort Worth, Texas

in capturing game, and it also served as a container for potent substances or medicines, contributing an additional element to his arsenal of impressive traits. The sculpture conveys the valued attributes of authority, potency, and restraint that made this celebrated hunter a model leader.

Manual labor relies on strength and endurance, which have traditionally been considered distinctly masculine, allowing laborers to be seen as heroic through their hard work. Shortly after World War I, the American sociologist and photographer Lewis Wickes Hine (1874–1940) made a series of *Work Portraits*. Unlike some of his earlier projects, which condemned the exploitation of children in factories and mines, this series celebrated the positive connection between the worker and the machines he used. *Power House Mechanic Working on Steam Pump* salutes the man's muscular physique and its complementary relationship with the tools of his trade (**4.149**). Hine's visual commentary records the commanding role the worker played as the driving force behind the progressive industrial era. (As a counterpoint to Hine, see Gateway Box: Lange, **4.151**, p. 570.)

4.149 Lewis Wickes Hine, *Power House Mechanic Working on Steam Pump*, 1920. Silver gelatin print, sheet: 9½ × 6¾". National Archives and Records Administration, Records of the Work Projects Administration

4.150 John Coplans, *Self-portrait Sideways No. 3*, 2001. Gelatin silver print, 4'2" × 6'8".

The British photographer John Coplans (1920–2003) directly challenges traditional views of the ideal male **nude**. He frankly shows wrinkles, sags, and rolls of skin. *Self-portrait Sideways No. 3* is part of a series of self-portraits the artist began when he was in his sixties (**4.150**). These self-portraits highlight the realities of the aging body in direct and personal but also enigmatic ways. The photographs often transform actual body parts through extreme close-ups, making it hard to tell if we are looking at the crook of a finger, the crease of an elbow, or the bend of a leg. These images, which rarely include Coplans's face, give an edge of humility, and an unexpected voice, to the artist's self-examination, and expand the depictions of male figures and aging bodies in art.

The American photographer Cindy Sherman (b. 1954) plays the roles of all of the women

Gateway to Art: Lange, *Migrant Mother*
The Image of Motherhood

Byzantine, medieval, and **Renaissance** depictions of mothers and children generally focus on the ideal mother. Later artists show

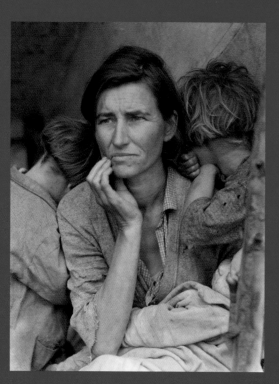

4.151 Dorothea Lange, *Migrant Mother*, 1936. Library of Congress, Washington, D.C.

children as more precious than jewels (for example, see p. 404, **3.152**, Angelica Kauffmann's *Cornelia Pointing to Her Children as Her Treasures*) and reveal the sweet interactions of ordinary moments (see, for example, p. 345, **3.76**, Mary Cassatt's *Child's Bath*). Lange captured a slightly different view, showing the intimacy of a family that has very little but each other.

Migrant Mother offers poignant evidence of a mother's strength and determination in a time of extreme need (**4.151**). Because the early pea crop had failed, this migrant worker and her three young children were starving. Photographer Dorothea Lange found the family surviving on frozen vegetables from the surrounding fields and birds they were able to kill. Like other mother and child images, *Migrant Mother* draws attention to the nature and enduring quality of the bond. This photograph resonates because of the way the mother's face reflects the pressures placed on the family unit.

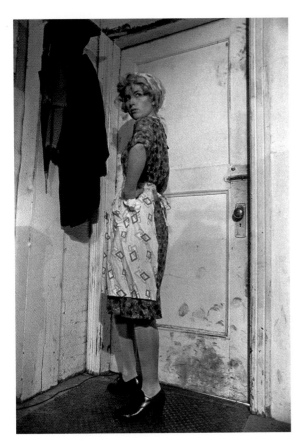

portrayed in her acclaimed *Untitled Film Stills* series, creating an intriguing visual puzzle as we try to uncover the "real" Cindy Sherman. The images she makes are not, however, intended to be self-portraits in the way that Coplans's photographs are. Sherman has explained that the images are not about her, but are about the representations of the women being shown and the ways that each viewer interprets them (see Perspectives on Art Box: Cindy Sherman: The Artist and her Identity).

For the *Untitled Film Stills*, Sherman fabricated backdrops and costumes for imagined characters from nonexistent 1950s B-movies. At that time, the film roles for women were limited to such stereotyped characters as housewife, starlet, country girl come to the city, and so on. In *Untitled Film Still #35* we see a woman—perhaps a housewife or a maid—with a distinctly bad attitude (**4.152**). The circumstances of the scene are far from clear, though. Is she sulking about

Nude: an artistic representation of the naked human figure
Renaissance: a period of cultural and artistic change in Europe from the fourteenth to the seventeenth century

4.152 Cindy Sherman, *Untitled Film Still #35*, 1979. Black and white photograph, 10 × 8". MOMA, New York

Perspectives on Art: Cindy Sherman
The Artist and Her Identity

*The American photographer and film director Cindy Sherman is best known for her photographs in which she is dressed in costumes as if she were another person (see above, **4.152**). Here she explains her general working process and one specific image,* Untitled Film Still #35, *inspired by the Italian film actress Sophia Loren.*

There is a stereotype of a girl who dreams all her life of being a movie star. She tries to make it on the stage, in films, and either succeeds or fails. I was more interested in the types of characters that fail. Maybe I related to that. But why should I try to do it myself? I'd rather look at the reality of these kinds of fantasies, the fantasy of going away and becoming a star...

The black-and-white photographs were... fun to do. I think they were easy partly because throughout my childhood I had stored up so many images of role models. It was real easy to think of a different one in every scene. But they were so clichéd that after three years I couldn't do them anymore. I was really thinking about the movies, the characters are almost typecast from movies.

For the woman standing in front of my studio door, I was thinking of a film with Sophia Loren called *Two Women*. She plays this Italian peasant. Her husband is killed and she and her daughter are both raped. She is this tough strong woman, but all beaten-up and dirty. I liked that combination of Sophia Loren looking very dirty and very strong. So that's what I was thinking of....

I realized I had to become more specific in details, because that's what makes a person different from other people.

something, planning to leave, or about to pull a wallet from the jacket hanging on the hook? Why are there so many scuff marks on the door? More questions are raised than answered in the scenarios Sherman invents. Her *Untitled Film Stills*, which were created between 1977 and 1980, revisit these 1950s-inspired women in order to make it clear how narrow the representations of and expectations for women had been only a few short years before. At the time Sherman made *Untitled Film Still #35*, feminism was beginning to have a significant impact on artistic representations of women as well as on the possibilities for women in society. Sherman made sixty-nine photographs in the series and the women in them always seem as if they are being watched, the object of an unseen voyeur's gaze. These scenarios call attention to and question the way we look at these and all women.

Feminist Critique

In Western countries, for many centuries women had far fewer opportunities than men to become artists, and were rarely given the recognition granted to their male counterparts. For example, women were not allowed to draw from the nude in their art classes until the nineteenth century. It was also believed that "genius" was a trait exclusively available to men, and language with a gender bias—such as the word "masterpiece" to describe a great artwork—reinforced that belief. Before the 1970s few people even noticed that women had largely been excluded from the institutions and systems that produced serious artists.

In many cases, successful women had simply been written out of the history of art. The Italian artist Artemisia Gentileschi, for example, enjoyed an impressive reputation in the seventeenth century, but her efforts were eventually forgotten, only to be rediscovered in the early twentieth century (see Gateway Box: Gentileschi). The feminist movement of the 1960s and 1970s made a significant impact on the production and understanding of artworks made by women. It acknowledged that women artists had been left out of much of the history of art, and it introduced the possibility that this situation could be rectified. As a result, feminist artists expanded the subject matter of art, making it more relevant to women's issues, and many more works made by women were included in museums and galleries.

The American artist Judy Chicago (b. 1939) appreciated the achievement of such women as Gentileschi. She realized that many women had been forgotten over time and, likewise, that women who seem prominent today might in the future also be omitted from history. From 1974 to 1979, Chicago worked on an epic sculpture called *The Dinner Party* (**4.153**), which honors women from the past and present. Her huge triangular dinner table has thirteen place settings on each side. Every setting features a placemat, on which is embroidered the name of a famous historical or mythical woman, and an elaborate plate designed intentionally to resemble the shape of a butterfly or a vagina. The appearance of all the elements on each setting was inspired by the woman whose place it is. Layers of lace designate the place of the nineteenth-century poet Emily Dickinson, while the plate for the artist Georgia O'Keeffe (**4.153**) resembles a sculpted version of one of her **abstract** flower paintings. Artemisia Gentileschi's place setting has a brightly colored plate surrounded by lush fabric similar to the kind shown in her paintings.

Abstract: an artwork the form of which is simplified, distorted, or exaggerated in appearance. It may represent a recognizable form that has been slightly altered, or it may be a completely non-representational depiction

Baroque: European artistic and architectural style of the late sixteenth to early eighteenth centuries, characterized by extravagance and emotional intensity

Medium (plural **media**): the material on or from which an artist chooses to make a work of art

Ceramics: fire-hardened clay, often painted, and normally sealed with shiny protective coating

4.153 Judy Chicago, *The Dinner Party*, 1974–9. Installation view showing Georgia O'Keeffe placesetting. Embroidery on linen and china paint on porcelain, entire work 48 × 48'. Brooklyn Museum, New York

Gateway to Art: Gentileschi, *Judith Decapitating Holofernes*
Professional Artist and Painter of Women

At a time when there were very few women professional artists, the Italian Artemisia Gentileschi (1593–*c.* 1656) earned a reputation as a talented and accomplished **Baroque** painter. While women were accepted as portrait artists in the seventeenth century, Gentileschi also worked in the more highly esteemed genres of historical, mythological, and religious paintings. Women were not allowed to follow the traditional avenues of apprenticeship to complete their training as painters and sculptors, but Gentileschi was the daughter of an artist, and her talent was recognized and fostered by her father. Unlike her male contemporaries, Gentileschi often depicted strong female figures with emotion, intensity, and power.

One of the subjects she painted was the story of Judith Decapitating Holofernes, from the Bible (**4.154**). Judith became a heroine of the Israelite people when she murdered Holofernes, an Assyrian general sent by King Nebuchadnezzar II to punish the western nations of his empire—including the Israelites—for not supporting his reign. After Holofernes became intoxicated, Judith used his sword to cut off his head. The Hebrews were then able to defeat the Assyrian army and avoid surrender. Scholars generally agree that such scenes of powerful women taking vengeance on immoral men are connected to events in Gentileschi's own life. At the age of eighteen

Gentileschi was sexually assaulted by her painting teacher and had to endure a humiliating public rape trial in her attempts to bring her attacker to justice.

4.154 Artemisia Gentileschi, *Judith Decapitating Holofernes*, *c.* 1620. Oil on canvas, 6'6⅜" × 5'3¾". Uffizi Gallery, Florence, Italy

Chicago made the table an equilateral triangle not only because the shape was an ancient sign for both woman and goddess, but also because it could be used here to symbolize the world of fairness and equality that feminists sought. She chose to have thirteen guests to a side both because there were thirteen witches in a coven and because it was an important number for those ancient religions that worshiped a mother goddess. The number is also a reference to the biblical Last Supper, here reconfigured with women as the guests instead of Jesus and his twelve disciples. The idea of a dinner party—as well as the **media**, such as needlework and **ceramics**, which are included in her piece—evokes the role of woman as homemaker, which Chicago and other feminists believed should be admired and praised.

In 1985, a group of women artists in New York City formed a collective organization called the Guerrilla Girls to protest at the unequal treatment of female artists in the art world. Their name indicates their willingness to engage in unconventional tactics in their fight for equality. The Guerrilla Girls, who are still active, are known for the gorilla masks the members wear to avoid being recognized by the art world establishment and institutions they might criticize. Their productions take the form of public protests and lectures as well as flyers and posters. One of their best-known posters, *Do Women Have to be Naked to Get into the Met. Museum?* (**4.155**), includes statistics to highlight the disproportionate representation of women artists (5 percent) compared to female nudes (85 percent) in the collection of the Metropolitan Museum of Art in New York. As this poster shows, one of their principal goals is to oppose the lack of representation of women artists in major museum collections.

The American artist Lorna Simpson (b. 1960) has confronted similar issues about the treatment of women, as well as assumptions regarding race, in art and society. Her combinations of text and imagery raise questions about gendered and racial identity, both verbal and visual. *You're Fine* shows a woman lying on an examination table (**4.156**). She wears a nondescript white slip and has her back to us, so we are not able to identify her by the usual means of looking at her face. The text accompanying the image indicates multiple levels of meaning. This woman, whose pose recalls a reclining nude from Classical art, is lying down here for the purposes of a medical inspection. The plaques on the left list procedures and tests, probably ones she is undergoing. Those on the right, however, suggest that she is being subjected to this scrutiny in order to gain a secretarial position. Finally, the lettering above and below the picture reveals that her body has passed inspection: "You're Fine. You're Hired." Unlike all those images that the Guerrilla Girls noted, Simpson's model is not nude and her identity has not been exposed.

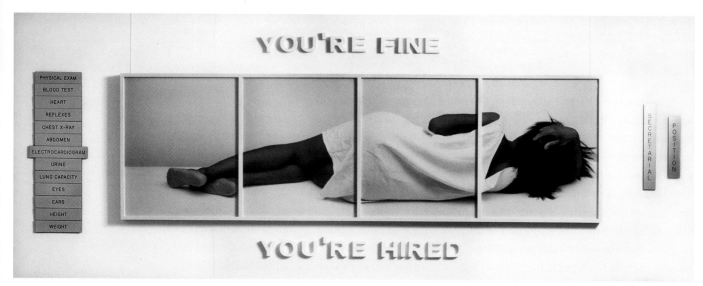

Blurring the Lines: Ambiguous Genders

We frequently assign roles to men and women according to our ideas of "normal" gender. Of course, traditional roles are frequently reversed: women have been primary breadwinners, worked in mines or gone to war, and men have been nurturers and raised children. But in recent years it has become more acceptable to address other ways of transcending the conventional gender boundaries. Public awareness of such issues as transvestism and transgender surgery has been raised by more open discussion. The investigation of the ways that bodies and identities can assume various levels of masculinity and femininity, however, is not entirely new to art. It is a question that artists from many cultures and eras of history have sought to address.

Almost 3,500 years ago, ancient Egypt was governed by a woman called Hatshepsut. She was arguably the most powerful of the handful of female rulers in Egyptian history. Hatshepsut controlled the kingdom for about twenty years in the fifteenth century BCE, first as regent for her stepson and nephew Thutmose III, and then as pharaoh in her own right. To legitimize her reign, Hatshepsut emphasized that she was her father's choice as successor, ahead of her two brothers and half-brother. She also claimed direct lineage from Amun, the sun god who was worshiped at that time.

Like all Egyptian rulers, Hatshepsut commissioned many sculptures and relief carvings to replicate and immortalize her image. A few show her as a woman, but she is most often depicted in the conventional poses and clothing of a male king. The image in **4.157** is one of a group of sphinxes that possess Hatshepsut's face. It was not uncommon for pharaohs to be represented in the form of a sphinx, a creature with the body of a lion and the head of a human. The artist has clearly followed the customary guidelines for depicting male pharaohs, including the traditional headcloth and royal beard. But, although the portrait is idealized, the sculptor has not attempted to disguise the delicate lines of Hatshepsut's features.

4.157 Sphinx of Hatshepsut, 18th Dynasty, 1479–1458 BCE. Granite and paint, 5'4⅝" × 11'3". Metropolitan Museum of Art, New York

The American photographer Diane Arbus (1923–71) was fascinated by subjects that crossed established boundaries, including conventional gender distinctions. She made direct, even confrontational pictures of people outside the mainstream, such as the midgets, giants, twins, and sword swallowers that she met at sideshows, carnivals, and circuses. Her photograph *Hermaphrodite with a Dog* conveys a fascination with, and a kind of reverence for, extreme difference (**4.158**). Her subject's experience of being both male and female and, at the same time, not conforming to either gender, adds up to a shocking reality. The spectacle of the hermaphrodite's dual nature is highlighted in the visible juxtaposition between the feminine costume, make-up, and clean-shaven right side and the masculine tattoo, wrist watch, and hairy body on the left.

4.158 (below) Diane Arbus, *Hermaphrodite with a Dog*, 1968. Gelatin silver print, 20 × 16".

Unlike Arbus, the American artist Robert Mapplethorpe (1946–89) photographed a lifestyle of which he was himself a part. The issue of gender affects his photographic work because he chose subjects that were highly sexualized and often related to his own interests as a gay man. His photographs are carefully composed, elegantly lit, and technically perfect, making subjects that might previously have been seen as deviant appear normal, even beautiful. A national controversy was sparked by the exhibition of Mapplethorpe's work that traveled to several museums across the U.S. shortly after the artist died of AIDS-related illness. Some museum officials and politicians considered the graphic sexual nature of Mapplethorpe's *X Portfolio* to be problematic because the artist had been awarded a grant from public funds.

Mapplethorpe, however, did not see a significant difference between a flower, a Classical sculpture, or a nude male figure.

In Mapplethorpe's 1980 *Self-portrait (#385)*, his hair is curled and he wears eye shadow, blush, and lipstick (**4.159**). If one looks solely at his face, he seems to be a woman. His bare chest, however, tells us that he is a man. Mapplethorpe's appearance raises many questions about the assumptions we make based on the way people look. It also reveals the degree to which gender is a construction and suggests that not all people fit the conventional distinctions between the sexes. Mapplethorpe photographed what he wanted to see, the things that he considered visually interesting but did not find elsewhere in the art world. Through his carefully crafted compositions and technically masterful prints

4.159 Robert Mapplethorpe, *Self-portrait (#385)*, 1980. Gelatin silver print, 20 × 16"

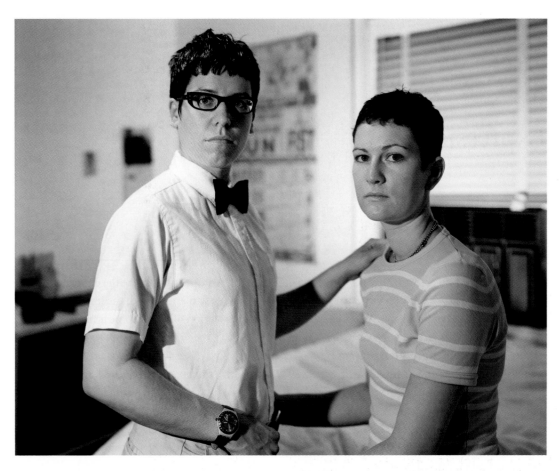

4.160 Catherine Opie, *Melissa & Lake, Durham, North Carolina*, 1998. Chromogenic print, 40 × 50"

he ensured his models (including himself) looked their absolute best.

The American artist Catherine Opie (b. 1961) uses photography to investigate the nuances of gender and identity. Her pictures include studio portraits of her lesbian friends dressed in leather or wearing false facial hair, staged depictions of radical performance artists, high school football games, and landscapes. Opie created her *Domestic* series while traveling across the U.S. in order to photograph lesbian couples, such as Melissa and Lake, in their everyday settings (**4.160**). This photograph accentuates some of the similarities in the couple's appearance, such as their short haircuts with bangs. The point of the picture, however, is their bond, not their gender or sexual identity. Opie's portraits, by highlighting the lesbian community, introduce some viewers to new ways of life. They remind others that the familiar people, places, and things we see each day can be thought of in new ways. Such pictures are not about difference, they are celebrations of individuality.

Discussion Questions

1   What kind of words can you think of that are specifically gendered? Come up with a list of five "male" and five "female" adjectives. Are they based on facts or opinions? Find an artwork to illustrate each of your terms. Find an artwork that contradicts each of your terms. Make sure that at least half the artworks you choose are not from this chapter.

2   What obstacles have women faced in being taken seriously as professional artists? What has been done to counteract that inequity? What artworks, either in this chapter or elsewhere, effectively express either these challenges or the changes in institutional practices toward women in the arts?

3   Consider the artworks you have studied and then describe an artwork that expresses your personal experience as a man or woman. What roles have you played in your life that conform to or deviate from established norms? How can you communicate that experience to your audience in an artwork?

4.11

Expression

Throughout this book, as you have looked at artworks, you have probably realized that they have something in common: they make visual or **conceptual** statements. In other words, art is at its core a medium of expression, a means by which an artist communicates with an audience. In fact, art is such a powerful form of expression that there is virtually no limit to what artists can address through their work. In this chapter we will examine what some artworks can tell us about an artist's creative intentions.

Art often conveys something personal, even intimate, about the artist, such as deeply held beliefs or emotions. Consider a very directly personal form of expression, the self-portrait. In theory, a self-portrait presents a picture of the artist, but does it give an accurate portrayal of the artist's physical appearance? Does it show the way the artist wants to be seen? Does it somehow reveal anything that the artist thinks or feels in addition to (or instead of) showing the artist's likeness? Alternately, some artists use their artworks to make a statement about the world around them rather than about themselves. For example, in this chapter we will see how artists use visual language to comment on the expectations that society imposes on women, to address issues of national or cultural identity, or to refer to current events.

Visual expression is certainly not limited to comment about one's own feelings or opinions. Art can be a powerful medium for exploring even non-visual experience. Art can, for example, explore the sensations of hearing music, experiencing nature, or contemplating human thought. Art can also explore the character of art itself by experimenting with the impact of color or the distortion of form. Some artists have defined art as being something original, and, as such, many artworks are unique creations by an individual. Others have actively challenged the idea that originality is an essential aspect of art. Some artists have gone so far as consciously to borrow the existing imagery of other artists in order to question the very idea of originality.

Expression is fundamental to art, but it is also a very complicated subject, as we will continue to discover when we examine some of the many means by which artists have expressed themselves.

Making a Self-portrait

One definition of a self-portrait is an artwork that represents the physical appearance of the artist. In practice, however, self-portraits are never quite that simple. As well as depicting the likeness of the artist, self-portraits often tell us something about the artist's personality, experiences, or choices. Another form of self-portraiture involves the artist assuming the role or persona of someone else, much as an actor portrays another person on the stage.

The Dutch artist Vincent van Gogh (1853–90) made a specialty out of self-portraiture in which he emphasized the internal reality of what he felt rather than simply recording what he saw. His *Self-portrait with Bandaged Ear and Pipe*, one of approximately thirty self-portraits that

Conceptual: relating to or concerning ideas

4.161 Vincent van Gogh, *Self-portrait with Bandaged Ear and Pipe*, 1889. Oil on canvas, 25¼ × 19¾".
Private collection

suffering. Kahlo is perhaps best known for her self-portraits, which comprise up to one-third of her artistic output.

The women in *The Two Fridas* are almost mirror images of one another (**4.162**). They depict distinct aspects of the artist's identity. Kahlo's mixed cultural background is represented in the clothes worn by the two figures. The Frida on the right wears a Mexican dress (related to her mother's heritage); the one on the left, a European gown (reflecting her father's German roots). Another complicated element in Kahlo's life was her turbulent relationship with her husband, fellow Mexican artist Diego Rivera (1886–1957). When this painting was being made, Kahlo was in the process of divorcing Rivera (subsequently, a year after the divorce, they remarried). While the Mexican Frida holds a small picture of Rivera, the German Frida has a broken heart and tries with surgical pincers to stop the flow of blood from the artery that joins the two women together. The presentation of the hearts on the outside of the bodies emphasizes the sensitive emotional content of the painting.

he made, refers to a notorious incident in his life (**4.161**). At the time this painting was made Van Gogh lived in Arles, in the south of France, and hoped to realize his dream of starting an artists' colony there. When he learned that his fellow artist and close friend Paul Gauguin was planning to return to Paris, they had an intense argument, during which Van Gogh threatened Gauguin's life. Afterward Van Gogh cut off a portion of his own ear. He then wrapped the severed lobe in newspaper and presented it to a prostitute in a brothel before he was hospitalized and treated for acute blood loss. The *Self-portrait with Bandaged Ear and Pipe* displays, in its restrained but nervous lines and bold, contrasting colors, some of the agitation that the artist certainly experienced during the episode.

Self-reflection in the work of the Mexican artist Frida Kahlo (1907–54) is presented by combining depictions of her physical appearance with metaphorical references to her feelings. Kahlo began making art around the age of eighteen, while recuperating from a devastating trolley-car accident that left her bedridden for three months and in pain for the rest of her life. As a result, her paintings tend to be very personal portrayals of psychological and physical

4.162 Frida Kahlo, *The Two Fridas*, 1939. Oil on canvas, 5'8" × 5'8". Museo de Arte Moderno, Mexico City, Mexico

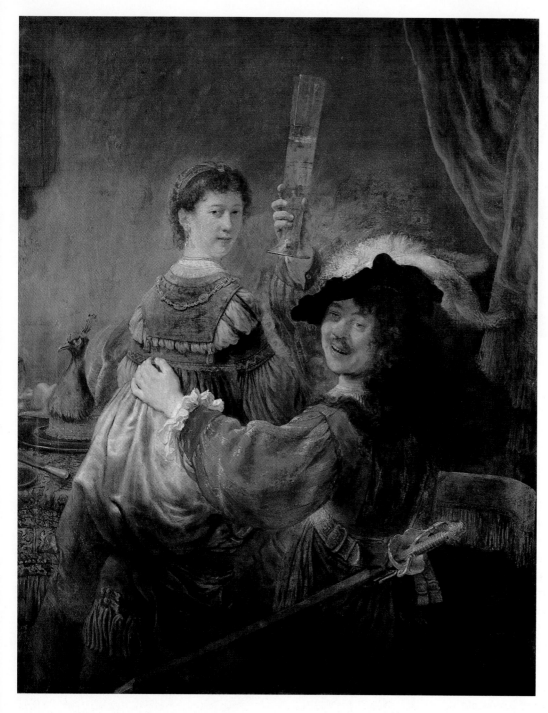

More than two centuries before van Gogh, another Dutch painter, Rembrandt van Rijn (1606–69), known as Rembrandt, was one of the first artists to dedicate a significant portion of his output to self-portraits. He made more than ninety of them over the course of forty years, reflecting the changes that occurred both in his appearance and in the style of his artworks across his lifetime. Rembrandt's self-portraits portrayed him in many guises, from a peasant to an aristocrat, and gave him the opportunity to examine different facial expressions and character types. In *Self-portrait with Saskia in the Scene of the Prodigal Son in the Tavern*, Rembrandt appears as the prodigal son, from the biblical story of a young man who rebels against his father's wishes by squandering his inheritance on wasteful living (**4.163**). Rembrandt creates a lively mood in the tavern: he raises his glass toward the viewer, as the barmaid, modeled on his wife Saskia, looks on.

A slightly different (and much later) take on the story of the Prodigal Son is provided by the

4.164 Duane Michals, *The Return of the Prodigal Son*, 1982

American photographer Duane Michals (b. 1932). Like Rembrandt, Michals includes himself in the scene, although he plays the part of the forgiving father rather than the wayward son (**4.164**). The reconciliation between father and son is shown in five frames. In the first scene, the father is reading the newspaper by a window as his son enters the room, naked and with his head hanging in shame. In the second frame, the father stands up, while the son hides his face and body, not sure what kind of reaction to expect. By the final frame the father and son have switched places: the father is now naked and the son is wearing his clothes as they embrace. This reversal suggests that the father, in addition to welcoming his son back into his life, also accepts some of the blame for his son's failings.

The British painter Jenny Saville (b. 1970) is another artist who has chosen an unconventional approach to the self-portrait. In such larger-than-lifesize paintings as *Branded*, which is 7 feet tall, she appears as a monumental nude (**4.165**). From this vantage point Saville's breasts and stomach are far more prominent than her head, which is barely squeezed into the frame. She glances down with a look of disdain as she pinches a roll of flesh with her left hand, as if peering into a mirror. Not only does her nude figure appear fat, countering contemporary society's bias toward thin women (and noticeably exaggerating Saville's actual size), but her discolored skin is also far from ideal. To make

her paintings, Saville refers to photographs and medical illustrations of flesh tones, bruises, dimples, and pockmarks. Such words as "delicate," "supportive," "irrational," "decorative," and "petite," inscribed on her body, comment on society's expectations of the kind of body a

4.165 Jenny Saville, *Branded*, 1992. Oil on canvas, 7 × 6′

Performance artist: an artist whose work involves the human body (often including their own)
Patron: an organization or individual who sponsors the creation of works of art

woman should have. Saville has said that she uses her body as a prop that she is willing to distort and manipulate. The results are direct, if harsh and critical. By confronting—even exaggerating—the imperfections of reality, Saville comments on the conflicted relationship women sometimes have with their own body image.

The French **performance artist** ORLAN (b. 1947) adopted an even more extreme approach to constructing the self. ORLAN's artistic medium is her own body: in order to create a completely new persona, she underwent a series of plastic surgeries that transformed her appearance, and documented the entire process (**4.166a** and **4.166b**). An operating room became the stage for ORLAN's "performance." She was the star, the medical team the cast, with costumes created by famous fashion designers. Because she was given only a local anesthetic, ORLAN was able to remain conscious and read aloud from philosophical and poetic texts while the surgical procedures were carried out. Video cameras in the operating room transmitted a live feed of the surgery to CBS News, the Sandra Gering Gallery in New York, and the Centre Georges Pompidou in Paris. ORLAN also documented the stages of her transformation with photographs taken as she healed.

In her final incarnation, ORLAN had become a composite woman. Her features were modeled after several famously beautiful paintings of women: her chin was copied from Botticelli's Venus (in *The Birth of Venus*); her mouth from the Roman deity Diana in a renowned French

Renaissance canvas; her nose from Psyche, the mythical lover of Cupid, in a later French painting by François Gérard; and her brow from Leonardo da Vinci's *Mona Lisa*. ORLAN has said her work has several aims: to intervene in the historical representation of women in art by actively determining her own appearance; to comment on the ways technology empowers us to transcend our human limitations; to critique the cult of beauty that imposes unfair standards on women; and to make a statement about the impossibility of physical perfection even in an age when plastic surgery is performed routinely. Ultimately, ORLAN has used her own body to raise questions about cultural perceptions as well as about what constitutes art.

Finding an Artistic Voice

In addition to depicting themselves directly or indirectly in their artworks, artists often use their own experiences, dreams, fears, or confusions as inspiration. Sometimes the result is very different from the way other people might have experienced a similar emotion or event. Learning about the original context of a piece of art, such as the circumstances surrounding its making, can help us to understand the artist's intentions and the ways that their work might contain more than meets the eye. (See Gateway Box: Gentileschi; and Perspectives on Art Box: Mona Hatoum: Art, Personal Experience, and Identity, p. 585.)

Gateway to Art: Gentileschi, *Judith Decapitating Holofernes*
Self-Expression in the *Judith* Paintings

The powerful heroines in the paintings of Artemisia Gentileschi (1593–*c*. 1656), such as Judith, who beheads Holofernes with steadfast determination, have a strong correlation with events in the artist's own life. Gentileschi was the victim of a sexual assault by Agostino Tassi, who was her painting teacher and a colleague of her father. During the public rape trial that followed, Tassi claimed that Gentileschi was not only a willing lover, but also quite promiscuous. Gentileschi and her father felt that, in addition to the physical violence she had suffered in the assault, their family name and reputation had been attacked. They feared that her prospects of marrying had been damaged both by the rape and the trial. Tassi was eventually sentenced to exile, and Gentileschi married another man, with whom she had five children.

Gentileschi is known to have painted seven works showing different events from the biblical story of Judith's encounter with Holofernes. The first, depicting Judith and her maidservant cutting off his head, was painted about a year after the Tassi trial (**4.167**). The painting of this violent assault by a woman on an invader has been interpreted as both an expression of the artist's anger at her own attacker, and as a cathartic way of healing the effects of her ordeal. In fact, Gentileschi's heroines in the Judith paintings resemble her own features.

Another of the painter's depictions of the story, made about a decade later, shows Judith and her maidservant by candlelight while making their escape from the murder scene with the bloody head (**4.168**). While there may indeed be an element of autobiography at least in Gentileschi's earlier paintings, the various versions of the story that she made over a thirty-year period were probably created for a variety of other reasons. The beheading of Holofernes was a popular theme with other artists of the time, suggesting that the **patron** who commissioned Gentileschi's painting may have requested the subject, or that some of her later representations may have been intended for purchasers who had seen and admired her earlier work.

4.168 Artemisia Gentileschi, *Judith and Her Maidservant with the Head of Holofernes*, 1623–5. Oil on canvas, 6'³⁄₈" × 4'7¾". Detroit Institute of Arts

4.167 (left) Artemisia Gentileschi, *Judith Decapitating Holofernes*, *c*. 1620. Oil on canvas, 6'6⅜" × 5'3¾". Uffizi Gallery, Florence, Italy

Chiaroscuro: the use of light and dark in a painting to create the impression of volume
Installation: an artwork created by the assembling and arrangement of objects in a specific location
Found object: an object found by an artist and presented, with little or no alteration, as part of a work or as a finished work of art in itself

4.169 Henry Fuseli, *The Nightmare*, 1781. Oil on canvas, 40 × 50″. Detroit Institute of Arts

Henry Fuseli (1741–1825), a Swiss-born artist who lived in England after 1779, was inspired by gruesome elements from folklore, horror stories, and the occult to make his own uniquely disturbing paintings. In one of his most famous images, *The Nightmare,* a woman in white is stretched out on a divan with an incubus on top of her body (**4.169**). In the background, a fiendish horse peers around the curtain. According to legend, an incubus is a male demon who comes to people, usually women, while they sleep and has sex with them. Fuseli depicts a moment somewhere between sleep and death when the woman's nightmare seems to come to life around her. Fuseli's use of **chiaroscuro**, or contrasted light and dark colors, enhances the sinister mood created by the expressions on the faces of the incubus and the horse. At the time it was made, the painting's sexual implications were considered scandalous.

The American artist James Abbott McNeill Whistler (1834–1903) used music as the inspiration for an artwork that exemplified an approach known as "Art for Art's Sake." He titled his painting *Nocturne in Black and Gold: The Falling Rocket* because, like a "nocturne" or a musical composition inspired by the night,

it communicates the rhythm, patterns, and mood of a darkened landscape (**4.170**).

Nocturne in Black and Gold: The Falling Rocket was controversial in its time. Viewers and critics, unsure of what they were seeing, accused

4.170 James Abbott McNeill Whistler, *Nocturne in Black and Gold: The Falling Rocket*, 1875. Oil on wood panel, 23¾ × 18⅜″. Detroit Institute of Arts

Perspectives on Art: Mona Hatoum
Art, Personal Experience, and Identity

Mona Hatoum is a native of Lebanon (b. 1952) and now lives in London. Her work is exhibited all over the world. Here the art historian Professor Whitney Chadwick, of San Francisco State University, explains some of the connections between Hatoum's art and her personal experiences.

Mona Hatoum's *Untitled* (*Baalbek Bird Cage*) (1999) is one of a series of sculptural works on the theme of cages and caging (**4.171**). An international artist, Hatoum travels extensively and her **installations** often incorporate **found objects** that affect her emotionally and/or psychologically. Often her works recall the dislocations of her own life, much of it lived far from her family and the land of her birth. This sculpture originated in a beautiful Victorian birdcage that she discovered in a market while on a trip to Baalbek, Lebanon. Perhaps it reminded her of the loss of her childhood home. Enlarged to ten times its normal size, her sculpture may suggest a giant birdcage, or a large wooden bed, or perhaps a house. The work's shifts of scale may feel confusing or threatening to the viewer. Approaching the sculpture, one often feels disoriented, or disconnected. Is this object—so familiar and yet so strange because of its size—a common household object that just happens to suggest a prison? Are its associations friendly or threatening?

The actual dimensions of the birdcage were, in fact, based on the measurements of the cells at Alcatraz Prison in California. The most famous inhabitant of that prison, whose story became the subject of a well-known Hollywood film, was the so-called "Bird Man of Alcatraz," an incarcerated murderer who raised canaries as a hobby in his cell. In literature, from nineteenth-century English poetry to twentieth-century autobiography, women authors have often identified domestic life with feelings of being a caged bird. Here, as elsewhere in Hatoum's work, the birdcage occupies both a physical and a psychic space that incorporates a wide range of associations—from containment and femininity to liberation.

The feelings of dislocation that accompany the experience of Hatoum's installations and objects, including *Untitled* (*Baalbek Bird Cage*), often evoke the artist's own sense of having been "displaced" and "unsettled" by world events. Born in Lebanon of Palestinian parents, who had themselves been uprooted from Haifa in 1948, Hatoum was visiting London when civil war broke out in Lebanon in 1975. The war prevented her return to Beirut and she did not see her family for some years. Much of her work since the early 1980s has been produced in geographically far-flung locations and under conditions of exile that have encouraged her to reconsider what it means to be "settled" or "at home." *Baalbek Bird Cage* is one among many of Hatoum's sculptures and installations that fuses individual experience and geopolitical reality.

4.171 Mona Hatoum, *Untitled* (*Baalbek Bird Cage*), 1999. Wood and galvanized steel, 10'2⁷/₁₆" × 9'9" × 6' 5"

Whistler of trying to deceive the public by presenting a work that was incomplete or carelessly done. The critic John Ruskin wrote that with this painting Whistler was "flinging a pot of paint in the public's face." In reality, Whistler was depicting a fireworks display he had seen in London. He departed from the accepted standards of detailed realism in order to convey his sense of the rhythmic scene with bright sparks in a darkened night sky. About this painting, Whistler said that he was not interested in conveying a story or a recognizable moment, but instead had wanted to focus on line, form, and color. Whistler was also influenced by the way in which music communicates. He appreciated the flow of music and the fact that it does not depend on recognizable words or images.

The Norwegian artist Edvard Munch (1863–1944) used the realm of his own mind as inspiration for *The Scream* (**4.172**). As a child he endured the death of his mother and sister and throughout his life suffered from physical illness and depression. These tragic experiences and psychological disturbances motivated his art. Munch reported that he felt psychologically driven to make art. His painting *The Scream* presents a ghoul-like figure on a bridge with a vibrant red sky in the background. At first glance it appears to be a fictional scene. Entries in Munch's diary, however, indicate that his painting in fact represents his interpretation of an actual event. While walking on a bridge with two friends (the figures looming in the distance), Munch saw the sky turn red, and he froze with anxiety. Scholars have suggested Munch witnessed an incredibly intense sunset caused by the dust thrown into the atmosphere during a volcanic eruption that had occurred years before he made the painting. Others believe he experienced an attack of agoraphobia, or fear of open spaces. Like many **Expressionist** artworks, this painting does not depict what Munch actually saw, but what he felt.

Many artists, like Munch, have found new ways to follow their creative impulses. During the 1940s the American painter Jackson Pollock (1912–56) was undergoing Jungian **psychoanalysis**, a type of therapy that stresses

the importance of the collective unconscious and archetypes, or psychological models that we inherit through our unconscious minds. A notably enigmatic work, *Male and Female* (1942), when interpreted through Jungian analysis, has been understood as an integration of the masculine and feminine elements, and thus a reflection of a balanced psyche (**4.173**). The female figure, on the left, can be related to the feminine archetype, with its **paisley** shaped eyes, flowing eyelashes, bright colors, and curving body parts. The male figure, seen on the right, can be connected to the masculine archetype because of its more angular facial features, rigid form, and a mathematical script written on the body. In this painting, Pollock, inspired by **Surrealist** approaches for tapping into the unconscious mind, began to explore unfamiliar

Expressionism: an artistic style, at its height in 1920s Europe, which aimed to portray the world in terms of vivid extremes of personal experience and feeling

Psychoanalysis: a method of treating mental illness by making conscious the patient's subconscious fears or fantasies

Paisley: teardrop-shaped motif of Iranian origin, popular on European textiles since the nineteenth century

Surrealism: an artistic movement in the 1920s and later, the art of which was inspired by dreams and the subconscious

4.173 Jackson Pollock, *Male and Female, c.* 1942. Oil on canvas, 6'1⅜" × 4'1". Philadelphia Museum of Art

regions of his own psyche in order to access what might be seen as universal ideas about humanity.

The American artist and filmmaker Julian Schnabel (b. 1951) first made his mark on the art world with innovative mixed-media paintings. Schnabel's unconventional approach to painting included attaching broken plates to his canvases and painting on velvet. His work *The Exile* contains antlers along with a seemingly random assortment of images, both realistic and **abstract** (**4.174**). The figure on the left is copied from a portrait of a boy with a fruit basket by the **Baroque** painter Caravaggio. To the right is a wooden figurine that resembles a *kachina* doll made by the Native American Hopi. On the upper right is a bearded man with a turban, who is probably a reference to the Ayatollah Khomeini, the political and spiritual leader of the Islamic Revolution in Iran, which was happening about the time that Schnabel made his painting. Through this unlikely collection of imagery, Schnabel blends together influences from art history and current events in order to convey his own experience of life in the present moment.

4.174 Julian Schnabel, *The Exile*, 1980. Oil, antlers, gold leaf, and mixed media on wood, 7'6" × 12'

Abstract: an artwork the form of which is simplified, distorted, or exaggerated in appearance. It may represent a recognizable form that has been slightly altered, or it may be a completely non-representational depiction
Baroque: European artistic and architectural style of the late sixteenth to early eighteenth centuries, characterized by extravagance and emotional intensity
Kachina: carved wooden doll made by the Native American Hopi, representing a supernatural being in human form as a masked dancer

Borrowing an Image

Many artworks are personal statements, and those statements can take many forms. Some artworks are created by borrowing objects, figures, or entire compositions from the work of other artists. This practice, known as **appropriation,** can be traced to the invention by French artist Marcel Duchamp (1887–1968) of **readymades** (see p. 270), which consist of ordinary objects transformed into artworks simply by the decision of the artist.

Duchamp appropriated such objects as urinals, bicycle wheels, snow shovels, and even other artworks as viable material for his art. Over time, other artists followed in his footsteps by continuing to appropriate artworks (including ones by Duchamp). Some also borrowed images from the realms of popular culture, advertising, and even social stereotypes. Thus an artist can make a personal statement by appropriating the work of another.

The American artist Sherrie Levine (b. 1947) is known for her appropriation of famous paintings, sculptures, and photographs from the past. These pieces raise many questions: Who can be an artist? What role does the artist play? How has that role changed over time? What is originality? Who can be original? The pieces Levine appropriates are generally by male artists who worked at a time when there were very few women in the art world, as has been the case throughout most of history. Levine's work leads us to reconsider the structures of art institutions as they existed in the past. Her sculpture *Fountain (After Marcel Duchamp: A. P.)* (**4.175**) recalls Duchamp's famous porcelain urinal from 1917. Unlike Duchamp, though, who took an existing urinal and declared it to be art, Levine had a urinal cast in bronze, a material traditionally used for fine art sculptures. Levine encourages the viewer not just to interact with her own piece, but also to consider his or her attitude toward Duchamp's urinal. Her quotation of a past artwork makes Levine's sculpture most meaningful for viewers who are familiar with Duchamp's work.

In the 1960s, **Pop** artists began using appropriation to bring recognizable and familiar imagery into galleries and museums. Their sources included comic-book characters, movie stars, popular commercial products, and everyday household items. The *Brillo Box* sculptures by the American artist Andy Warhol (1928–87) exactly copied the design of the product's packaging (**4.176**). He had the plywood boxes built in his studio, The Factory, and then **silkscreened** by hand (although they look manufactured rather than hand-made). The square shape of the boxes and the blue, red, and white of the labels recall some of the formal **elements** in abstract artworks. By combining the practices of what was then considered "high art" at the time with the "low art" of **graphic design**, Warhol was able to bridge the gap between the two and expand the boundaries of acceptable fine art practices to include popular imagery and commercial printing processes.

Even though Warhol's work challenged accepted practices, many people in the art world readily embraced his approach. An even more controversial line was adopted by the Panamanian-

4.175 Sherrie Levine, *Fountain (After Marcel Duchamp: A. P.)*, 1991. Bronze, 26 × 14½ × 14˝

4.176 Andy Warhol, *Brillo Box*, 1964. Synthetic polymer paint and silkscreen ink on painted wood, 17 × 17 × 14˝. Collection Andy Warhol Foundation

Appropriation: the deliberate incorporation in an artwork of material originally created by other artists
Readymade: an everyday object presented as a work of art
Pop art: mid-twentieth-century artistic movement inspired by commercial art forms and popular culture
Silkscreen: method of printmaking using a stencil and paint pushed through a screen
Elements: the basic vocabulary of art—including line, form, shape, volume, mass, color, texture, space, time and motion, and value (lightness/darkness)
Graphic design: the use of images, typography, and technology to communicate ideas for a client or to a particular audience

4.177 Richard Prince, *Untitled (Cowboys)*, 1980. Ektacolor print, 27 × 40", edition 1/2. Museum of Contemporary Art, Los Angeles

born American artist Richard Prince (b. 1949). While working for Time Life publications in the 1980s, Prince began to use advertisements as the basis for his artworks. His *Cowboys* series focused on the Marlboro man from the cigarette company's print ads (**4.177**). He cropped the images in such a way that the logos were not included, but otherwise, the color, composition, and vantage point of Prince's artworks were predetermined by the advertisements. When the images were enlarged to fit an art gallery wall they became grainy and blurry, revealing that they were copies, not originals. Prince's photographs were considered sufficiently different from the source to have their own artistic merit.

4.178 Nikki S. Lee, *Hip Hop Project (25)*, 2001. Fujiflex print

For her *Projects* series, the Korean artist Nikki S. Lee (b. 1970) joined a number of different communities, from yuppies and tourists to Hispanics and senior citizens, shopping in the stores they frequented and adopting their mannerisms. Lee said, "My goal is not to become black, white, or Hispanic. It's more like becoming an Asian person who really likes that culture." Once she felt she had become a genuine member of the group, she would have a snapshot self-portrait of herself taken with her new peers. For the *Hip Hop Project* in 2001, Lee went to a tanning salon three times a week to darken her skin, and then immersed herself in the subculture of the hip hop music scene (**4.178**). Although she told the people in the close-knit group depicted in this image that she was an artist, most of them did not believe her. It is surprising to learn that her interaction with these people is temporary, because there are no clues to suggest that she is not one of them. Such guises as this one become borrowed personalities for Lee, who considers her identity to be very fluid.

Discussion Questions

1 Several artists created multiple self-portraits. Select three self-portraits by the same artist and study them closely. What are the differences between your three selections? What do you think the artist was exploring or conveying in each example?

2 In this chapter we have studied artists who appropriate imagery. Elsewhere in this book you will see examples of artworks that have been influenced by another artist or culture (see for example **3.76**, **3.184**, and **4.130**). How does influence differ from appropriation? How do the two groups of artwork relate to the earlier work that influenced them or that was appropriated?

3 Consider artworks in this chapter that were inspired by the artist's personal experience. Now think of a specific event in your life or a set of circumstances that would be interesting to translate into an artwork. What would you want people to know? What feelings stand out in your mind? What kinds of colors and imagery relate to your experience?

Images related to 3.1:
The Prehistoric and Ancient Mediterranean

4.129 *Woman from Willendorf*, c. 24,000–22,000 BCE, p. 554

4.96a, 4.96b Palette of Narmer, c. 2950–2775 BCE, p. 526

4.3 Stonehenge, c. 3200–1500 BCE, p. 456

1.136 *Poseidon* [or *Zeus*], c. 460–450 BCE, p. 134

2.152 *Riace Warrior A*, c. 450 BCE, p. 266

4.14 Sumerian bull lyre, c. 2550–2450 BCE, p. 464

4.131b *Menkaure and his Wife, Queen Khamerernebty*, c. 2520 BCE, p. 556

4.27 Stela of Naram-Sin, c. 2254–2218 BCE, p. 474

4.7 Ziggurat at Ur, c. 2100 BCE, p. 459

4.99 Stela of Hammurabi, c. 1792–1750 BCE, p. 528

4.157 Sphinx of Hatshepsut, 1479–1458 BCE, p. 575

2.171 Temple of Amun-Re, 1417–1379 BCE, p. 278

4.95 Akhenaten, Nefertiti, and three daughters, c. 1353–1335 BCE, p. 525

2.151 Sarcophagus from Cerveteri, c. 520 BCE, p. 266

4.132 Myron, *Discus Thrower (Discobolos)*, c. 450 BCE, p. 557

1.34 Imperial Procession from the Ara Pacis Augustae, 13 BCE, p. 67

4.97 *Augustus of Primaporta*, early 1st century CE (after original from 20 BCE), p. 527

4.5 Colosseum, 72–80 CE, p. 458

1.161 Equestrian statue of Marcus Aurelius, c. 175 CE, p. 152

4.100 Remnants of colossal statue of Constantine, 325–6 CE, p. 528

Images related to 3.2:
Art of the Middle Ages

2.179 Hagia Sophia, 532–5 CE, p. 282

1.10 *Pentateuch with Prophetical Readings and the Five Scrolls*, 13th–14th century, p. 52

4.22a Doors depicting scenes from Genesis and the Life of Christ, 1015, p. 471

1.27 *Banner of Las Navas de Tolosa*, 1212–50, p. 61

1.32 *Vesperbild* (Pietà), *c.* 1330, p. 65

1.156 Great Mosque of Córdoba, 784–6, p. 148

4.89 Justinian mosaic, *c.* 547 CE, p. 521

4.110 Detail of Battle of Hastings, Bayeux Tapestry, *c.* 1066–82, p. 536

2.176 Interior, nave, Sainte-Foy, *c.* 1050–1120, p. 280

4.28 *Virgin of Vladimir*, 12th century (before 1132), p. 475

4.57 Gislebertus, *Last Judgment*, *c.* 1120–35, p. 494

4.125 Icon of *Virgin and Child with Saints*, 6th century, p. 550

4.2 Notre Dame Cathedral, 1163–1250, p. 455

2.133 Rose window and lancets, Chartres Cathedral, 13th century, p. 254

4.34 Main entrance portal, Masjid-i-Shah, 17th century, p.480

Images related to 3.3:
Art of India, China, and Japan

1.122 Ritual container from Gui, China, 1600–1100 BCE, p. 125

4.11 Soldiers from mausoleum of Qin Shi Huangdi, *c.* 210 BCE, p. 462

4.35 Ise Jingu, 4th century CE, rebuilt 1993, p. 481

1.118 *Vishnu Dreaming the Universe*, *c.* 450–500 CE, p. 122

4.23 *Life of Buddha*, *c.* 475 CE, p. 472

4.124a and **b** Colossal Buddha from Bamiyan (before and after destruction), 6th or 7th century CE, destroyed 2001, p. 549

4.45 *Shiva Nataraja* (*Lord of the Dance*), 11th century, p. 488

1.123 Muqi, *Six Persimmons*, *c.* 1250, p. 126

4.111 *Night Attack on the Sanjo Palace*, late 13th century, p. 537

2.129 Porcelain flask with decoration in blue underglaze, 1425–35, p. 252

1.125 Amitayas mandala created at Drepung Loseling Monastery, Tibet, p. 127

1.146 *The Emperor Babur Overseeing his Gardeners*, *c.* 1590, p. 140

1.152 Pashmina carpet with millefleur pattern, second half of 17th century, p. 144

4.90 Portrait of the Yongzheng Emperor in court dress, 1723–35, p. 521

2.43 Kitagawa Utamaro, *Lovers in an Upstairs Room*, 1788, p. 194

1.148 Ando Hiroshige, *Riverside Bamboo Market, Kyōbashi*, 1857, p. 141

4.101 Mao Zedong's portrait over Tiananmen Square, p. 529

2.32 Hung Liu, *Interregnum*, 2002, p. 186

Images related to 3.4:
Art of the Americas

2.154 Great Serpent Mound, *c.* 800 BCE–100 CE, p. 267

4.12 Cahokia, Illinois, *c.* 1150 (reconstruction drawing), p. 463

2.128 Baby Figure, 12th–9th century BCE, p. 251

1.1 Spider, *c.* 500 BCE–500 CE, p. 47

4.49 Sarcophagus lid, tomb of Lord Pacal, *c.* 680 CE, p. 490

2.127 *Seated Figure*, 300 BCE–700 CE, p. 250

1.35 Stela with supernatural scene, 761 CE, p. 67

1.141 Double-chambered vessel with mouse, 4th–8th century, p. 136

4.92 Shield Jaguar and Lady Xoc, *c.* 725 CE, p. 523

4.59 Eccentric flint depicting a crocodile canoe with passengers, 600–900 CE, p. 497

2.168 Temple I in the Great Plaza, Tikal, *c.* 300–900 CE, p. 276

4.108 Tula warrior columns, 900–1000 CE, p. 534

4.60 Calendar stone, late postclassic, p. 497

4.51 Vessel with mask of Tlaloc, *c.* 1440–69, p. 491

4.46 Mummy of a boy, *c.* 1500, p. 488

2.139 Tlingit Chilkat dancing blanket, 19th century, p. 258

4.50 Hopi kachina doll, *c.* 1925, p. 491

4.16 Navajo medicine man in healing ceremony, *c.* 1908, p. 465

Images related to 3.5:
Art of Africa and the Pacific Islands

0.18 Benin hip pendant, mid-16th century, p. 43

1.116 Romare Bearden, *The Dove*, 1964, p. 120

1.133 Figure of Oni, early 14th–15th century, p. 132

4.134 Head, possibly a king, 12th–14th century, p. 559

4.39 Ritual vessel, 13th–14th century, p. 484

4.98 Plaque with warrior and attendants, 16th–17th century, p. 527

1.158 Bai-ra-Irrai, originally built *c.* 1700, p. 149

2.150 Figure of the war god Ku-ka'ili-moku, 18th or 19th century, p. 265

4.24 Mother and child figure, late 19th–mid-20th century, p. 472

4.148 *Chibinda Ilunga*, mid-19th century, p. 569

4.44 Kneeling female figure with bowl and child, 19th–20th century, p. 487

4.43 Bis ancestor poles, late 1950s, p. 487

4.16 Pair of Gèlèdé masqueraders, 1970, p. 465

4.26 Chair, early 20th century, p. 473

Images related to 3.6:
Art of Renaissance and Baroque Europe (1400–1750)

0.8 Leonardo da Vinci, *Mona Lisa*, 1503–6, p. 33

1.65 Masaccio, *Trinity*, c. 1425–26, p. 88

1.115 Piero della Francesca, *The Flagellation*, c. 1649, p. 119

2.28 Jan van Eyck, *The Madonna of Chancellor Rolin*, 1430–34, p. 185

4.133 Sandro Botticelli, *The Birth of Venus*, c. 1482–6, p. 558

1.70 Andrea Mantegna, *The Lamentation over the Dead Christ*, c. 1480, p. 91

2.42 Albrecht Dürer, *Four Horsemen of the Apocalypse*, c. 1497–8, p. 193

2.2 Leonardo da Vinci, Studies of the foetus in the womb, c. 1510–13, p. 167

2.148 Michelangelo, *Creation of the Sun and the Moon*, 1508–10, p. 264

4.77 Parmigianino, *Self-portrait in a Convex Mirror*, c. 1524, p. 511

4.136 Titian, *Venus of Urbino*, 1538, p. 560

1.144 Peter Bruegel the Elder, *Landscape with the Fall of Icarus*, c. 1555–8, p. 138

1.124 Andrea Palladio, Plan and part elevation/section of the Villa Rotonda, begun 1565/6, p. 127

1.52 Caravaggio, *The Calling of St. Matthew*, c. 1599–1600, p. 79

4.163 Rembrandt van Rijn, *Self-portrait with Saskia in the Scene of the Prodigal Son at the Tavern*, c. 1635, p. 580

2.34 Artemisia Gentileschi, *Self-portrait as the Allegory of Painting (La Pittura)*, 1638–9, p. 187

2.16 Claude Lorrain, *The Tiber from Monte Mario Looking South*, 1640, p. 176

4.29 Gianlorenzo Bernini, *The Ecstasy of St. Teresa*, 1645–52, p. 475

1.169 Diego de Silva y Velázquez, *Las Meninas*, c. 1656, p. 160

4.58 Johannes Vermeer, *Woman Holding a Balance*, c. 1664, p. 495

Images related to 3.7:
Art of Europe and America (1700–1900)

4.93 Hyacinthe Rigaud, *Louis XIV*, 1701, p. 524

4.62 Joseph Wright of Derby, *An Experiment on a Bird in the Air Pump*, 1768, p. 499

4.169 Henry Fuseli, *The Nightmare*, 1781, p. 584

4.94 Élisabeth-Louise Vigée-Lebrun, *Marie Antoinette and Her Children*, 1787, p. 524

1.166 Jean-Auguste-Dominique Ingres, *Grande Odalisque*, 1814, p. 157

4.116 Théodore Géricault, *Raft of the Medusa*, 1819, p. 542

2.54 Honoré Daumier, *Rue Transnonain, April 15, 1834*, p. 200

2.79 Louis-Jacques-Mandé Daguerre, *The Artist's Studio*, 1837, p. 218

4.137 Édouard Manet, *Olympia*, 1863, p. 561

4.170 James Abbott McNeill Whistler, *Nocturne in Black and Gold: The Falling Rocket*, 1875, p. 584

4.63 Thomas Eakins, *Portrait of Dr. Samuel D. Gross (The Gross Clinic)*, 1875, p. 499

2.96 Eadweard Muybridge, *The Horse in Motion*, June 18, 1878, p. 229

4.66 Georges Seurat, *Sunday on La Grande Jatte*, 1884–6, p. 501

1.160 Rosa Bonheur, *Plowing in the Nivernais: The Dressing of the Vines*, 1849, p. 151

1.18 Vincent van Gogh, *The Bedroom*, 1889, p. 56

4.172 Edvard Munch, *The Scream*, 1893, p. 586

4.143 Auguste Rodin, *Walking Man*, c. 1890–95, p. 565

2.65 William Morris and Edward Burne-Jones, Page from *Works of Geoffrey Chaucer*, 1896, p. 208

2.184 Joseph Paxton, Crystal Palace, 1851, p. 284

3.76 Mary Cassatt, *The Child's Bath*, 1893, p. 345

Images related to 3.8:
Twentieth and Twenty-First Centuries, The Age of Global Art

2.159 Marcel Duchamp, *Fountain*, 1917, p. 270

1.24 Georgia O'Keeffe, *Music—Pink and Blue II*, 1919, p. 59

2.188 Le Corbusier, Villa Savoye, 1931, p. 286

4.70 Salvador Dalí, *Persistence of Memory*, 1931, p. 504

4.119 Pablo Picasso, *Guernica*, 1937, p. 545

4.162 Frida Kahlo, *The Two Fridas*, 1939, p. 579

4.147 Alberto Giacometti, *Man Pointing*, 1947, p. 567

4.130 Willem de Kooning, *Woman I*, 1950–52, p. 555

2.155 Robert Smithson, *Spiral Jetty*, 1969–70, p. 268

1.106 Alexander Calder, *Untitled*, 1976, p. 113

2.104 George Lucas, still from *Star Wars Episode IV—A New Hope*, 1977, p. 234

4.152 Cindy Sherman, *Untitled Film Still #35*, 1979, p. 571

1.168 Edward Hopper, *Nighthawks*, 1942, p. 159

4.153 Judy Chicago, *The Dinner Party*, 1974–9, p. 572

2.157 Damien Hirst, *The Physical Impossibility of Death in the Mind of Someone Living*, 1991, p. 269

1.45 Frank Gehry, Guggenheim Museum, 1997, p. 74

1.153 Chuck Close, *Self Portrait*, 1997, p. 145

2.134 Dale Chihuly, *Fiori di Como*, 1998, p. 255

2.124 Kara Walker, *Insurrection! (Our Tools were Rudimentary, Yet We Pressed On)*, 2000, p. 247

4.4 Christo and Jeanne-Claude, *The Gates*, 1979–2005, p. 457

Glossary

NOTE: *A few terms have more than one definition, depending on the context in which they are used.*

Abstract: (1) art imagery that departs from recognizable images from the natural world; (2) an artwork the form of which is simplified, distorted, or exaggerated in appearance. It may represent a recognizable form that has been slightly altered, or it may be a completely non-representational depiction

Abstraction: the degree to which an image is altered from an easily recognizable subject

Abstract Expressionism: a mid-twentieth-century artistic style characterized by its capacity to convey intense emotions using non-representational images

Academies: institutions training artists in both the theory of art and practical techniques

Acropolis: a high place in a Greek city on which a temple is located

Action painting: application of paint to canvas by dripping, splashing, or smearing that emphasizes the artist's gestures

Actual and Implied lines: actual lines are solid lines. Implied lines are impressions of lines created from a series of points that orient our gaze along a visual path

Actual line: a continuous, uninterrupted line

Aesthetic: related to beauty, art, and taste

A-frame: an ancient form of structural support, made out of beams arranged so that the shape of the building resembles a capital letter A

Afterimage effect: when the eye sees the complementary color of something that the viewer has spent an extended time viewing (also known as successive contrasts)

Aisles: in a basilica or other church, the spaces between the columns of the nave and the side walls

Altar: an area where sacrifices or offerings are made

Altarpiece: an artwork that is placed behind an altar in a church

Ambulatory: a covered walkway, particularly around the apse of a church

Analogous colors: colors adjacent to each other on the color wheel

Anamorphosis: the distorted representation of an object so that it appears correctly proportioned only when viewed from one particular position

Appropriation: the deliberate incorporation in an artwork of material originally created by other artists

Apse: semicircular vaulted space in a church

Aquatint: an intaglio printmaking process that uses melted rosin or spray paint to create an acid-resistant ground

Aqueduct: a structure designed to carry water, often over long distances

Arabesque: an abstract pattern derived from geometric and vegetal lines and forms

Archaic: Greek art of the period *c.* 620–480 BCE

Arches: structures, usually curved, that span an opening

Architectural order: a style of designing columns and related parts of a Greek or Roman building

Architrave: a beam that rests on the top of a row of columns

Armature: a framework or skeleton used to support a sculpture

Art Brut: "raw art," artworks made by untrained artists, and having a primitive or childlike quality

Articulate: to make smaller shapes or spaces within a larger composition

Artifact: an object made by a person

Artist's book: a book produced by an artist, usually an expensive limited edition, often using specialized printing processes

Assemblage: artwork made of three-dimensional materials including found objects

Asymmetry: a type of design in which balance is achieved by elements that contrast and complement one another without being the same on either side of an axis

Atmospheric perspective: use of shades of color and clarity to create the illusion of depth. Closer objects have warmer tones and clear outlines, while objects set further away are cooler and become hazy

Atrium: a central, normally public, interior space, first used in Roman houses

Automatic: suppressing conscious control to access subconscious sources of creativity and truth

Avant-garde: early twentieth-century emphasis on artistic innovation, which challenged accepted values, traditions, and techniques

Axis: an imaginary line showing the center of a shape, volume, or composition

Background: (1) the part of a work depicted as behind the main figures; (2) the part of a work depicted furthest from the viewer's space, often behind the main subject matter

Balance: a principle of art in which elements are used to create a symmetrical or asymmetrical sense of visual weight in an artwork

Balustrade: a railing supported by short pillars

Baroque: European artistic and architectural style of the late sixteenth to early eighteenth century, characterized by extravagance and emotional intensity

Base: the projecting series of blocks between the shaft of a column and its plinth

Basilica: an early Christian church, either converted from or built to resemble a type of Roman civic building

Bas-relief: a sculpture carved with very little depth

Bauhaus: design school founded in Weimar, Germany, in 1919

Binder: a substance that makes pigments adhere to a surface

Bohemian: derived from the gypsies of the former Czech Kingdom of Bohemia who moved around; a wanderer; an artist or writer who functions outside the bounds of conventional rules and practices

Boldface: a darker and heavier typeface than its normal instance

Bust: a statue of a person depicting only his or her head and shoulders

Byzantine: relating to the East Roman Empire, centered on Constantinople (modern-day Istanbul) from the fifth century CE to 1453

Calligraphy: the art of emotive or carefully descriptive hand lettering or handwriting

Canon of proportions: a set of ideal mathematical ratios in art used to measure the various parts of the human body in relation to one another

Canopic jar: a jar used by ancient Egyptians to hold the embalmed internal organs removed from the body during mummification

Capital: the architectural feature that crowns a column

Capstone: a final stone forming the top of a structure; on a pyramid, it is pyramid-shaped

Cast: a sculpture or artwork made by pouring a liquid (for example molten metal or plaster) into a mold

Catacombs: an underground system of tunnels used for burying and commemorating the dead

Central-plan church: Eastern Orthodox church design, often in the shape of a cross with all four arms of equal length

Ceramic(s): fire-hardened clay, often painted, and normally sealed with shiny protective coating

Ceramist: a person who makes ceramics

Chevron: a V-shaped stripe, often reproduced upside down or on its side in decorative patterns

Chiaroscuro: the use of light and dark in a painting to create the impression of volume

Choir: part of a church traditionally reserved for singers and clergy, situated between the nave and the apse

Classical: (1) ancient Greek and Roman; (2) artworks from ancient Greece or Rome; (3) art that conforms to Greek and Roman models, or is based on rational construction and emotional equilibrium; (4) Greek art of the period *c.* 480–323 BCE

Classical period: a period in the history of Greek art, *c.* 480–323 BCE

Clerestory windows: a row of windows high up in a church to admit light into the nave

Coffered: decorated with recessed paneling

Coiling: the use of long coils of clay – rather than a wheel – to build the walls of a pottery vessel

Collage: a work of art assembled by gluing materials, often paper, onto a surface. From the French *coller*, to glue

Colophon: comment written on a Chinese scroll by the creator, owner, or a viewer

Color: the optical effect caused when reflected white light of the spectrum is divided into a separate wavelength

Color field: a term used by a group of twentieth-century abstract painters to describe their work with large flat areas of color and simple shapes

Color theory: the understanding of how colors relate to each other, especially when mixed or placed near one another

Column: freestanding pillar, usually circular in section

Complementary colors: colors opposite one another on the color wheel

Composite view: representation of a subject from multiple viewpoints at one time

Composition: the overall design or organization of a work

Concentric: identical shapes stacked inside each other sharing the same center, for example the circles of a target

Conceptual: relating to or concerning ideas

Conceptual art: a work in which the ideas are often as important as how it is made

Concrete: a hard, strong, and versatile construction material made up of powdered lime, sand, and rubble

Constructivism: an art movement in the Soviet Union in the 1920s, primarily concerned to make art of use to the working class

Continuous narrative: when different parts of a story are shown within the same visual space

Contour: the outline that defines a form

Contour rivalry: a design in which the lines can be read in more than one way at the same time, depending on the angle from which it is viewed

Contrapposto: a pose in sculpture in which the upper part of the body twists in one direction and the lower part in another

Contrast: a drastic difference between such elements as color or value (lightness/darkness)

Convention: a widely accepted way of doing something; using a particular style, following a certain method, or representing something in a specific way

Convex: curved inward, like the exterior of a sphere

Corbeled: with a series of corbels— architectural feature made of stone, brick, wood, etc.—each projecting beyond the one below

Cornice: molding round the top of a building

Cor-ten steel: a type of steel that forms a coating of rust that protects it from the weather and further corrosion

Course: a single row of stones or bricks forming a horizontal layer of a structure

Cropping: trimming the edges of an image, or composing it so that part of the subject matter is cut off

Cross-hatching: the use of overlapping parallel lines to convey darkness or lightness

Cubism: a twentieth-century art movement that favored a new perspective emphasizing geometric forms

Curator: a person who organizes the collection and exhibition of objects/artworks in a museum or gallery

Dada: anarchic anti-art and anti-war movement, dating back to World War I, that reveled in absurdity and irrationality

Deposition: a scene showing the taking down of Christ's body from the cross

Depth: the degree of recession in perspective

De Stijl: a group of artists originating in the Netherlands in the early twentieth century, associated with a utopian style of design that emphasized primary colors and straight lines

Diagonal: a line that runs obliquely, rather than horizontally or vertically

Didactic: with the aim of teaching or educating

Directional line: implied line within a composition, leading the viewer's eye from one element to another

Dissonance: a lack of harmony

Documentary: non-fiction film based on actual people, settings, and events

Dome: an evenly curved vault

Drypoint: an intaglio printmaking process where the artist raises a burr when gouging the printing plate

Edition: all the copies of a print made from a single printing

Elements: the basic vocabulary of art—line, form, shape, volume, mass, color, texture, space, time and motion, and value (lightness/darkness)

Embroidery: decorative stitching generally made with colored thread applied to the surface of a fabric

Emphasis: the principle of drawing attention to particular content within a work

Engraving: a printmaking technique where the artist gouges or scratches the image into the surface of the printing plate

Enlightenment: an intellectual movement in eighteenth-century Europe that argued for science, reason, and individualism, and against tradition

Entablature: the part of a Greek or Roman building that rests on top of a column

Entasis: the slight swelling or bulge at the midpoint of a column

Etching: (1) a printmaking process that uses acid to bite (or etch) the engraved design into the printing surface; (2) an intaglio printmaking process that uses acid to bite (or etch) the engraved design into the printmaking surface

Eucharist: Christian ceremony that commemorates the death of Jesus Christ

Experimental film: films the style and content of which are very different from mainstream commercial films

Expressionism: an artistic style at its height in 1920s Europe, aiming to portray the world in terms of vivid extremes of personal experience and feeling

Expressive: capable of stirring the emotions of the viewer

Facade: any side of a building, usually the front or entrance

Fauves: a group of early twentieth-century French artists whose paintings used vivid colors. From the French *fauve*, wild beast

Figuration: the portrayal of things in the visible world

Figurative: art that portrays items perceived in the visible world, especially human or animal forms

Figure–ground reversal: the reversal of the relationship between one shape (the figure) and its background (the ground), so that the figure becomes background and the ground becomes the figure

Firing: heating ceramic, glass, or enamel objects in a kiln, to harden them, fuse the components, or fuse a glaze to the surface

Fixing: the chemical process used to ensure a photographic image becomes permanent

Flint: an object or tool made from the very hard, sharp-edged stone of the same name

Flying buttress: an arch built on the exterior of a building that transfers some of the weight of the vault

Focal point: (1) the center of interest or activity in a work of art, often drawing the viewer's attention to the most important element; (2) the area in a composition to which the eye returns most naturally

Foreground: the part of a work depicted as nearest to the viewer

Foreshortening: a perspective technique that depicts a form at a very oblique (often dramatic) angle to the viewer in order to show depth in space

Form: an object that can be defined in three dimensions (height, width, and depth)

Format: the shape of the area an artist uses for making a two-dimensional artwork

Found image: an image found by an artist and presented with little or no alteration as a work of art

Found object: an object found by an artist and presented, with little or no alteration, as part of a work or as a finished work of art in itself

Fresco: (1) a technique where the artist paints onto freshly applied plaster. From the Italian fresco, *fresh*; (2) paintings made on freshly applied plaster

Frieze: the strip that goes around the top of a building, often filled with sculptural ornamentation

Futurism: an artistic and social movement, originating in Italy in 1909, passionately in favor of everything modern

Gèlèdé ritual: ritual performed in Nigeria's Yoruba society to celebrate and honor women

Genre: categories of artistic subject matter, often with strongly influential histories and traditions

Gestalt: complete order and indivisible unity of all aspects of an artwork's design

Glazing: in oil painting, adding a transparent layer of paint to achieve a richness in texture, volume, and form

Golden Section: a unique ratio of a line divided into two parts so that $a + b$ is to a as a is to b. The result is 1:1.618

Gothic: Western European architectural style of the twelfth to sixteenth centuries, characterized by the use of pointed arches and ornate decoration

Graphic design: the use of images, typography, and technology to communicate ideas for a client or to a particular audience

Grid: a network of horizontal and vertical lines; in an artwork's composition, the lines are implied

Ground: the surface or background onto which an artist paints or draws

Guilds: medieval associations of artists, craftsmen, or tradesmen

Gypsum: fine grained, powdery mineral often used to make a smooth plaster

Happening: impromptu art actions, initiated and planned by an artist, the outcome of which is not known in advance

Hatching: the use of non-overlapping parallel lines to convey darkness or lightness

Hellenistic: Greek art from *c.* 323–100 BCE

Hierarchical scale: the use of size to denote the relative importance of subjects in an artwork

Hieroglyph: written language involving sacred characters that may be pictures as well as letters

Highlight: an area of lightest value in a work

High relief: a carved panel where the figures project with a great deal of depth from the background

Hue: general classification of a color; the distinctive characteristics of a color as seen in the visible spectrum, such as green or red

Humanism: the study of such subjects as history, philosophy, languages, and literature, particularly in relation to those of ancient Greece and Rome

Hypostyle hall: a large room with a roof supported by a forest of columns

Icon: a small, often portable, religious image venerated by Christian believers; first used by the Eastern Orthodox Church

Iconic: a sign, the form of which directly suggests its meaning

Iconoclast: someone who destroys imagery, often out of religious belief

Ideal: more beautiful, harmonious, or perfect than reality

Idealism: elevating depictions of nature to achieve more beautiful, harmonious, and perfect depictions

Idealized: represented as perfect in form or character, corresponding to an ideal

Ideogram: a symbol that expresses an idea or a thing without representing the sounds in its name (for example, "8")

Illuminated characters: highly decorated letters, usually found at the beginning of a page or paragraph

Illuminated manuscript: a hand-lettered text with hand-drawn pictures

Illuminations: illustrations and decorations in a manuscript

Illusionism (adjective **illusionistic**): the artistic skill or trick of making something look real

IMAX: a format for film presentation that records at such high resolution that it allows presentation of films at far larger sizes than the conventional one

Impasto: paint applied in thick layers

Implied line: a line not actually drawn but suggested by elements in the work

Implied texture: a visual illusion expressing texture

Impression: an individual print, or pull, from a printing press

Impressionism: a late nineteenth-century painting style conveying the impression of the effects of light

Incised: cut

Inlay: substance embedded in another, contrasting material

Installation: an artwork created by the assembling and arrangement of objects within a specific location

Intaglio: any print process where the inked image is lower than the surface of the printing plate; from the Italian for "cut into"

Intarsia: the art of setting pieces of wood into a surface to create a pattern

Intensity: the relative clarity of color in its purest raw form, demonstrated through luminous or muted variations

In the round: a freestanding sculpted work that can be viewed from all sides

Isometric perspective: a system using diagonal parallel lines to communicate depth

Ivory: hard, creamy-colored material from the tusks of such mammals as elephants

Kachina: carved wooden doll made by the Native American Hopi, representing a supernatural being in human form as a masked dancer

Kinetic art: a work that contains moving parts

Kinetic sculpture: three-dimensional art that moves, impelled by air currents, motors, or people

Kouros: sculpture of a nude Greek youth

Lapis lazuli: bright-blue semiprecious stone containing sodium aluminum silicate and sulphur

Latitude: a point on the earth's circumference measured to the east or west

Levering: to move or raise an object

using a leverlike action

Line: a mark, or implied mark, between two endpoints

Linear outline: a line that clearly separates a figure from its surroundings

Linear perspective: a system using imaginary sight lines to create the illusion of depth

Lintel: the horizontal beam over the doorway of a portal

Low relief: carving in which the design stands out only slightly from the background surface

Luminosity: a bright, glowing quality

Lyre: a stringed instrument that is played by being plucked; the strings hang from a crossbar that is supported by two arms connected to a hollow box, which amplifies the sound

Mandala: a sacred diagram of the universe, often involving a square and a circle

Mannerism: from Italian *di maniera*, meaning charm, grace, playfulness; mid- to late sixteenth-century style of painting, usually with elongated human figures elevating grace as an ideal

Mantle: sleeveless item of clothing—a cloak or cape

Manuscripts: handwritten texts

Mask: a barrier, in spray painting or silkscreen printing, the shape of which blocks the paint or ink from passing through

Masquerade: performance in which participants wear masks and costumes for a ritual or cultural purpose

Mass: a volume that has, or gives the illusion of having, weight, density, and bulk

Medieval: relating to the Middle Ages; roughly, between the fall of the Roman Empire and the Renaissance

Medium (plural **media**)**:** the material on or from which an artist chooses to make a work of art, for example canvas and oil paint, marble, engraving, video, or architecture

Metope: a square space between triglyphs, often decorated with sculpture

Mezzotint: an intaglio printmaking process based on roughening the entire printing plate to accept ink; the artist smoothes non-image areas

Middle ground: the part of a work between the foreground and background

Mihrab: a niche in a mosque that is in a wall oriented towards Mecca

Mime: a silent performance work; actors use only body movements and facial expressions

Minaret: a tall slender tower, particularly on a mosque, from which the faithful are called to prayer

Minimalist: a mid-twentieth-century artistic style characterized by its simple, unified, and impersonal look, and often employing geometrical or massive forms

Mobile: suspended moving sculptures, usually impelled by natural air currents

Modeling: the representation of three-dimensional objects in two dimensions so that they appear solid

Modernist: a radically new twentieth-century architectural movement that embraced modern industrial materials and a machine aesthetic

Monochromatic: having one or more values of one color

Monolith: a monument or sculpture made from a single piece of stone

Monumental: having massive or impressive scale

Mosaic: a picture or pattern created by fixing together small pieces of stone, glass, tile, etc.

Motif: a distinctive visual element, the recurrence of which is often characteristic of an artist's work

Motion: the effect of changing placement in time

Mural: a painting executed directly on to a wall

Narrative: an artwork that tells a story

Naturalism (adjective **naturalistic**)**:** a very realistic or lifelike style of making images

Nave: the central space of a cathedral or basilica

Necropolis: cemetery or burial place

Negative: a reversed image, in which light areas are dark, and dark areas are light (opposite of a positive)

Negative space: an empty space given shape by its surround, for example the right-pointing arrow between the **E** and **x** in **FedEx**

Neutral: colors (such as blacks, whites, grays, and dull gray-browns) made by mixing complementary hues

Non-objective: art that does not depict a recognizable subject

Nude: an artistic representation of the naked human figure

Oculus: a round opening at the center of a dome

Octagonal: eight-sided

Oil paint: paint made of pigment floating in oil

One-point perspective: a perspective system with a single vanishing point on the horizon

Opaque: not transparent

Op art: a style of art exploiting the physiology of seeing to create illusory optical effects

Optical mixture: when the eye blends two colors that are placed near one another, creating a new color

Organic: having forms and shapes derived from living organisms

Origami: the Japanese art of paperfolding

Orthogonals: in perspective systems, imaginary sightlines extending from forms to the vanishing point

Outline: the outermost line of an object or figure, by which it is defined or bounded

Paisley: teardrop-shaped motif of Iranian origin, popular on European textiles since the nineteenth century

Paleolithic: prehistoric period,

extending from 2.5 million to 12,000 years ago

Palette: (1) the range of colors used by an artist; (2) a smooth slab or board used for mixing paints or cosmetics

Passion: the arrest, trial, and execution of Jesus Christ, and his sufferings during them

Patina: surface color or texture on a metal caused by aging

Patron: an organization or individual who sponsors the creation of works of art

Pattern: an arrangement of predictably repeated elements

Pectoral: a large ornament worn on the chest

Pediment: the triangular space, situated above the row of columns, at the end of a building in the Classical style

Pendentive: a curving triangular surface that links a dome to a square space below

Performance art: a work involving the human body, usually including the artist, in front of an audience

Performance artist: an artist whose work involves the human body (often including his or her own)

Perspective: the creation of the illusion of depth in a two-dimensional image by using mathematical principles

Photomontage: a single photographic image that combines (digitally or using multiple film exposures) several separate images

Physiology: a science that studies the workings of the body and its organs

Pictograph: picture used as a symbol in writing

Picture plane: the surface of a painting or drawing

Piece mold casting: a process for casting metal objects in which a mold is broken into several pieces that are then reassembled into a final sculpture

Pigment: the colored material used in paints. Often made from finely ground minerals

Pilaster: a vertical element, square in shape, that provides architectural support for crossing horizontal elements in post-and-lintel construction; also used for decoration

Plane: a flat surface

Planography: a print process—lithography and silkscreen printing—where the inked image area and non-inked areas are at the same height

Plastic: referring to materials that are soft and can be manipulated

Pointed arches: arches with two curved sides that meet to form a point at the apex

Pointillism: a late nineteenth-century painting style using short strokes or points of differing colors that optically combine to form new perceived colors

Pop art: mid-twentieth-century artistic movement inspired by commercial art forms and popular culture

Portico: a roof supported by columns at the entrance to a building

Portrait: image of a person or animal, usually focusing on the face

Positive: an image in which light areas are light and dark areas are dark (opposite of a negative)

Positive–negative: the relationship between contrasting opposites

Positive shape: a shape defined by its surrounding empty space

Post-and-lintel construction: a horizontal beam (the lintel) supported by a post at either end

Post-Impressionists: artists either from or living in France, c. 1885–1905, who moved away from the Impressionist style – notably Cezanne, Gauguin, Seurat, and Van Gogh

Postmodernism: a late twentieth-century style of architecture playfully adopting features of earlier styles

Predella: an artwork designed as a companion piece to a more important work

Prehistoric: dating from the period of human existence before the invention of writing

Pre-Raphaelite Brotherhood: English art movement formed in 1848 by painters who rejected the academic rules of art, and often painted medieval subjects in a naïve style

Primary colors: three basic colors from which all others are derived

Principles: the "grammar" applied to the elements of art—contrast, balance, unity, variety, rhythm, emphasis, pattern, scale, proportion, and focal point

Print: a picture reproduced on paper, often in multiple copies

Profile: the outline of an object, especially a face or head, represented from the side

Propaganda: art that promotes an ideology or a cause

Proportion: the relationship in size between a work's individual parts and the whole

Provenance: the record of all known previous owners and locations of a work of art

Psychoanalysis: a method of treating mental illness by making conscious the patient's subconscious fears or fantasies

Psychology: a science that studies the nature, development, and operation of the human mind

Pueblos: word meaning "town" that refers to Anasazi settlements throughout the Four Corners area of Utah, Colorado, New Mexico, and Arizona; also the name of groups descending from the Anasazi

Putto (plural **putti**): a representation of a nude or scantily clad infant angel or boy, common in Renaissance and Baroque art

Pyramid: ancient structure, usually massive in scale, consisting of a square base with four sides that meet at a point or apex with each side forming a triangular shape

Qibla: the direction Muslims face when praying

Raku: handmade and fired ceramic, made for a tea ceremony

Readymade: an everyday object presented as a work of art

Realism: nineteenth-century artistic style that aimed to depict nature and everyday subjects in an unidealized manner

Realistic: artistic style that aims to represent appearances as accurately as possible

Register: one of two or more horizontal sections into which a space is divided in order to depict the episodes of a story

Relief: (1) a raised form on a largely flat background. For example, the design on a coin is "in relief"; (2) a print process where the inked image is higher than the non-printing areas; (3) a sculpture that projects from a flat surface

Renaissance: a period of cultural and artistic change in Europe from the fourteenth to the seventeenth century

Repoussé: a technique of hammering metal from the back

Representation: the depiction of recognizable figures and objects

Representational: art that depicts figures and objects so that we recognize what is represented

Rhythm: the regular or ordered repetition of elements in the work

Rib vault: an archlike structure supporting a ceiling or roof, with a web of protruding stonework

Romanesque: an early medieval European style of architecture based on Roman-style rounded arches and heavy construction

Romanticism: movement in nineteenth-century European culture, concerned with the power of the imagination and greatly valuing intense feeling

Rosin: a dry powdered resin that melts when heated, used in the aquatint process

Salon: (1) official annual exhibition of French painting, first held in 1667; (2) a French term for an exhibition of work by multiple artists; (3) the routine gathering of a circle of notable people—often figures from the worlds of art, literature, and politics—at the home of one member of the group

Sand painting: also known as dry painting, a labor-intensive method of painting using grains of sand as the medium

Sarcophagus (plural sarcophagi): a coffin (usually made of stone or baked clay)

Sarsen: a type of hard, gray sandstone

Satire: a work of art that exposes the weaknesses and mistakes of its subjects to ridicule

Saturation: the degree of purity of a color

Scale: the size of an object or an artwork relative to another object or artwork, or to a system of measurement

Secondary color: a color mixed from two primary colors

Sfumato: in painting, the application of layers of translucent paint to create a hazy or smoky appearance and unify the composition

Shade: a color darker in value than its purest state

Shading: the use of gradated light and dark tones to represent a three-dimensional object in two dimensions

Shaft: the main vertical part of a column

Shaman: a priest or priestess regarded as having the ability to communicate directly with the spiritual world

Shape: a two-dimensional area, the boundaries of which are defined by lines or suggested by changes in color or value

Silhouette: a portrait or figure represented in outline and solidly colored in

Silueta: series of images by Ana Mendieta in which the artist's body is situated in outdoor environments

Silkscreen: method of printmaking using a stencil and paint pushed through a screen

Sketch: a rough preliminary version of a work or part of a work

Slip: clay mixed with water used to decorate pottery

Space: the distance between identifiable points or planes

Span: the distance bridged between two supports, such as columns or walls

Stained glass: colored glass used for windows or decorative applications

Stela: upright stone slab decorated with inscriptions or pictorial relief carvings

Stencil: a perforated template allowing ink or paint to pass through to print a design

Stepped pyramid: a pyramid consisting of several rectangular structures placed on top of one another

Stereotypes: oversimplified notions, especially about marginalized groups, that can lead to prejudiced judgments

Still life: a scene of inanimate objects, such as fruits, flowers, or motionless animals

Stucco: a coarse plaster designed to give the appearance of stone

Style: a characteristic way in which an artist or group of artists uses visual language to give a work an identifiable form of visual expression

Stylized: art that represents objects in an exaggerated way to emphasize certain aspects of the object

Stylobate: the uppermost platform on a Classical temple, on which the columns stand

Subject: the person, object, or space depicted in a work of art

Sublime: feeling of awe or terror, provoked by the experience of limitless nature and the awareness of the smallness of an individual

Subordination: the opposite of emphasis; it draws our attention away from particular areas of a work

Sunken relief: a carved panel where the figures are cut deeper into the stone than the background

Support: the material on which painting is done

Surreal: reminiscent of the Surrealist movement in the 1920s and later, whose art was inspired by dreams and the subconscious

Surrealism: an artistic movement in the 1920s and later, the art of which was inspired by dreams and the subconscious

Surrealist: an artist belonging to the Surrealist movement in the 1920s and later, whose art was inspired by dreams and the subconscious

Symbolism: movement in European art and literature, *c.* 1885–1910, that conveyed meaning by the use of powerful yet ambiguous symbols

Symmetry: the correspondence in size, form, and arrangement of items on opposite sides of a plane, line, or point that creates direct visual balance

Synesthesia: when one of the five senses perceives something that was stimulated by a trigger from one of the other senses

Tableau: a stationary scene arranged for artistic impact

Tapestry: hand-woven fabric—usually silk or wool—with a non-repeating, usually figurative, design woven into it

Tattoos: designs marked on the body by injecting dye under the skin

Temperature: a description of color based on our associations with warmth or coolness

Tenebrism: dramatic use of intense darkness and light to heighten the impact of a painting

Terracotta: iron-rich clay, fired at a low temperature, which is traditionally brownish-orange in color

Tesserae: small pieces of stone or glass or other materials used to make a mosaic

Texture: the surface quality of a work, for example fine/coarse, detailed/lacking in detail

Three-dimensional: having height, width, and depth

Three-dimensionality: the condition of having height, width, and depth

Three-point perspective: a perspective system with two vanishing points on the horizon and one not on the horizon

Throwing: the process of making a ceramic object on a potter's wheel

Tint: a color lighter in value than its purest state

Tipi or **teepee:** portable dwelling used by Plains groups

Tracery: a complex but delicate pattern of interwoven lines

Transept: structure crossing the main body of a cruciform church

Triglyph: a projecting block carved with three raised bands, which alternates with figurative reliefs in a frieze

Triptych: an artwork comprising three painted or carved panels, normally joined together and sharing a common theme

Trompe l'oeil: an extreme kind of illusion meant to deceive the viewer

Tumbling: the use of levers to roll heavy objects over short distances

Twisted perspective, also known as **composite view:** a representation of a figure, part in profile and part frontally

Two-dimensional: having height and width

Tympanum: an arched recess above a doorway, often decorated with carvings

Typography: the art of designing, arranging, and choosing type

Unity: the imposition of order and harmony on a design

Value: the lightness or darkness of a plane or area

Vanishing point: the point in a work of art at which imaginary sight lines appear to converge, suggesting depth

Vanitas: an artwork in which the objects remind the viewer of the transience of life

Variety: the diversity of different ideas, media, and elements in a work

Vault: an archlike structure supporting a ceiling or roof

Vaulted: arched

Visionary art: art made by self-taught artists following a personal vision

Void: an area in an artwork that seems empty

Volume: the space filled or enclosed by a three-dimensional figure or object

Voodoo: a religion based on Roman Catholic and traditional African rituals, practiced in the West Indies and southern U.S.

Watercolor: transparent paint made from pigment and a binder dissolved in water

White space: in typography, the empty space around type or other features in a layout

Woodblock: a relief print process where the image is carved into a block of wood

Woodcut: a print created from an incised piece of wood

Ziggurat: Mesopotamian stepped tower, roughly pyramid-shaped, that diminishes in size toward a platform summit

Further Reading

PART 1

Chapter 1.1 Art in Two Dimensions: Line, Shape, and the Principle of Contrast

de Zegher, Catherine, and Cornelia Butler, *On Line: Drawing Through the Twentieth Century*. New York (The Museum of Modern Art) 2010.
Ocvirk, Otto, Robert Stinson, Philip Wigg, and Robert Bone, *Art Fundamentals: Theory and Practice*, 11th edn. New York (McGraw-Hill) 2008.

Chapter 1.2 Three-Dimensional Art: Form, Volume, Mass, and Texture

Ching, Francis D. K., *Architecture: Form, Space, and Order*, 3rd edn. Hoboken, NJ (Wiley) 2007.
Wong, Wucius, *Principles of Three-Dimensional Design*. New York (Van Nostrand Reinhold) 1977.

Chapter 1.3 Implied Depth: Value and Space

Auvil, Kenneth W., *Perspective Drawing*, 2nd edn. New York (McGraw-Hill) 1996.
Curtis, Brian, *Drawing from Observation*, 2nd edn. New York (McGraw-Hill) 2009.

Chapter 1.4 Color

Albers, Josef and Nicholas Fox Weber, *Interaction of Color: Revised and Expanded Edition*. New Haven, CT (Yale University Press) 2006.
Bleicher, Steven, *Contemporary Color: Theory and Use*, 2nd edn. Clifton Park, NY (Delmar Cengage Learning) 2011.

Chapter 1.5 Time and Motion

Krasner, Jon, *Motion Graphic Design: Applied History and Aesthetics*, 2nd edn. Burlington, MA (Focal Press [Elsevier]) 2008.
Stewart, Mary, *Launching the Imagination*, 3rd edn. New York (McGraw-Hill) 2007.

Chapter 1.6 Unity, Variety, and Balance

Bevlin, Marjorie Elliott, *Design Through Discovery: An Introduction*, 6th edn. Orlando, FL (Harcourt Brace & Co./Wadsworth Publishing) 1993.
Lauer, David A., and Stephen Pentak, *Design Basics*, 8th edn. Boston, MA (Wadsworth Publishing) 2011.

Chapter 1.7 Scale and Proportion

Bridgman, George B., *Bridgman's Life Drawing*. Mineola, NY (Dover Publications) 1971.
Elam, Kimberly, *Geometry of Design: Studies in Proportion and Composition*, 1st edn. New York (Princeton Architectural Press) 2001.

Chapter 1.8 Emphasis and Focal Point

Lauer, David A., and Stephen Pentak, *Design Basics*, 8th edn. Boston, MA (Wadsworth Publishing) 2011.
Stewart, Mary, *Launching the Imagination*, 3rd edn. New York (McGraw-Hill) 2007.

Chapter 1.9 Pattern and Rhythm

Ocvirk, Otto, Robert Stinson, Philip Wigg, and Robert Bone, *Art Fundamentals: Theory and Practice*, 11th edn. New York (McGraw-Hill) 2008.
Wong, Wucius, *Principles of Two-Dimensional Design*, 1st edn. New York (Wiley) 1972.

Chapter 1.10 Content and Analysis

Barnet, Sylvan, *Short Guide to Writing About Art*. Harlow, UK (Pearson Education) 2010.
Hatt, Michael, and Charlotte Klonk, *Art History: A Critical Introduction to Its Methods*. New York (Manchester University Press; distributed exclusively in the USA by Palgrave) 2006.

PART 2

Chapter 2.1 Drawing

Faber, David L., and Daniel M. Mendelowitz, *A Guide to Drawing*, 8th edn. Boston, MA (Wadsworth Publishing) 2011.
Sale, Teel and Claudia Betti, *Drawing: A Contemporary Approach*, 6th edn. Boston, MA (Wadsworth Publishing) 2007.

Chapter 2.2 Painting

Gottsegen, Mark David, *Painter's Handbook: Revised and Expanded*. New York (Watson-Guptill) 2006.
Robertson, Jean, and Craig McDaniel, *Painting as a Language: Material, Technique, Form, Content*, 1st edn. Boston, MA (Wadsworth Publishing) 1999.

Chapter 2.3 Printmaking

Hunter, Dard, *Papermaking*. Mineola, NY (Dover Publications) 2011.
Ross, John, *Complete Printmaker*, revised expanded edn. New York (Free Press) 1991.

Chapter 2.4 Visual Communication Design

Craig, James, William Bevington, and Irene Korol Scala, *Designing with Type, 5th Edition: The Essential Guide to Typography*. New York (Watson-Guptill) 2006.
Meggs, Philip B. and Alston W. Purvis, *Meggs' History of Graphic Design*, 4th edn. Hoboken, NJ (Wiley) 2005.

Chapter 2.5 Photography

Hirsch, Robert, *Light and Lens: Photography in the Digital Age*. London (Elsevier) 2007.

Jeffrey, Ian, *How to Read a Photograph.* New York (Abrams) 2010.

London, Barbara, John Upton, and Jim Stone, *Photography,* 10th edn. Upper Saddle River, NJ (Pearson) 2010.

Marien, Mary Warner, *Photography: A Cultural History,* 3rd edn. Upper Saddle River, NJ (Prentice Hall) 2010.

Rosenblum, Naomi, *A World History of Photography,* 4th edn. New York (Abbeville Press) 2008.

Trachtenberg, Alan, ed., *Classic Essays on Photography.* New York (Leete's Island Books) 1980.

Chapter 2.6 Film/Video and Digital Art

Cook, David A., *A History of Narrative Film,* 4th edn. New York (W. W. Norton) 2004.

Corrigan, Timothy, and Patricia White, *The Film Experience,* 2nd edn. New York (Bedford/St. Martin's) 2008.

Monaco, James, *How to Read a Film: Movies, Media, and Beyond.* New York (Oxford University Press) 2009.

Wands, Bruce, *Art of the Digital Age.* New York (Thames & Hudson) 2007.

Chapter 2.7 Alternative Media and Processes

Alberro, Alexander, and Black Stimson, *Conceptual Art: A Critical Anthology.* Cambridge, MA (MIT Press) 2000.

Bishop, Claire, *Installation Art,* 2nd edn. London (Tate Publishing) 2010.

Goldberg, Rosalee, *Performance Art: From Futurism to the Present,* 2nd edn. New York (Thames & Hudson) 2001.

Lippard, Lucy, *Six Years: The Dematerialization of the Art Object from 1966 to 1972.* Berkeley, CA (University of California Press) 1997.

Osborne, Peter, *Conceptual Art (Themes and Movements).* New York and London (Phaidon) 2011.

Rosenthal, Mark, *Understanding Installation Art: From Duchamp to Holzer.* New York (Prestel) 2003.

Chapter 2.8 The Tradition of Craft

Speight, Charlotte, and John Toki, *Hands in Clay : An Introduction to Ceramics,* 5th edn. New York (McGraw-Hill) 2003.

Wight, Karol, *Molten Color: Glassmaking in Antiquity.* Los Angeles, CA (J. Paul Getty Museum) 2011.

Chapter 2.9 Sculpture

Rich, Jack C., *The Materials and Methods of Sculpture,* 10th edn. Mineola, NY (Dover Publications) 1988.

Tucker, William, *The Language of Sculpture.* London (Thames & Hudson) 1985.

Chapter 2.10 Architecture

Ching, Francis D. K., *Architecture: Form, Space, and Order,* 3rd edn. Hoboken, NJ (Wiley) 2007.

Glancey, Jonathan, *Story of Architecture.* New York (Dorling Kindersley/Prentice Hall) 2006.

PART 3

Chapter 3.1 The Prehistoric and Ancient Mediterranean

Alfred, Cyril, *Egyptian Art.* New York (Oxford University Press) 1980.

Aruz, Joan, *Art of the First Cities: The Third Millennium B.C. from the Mediterranean to the Indus.* New York (The Metropolitan Museum of Art); New Haven, CT (Yale University Press) 2003.

Boardman, John, *The World of Ancient Art.* New York (Thames & Hudson) 2006.

Pedley, John Griffiths, *Greek Art and Archeology,* 5th edn. Upper Saddle River, NJ (Pearson/Prentice Hall) 2007.

Wheeler, Mortimer, *Roman Art and Architecture.* New York (Thames & Hudson) 1985.

Chapter 3.2 Art of the Middle Ages

Benton, Janetta, *Art of the Middle Ages.*

New York (Thames & Hudson) 2002.

Camille, Michael, *Gothic Art: Glorious Visions.* New York (Abrams) 1996.

Lowden, John, *Early Christian & Byzantine Art.* London (Phaidon) 1997.

Chapter 3.3 Art of India, China, and Japan

Craven, Roy, *Indian Art.* New York (Thames & Hudson) 1997.

Lee, Sherman, *History of Far Eastern Art.* New York (Abrams) 1994.

Stanley-Baker, Joan, *Japanese Art.* New York (Thames & Hudson) 2000.

Tregear, Mary, *Chinese Art.* New York (Thames & Hudson) 1997.

Chapter 3.4 Art of the Americas

Berlo, Janet Catherine, and Ruth B. Phillips, *Native North American Art.* New York (Oxford University Press) 1998.

Coe, Michael D., and Rex Koontz, *Mexico: From the Olmecs to the Aztecs,* 6th edn. New York (Thames & Hudson) 2008.

Miller, Mary Ellen, *The Art of Ancient Mesoamerica,* 4th edn. New York (Thames & Hudson) 2006.

Rushing, Jackson III, *Native American Art in the Twentieth Century: Makers, Meanings, Histories.* New York (Taylor and Francis) 1999.

Stone-Miller, Rebecca, *Art of the Andes: From Chavin to Inca,* 2nd edn. New York (Thames & Hudson) 2002.

Chapter 3.5 Art of Africa and the Pacific Islands

Bacquart, Jean-Baptiste, *The Tribal Arts of Africa.* New York (Thames & Hudson) 2002.

Berlo, Janet Catherine, and Lee Anne Wilson, *Arts of Africa Oceania and the Americas.* Upper Saddle River, NJ (Prentice Hall) 1992.

D'Alleva, Anne, *Arts of the Pacific Islands.* New Haven, CT (Yale University Press) 2010.

Willet, Frank, *African Art,* 3rd edn. New York (Thames & Hudson) 2003.

Chapter 3.6 Art of Renaissance and Baroque Europe (1400–1750)

Bazin, Germain, and Jonathan Griffin, *Baroque and Rococo*. New York (Thames & Hudson) 1985.

Garrard, Mary, *Artemisia Gentileschi*. Princeton, NJ (Princeton University Press) 1991.

Hartt, Frederick, *History of Italian Renaissance Art*, 7th edn. Upper Saddle River, NJ (Pearson) 2010.

Welch, Evelyn, *Art in Renaissance Italy: 1350–1500*. New York (Oxford University Press) 2001.

Chapter 3.7 Art of Europe and America 1700–1900

Chu, Petra ten-Doesschate, *Nineteenth Century European Art*. New York (Abrams) 2003.

Denvir, Bernard, *Post-Impressionism*. New York (Thames & Hudson) 1992.

Irwin, David, *Neoclassicism*. London (Phaidon) 1997.

Levey, Michael, *Rococo to Revolution: Major Trends in Eighteenth-Century Painting*. New York (Thames & Hudson) 1985.

Thomson, Belinda, *Impressionism: Origins, Practice, Reception*. New York (Thames & Hudson) 2000.

Vaughan, William, *Romanticism and Art*. London (Thames & Hudson) 1994.

Chapter 3.8 Twentieth and Twenty-First Centuries: The Age of Global Art

Arnason, H. H., and Elizabeth C. Mansfield, *History of Modern Art*, 6th edn. Upper Saddle River, NJ (Pearson) 2009.

Barrett, Terry, *Why is that Art?: Aesthetics and Criticism of Contemporary Art*. New York (Oxford University Press) 2007.

Fineberg, Jonathan, *Art Since 1940: Strategies of Being*, 3rd edn. Upper Saddle River, NJ (Prentice Hall) 2010.

Jones, Amelia, *A Companion to Contemporary Art Since 1945*. Malden, MA (Blackwell Publishing) 2006.

Stiles, Kristine, and Peter Selz, *Theories and Documents of Contemporary Art: A Sourcebook of Artists' Writings*, 2nd edn, revised and expanded. Berkeley, CA (University of California Press) 2011.

PART 4

Chapter 4.1 Art and Community

Art in Action: Nature, Creativity, and Our Collective Future. San Rafael, CA (Earth Aware Editions) 2007.

Iosifidis, Kiriakos, *Mural Art: Murals on Huge Public Surfaces Around the World from Graffiti to Trompe l'oeil*. Vancouver, BC (Adbusters) 2009.

Kwon, Miwon, *One Place After Another: Site-Specific Art and Location Identity*. Cambridge, MA (MIT Press) 2004.

Witley, David S., *Cave Paintings and the Human Spirit*. Amherst, NY (Prometheus Books) 2009.

Chapter 4.2 Spirituality and Art

Azara, Nancy J., *Spirit Taking From: Making a Spiritual Practice of Making Art*. Boston, MA (Red Wheel) 2002.

Bloom, Jonathan, and Sheila S. Blair, *Islamic Arts*. London (Phaidon) 1997.

Fisher, Robert E., *Buddhist Art and Architecture*. New York (Thames & Hudson) 1993.

Guo, Xi, *Essay on Landscape Painting*. London (John Murray) 1959.

Lyle, Emily, *Sacred Architecture in the Traditions of India, China, Judaism, and Islam*. Edinburgh (Edinburgh University Press) 1992.

Williamson, Beth, *Christian Art: A Very Short Introduction*. New York (Oxford University Press) 2004.

Chapter 4.3 Art and the Cycle of Life

Dijkstra, Rineke, *Portraits*. Boston, MA (Institute of Contemporary Art) 2005.

Gearon, Tierney, *The Mother Project* (DVD). New York (Zeitgeist Films) 2007.

Germer, Renate, Fiona Elliot, and Artwig Altenmuller, *Mummies: Life after Death in Ancient Egypt*. New York (Prestel) 1997.

Miller, Mary Ellen, and Karl Taube, *An Illustrated Dictionary of the Gods and Symbols of Ancient Mexico and the Maya*. New York (Thames & Hudson) 1997.

Ravenal, John B., *Vanitas: Meditations on Life and Death in Contemporary Art*. Richmond, VA (Virginia Museum of Fine Arts) 2000.

Steinberg, Leo, *The Sexuality of Christ in Renaissance Art and in Modern Oblivion*. Chicago, IL (University of Chicago Press) 1996.

Chapter 4.4 Art and Science

Bordin, Giorgio, *Medicine in Art*. Los Angeles (J. Paul Getty Museum) 2010.

Brouger, Kerry, et. al., *Visual Music: Synaesthesia in Art and Music Since 1900*. London (Thames & Hudson); Washington, D.C. (Hirshhorn Museum); Los Angeles, CA (Museum of Contemporary Art) 2005.

Gamwell, Lynn, and Neil deGrasse Tyson, *Exploring the Invisible: Art, Science, and the Spiritual*. Princeton, NJ (Princeton University Press) 2004.

Milbrath, Susan, *Star Gods of the Maya: Astronomy in Art, Folklore, and Calendars*. Austin, TX (University of Texas Press) 2000.

Pietrangeli, Carlo et al., *The Sistine Chapel: A Glorious Restoration*. New York (Abrams) 1999.

Rhodes, Colin, *Outsider Art: Spontaneous Alternatives*. New York (Thames & Hudson) 2000.

Chapter 4.5 Art and Illusion

Ades, Dawn, *In the Mind's Eye: Dada and Surrealism*. Chicago, IL (Museum of Contemporary Art); New York (Abbeville Press) 1986.

Battistini, Matilde, *Astrology, Magic and*

Alchemy in Art. Los Angeles, CA (J. Paul Getty Museum) 2007.

Ebert-Schifferer, Sybille, et al., *Deceptions and Illusions: Five Centuries of Trompe L'Oeil Painting.* Washington, D.C. (National Gallery of Art) 2003.

Gablik, Suzi, *Magritte.* New York (Thames & Hudson) 1985.

Kemp, Martin, *The Science of Art: Optical Themes in Western Art from Brunelleschi to Seurat.* New Haven, CT (Yale University Press) 1992.

Seckel, Al and Douglas Hofstadter, *Masters of Deception: Escher, Dali & The Artists of Optical Illusion.* New York (Sterling Publishing) 2007.

Chapter 4.6 Art and Rulers

Berzock, Kathleen Bickford, *Benin: Royal Arts of a West African Kingdom.* Chicago, IL (Art Institute of Chicago); New Haven, CT (distributed by Yale University Press) 2008.

Freed, Rita, *Pharaohs of the Sun: Akhenaten, Nevertiti: Tutankhamen.* Boston, MA (Museum of Fine Arts in association with Bulfinch Press/Little, Brown and Co.) 1999.

Rapelli, Paola, *Symbols of Power in Art.* Los Angeles, CA (J. Paul Getty Museum, Getty Publications) 2011.

Rawski, Evelyn, *China: The Three Emperors 1662–1795.* London (Royal Academy of Arts) 2006.

Schele, Linda, *The Blood of Kings: Dynasty and Ritual in Maya Art.* New York (G. Braziller) and Fort Worth, TX (Kimball Art Museum) 1992.

Spike, John T., *Europe in the Age of Monarchy.* New York (The Metropolitan Museum of Art) 1987.

Zanker, Paul, *The Power of Images in the Age of Augustus.* Ann Arbor, MI (University of Michigan Press) 1990.

Chapter 4.7 Art and War

Auping, Michael, *Anselm Kiefer Heaven and Earth.* Fort Worth, TX (Modern Art Museum of Fort Worth, in association with Prestel) 2005.

Barron, Stephanie, *Degenerate Art.* Los Angeles, CA (Los Angeles County Museum of Art) and New York (Abrams) 1991.

Hughes, Robert, *Goya.* New York (Alfred A. Knopf) 2003.

Steel, Andy, *The World's Top Photographers: Photojournalism: And the Stories Behind Their Greatest Images.* Mies, Switzerland, and Hove, UK (RotoVision) 2006.

Wilson, David, *The Bayeux Tapestry.* London (Thames & Hudson) 2004.

Chapter 4.8 Art of Social Conscience

Alhadeff, Albert, *The Raft of the Medusa: Gericault, Art, and Race.* Munich and London (Prestel) 2002.

Blais, Allison, et al., *A Place of Remembrance: Official Book of the National September 11 Memorial.* Washington, D.C. (National Geographic) 2011.

Kammen, Michael, *Visual Shock: A History of Art Controversies in American Culture.* New York (Alfred A. Knopf) 2007.

Van Hensbergen, Gijs, *Guernica: The Biography of a Twentieth-Century Icon.* New York (Bloomsbury) 2005.

Chapter 4.9 The Body in Art

Clark, Kenneth, *The Nude: A Study in Ideal Form.* Princeton, NJ (Yale University Press) 1990/1956.

Dijkstra, Bram, *Naked: The Nude in America.* New York (Rizzoli) 2010.

Jones, Amelia, *Body Art/Performing the Self.* Minneapolis, MN (University of Minnesota Press) 1998.

Nairne, Sandy, and Sarah Howgate, *The Portrait Now.* New Haven, CT (Yale University Press) and London (National Portrait Gallery) 2006.

Chapter 4.10 Art and Gender

Broude, Norma, and Mary Garrard, *Feminism and Art History: Questioning the Litany.* New York (Harper & Row) 1982.

Hickey, Dave, *The Invisible Dragon: Essays on Beauty,* revised and expanded edition. Chicago, IL (University of Chicago Press) 2009.

hooks, bell, *Feminism is for Everybody: Passionate Politics.* Cambridge, MA (South End Press) 2000.

Jones, Amelia, *Feminism and Visual Culture Reader.* New York (Routledge) 2010.

Perry, Gill, *Gender and Art.* New Haven, CT (Yale University Press) 1999.

Valenti, Jessica, *Full Frontal Feminism: A Young Woman's Guide to Why Feminism Matters.* Emeryville, CA (Seal Press) 2007.

Chapter 4.11 Expression

Dempsey, Amy, *Styles, Schools, and Movements,* 2nd edn. New York (Thames & Hudson) 2011.

Doy, Gen, *Picturing the Self: Changing Views of the Subject in Visual Culture.* London (I. B. Tauris) 2004.

Evans, David, *Appropriation.* Cambridge, MA (MIT Press) and London (Whitechapel Gallery) 2009.

Rebel, Ernst, *Self-Portraits.* Los Angeles, CA (Taschen) 2008.

Rugg, Linda Haverty, *Picturing Ourselves: Photography and Autobiography.* Chicago, IL (University of Chicago Press) 1997.

Sources of Quotations

Introduction

p. 27: William Wall quoted from http://www.library.yale.edu/beinecke/br blevents/spirit1.htm

p. 40: Label from Nazi exhibition from Stephanie Barron, *Degenerate Art: The Fate of the Avant-Garde in Nazi Germany* (New York: Harry N. Abrams, 1991), 390.

p. 40: Otto Dix from *The Dictionary of Art*, vol. 9 (Basingstoke: Macmillan Publishers, 1996), 42.

PART I

Chapter 1.1

p. 50: Barbara Hepworth from Abraham Marie Hammacher, *The Sculpture of Barbara Hepworth* (New York: Harry N. Abrams, 1968), 98.

Chapter 1.2

p. 62: Vivant Denon from http://www.ancient-egypt-history.com/2011/04/napoleon-bonapartes-wise-men-at.html.

p. 66: Lino Tagliepietra from the artist's website at http://www.linotagliapietra.com/batman/index.htm.

Chapter 1.3

p. 76: Albert Einstein from Thomas Campbell, *My Big TOE: Inner Workings* (Huntsville, AL: Lightning Strike Books, 2003), 191.

Chapter 1.4

p. 92: Vasily Kandinsky from Robert L. Herbert, *Modern Artists on Art* (New York: Dover Publications, 1999), 19.

p. 97: Matisse from Dorothy M. Kosinski, Jay McKean Fisher, Steven A. Nash, and Henri Matisse, *Matisse: Painter as Sculptor* (New Haven, CT: Yale University Press, 2007), 260.

p. 102: Van Gogh quoted in Ian Chilvers, Harold Osborne, and Denis Farr (eds.), *The Oxford Dictionary of Art* (New York: Oxford University Press, 2009), 298.

Chapter 1.5

p. 108: William Faulkner from Philip Gourevitch (ed.), *The Paris Review: Interviews, Volume 2* (New York: Picador USA, 2007), 54.

Chapter 1.6

p. 126: Palladio from Rob Imrie and Emma Street, *Architectural Design and Regulation* (Chichester, UK: Wiley-Blackwell, 2011), section 1.2.

Chapter 1.7

p. 128: Baudelaire from Charles Baudelaire, *Flowers of Evil and Other Works*, ed. and trans. Wallace Fowlie (New York: Dover Publications, 1992), 201.

Chapter 1.8

p. 137: Mark Tobey from Tate Collection, *Northwest Drift 1958* (quoted from the display caption, November 2005).

Chapter 1.9

p. 146: Elvis Presley from Dave Marsh and James Bernard, *The New Book of Rock Lists* (New York: Simon & Schuster [Fireside], 1994), 9.

PART 2

Chapter 2.1

p. 166: William Blake from *The Complete Poetry and Prose of William Blake* (Berkeley and Los Angeles, CA: Anchor/University of California Press 1997), 574.

Chapter 2.2

p. 183: Andrew Wyeth from William Scheller, *America, a History in Art: The American Journey Told by Painters, Sculptors ...* (New York: Black Dog & Leventhal Publishers, 2008), 22.

Chapter 2.5

p. 216: Dorothea Lange from Dorothea Lange, "The Assignment I'll Never Forget: Migrant Mother," in *Popular Photography* (February 1960); reprinted in James Curtis, *Mind's Eye, Mind's Truth: FSA Photography Reconsidered* (Philadelphia: Temple University Press, 1989).

p. 227: Edward Burtynsky from *Manufactured Landscapes (U.S. Edition)*, directed by Jennifer Baichwal (Zeitgeist Films, 2006).

Chapter 2.7

p. 242: Vito Acconci's description of *Following Piece* from documentation accompanying the photographs; reprinted in Lucy Lippard, *Six Years: The Dematerialization of the Art Object* (Berkeley, CA: University of California Press, 1973/1997), 117.

p.244: Yoko Ono's text accompanying *Wish Tree* from Jessica Dawson, "Yoko Ono's Peaceful Message Takes Root," *Washington Post* (April 3, 2007); washingtonpost.com.

p.247: Kara Walker from "Interview: Projecting Fictions: 'Insurrection! Our Tools Were Rudimentary, Yet We Pressed On,'" *ART21* "Stories" Episode, Season 2 (PBS: 2003); http://www.pbs.org/art21/artists/walker/clip1.html.

Chapter 2.8

p. 248: Geoffrey Chaucer from *The Works of Geoffrey Chaucer, Volume 5* (New York: Macmillan and Co., Limited, 1904), 341.

p. 257: Tilleke Schwarz from her website: http://mytextilefile.blogspot.com/2011/02/tilleke-schwarz.html.

Chapter 2.9

p. 260: Michelangelo quoted by Henry Moore from Henry Moore and Alan G. Wilkinson, *Henry Moore–Writings and Conversations* (Berkeley, CA: University of California Press, 2002), 238.

p. 264: Michelangelo from Howard Hibbard, *Michelangelo* (New York: Harper & Row, 1985), 119.

p. 273: Ilya Kabakov from H. H. Arnason and Peter Kalb, *History of Modern Art* (Chicago: Prentice Hall, 2003), 715.

Chapter 2.10

p. 285: Le Corbusier from Nicholas Fox Weber, *Le Corbusier: A Life* (New York: Alfred A. Knopf, 2008), 171.

p. 286: Mies van der Rohe from E. C. Relph, *The Modern Urban Landscape* (Baltimore, MD: The Johns Hopkins University Press, 1987), 191.

PART 3

Chapter 3.1

p. 299: Inscription from Assyrian palace from Met Museum website and object file:
http://www.metmuseum.org/works_of_art/collection_database/ancient_near_eastern_art/human_headed_winged_bull_and_winged_lion_lamassu/objectview.aspx?collID=3&OID=30009052

p. 304: Protagoras from Kenneth Clark, *Protagoras* (New York: Harper and Row, 1969), 57.

Chapter 3.2

p. 322: Hildegard of Bingen from *Hildegard von Bingen's Mystical Visions*, trans. by Bruce Hozeski from *Scivias* (I,1), 8.

Chapter 3.4

p. 354: David Grove from David Grove, *In Search of The Olmec* (unpublished work), © David Grove.

Chapter 3.7

p. 403: Jacques-Louis David from the Revolutionary Convention, 1793, quoted in Robert Cumming, *Art Explained* (New York: DK Publishing, 2005), 70.

p. 406: Unspecified critic on Goya from Lucien Solvay, *L'Art espagnol* (Paris and London, 1887), 261.

p. 408: Unspecified critic on Frederic Erwin Church from Pierre Berton, *Niagara: A History of the Falls* (New York: State University of New York, Albany,1992), 119.

p. 408: Gustave Courbet from Robert Williams, *Art Theory: An Historical Introduction* (Malden, MA: Blackwell Publishing, 2004), 127.

p. 414: Unspecified critic on Claudel from Ruth Butler, *Rodin: The Shape of Genius* (New Haven, CT and London: Yale University Press, 1993), 271.

p. 416: Paul Gauguin from Charles Estienne, *Gauguin: Biographical and Critical Studies* (Geneva: Skira, 1953), 17.

p. 418: Unspecified critic on the Eiffel Tower from Joseph Harriss, *The Tallest Tower: Eiffel and the Belle Epoque* (Bloomington, Indiana: Unlimited Publishing, 2004), 15.

Chapter 3.8

p. 424: Henri Matisse from Jack Flam, *Matisse: The Man and His Art, 1869–1918* (Ithaca, NY: Cornell University Press, 1986), 196.

p. 431: Marcel Duchamp from Arturo Schwarz, *The Complete Works of Marcel Duchamp* (New York: Delano Greenidge Editions, 1997), II, 442.

p. 434: Filippo Marinetti from his "Manifesto for the Italo-Abyssinian War," (1936), quoted in Walter Benjamin, "The Work of Art in the Age of Mechanical Reproduction," in Walter Benjamin, *Illuminations: Essays and Reflections*, ed. Hannah Arendt (New York: Schocken Books,1968), 241.

p. 438: Mark Rothko from Selden Rodman, *Conversations with Artists* (New York: Devin-Adair, Co., 1957).

p. 450: Matthew Ritchie from his interview about *Proposition Player*, ART21, Season 3, Episode 1 (PBS: 2005); http://www.pbs.org/art21/series/seasonthree/index.html.

PART 4

Chapter 4.1

p. 454: Susan Cervantes from Tyce Hendricks, "Celebrating Art that Draws People Together," *San Francisco Chronicle* (May 6, 2005), F1.

p. 454: Aliseo Purpura-Pontoniere from Tyce Hendricks, "Celebrating Art that Draws People Together," *San Francisco Chronicle* (May 6, 2005), F1.

p. 457: Christo and Jeanne-Claude, "Selected Works: The Gates," The Art of Christo and Jeanne-Claude (© 2005; access date September 7, 2007) www.christojeanneclaude.net

p. 459: Hilla Rebay (the curator of the foundation and director of the Guggenheim museum) from the Solomon R. Guggenheim website: http://www.guggenheim.org/guggenheim-foundation/architecture/new-york.

pp. 460–61: Mark Lehner from "Explore the Pyramids," © 1996–2007 National Geographic Society <access date September 13, 2007>: http://www.nationalgeographic.com/pyramids/pyramids.html

p. 468: Diego Rivera from Bertram D. Wolfe, *The Fabulous Life of Diego Rivera* (New York: Stein and Day, 1963), 423.

Chapter 4.2

p. 473: Betye Saar from Beryl Wright, *The Appropriate Object* (Buffalo, NY: Albright-Knox Gallery, 1989), 58.

p. 480: Description of the Mosque of the Imam, Isfahan from The Metropolitan Museum of Art, "Works of Art: Islamic Highlights: Signatures, Inscriptions, and Markings", accessed September 13, 2010: www.metmuseum.org/works_of_art/collection_database/islamic?art/mihrab/objectview.aspx?collID=14OID=140006815

Chapter 4.3

p. 484: Albert Einstein from "The World As I See It," *Forum and Century*, vol. 84 (October, 1930), 193–4; reprinted in *Living Philosophies*, vol. 13 (New York: Simon and Schuster, 1931), 3–7; also reprinted in Albert Einstein, *Ideas and Opinions, based on Mein Weltbild*, ed. Carl Seeling (New York: Bonanza Books, 1954), 8–11.

p. 486: Tierney Gearon, from Brett Leigh Dicks, "Tierney Gearon's *Mother Project*,"

The Santa Barbara Independent (February 14, 2008).

Chapter 4.4

p. 500: Willard Wigan from *The Telegraph* article by Benjamin Secher on July 7, 2007: http://www.telegraph.co.uk/culture/art/3666352/The-tiny-world-of-Willard-Wigan-nano-sculptor.html.

p. 502: Jasper Johns from Martin Friedman, *Visions of America: Landscape as Metaphor in the Late Twentieth Century* (Denver, CO: Denver Art Museum, 1994), 146.

p. 503: Marcia Smilack from Artist's Statement on her own website: http://www.marciasmilack.com/artist-statement.php

p. 503: Jean Dubuffet from John Maizels, *Raw Creation: Outsider Art and Beyond* (London: Phaidon, 2000), 33.

p. 504: Salvador Dali from Dawn Ades et al., *Dali* (Venice, Italy: Rizzoli, 2004), 559.

Chapter 4.5

p. 508: Pliny the Elder from Jerome Jordon Pollitt, *The Art of Ancient Greece: Sources and Documents* (Cambridge: Cambridge University Press, 1990), 150.

p. 512: Ovid from *Metamorphoses*, trans. A. D. Melville and E. J. Kenney (New York and Oxford: Oxford World's Classics, 2009), 232.

p. 519: Magritte from Paul Crowther, *Language of 20th-Century Art* (New Haven, CT: Yale University Press, 1997), 116.

Chapter 4.7

p. 533: Nick Ut from William Kelly, *Art and Humanist Ideals: Contemporary Perspectives* (Australia: Palgrave Macmillan, 2003), 284.

Chapter 4.8

p. 545: Picasso from Charles Harrison and Paul Wood, *Art in Theory, 1900–2000: An Anthology of Changing Ideas* (Oxford: Blackwell Publishing, 2003), 508.

p. 546: Florence Owens Thompson, and one of her children, both from Kiku Adatto, *Picture Perfect: Life in the Age of the Photo Op.* (Princeton, NJ: Princeton University Press, 2008), 247 and 248.

p. 548: Mary Richardson from June Purvis, *Emmeline Pankhurst: A Biography* (London and New York: Routledge, 2002), 255.

p. 549: Eric Fischl poem from Laura Brandon, *Art and War* (London: I.B. Tauris & Co Ltd, 2007), 129; and Fischl's remarks from Daniel Sherman and Terry Nardin, *Terror, Culture, Politics: Rethinking 9/11* (Indiana: Indiana University Press, 2006), 60.

p. 552: Maya Lin from Marilyn Stokstad, *Art History* (place?: Pearson Education, 2008), xliv.

p. 553: Translation of text on artwork by Wenda Gu from discussion of the exhibition by the Asia Society: http://sites.asiasociety.org/arts/insideout/commissions.html.

Chapter 4.9

p. 554: Willem de Kooning from an interview with David Sylvester (BBC, 1960), "Content is a Glimpse…" in *Location I* (Spring, 1963) and reprinted in David Sylvester, "The Birth of 'Woman I,'" *Burlington Magazine* 137, no. 1105 (April, 1995), 223.

p. 566: Matisse from "Exactitude is not Truth," 1947, essay by Matisse written for an exhibition catalog (Liège: Association pour le progrès intellectuel et artistique de la Wallonie, with the participation of Galerie Maight, Paris); English translation (Philadelphia Museum of Art, 1948); reprinted in Jack Flam, *Matisse on Art* (Berkeley, CA: University of California Press, 1995/1973), 179–181.

Chapter 4.10

p. 571: Cindy Sherman from "Interview with Els Barents," in *Cindy Sherman* (Munich: Schirmer und Mosel, 1982); reprinted in Kristine Stiles and Peter Selz, eds., *Theories and Documents of Contemporary Art: A Sourcebook of Artists' Writings* (Berkeley, CA: University of California Press, 1996), 792–3.

Chapter 4.11

p. 584: John Ruskin, letter 79 (18 June 1877) from *Fors Clavigera: Letters to the Workmen and Labourers of Great Britain*, vol. 7 (Orpington, Kent: George Allen, July 2, 1877), 201; reprinted in E. T. Cook and Alexander Wedderburn, eds., *The Works of John Ruskin*, vol. 29 (London: George Allen, 1907), 160.

p. 589: Nikki S. Lee from Erica Schlaikjer, "Woman's Art Requires Becoming a Chameleon," *The Daily Northwestern* (February 24, 2006), Campus Section.

Illustration Credits

p. 16 (above) Stanza della Segnatura, Vatican Museums, Rome; (center) Library of Congress, Washington, D.C. Prints & Photographs Division, H. Irving Olds collection, LC-DIG-jpd-02018; (below) Photo Irmgard Groth-Kimball © Thames & Hudson Ltd, London; **p. 18** iStockphoto.com; **p. 19** Photo Irmgard Groth-Kimball © Thames & Hudson Ltd, London; **p. 20** Stanza della Segnatura, Vatican Museums, Rome; **p. 21** Galleria degli Uffizi, Florence; **p. 22** Museo Nacional del Prado, Madrid; **p. 23** Library of Congress, Washington, D.C.. Prints & Photographs Division, H. Irving Olds collection, LC-DIG-jpd-02018; **p. 24** Library of Congress, Washington, D.C.. Prints & Photographs Division, FSA/OWI Collection, LC-DIG-fsa-8b29516; **p. 25** Teriade Editeur, Paris, 1947. Printer Edmond Vairel, Paris. Edition 250. Museum of Modern Art, New York, The Louis E. Stern Collection, 930.1964.8. Digital image 2012, Museum of Modern Art, New York/Scala, Florence. © Succession H. Matisse/DACS 2012; **0.1** Fitzwilliam Museum, University of Cambridge/Bridgeman Art Library; **0.2** Spencer Collection, New York Public Library, Astor, Lenox and Tilden Foundations; **0.3** Solomon R. Guggenheim Museum, New York, Gift, Mr. and Mrs. James J. Shapiro, 85.3266. Photo David Heald © Solomon R. Guggenheim Foundation. © ARS, NY and DACS, London 2012; **0.4** © Nik Wheeler/Corbis; **0.5** © Ian Dagnall/Alamy; **0.6** © Jeff Koons; **0.7** Indianapolis Museum of Art, Gift of Charles L. Freer/Bridgeman Art Library; **0.8** Musée du Louvre, Paris; **0.9** Kunsthistorisches Museum, Vienna; **0.10** Private Collection; **0.11** Photo © Erik Cornelius/Nationalmuseum, Stockholm; **0.12** © Ian Dagnall/Alamy; **0.13** Mauritshuis, The Hague; **0.14** Photo Marc Quinn Studio. Courtesy White Cube. © the artist; **0.15** Publisher Heinar Schilling, Dresden. Printer unknown. Edition 15. Museum of Modern Art, New York, Purchase, Acc. no. 480.1949. Photo 2012, Museum of Modern Art, New York/Scala, Florence. © DACS 2012; **0.16** Metropolitan Museum of Art, Gift of Mrs. Frank B. Porter, 1922, Acc. no. 22.207. Photo Metropolitan Museum of Art/Art Resource/Scala, Florence; **0.17** Musée du Louvre, Paris; **0.18** André Held /akg-images; **p. 44** (above) Photo Andrew Hawthorne. Courtesy the artists; (center) © 2012 The M.C. Escher Company-Holland. All rights reserved. www.mcescher.com; (below) Museo Nacional del Prado, Madrid; **1.1** Photo Jarno Gonzalez Zarraonandia/iStockphoto.com; **1.2a** Slow Images/Getty Images; **1.2b** National Gallery of Art, Washington, D.C., Wolfgang Ratjen Collection, Paul Mellon Fund, 2007.111.55; **1.3** © CLAMP/Kodansha Ltd; **1.4** Image courtesy Peter Freeman, Inc., New York; **1.5** © Bowness, Hepworth Estate; **1.6** © ADAGP, Paris and DACS, London 2012; **1.7**

Fondation Dubuffet. © ADAGP, Paris and DACS, London 2012; **1.8** National Gallery of Art, Washington, D.C., Collection of Mr. and Mrs. Paul Mellon, 1983.1.81; **1.9** Ralph Larmann; **1.10**, **1.11** British Library, London; **1.12** © Sauerkids; **1.13** Museo Nacional del Prado, Madrid; **1.14** British Museum, London; **1.15** Private Collection; **1.16** Ralph Larmann; **1.17** © Nike; **1.18** Art Institute of Chicago, Helen Birch Bartlett Memorial Collection, 1926.417; **1.19** Ralph Larmann; **1.20** Courtesy Flomenhaft Gallery, New York; **1.21** Ralph Larmann; **1.22** Courtesy AT&T Archives and History Center; **1.23a** © 1996 Shepard Fairey/ObeyGiant.com; **1.23b** © 1996 Shepard Fairey/ObeyGiant.com. Photo © Elizabeth Daniels, www.elizabethdanielsphotography.com; **1.24** © Georgia O'Keeffe Museum/DACS 2012; **1.25** © Big Ten Conference; **1.26** © 2012 The M.C. Escher Company-Holland. All rights reserved. www.mcescher.com; **1.27** Monasterio de las Huelgas, Museo de Telas Medievales, Burgos; **1.28** Ralph Larmann; **1.29**, **1.30** Photo Heidi Grassley © Thames & Hudson Ltd, London; **1.31** Photo courtesy the Marlborough Gallery Inc., New York. © Estate of David Smith/DACS, London/VAGA, New York 2012; **1.32** Rheinisches Landesmuseum, Bonn; **1.33** Photo Russell Johnson. Courtesy Lino Tagliapietra, Inc.; **1.34** Museo dell'Ara Pacis, Rome; **1.35** Fine Arts Museum of San Francisco, Museum Purchase, Gift of Mrs Paul Wattis 1999, 42 a-k; **1.36** Ralph Larmann; **1.37a**, **1.37b** Photo Clements/Howcroft, MA, USA. Courtesy the artists; **1.38** Photo Nationalmuseum, Stockholm; **1.39** Photo Andrew Hawthorne. Courtesy the artists; **1.40** Photo Irmgard Groth-Kimball © Thames & Hudson Ltd, London; **1.41** Photo Sue Ormerod. © Rachel Whiteread. Courtesy Gagosian Gallery, London; **1.42** © Marisol, DACS, London/VAGA, New York 2012; **1.43** Stedelijk Museum, Amsterdam; **1.44** Museum of Modern Art, New York, Purchase, Acc. no. 130.1946.a-c. Photo 2012, Museum of Modern Art, New York/Scala, Florence. © DACS 2012; **1.45** © Romain Cintract/Hemis/Corbis; **1.46** © Louise Bourgeois Trust/DACS, London/VAGA, New York 2012; **1.47** Los Angeles County Museum of Art (LACMA). Purchased with funds provided by the Mr. and Mrs. William Preston Harrison Collection, 78.7. © ADAGP, Paris and DACS, London 2012; **1.48** Special Collections & Archives, Eric V. Hauser Memorial Library, Reed College, Portland, Oregon; **1.49**, **1.50** Ralph Larmann; **1.51** Sterling & Francine Clark Art Institute, Williamstown; **1.52** Contarelli Chapel, Church of San Luigi dei Francesci, Rome; **1.53** Ralph Larmann; **1.54** Musée du Louvre, Paris; **1.55** Library of Congress, Washington, D.C. Prints & Photographs Division, H. Irving Olds collection, LC-DIG-jpd-02018; **1.56** National Palace Museum, Taipei; **1.57** © T. H. Benton and R. P. Benton Testamentary Trusts/DACS, London/VAGA, New York 2012; **1.58** Ralph Larmann; **1.59** Crystal Bridges Museum of American Art, Arkansas; **1.60** Metropolitan Museum of Art, Purchase, The Dillon Fund Gift, 1988. Photo

Metropolitan Museum of Art/Art Resource/Scala, Florence 2012; **1.61** Ralph Larmann; **1.62** The Sims © 2012 Electronic Arts Inc. The Sims and The Sims plumbob design are trademarks or registered trademarks of Electronic Arts Inc. in the US and/or other countries. All Rights Reserved. Used with permission; **1.63** Private Collection; **1.64** Ralph Larmann; **1.65** Santa Maria Novella, Florence; **1.66a**, **1.66b** Stanza della Segnatura, Vatican Museums, Rome; **1.67** Ralph Larmann; **1.68** © 2012 The M.C. Escher Company-Holland. All rights reserved. www.mcescher.com; **1.69** Graphische Sammlung Albertina, Vienna; **1.70** Pinacoteca di Brera, Milan; **1.71**, **1.72** Ralph Larmann; **1.73** Fine Arts Museum of San Francisco, Gift of Vivian Burns, Inc., 74.8; **1.74** Ralph Larmann; **1.75** © Mark Tansey. Courtesy Gagosian Gallery, New York; **1.76** Ralph Larmann; **1.77** Museum of Modern Art, New York, Gift of Mr. and Mrs. Ben Heller, Acc. no. 240.1969. Photo 2012, Museum of Modern Art, New York/Scala, Florence. © ARS, NY and DACS, London, 2012; **1.78** The Museum of Fine Arts, Houston, Gift of Audrey Jones Beck. © ADAGP, Paris and DACS, London 2012; **1.79** Ralph Larmann; **1.80** Teriade Editeur, Paris, 1947. Printer Edmond Vairel, Paris. Edition 250. Museum of Modern Art, New York, The Louis E. Stern Collection, 930.1964.8. Photo 2012, Museum of Modern Art, New York/Scala, Florence. © Succession H. Matisse/DACS 2012; **1.81** Cleveland Museum of Art, Mr. and Mrs. William H. Marlatt Fund, 1965.233; **1.82** National Gallery of Art, Washington, D.C., Chester Dale Collection, 1963.10.94; **1.83** © Howard Hodgkin; **1.84** British Museum, London; **1.85** Ralph Larmann; **1.86**, **1.87** Musée d'Orsay, Paris; **1.88** Ralph Larmann; **1.89** Private Collection (color artwork by Ralph Larmann); **1.90**, **1.91** Ralph Larmann; **1.92** Courtesy Charles Csuri; **1.93** Yale University Art Gallery, New Haven, Bequest of Stephen Carlton Clark, B.A. 1903, 1961.18.34; **1.94** Albright-Knox Art Gallery, Buffalo, New York, General Purchase Funds, 1946; **1.95** National Gallery of Art, Washington, D.C., Samuel H. Kress Collection, 1939.1.293; **1.96** Photo University of South Florida. © Nancy Holt/DACS, London/VAGA, New York 2012; **1.97** Library of Congress, Washington, D.C.. Prints & Photographs Division, LC-USZ62-536; **1.98** Galleria Borghese, Rome; **1.99** Albright-Knox Art Gallery, Buffalo, New York, Bequest of A. Conger Goodyear and Gift of George F. Goodyear, 1964. © DACS 2012; **1.100** Solomon R. Guggenheim Museum, New York, Partial gift of the artist, 1989, 89.3626. Photo David Heald © Solomon R. Guggenheim Foundation, New York. © ARS, NY and DACS, London 2012; **1.101** Copyright Bridget Riley, 2012. All rights reserved; **1.102** Courtesy the Bill Douglas Centre for the History of Cinema and Popular Culture, University of Exeter; **1.103** Disney Enterprises/Album/akg-images; **1.104** Double Indemnity, © Paramount Pictures; **1.105** © Blaine Harrington III/Alamy; **1.106** Photo © B. O'Kane/Alamy. © 2012 Calder Foundation, New York/DACS, London; **1.107a** Library of Congress, Washington, D.C. Prints & Photographs Division,

FSA/OWI Collection, LC-USZ62-58355; **1.107b** © The Dorothea Lange Collection, Oakland Museum of California, City of Oakland. Gift of Paul S. Taylor; **1.107c** Library of Congress, Washington, D.C. Prints & Photographs Division, FSA/OWI Collection, LC-USF34-9097-C; **1.107d** Library of Congress, Washington, D.C. Prints & Photographs Division, FSA/OWI Collection, LC-USF34-9093-C; **1.107e** Library of Congress, Washington, D.C. Prints & Photographs Division, FSA/OWI Collection, LC-USF34-9095; **1.107f** Library of Congress, Washington, D.C. Prints & Photographs Division, FSA/OWI Collection, LC-DIG-fsa-8b29516; **1.108** Courtesy the artists; **1.109** © the artist. Courtesy Catherine Person Gallery, Seattle, WA; **1.110** Ralph Larmann; **1.111** Library of Congress, Washington, D.C.. Prints & Photographs Division, H. Irving Olds collection, LC-DIG-jpd-02018; **1.112** I. Michael Interior Design; **1.113** Ralph Larmann; **1.114** Courtesy Galerie Berès, Paris. © ADAGP, Paris and DACS, London 2012; **1.115** Galleria Nazionale delle Marche, Urbino; **1.116** Museum of Modern Art, New York, Blanchette Hooker Rockefeller Fund, Acc. no. 377.1971. Photo 2012, Museum of Modern Art, New York/Scala, Florence. © Romare Bearden Foundation/DACS, London/VAGA, New York 2012; **1.117** © The Joseph and Robert Cornell Memorial Foundation/DACS, London/VAGA, New York 2012; **1.118** Photo John Freeman; **1.119** Ralph Larmann; **1.120** © Estate of Robert Rauschenberg. DACS, London/VAGA, New York 2012; **1.121** Private Collection; **1.122** The University of Hong Kong Museum; **1.123** Photo Shimizu Kohgeisha Co., Ltd. Permission Ryoko-in Management; **1.124** pl. XIII, Book II from Wade, I. (ed.) *Palladio: Four Books of Architecture*, 1738; **1.125** Courtesy Drepung Loseling Monastery, Inc.; **1.126** Photo Attilio Maranzano. Photo courtesy the Oldenburg van Bruggen Foundation. Copyright 1992 Claes Oldenburg and Coosje van Bruggen; **1.127** Courtesy the artist; **1.128** Werner Forman Archive, line artwork Ralph Larmann; **1.129** Gemäldegalerie, Staatliche Museen, Berlin; **1.130** Purchased with assistance from the Art Fund and the American Fund for the Tate Gallery 1997 © Tate, London, 2012. © ADAGP, Paris and DACS, London 2012; **1.131, 1.132** Ralph Larmann; **1.133** National Museum, Ife, Nigeria; **1.134** Stanza della Segnatura, Vatican Museums, Rome; **1.135** Ralph Larmann; **1.136** National Archaeological Museum, Athens; **1.137** Ralph Larmann; **1.138a** George Eastman House, New York; **1.138b** Ralph Larmann; **1.139** iStockphoto.com; **1.140** Ralph Larmann; **1.141** Metropolitan Museum of Art, Gift of Nathan Cummings, 1966, 66.30.2. Photo Metropolitan Museum of Art/Art Resource/Scala, Florence; **1.142** Photo © Museum of Fine Arts, Boston. Courtesy Jules Olitski Warehouse LLC. © Estate of Jules Olitski, DACS, London/VAGA, New York 2012; **1.143** © Estate of Mark Tobey, ARS, NY/DACS, London 2012. Courtesy Sotheby's; **1.144** Musées Royaux des Beaux-Arts de Belgique, Brussels; **1.145** Galleria degli Uffizi, Florence; **1.146** Victoria

& Albert Museum, London; **1.147** Musée du Louvre, Paris; **1.148** James A. Michener Collection, Honolulu Academy of Arts; **1.149** Ralph Larmann; **1.150** Musée National d'Art Moderne, Centre Georges Pompidou, Paris; **1.151** Metropolitan Museum of Art, Louis E. and Theresa S. Seley Purchase Fund for Islamic Art, and Rogers Fund, 1984. Photo Metropolitan Museum of Art/Art Resource/Scala, Florence; **1.152** Ashmolean Museum, Oxford; **1.153a, 1.153b, 1.153c** Museum of Modern Art, New York, Gift of Agnes Gund, Jo Carole and Ronald S. Lauder, Donald L. Bryant, Jr., Leon Black, Michael and Judy Ovitz, Anna Marie and Robert F. Shapiro, Leila and Melville Straus, Doris and Donald Fisher, and purchase, Acc. no. 215.2000. Photo Ellen Page Wilson, courtesy The Pace Gallery © Chuck Close, The Pace Gallery; **1.154** © DACS 2012; **1.155** Kunsthistorisches Museum, Vienna; **1.156** iStockphoto.com; **1.157** Collection Center for Creative Photography © 1981 Arizona Board of Regents; **1.158** © WaterFrame/Alamy; **1.159** Museo Nacional del Prado, Madrid; **1.160a** Musée d'Orsay, Paris; **1.160b** Ralph Larmann; **1.161** iStockphoto.com; **1.162** © Andia/Alamy; **1.163** Allan Houser archives © Chiinde LLC; **1.164** Collection University of Arizona Museum of Art, Tucson, Museum purchase with funds provided by the Edward J. Gallagher, Jr Memorial Fund 1982.35.1. © the artist; **1.165** The Art Institute of Chicago, Gift of Arthur Keating and Mr. and Mrs. Edward Morris by exchange, April 1988. © The Estate of Eva Hesse. Hauser & Wirth. Photo Susan Einstein, courtesy The Art Institute of Chicago; **1.166** Musée du Louvre, Paris; **1.167** Courtesy Archiv LRP; **1.168** The Art Institute of Chicago, Friends of American Art Collection, 1942.51; **1.169** Museo Nacional del Prado, Madrid; **1.170** Museo Nacional del Prado, Madrid; **1.171** © Succession Picasso/DACS, London 2012; **1.172** © 2012 Thomas Struth; **p. 164** (above) National Palace Museum, Taipei; (center) Printed by permission of the Norman Rockwell Family Agency. Book Rights Copyright © 1943 The Norman Rockwell Family Entities; (below) © Free Agents Limited/Corbis; **2.1** Biblioteca Ambrosiana, Milan; **2.2** The Royal Collection © Her Majesty The Queen; **2.3a** Biblioteca Ambrosiana, Milan; **2.3b** Stanza della Segnatura, Vatican Museums, Rome; **2.4** Ralph Larmann; **2.5** © DACS 2012; **2.6** Museum of Modern Art, New York, The Judith Rothschild Foundation Contemporary Drawings Collection Gift. Courtesy Daniel Reich Gallery, New York; **2.7** British Museum, London; **2.8** © DACS 2012; **2.9** Photo Peter Nahum at The Leicester Galleries, London/Bridgeman Art Library; **2.10** Metropolitan Museum of Art, Purchase, Joseph Pulitzer Bequest, 1924, Acc. no. 24.197.2. Photo Metropolitan Museum of Art/Art Resource/Scala, Florence; **2.11** Musée d'Orsay, Paris; **2.12** The Art Institute of Chicago, Helen Regenstein Collection, 1966.184; **2.13** San Francisco Museum of Modern Art, Purchased through a gift of Phyllis Wattis. © Estate of Robert Rauschenberg. DACS, London/VAGA, New York 2012; **2.14** Van Gogh

Museum (Vincent Van Gogh Foundation), Amsterdam; **2.15** National Palace Museum, Taipei; **2.16** British Museum, London; **2.17** from *Wakoku Shōshoku Edzukushi*, 1681; **2.18** Ralph Larmann; **2.19** Musée des Beaux-Arts de Lyon. © Succession H. Matisse/DACS 2012; **2.20** Teriade Editeur, Paris, 1947. Printer Edmond Vairel, Paris. Edition 250. Museum of Modern Art, New York, The Louis E. Stern Collection, 930.1964.8. Photo 2012, Museum of Modern Art, New York/Scala, Florence. © Succession H. Matisse/DACS 2012; **2.21** Museum of Modern Art, New York, Purchase, 330.1949. Photo 2012, Museum of Modern Art, New York/Scala, Florence; **2.22** Ralph Larmann; **2.23** Metropolitan Museum of Art, Gift of Edward S. Harkness, 1918, 18.9.2. Photo Metropolitan Museum of Art/Art Resource/Scala, Florence; **2.24** National Gallery of Scotland, Edinburgh; **2.25** Metropolitan Museum of Art, Purchase, Francis M. Weld Gift, 1950, Inv. 50.164. Photo Metropolitan Museum of Art/Art Resource/Scala, Florence; **2.26** Museum of Modern Art, New York, Purchase, 16.1949. Photo 2012, Museum of Modern Art, New York/Scala, Florence. © Andrew Wyeth; **2.27** Vatican Museums, Rome; **2.28** Philadelphia Museum of Art, Gift of Mr. and Mrs. Herbert Cameron Morris, 1943. © 2012 Banco de México Diego Rivera Frida Kahlo Museums Trust, Mexico, D.F./DACS; **2.29** Photo Steven Ochs; **2.30** Musée du Louvre, Paris; **2.31** Los Angeles County Museum of Art, Gift of Mr. and Mrs. Robert H. Ginter, M.64.49. Digital Image Museum Associates/LACMA/Art Resource NY/Scala, Florence. Courtesy Gallery Paule Anglim; **2.32** Kemper Museum of Contemporary Art, Kansas City. Bebe and Crosby Kemper Collection, Gift of the William T. Kemper Charitable Trust, UMB Bank, n.a., Trustee 2006.7. Photo Ben Blackwell © the artist; **2.33** Galleria degli Uffizi, Florence; **2.34** The Royal Collection © Her Majesty The Queen; **2.35** Kemper Museum of Contemporary Art, Kansas City. Bebe and Crosby Kemper Collection, Kansas City, Missouri. Museum Purchase, Enid and Crosby Kemper and William T. Kemper Acquisition Fund 2000.13. © the artist; **2.36** Photo Austrian Archives/Scala Florence; **2.37** Photo Tate, London 2012. © L&M Services B.V. The Hague 20110512. © Miriam Cendrars; **2.38** Clark Family Collection. Image courtesy The Clark Center for Japanese Art & Culture; **2.39** Courtesy Art Link International, Florida. © the artist; **2.40** Photo Sybille Prou; **2.41** Ralph Larmann; **2.43** British Museum, London; **2.44** Museum of Modern Art, New York. Given anonymously (by exchange), Acc. no. 119.1956. Photo 2012, Museum of Modern Art, New York/Scala, Florence. © Nolde Stiftung Seebüll; **2.45** Library of Congress, Washington, D.C. Prints & Photographs Division, H. Irving Olds collection, LC-DIG-jpd-02018; **2.46** Ralph Larmann; **2.47** Victoria & Albert Museum, London; **2.48** © DACS 2012; **2.49** Kupferstichkabinett, Museen Preussiches Kulturbesitz, Berlin; **2.50** Metropolitan Museum of Art, Harris Brisbane Dick Fund, 1935, Acc. no. 35.42. Photo Metropolitan Museum of Art/Art

Resource/Scala, Florence; **2.51a** Museo Nacional del Prado, Madrid; **2.51b** Private Collection; **2.52** Print and Picture Collection, Free Library of Philadelphia. Courtesy Fine Arts Program, Public Buildings Service, U.S. General Services Administration. Commissioned through the New Deal art projects; **2.53** Ralph Larmann; **2.54** Private Collection; **2.55** © The Andy Warhol Foundation for the Visual Arts/Artists Rights Society (ARS), New York/DACS London 2012; **2.56** Fogg Art Museum, Harvard Art Museums, Margaret Fisher Fund, M25276. Photo Imaging Department © President & Fellows of Harvard College. © ARS, NY and DACS, London 2012; **2.57** © Kathy Strauss 2007; **2.58** British Museum, London; **2.59** Tokyo National Museum; **2.60** Koninklijke Bibliotheek, The Hague, Folio 8r., shelf no. 69B 10; **2.61** V&A Images/Victoria & Albert Museum; **2.62** Ralph Larmann; **2.63** Courtesy Ford Motor Company; **2.64** General Motors Corp. Used with permission, GM Media Archives; **2.65** from *Works of Geoffrey Chaucer*, Kelmscott Press, 1896; **2.66** Printed by permission of the Norman Rockwell Family Agency. Book Rights Copyright © 1943 The Norman Rockwell Family Entities; **2.67** Courtesy Kok Cheow Yeoh; **2.68** The Art Institute of Chicago, Mr. and Mrs. Carter H. Harrison Collection, 1954.1193; **2.69** Taesam Do/FoodPix/Getty. Image courtesy Hill Holiday; **2.70** School of Journalism and Mass Communication, University of North Carolina at Chapel Hill. Photo Eileen Mignoni; **2.71** Gernsheim Collection, London; **2.72** Image appears courtesy Abelardo Morell; **2.73** British Library, London; **2.74** Metropolitan Museum of Art, The Rubel Collection, Purchase, Ann Tenenbaum and Thomas H. Lee and Anonymous Gifts, 1997, Acc. no. 1997.382.1. Photo The Metropolitan Museum of Art/Art Resource/Scala, Florence; **2.75** Ralph Larmann; **2.76** Bibliothèque nationale, Paris; **2.77** Library of Congress, Washington, D.C.. Prints & Photographs Division, FSA/OWI Collection, LC-DIG-fsa-8b29516; **2.78** © Ansel Adams Publishing Rights Trust/Corbis; **2.79** Collection of the Société Française de Photographie, Paris; **2.80** Collection Center for Creative Photography © 1981 Arizona Board of Regents; **2.81** Library of Congress, Washington, D.C.. Prints & Photographs Division, LC-DIG-nclc-01555; **2.82a**, **2.82b** Copyright Steve McCurry/Magnum Photos; **2.83** © Hiroko Masuike/New York Times/Eyevine; **2.84** Copyright Steve McCurry/Magnum Photos; **2.85** Royal Photographic Society, Bath; **2.86** Courtesy Yossi Milo Gallery, New York. © DACS 2012; **2.87** The Art Institute of Chicago, Alfred Stieglitz Collection, 1949.705 © Georgia O'Keeffe Museum/DACS, 2012; **2.88** © Estate of Garry Winogrand, courtesy Fraenkel Gallery, San Francisco; **2.89** Nationalgalerie, Staatliche Museen, Berlin. © DACS 2012; **2.90** © Stephen Marc; **2.91** Gernsheim Collection, Harry Ransom Humanities Research Centre, University of Texas at Austin; **2.92** Courtesy Gagosian Gallery © Sally Mann; **2.93** Sandy Skoglund, Radioactive Cats © 1980; **2.94** Photo © Edward Burtynsky, courtesy Flowers, London & Nicholas Metivier, Toronto; **2.95** Ralph Larmann; **2.96** Library of Congress, Washington, D.C. Prints & Photographs Division, LC-USZ62-45683; **2.97** Star Film Company; **2.98** akg-images; **2.99**, **2.100** British Film Institute (BFI); **2.101** M.G.M/Album/akg-images; **2.102** British Film Institute (BFI); **2.103** Disney Enterprises/Album/akg-images; **2.104** Lucasfilm/20th Century Fox/The Kobal Collection; **2.105**, **2.106**, **2.107**, **2.108** British Film Institute (BFI); **2.109** Image copyright of the artist, courtesy Video Data Bank, www.vdb.org; **2.110** Courtesy Electronic Arts Intermix (EAI), New York; **2.111** Image courtesy Dia Art Foundation. Courtesy Tony Oursler, Stephen Vitiello and Constance de Jong; **2.112** Courtesy exonemo; **2.113a** Photo Mathias Schormann © Bill Viola; **2.113b**, **2.113c** Photo Kira Perov © Bill Viola; **2.114** © DACS 2012; **2.115** Photo Betsy Jackson. Courtesy the artist; **2.116** © Marina Abramović. Courtesy Marina Abramović and Sean Kelly Gallery, New York. DACS 2012; **2.117** © Barbara Kruger. Courtesy Mary Boone Gallery, New York; **2.118** © ARS, NY and DACS, London 2012; **2.119** Photo Karla Merrifield © Yoko Ono; **2.120**, **2.121** Courtesy The Fundred Dollar Bill Project; **2.122** Photo courtesy the Oldenburg van Bruggen Foundation. Photo © Robert McElroy/Licensed by VAGA, New York, NY; **2.123** © Fred Wilson, courtesy PaceWildenstein, New York. Photo courtesy PaceWildenstein, New York; **2.124** Courtesy Sikkema Jenkins & Co., NY; **2.125** (above) Courtesy Trudy Labell Fine Art, Florida. © the artist; **2.125** (below) Photo Trudy Labell; **2.126** Photos Ralph Larmann; **2.127** Cleveland Museum of Art, Gift of the Hanna Fund, 1954.857; **2.128a** Metropolitan Museum of Art, New York. The Michael C. Rockefeller Memorial Collection, Bequest of Nelson A. Rockefeller, 1979, Acc. no. 1979.206.1134. Photo Schecter Lee. Photo Metropolitan Museum of Art/Art Resource/Scala, Florence; **2.128b** Photo Irmgard Groth-Kimball © Thames & Hudson Ltd, London; **2.129** Palace Museum, Beijing; **2.130** Courtesy Arizona State University Art Museum, photo Anthony Cunha; **2.131** Courtesy the Voulkos & Co. Catalogue Project, www.voulkos.com; **2.132** British Museum, London; **2.133** © Angelo Hornak/Corbis; **2.134** Photo Teresa Nouri Rishel © Dale Chihuly; **2.135** National Archaeological Museum, Athens; **2.136** Kunsthistorisches Museum, Vienna; **2.137** © the artist www.tillekeschwarz.com; **2.138** The Solomon R. Guggenheim Foundation, 88.3620; Faith Ringgold © 1988; **2.139** © Christie's Images/Corbis; **2.140** Metropolitan Museum of Art, Rogers Fund, 1939, Acc. no. 39.153. Photo Metropolitan Museum of Art/Art Resource/Scala, Florence; **2.141** Seattle Art Museum, Gift of John H. Hauberg and John and Grace Putnam, 86.278. Photo Paul Macapia; **2.142** Museum of Fine Arts, Boston, Massachusetts/Harvard University – Museum of Fine Arts Expedition/Bridgeman Art Library; **2.143a**, **2.143b** Photo Scala, Florence; **2.144** British Museum, London; **2.145** Photograph Jacqueline Banerjee, Associate Editor of the Victorian Web www.victorianweb.org; **2.146a**, **2.146b** © David Hilbert/Alamy; **2.147** Photo Scala, Florence, courtesy Ministero Beni e Att. Culturali; **2.148** Vatican Museums, Rome; **2.149** Photo Scala, Florence, courtesy Ministero Beni e Att. Culturali; **2.150** British Museum, London; **2.151** Museo Nazionale di Villa Guilia, Rome; **2.152** National Museum, Reggio Calabria, Italy; **2.153** Ralph Larmann; **2.154** © Richard A. Cooke/Corbis; **2.155** Photo Tom Smart; **2.156** Photo Tate, London 2012. The works of Naum Gabo © Nina Williams; **2.157** Photo Prudence Cuming Associates/© Hirst Holdings Limited and Damien Hirst. All rights reserved, DACS 2012; **2.158** © Succession Picasso/DACS, London 2012; **2.159** Philadelphia Museum of Art, The Louise and Walter Arensberg Collection. © ADAGP, Paris and DACS, London 2012; **2.160** Harvard Art Museums, Busch-Reisinger Museum, Hildegard von Gontard Bequest Fund, 2007.105. Photo Junius Beebe, President & Fellows of Harvard College © DACS 2012; **2.161** Photo Jens Ziehe 2004 © 2002 Olafur Eliasson; **2.162** Photo Mark Pollock/Estate of George Rickey. © Estate of George Rickey/DACS, London/VAGA, New York 2012; **2.163a** Photograph by Zhang Haier; **2.163b** Photo Dai Wei, Shanghai © the artist; **2.164** Courtesy the artists and Sprovieri Gallery, London; **2.165** Maki and Associates. Courtesy Silverstein Properties; **2.166**, **2.167** iStockphoto.com; **2.168** DeAgostini Picture Library/Scala, Florence; **2.169a** Ralph Larmann; **2.169b** iStockphoto.com; **2.170** Ralph Larmann; **2.171** Bridgeman Art Library; **2.172** Index/Bridgeman Art Library; **2.173** Ralph Larmann; **2.174** © Christophe Boisvieux/Corbis; **2.175** Ralph Larmann; **2.176** Photo Scala, Florence; **2.177** Gianni Dagli Orti/Basilique Saint Denis Paris/The Art Archive; **2.178a**, **2.178b** Ralph Larmann; **2.179** © Robert Harding Picture Library Ltd/Alamy; **2.180**, **2.181** Ralph Larmann; **2.182** © Photo Japan/Alamy; **2.183** Photo Shannon Kyles, ontarioarchitecture.com; **2.185** Photo Sandak Inc, Stamford, CT; **2.186** © INTERFOTO/Alamy; **2.187** © Robert Harding Picture Library Ltd/Alamy; **2.188** © Bildarchiv Monheim GmbH/Alamy; **2.189** © Richard A. Cooke/Corbis; **2.190** © Free Agents Limited/Corbis; **2.191** Photo courtesy Michael Graves & Associates; **2.192** © Chuck Eckert/Alamy; **2.193a** Courtesy Zaha Hadid Architects; **2.193b** © Roland Halbe/artur; **2.194** Courtesy CMPBS; **p. 292** (above) Egyptian Museum, Cairo; (center) iStockphoto.com; (below) Musée d'Orsay, Paris; **3.1** Drazen Tomic; **3.2** Photo Jean Clottes; **3.3** Images courtesy the Mellaarts/Çatalhöyük Research Project; **3.4** The J. Paul Getty Museum, Villa Collection, Malibu, California; **3.5** Photo Jeff Morgan Travel/Alamy; **3.6** Archaeological Museum, Heraklion; **3.7** British Museum, London; **3.8** Iraq Museum, Baghdad; **3.9** Metropolitan Museum of Art, Gift of John D. Rockefeller Jr., 1932, Acc. no. 32.143.2. Photo Metropolitan Museum of Art/Art Resource/Scala, Florence; **3.10** Photo Scala, Florence/BPK,

Bildagentur für Kunst, Kultur und Geschichte, Berlin; **3.11** iStockphoto.com; **3.12** Gianni Dagli Orti/Egyptian Museum, Cairo/The Art Archive; **3.13**, **3.14** Egyptian Museum, Cairo; **3.15** British Museum, London; **3.16** Peter Connolly/akg-images; **3.17** Nimatallah/akg-images; **3.18** Ralph Larmann; **3.19** British Museum, London; **3.20**, **3.21** Museum of Fine Arts, Boston, Henry Lillie Pierce Fund; **3.22** Metropolitan Museum of Art, Fletcher Fund, 1932, Acc. no. 32.11.1. Photo Metropolitan Museum of Art/Art Resource/Scala, Florence; **3.23** Minneapolis Institute of Arts; **3.24** Vatican Museums, Rome; **3.25** © Altair4 Multimedia Roma, www.altair.it; **3.26** Palazzo Torlonia, Rome; **3.27** Giovanni Caselli; **3.28** Image Source Pink/Alamy; **3.29** © Atlantide Phototravel/Corbis; **3.30** iStockphoto.com; **3.31** Drazen Tomic; **3.32**, **3.33** Zev Radovan/ www.BibleLandPictures.com; **3.34** Canali Photobank, Milan, Italy; **3.35** Photo Scala, Florence; **3.36** Monastery of St. Catherine, Sinai, Egypt; **3.37** Photo Scala, Florence; **3.38** Cameraphoto/ Scala, Florence; **3.39**, **3.40**, **3.41** British Library, London; **3.42** Biblioteca Governativa, Lucca; **3.43** British Library/akg-images; **3.44** Musées Royaux d'Art et d'Histoire, Brussels; **3.45** © Hanan Isachar/Corbis; **3.46** Mohamed Amin/Robert Harding; **3.47** Metropolitan Museum of Art, Harris Brisbane Dick Fund, 1939, Acc. no. 39.20. Photo Metropolitan Museum of Art/Art Resource/Scala, Florence; **3.48** © Matthew Lambley/Alamy; **3.49** Ralph Larmann; **3.50** © Rolf Richardson/Alamy; **3.51** Ralph Larmann; **3.52** Hervé Champollion/akg-images; **3.53** Sonia Halliday Photographs; **3.54**, **3.55** Galleria degli Uffizi, Florence; **3.56** Drazen Tomic; **3.57** iStockphoto.com; **3.58** © Tom Hanley/Alamy; **3.59** © Susanna Bennett/Alamy; **3.60** © Frédéric Soltan/Sygma/Corbis; **3.61** © Pep Roig/Alamy; **3.62** Freer Gallery of Art, Smithsonian Institution, Washington, D.C., Purchase F1942.15a; **3.63** iStockphoto.com; **3.64**, **3.65**, **3.66** Palace Museum, Beijing; **3.67** Brooklyn Museum, Gift of Mr. & Mrs. Alastair B. Martin, the Guennol Collection, 72.163a–b; **3.68** Hunan Museum, Changsha; **3.69** Courtesy the artist; **3.70** Photo Shunji Ohkura; **3.71** TRIP photographic library, photographer F. Good/Art Directors; **3.72** Sakai Collection, Tokyo; **3.73** Horyu-ji Treasure House, Ikaruga, Nara Prefecture, Japan; **3.74** The Tokugawa Art Museum, Nagoya; **3.75** V&A Images/ Alamy; **3.76** The Art Institute of Chicago, Robert A. Waller Fund, 1910.2; **3.77** Library of Congress, Washington, D.C. Prints & Photographs Division, H. Irving Olds collection, LC-DIG-jpd-02018; **3.78** iStockphoto.com; **3.79** Drazen Tomic; **3.80** Anton, F. *Ancient Peruvian Textiles*, Thames & Hudson Ltd, London, 1987; **3.81** Museo Arqueologia, Lima, Peru /Bridgeman Art Library; **3.82** Royal Tombs of Sipán Museum, Lambayeque; **3.83** iStockphoto.com; **3.84** American Museum of Natural History, New York; **3.85** Dumbarton Oaks Research Library and Collections, Washington, D.C.; **3.86** Drazen Tomic; **3.87** Richard Hewitt Stewart/

National Geographic Stock; **3.88a** Drazen Tomic; **3.88b** © aerialarchives.com/Alamy; **3.89** © Ken Welsh/Alamy; **3.90** © Gianni Dagli Orti/Corbis; **3.91** Dallas Museum of Art, Gift of Patsy R. and Raymond D. Nasher, 1983.148; **3.92** Peabody Museum, Harvard University, Cambridge, 48-63-20/17561; **3.93** Biblioteca Nazionale Centrale di Firenze; **3.94** Museo Nacional de Antropología, Mexico City; **3.95** Museo del Templo Mayor, Mexico City; **3.96** Drazen Tomic; **3.97** © Chris Howes/Wild Places Photography/Alamy; **3.98a**, **3.98b** Peabody Museum, Harvard University, Cambridge, 99-12-10/53121; **3.99** Missouri Historical Society, St. Louis, 1882.18.32; **3.100** American Museum of Natural History, New York; **3.101** Drazen Tomic; **3.102** National Museum, Lagos; **3.103** Linden Museum, Stuttgart; **3.104** Dallas Museum of Art, Foundation for the Arts Collection, Gift of the McDermott Foundation, 1996.184.FA; **3.105** National Museum of African Art, Smithsonian Institution, Washington, D.C.; **3.106** Musée Barbier-Mueller, Geneva; **3.107** © JTB Photo Communications, Inc./Alamy; **3.108** © Chris Howes/Wild Places Photography/Alamy; **3.109** Photo Barney Wayne; **3.110** Drazen Tomic; **3.111** pl. XVI from Parkinson, S., *A Journal of a Voyage to the South Seas*, 1784; **3.112** Photo Paul S. C. Tacon; **3.113** Bishop Museum, Honolulu, Hawaii; **3.114** iStockphoto.com; **3.115** Musée Barbier-Mueller, Geneva; **3.116** Collected by G.F.N. Gerrits, Vb 28418-28471 (1972). Photo Peter Horner 1981 © Museum der Kulturen, Basel, Switzerland; **3.117** Drazen Tomic; **3.118** from Vasari, G., *Lives of the Great Artists*, 1568; **3.119** © Michael S. Yamashita/Corbis; **3.120** Libreria dello Stato, Rome; **3.121** Brancacci Chapel, Church of Santa Maria del Carmine, Florence; **3.122** Refectory of Sta Maria delle Grazie, Milan; **3.123**, **3.124** Vatican Museums, Rome; **3.125** Stanza della Segnatura, Vatican Museums, Rome; **3.126** Vatican Museums, Rome; **3.127a**, **3.127b** National Gallery, London/Scala, Florence; **3.128**, **3.129a**, **3.129b**, **3.129c** Gemäldegalerie, Staatliche Museen, Berlin; **3.130** Musée d'Unterlinden, Colmar; **3.131** British Museum, London; **3.132** Museum Narodowe, Poznań/Bridgeman Art Library; **3.133** Galleria dell'Accademia, Venice; **3.134** Cameraphoto/Scala, Florence; **3.135** Capponi Chapel, Church of Santa Felicità, Florence; **3.136** National Gallery of Art, Washington, D.C., Samuel H. Kress Collection, 1946.18.1; **3.137** Photo Scala, Florence, courtesy Ministero Beni e Att. Culturali; **3.138** © nagelestock.com/Alamy; **3.139** Photo Scala, Florence, courtesy Ministero Beni e Att. Culturali; **3.140** The Earl of Plymouth. On loan to the National Museum of Wales, Cardiff; **3.141** Royal Institute for the Study and Conservation of Belgium's Artistic Heritage; **3.142** Galleria Nazionale d'Arte Antica, Rome; **3.143** Galleria degli Uffizi, Florence; **3.144** Rijksmuseum, Amsterdam; **3.145** © Bertrand Rieger/Hemis/Corbis; **3.146** © Florian Monheim/Arcaid/Corbis; **3.147** Gianni Dagli Orti/Musée du Château de Versailles/The Art Archive;

3.148 The Wallace Collection, London; **3.149** National Gallery, London/Scala, Florence; **3.150** Classic Image/Alamy; **3.151** Musée du Louvre, Paris; **3.152** Virginia Museum of Fine Arts, Richmond. The Adolf D. and Wilkins C. Williams Fund; **3.153** iStockphoto.com; **3.154** Musée du Louvre, Paris; **3.155**, **3.156** Museo Nacional del Prado, Madrid; **3.157** © Tate, London 2012; **3.158** Metropolitan Museum of Art, Gift of Mrs. Russell Sage, 1908, Acc. no. 08.228. Photo Metropolitan Museum of Art/Art Resource/Scala, Florence; **3.159** White Images/Scala, Florence; **3.161** Hampton University Museum, Virginia; **3.162** Musée d'Orsay, Paris; **3.163** © Tate, London 2012; **3.164** Musée Marmottan, Paris; **3.165** Musée d'Orsay, Paris; **3.166** Art Institute of Chicago, Charles H. and Mary F. S. Worcester Collection, 1964.336; **3.167** White Images/Scala, Florence; **3.168** BI, ADAGP, Paris/Scala, Florence. © ADAGP, Paris and DACS, London 2012; **3.169** Musée d'Orsay, Paris; **3.170** Courtauld Gallery, London; **3.171** National Gallery of Scotland, Edinburgh; **3.172** Museum of Modern Art, New York. Acquired through the Lillie P. Bliss Bequest. Acc. no. 472.1941. Photo 2012, Museum of Modern Art, New York/Scala, Florence; **3.173** Private Collection; **3.174** Musée Carnavalet, Paris; **3.175** Private Collection/ © Ackermann Kunstverlag/Bridgeman Art Library; **3.176** Österreichische Galerie Belvedere, Vienna; **3.177** Mark Edward Smith/photolibrary.com; **3.178** Photo Spectrum/Heritage Images/Scala, Florence; **3.179** Metropolitan Museum of Art, Harris Brisbane Dick Fund, 1966, 66.244.1-25. Photo Metropolitan Museum of Art/Art Resource/Scala, Florence; **3.180** The Barnes Foundation, Merion, PA. © Succession H. Matisse/DACS 2012; **3.181** Museum of Modern Art, New York, Mrs. Simon Guggenheim Fund, 8.1949. Photo 2012, Museum of Modern Art, New York/Scala, Florence. © Succession H. Matisse/DACS 2012; **3.182** Teriade Editeur, Paris, 1947. Printer Edmond Vairel, Paris. Edition 250. Museum of Modern Art, New York, The Louis E. Stern Collection, 930.1964.8. Photo 2012, Museum of Modern Art, New York/Scala, Florence. © Succession H. Matisse/DACS 2012; **3.183** Photograph by Hélène Adant/RAPHO/GAMMA, Camera Press, London; **3.184** Museum of Modern Art, New York, acquired through the Lillie P. Bliss Bequest, 333.1939. Photo 2012, Museum of Modern Art, New York/Scala, Florence. © Succession Picasso/DACS, London 2012; **3.185** Kunstmuseum, Bern; **3.186** Mildred Lane Kemper Art Museum, St. Louis, University purchase, Kende Sale Fund, 1946. © Succession Picasso/DACS, London 2012; **3.187** Metropolitan Museum of Art, Bequest of Gertrude Stein, 1946, Acc. no. 47.106. Photo Metropolitan Museum of Art/Art Resource/Scala, Florence. © Succession Picasso/DACS, London 2012; **3.188** Museum Folkwang, Essen; **3.189** Art Institute of Chicago, Arthur Jerome Eddy Memorial Collection, 1931.511. © ADAGP, Paris and DACS, London 2012; **3.190** Museum of Modern Art, New York, Purchase, 274.1939. Photo 2012, Museum of Modern Art, New

York/Scala, Florence; **3.192** Museum of Modern Art, New York, The Sidney and Harriet Janis Collection, 595.1967 a-b. Photo 2012, Museum of Modern Art, New York/Scala, Florence. © ADAGP, Paris and DACS, London 2012; **3.193** © The Heartfield Community of Heirs/VG Bild-kunst, Bonn and DACS, London 2012; **3.194** © DACS 2012; **3.195** Photo Hickey-Robertson, Houston. The Menil Collection, Houston. © ADAGP, Paris and DACS, London 2012; **3.196** Museum of Modern Art, New York, Gift of Mr. and Mrs. Pierre Matisse, 940.1965.a-c. Photo 2012, Museum of Modern Art, New York/Scala, Florence. © Succession Miro/ADAGP, Paris and DACS, London 2012; **3.197** Photo Francis Carr © Thames & Hudson Ltd, London; **3.198** Philadelphia Museum of Art, The Louise and Walter Arensberg Collection. © ADAGP, Paris and DACS, London 2012; **3.199**, **3.200** Stedelijk Museum, Amsterdam; **3.201** © ADAGP, Paris and DACS, London 2012; **3.202** © Romare Bearden Foundation/DACS, London/VAGA, New York 2012; **3.203** Courtesy Center for Creative Photography, University of Arizona © 1991 Hans Namuth Estate; **3.204** The University of Iowa Museum of Art, Iowa City, Gift of Peggy Guggenheim, OT 102. © The Pollock-Krasner Foundation ARS, NY and DACS, London 2012; **3.205** National Gallery of Art, Washington, D.C., Gift of the Mark Rothko Foundation, Inc., 1986.43.13. © 1998 Kate Rothko Prizel & Christopher Rothko ARS, NY and DACS, London, 2012; **3.206** © The Andy Warhol Foundation for the Visual Arts/Artists Rights Society (ARS), New York/DACS, London 2012; **3.207** © The Estate of Roy Lichtenstein/DACS 2012; **3.208** (above) Photo Smithsonian American Art Museum/Art Resource/Scala, Florence; **3.208** (below) Ralph Larmann; **3.209** Collection of the Modern Art Museum of Fort Worth, Museum purchase, The Benjamin J. Tillar Memorial Trust. Acquired in 1970. © Judd Foundation. Licensed by VAGA, New York/DACS, London 2012; **3.210** Photo Hickey-Robertson, Houston. The Menil Collection, Houston. © ARS, NY and DACS, London 2012; **3.211** Museum of Modern Art, New York, Larry Aldrich Foundation Fund, 393.1970.a-c. Photo 2012, Museum of Modern Art, New York/Scala, Florence. © ARS, NY and DACS, London 2012; **3.212** © The Estate of Ana Mendieta. Courtesy Galerie Lelong, New York; **3.213** Photo courtesy John Michael Kohler Arts Center © the artist and Stefan Stux Gallery, NY; **3.214** © EggImages/Alamy; **3.215** Photo courtesy Michael Graves & Associates; **3.216** (left) Museum of Modern Art, New York, Gift on behalf of The Friends of Education of The Museum of Modern Art, Acc. no. 70.1997.2. Photo 2012, Museum of Modern Art, New York/Scala, Florence. Courtesy the artist and Jack Shainman Gallery, New York; **3.216** (right) Museum of Modern Art, New York, Gift on behalf of The Friends of Education of The Museum of Modern Art, Acc. no. 70.1997.5. Photo 2012, Museum of Modern Art, New York/Scala, Florence. Courtesy the artist and Jack Shainman Gallery, New York; **3.217** William Sr.

and Dorothy Harmsen Collection, by exchange, 2007.47. Denver Art Museum. All Rights Reserved; **3.218a**, **3.218b** Courtesy Gladstone Gallery, New York. © Shirin Neshat; **3.219** Museum of Modern Art, New York, Fractional gift offered by Donald L. Bryant, Jr., Acc. no. 241.2000.b. Photo 2012, Museum of Modern Art, New York/Scala, Florence. © 1997 Pipilotti Rist. Image courtesy the artist, Luhring Augustine, New York and Hauser & Wirth; **3.220** Courtesy Gladstone Gallery, New York. Photo Michael James O'Brien. © 1997 Matthew Barney; **3.221** Contemporary Arts Museum, Houston. Photo Hester + Hardaway. Courtesy Andrea Rosen Gallery, NY; **p. 452** (above) Photo David Heald. The Solomon R. Guggenheim Foundation, New York. FLWW-10; (center) Courtauld Gallery, London; (below) Victor Chavez/WireImage/Getty; **4.1** Musée du Louvre, Paris; **4.2** © guichaoua/Alamy; **4.3** Martin Gray/National Geographic Stock; **4.4** Keith Bedford/epa/Corbis; **4.5** iStockphoto.com; **4.6** Photo David Heald. The Solomon R. Guggenheim Foundation, New York. FLWW-10; **4.7** Silvio Fiore/photolibrary.com; **4.8** iStockphoto.com; **4.9a**, **4.9b**, **4.9c**, **4.9d** © 1991 Ancient Egypt Research Associates ("AERA"). Photographs Mark Lehner; **4.10** © Taisei Corporation/NHK; **4.11** © Bob Krist/Corbis; **4.12** Cahokia Mounds State Historic Site, painting by William R. Iseminger; **4.13** David Hiser/National Geographic Stock; **4.14** Erich Lessing/akg-images; **4.15** University of Pennsylvania Museum of Archaeology and Anthropology, Philadelphia B17694; **4.16** © Peter Arnold, Inc./Alamy; **4.17** Henry John Drewal and Margaret Thompson Drewal Collection, EEPA D00639. Eliot Elisofon Photographic Archives, National Museum of African Art, Smithsonian Institution, Washington, D.C., courtesy Henry John Drewal; **4.18** Photo Anne Chauvet; **4.19** Photo Art Resource/Bob Schalkwijk/Scala, Florence. © 2012 Banco de México Diego Rivera Frida Kahlo Museums Trust, Mexico, D.F./DACS; **4.20** Precita Valley Vision © 1996 Susan Kelk Cervantes. Courtesy Precita Eyes Muralists, www.precitaeyes.org; **4.21** John Hios/akg-images; **4.22a**, **4.22b** Dom-Museum Hildesheim; **4.22c** Ralph Larmann; **4.23** India Museum, Calcutta; **4.24** The Cleveland Museum of Art, James Albert and Mary Gardiner Ford Memorial Fund, 1961.198; **4.25** National Museum of African Art, Smithsonian Institution, Washington, D.C., Museum purchase 90-4-1. Photograph Franko Khoury; **4.26** Smith College Museum of Art, Northampton, Massachusetts. Purchased with the proceeds from the sale of works donated by Mr. and Mrs. Alexander Rittmaster (Sylvian Goodkind, class of 1937) in 1958, and Adeline Flint Wing, class of 1898, and Caroline Roberta Wing, class of 1896, in 1961. Courtesy Michael Rosenfeld, LLC, New York, NY; **4.27** Musée du Louvre, Paris; **4.28** State Tretyakov Gallery, Moscow; **4.29** Photo Scala, Florence/Fondo Edifici di Culto – Min. dell'Interno; **4.30** Gianni Dagli Orti/The Art Archive; **4.31** Norbert Aujoulat; **4.32a** Ralph Larmann; **4.32b** Colorphoto Hans Hinz,

Allschwil, Switzerland; **4.33a** Ralph Larmann; **4.33b** © Araldo de Luca/Corbis; **4.34** © B. O'Kane/Alamy; **4.35** Courtesy Jingu Administration Office; **4.36** Photo Hickey-Robertson © 1998 Kate Rothko Prizel & Christopher Rothko ARS, NY and DACS, London; **4.37** Rainer Hackenberg/akg-images. © Succession H. Matisse/DACS 2012; **4.38** Teriade Editeur, Paris, 1947. Printer Edmond Vairel, Paris. Edition 250. Museum of Modern Art, New York, The Louis E. Stern Collection, 930.1964.8. Photo 2012, Museum of Modern Art, New York/Scala, Florence. © Succession H. Matisse/DACS 2012; **4.39** University Art Museum, Obafemi Awolowo University, Ife; **4.40** Dumbarton Oaks Museum, Washington, D.C.; **4.41** Courtesy the artist and Marian Goodman Gallery, New York/Paris; **4.42** © Tierney Gearon, Courtesy Yossi Milo Gallery, New York; **4.43** Metropolitan Museum of Art, The Michael C. Rockefeller Memorial Collection, Bequest of Nelson A. Rockefeller, 1979, Acc. no. 1979.206.1611. Photo Metropolitan Museum of Art/Art Resource/Scala, Florence; **4.44** Dallas Museum of Art, The Clark and Frances Stillman Collection of Congo Sculpture, Gift of Eugene and Margaret McDermott, 1969.S.22; **4.45** The Cleveland Museum of Art, Purchase from the J. H. Wade Fund 1930.331; **4.46** © Loren McIntyre/lorenmcintyre.com; **4.47** Pinoteca di Brera, Milan; **4.48** © Andres Serrano. Courtesy the artist and Yvon Lambert Paris, New York; **4.49** Copyright Merle Greene Robertson, 1976; **4.50** Courtesy National Museum of the American Indian, Smithsonian Institution (18/2023). Photo by Photo Services; **4.51** Museo del Templo Mayor, Mexico City, CONACULTA-INAH, 10-220302; **4.52** Dallas Museum of Art, Foundation for the Arts Collection, Mrs John B. O'Hara Fund; **4.53** British Museum, London; **4.54** Photo Heidi Grassley © Thames & Hudson Ltd, London; **4.55** Ralph Larmann; **4.56** Ivan Vdovin/Alamy; **4.57** Hervé Champollion/akg-images; **4.58** National Gallery of Art, Washington, D.C., Widener Collection, 1942.9.97; **4.59** Photograph K2822 © Justin Kerr; **4.60** National Museum of Anthropology, Mexico City; **4.61** National Maritime Museum, Greenwich, London; **4.62** National Gallery, London/Scala, Florence; **4.63** Gift of the Alumni Association to Jefferson Medical College in 1878, purchased by the Pennsylvania Academy of the Fine Arts and the Philadelphia Museum of Art in 2007 with the generous support of more than 3,600 donors, 2007, 2007-1-1; **4.64** Courtesy the David Lloyd Gallery; **4.65** Courtesy Institute for Plastination, Heidelberg, Germany; **4.66** Art Institute of Chicago, Helen Birch Bartlett Memorial Collection, 1926.224; **4.67** © Jasper Johns/VAGA, New York/DACS, London 2012; **4.68** Courtesy Marcia Smilack; **4.69** Museum of Modern Art, New York. Benjamin Scharps and David Scharps Fund, 288.1956. Photo 2012, Museum of Modern Art, New York/Scala, Florence. © ADAGP, Paris and DACS, London 2012; **4.70** Museum of Modern Art, New York. Given anonymously, 162.1934. Photo 2012, Museum of Modern Art, New York/Scala, Florence.

© Salvador Dali, Fundació Gala-Salvador Dalí, DACS, 2012; **4.71** High Museum of Art, Atlanta, 1999.93. Purchase with T. Marshall Hahn Folk Art Acquisition Fund for the T. Marshall Hahn Collection; **4.72** Victor R. Boswell, Jr./National Geographic Stock; **4.73** Photo Vatican Museums, Rome; **4.74** Metropolitan Museum of Art, Rogers Fund, 1903. Inv. 03.14.13a-g. Photo Metropolitan Museum of Art/Art Resource/Scala, Florence; **4.75** Photo Scala, Florence; **4.76** Photo Scala, Florence, courtesy Ministero Beni e Att. Culturali; **4.77** Kunsthistorisches Museum, Vienna; **4.78** National Gallery of Art, Washington, D.C. Gift of Mr. & Mrs. Richard Mellon Scaife in honour of Paul Mellon, 1993.15.1; **4.79** Courtesy Miran Fukuda; **4.80** Photo Anthony d'Offay, London; **4.81a** James Green/Robert Harding; **4.81b**, **4.81c**, **4.81d** Ralph Larmann; **4.82** Gianni Dagli Orti/Palazzo del Tè Mantua/The Art Archive; **4.83** Pietro Baguzzi/akg-images; **4.84a**, **4.84b** Courtesy the artist; **4.85** National Gallery of Art, Washington, D.C., Gift of Lila Acheson Wallace, 1987.2.1. Photo Ellen Page Wilson, courtesy The Pace Gallery. © Chuck Close, The Pace Gallery; **4.86** Courtauld Gallery, London; **4.87** from Kirby, J., *Dr Brook Taylor's Method of Perspective Made Easy*, 1754; **4.88** National Gallery of Art, Washington, D.C., Gift of the Collectors Committee, 1987.55.1. © ADAGP, Paris and DACS, London 2012; **4.89** Photo Scala, Florence; **4.90** The Palace Museum, Beijing; **4.91a** Photo Irmgard Groth-Kimball © Thames & Hudson Ltd, London; **4.91b** © World Pictures/Alamy; **4.92** British Museum, London; **4.93** Musée du Louvre, Paris; **4.94** Musée National de Château de Versailles; **4.95** Ägyptisches Museum, Staatliche Museen, Berlin; **4.96a**, **4.96b** Egyptian Museum, Cairo; **4.97** Photo Scala, Florence; **4.98** Metropolitan Museum of Art, Gift of Mr. and Mrs. Klaus G. Perls, 1990, Acc. no. 1990.332. Photo Metropolitan Museum of Art/Art Resource/Scala, Florence; **4.99** Musée du Louvre, Paris; **4.100** © Hubert Stadler/Corbis; **4.101** © Peter Guttman/Corbis; **4.102** Library of Congress, Washington, D.C. Prints & Photographs Division, LC-B8184-7964-A; **4.103** Photo Scala, Florence; **4.104**, **4.105** Museo Nacional del Prado, Madrid; **4.106** Nick Ut/AP/Press Association Images; **4.107** Dallas Museum of Art, purchased with funds donated by the Jolesch Acquisition Fund, The 500, Inc., the National Endowment for the Arts, Bradbury Dyer, III, Mr. and Mrs. Bryant M. Hanley, Jr., Mr. and Mrs Michael C. Mewhinney, Deedie and Rusty Rose, and Mr. and Mrs. William T. Solomon. Courtesy Gagosian Gallery; **4.108** Photograph Luidger; **4.109** National Archaeological Museum, Naples; **4.110** Centre Guillaume le Conquérant, Bayeux; **4.111** Museum of Fine Arts, Boston, Fenollosa-Weld Collection;

4.112 Courtesy the artist; **4.113** © DACS 2012; **4.114** Courtesy the artist; **4.115** © Anselm Kiefer; **4.116** Musée du Louvre, Paris; **4.117** Photo courtesy the artist and Jonathan Ferrara Gallery; **4.118** Museum of Fine Arts, Boston, Henry Lillie Pierce Fund, BJ385; **4.119** © Succession Picasso/ DACS, London 2012; **4.120** Lions Gate/The Kobal Collection; **4.121** Library of Congress, Washington, D.C. Prints & Photographs Division, FSA/OWI Collection, LC-DIG-fsa-8b29516; **4.122a** National Gallery, London/Scala, Florence; **4.123** Courtesy Mary Boone Gallery, New York; **4.124a** © Reuters/ Corbis; **4.124b** © Ton Koene/ZUMA Press/Corbis; **4.125** Monastery of St. Catherine, Sinai, Egypt; **4.126** Musées Royaux des Beaux-Arts de Belgique, Brussels; **4.127** © Maurice Savage/Alamy; **4.128** Courtesy the artist; **4.129** Naturhistorisches Museum, Vienna; **4.130** Museum of Modern Art, New York. Purchase, 478.1953. Photo 2012, Museum of Modern Art, New York/Scala, Florence. © ARS, NY and DACS, London 2012; **4.131a** Ralph Larmann; **4.131b** Erich Lessing/akg-images; **4.132** Museo delle Terme, Rome; **4.133** Uffizi Gallery, Florence; **4.134** Kimbell Art Museum, Fort Worth, Texas/Art Resource, NY/Scala, Florence; **4.135** Metropolitan Museum of Art, The Harry G. C. Packard Collection of Asian Art, Gift of Harry G. C. Packard, and Purchase, Fletcher, Rogers, Harris Brisbane Dick, and Louis V. Bell Funds, Joseph Pulitzer Bequest, and The Annenberg Fund Inc. gift, 1975, 1975.268.125. Photo Metropolitan Museum of Art/Art Resource/Scala, Florence; **4.136** Photo Scala, Florence, courtesy Ministero Beni e Att. Culturali; **4.137** Musée d'Orsay, Paris; **4.138** Courtesy the artist and Luhring Augustine, New York; **4.139a**, **4.139b** © ADAGP, Paris and DACS, London 2012; **4.140** Courtesy the artist and Luhring Augustine, New York; **4.141** © Vanessa Beecroft; **4.142a** Victor Chavez/WireImage/Getty; **4.142b** Alessandro della Valle/epa/Corbis; **4.143** Museum of Modern Art, New York. Fractional and promised gift of Malcom Wiener in memory of John Rewald, Acc. no. 183.1994. Photo 2012, Museum of Modern Art, New York/Scala, Florence; **4.144** Teriade Editeur, Paris, 1947. Printer Edmond Vairel, Paris. Edition 250. Museum of Modern Art, New York, The Louis E. Stern Collection, 930.1964.8. Photo 2012, Museum of Modern Art, New York/Scala, Florence. © Succession H. Matisse/DACS 2012; **4.145** Musée National d'Art Moderne, Centre Georges Pompidou, Paris. © Succession H. Matisse/DACS 2012; **4.146** © Tate, London, 2012. Reproduced by permission of The Henry Moore Foundation; **4.147** Museum of Modern Art, New York, Gift of Mrs. John D. Rockefeller III, 678.1954. Photo 2012, Museum of

Modern Art, New York/Scala, Florence. © ADAGP, Paris and DACS, London 2012; **4.148** Courtesy Christie's/Werner Forman Archive; **4.149** Records of the Work Projects Administration, U.S. National Archives and Records Administration; **4.150** © The John Coplans Trust; **4.151** Library of Congress, Washington, D.C. Prints & Photographs Division, FSA/OWI Collection, LC-DIG-fsa-8b29516; **4.152** Courtesy the artist and Metro Pictures; **4.153** Brooklyn Museum, Gift of the Elizabeth A. Sackler Foundation, 2002.10. Photo © Donald Woodman. © Judy Chicago, 1979. © ARS, NY and DACS, London 2012; **4.154** Galleria degli Uffizi, Florence; **4.155** Copyright © by Guerrilla Girls, Inc. Courtesy www.guerrillagirls.com; **4.156** Courtesy the artist; **4.157** Metropolitan Museum of Art, Rogers Fund, 1931, Acc. no. 31.3.166. Photo Metropolitan Museum of Art/Art Resource/Scala, Florence; **4.158** Copyright © 1972 The Estate of Diane Arbus; **4.159** © copyright The Robert Mapplethorpe Foundation. Courtesy Art + Commerce; **4.160** Courtesy Regen Projects, Los Angeles; **4.161** Private Collection; **4.162** Museo de Arte Moderno, Mexico City. © 2012 Banco de México Diego Rivera Frida Kahlo Museums Trust, Mexico, D.F./DACS; **4.163** Gemäldegalerie Alte Meister, Dresden; **4.164** Copyright Duane Michals. Courtesy Pace/MacGill Gallery, New York; **4.165** © Jenny Saville; **4.166a** Photo Vladimir Sichov, Sipa-Press. Courtesy the artist and galerie Michel Rein, Paris. © ORLAN; **4.166b** Courtesy ORLAN. © ORLAN; **4.167** Galleria degli Uffizi, Florence; **4.168** Detroit Institute of Arts, Gift of Mr. Leslie H. Green; **4.169** Detroit Institute of Arts, Founders Society Purchase with funds from Mr. and Mrs. Bert L. Smokler and Mr. and Mrs. Lawrence A. Fleischman; **4.170** Detroit Institute of Arts, Gift of Dexter M. Ferry, Jr.; **4.171** Photo Herbert Lotz © the artist. Courtesy White Cube; **4.172** © Munch Museum/Munch-Ellingsen Group, BONO, Oslo/DACS, London 2012; **4.173** Philadelphia Museum of Art, Gift of Mr. and Mrs. H. Gates Lloyd, 1974. © The Pollock-Krasner Foundation ARS, NY and DACS, London 2012; **4.174** Courtesy Bischofberger Collection, Switzerland. © 2012 Julian Schnabel/ARS, New York/DACS; **4.175** © Sherrie Levine. Courtesy Simon Lee Gallery, London; **4.176** © The Andy Warhol Foundation/Corbis. © The Andy Warhol Foundation for the Visual Arts/Artists Rights Society (ARS), New York/DACS, London 2012; **4.177** The Museum of Contemporary Art, Los Angeles. Purchased with funds provided by the National Endowment for the Arts, a Federal Agency, and Councilman Joel Wachs. © Richard Prince; **4.178** Courtesy the artist and Sikkema Jenkins & Co.

Image Numbering by Part and Chapter

The following list shows in which chapters images appear, cited by figure number:

Acknowledgments

The publisher would like to thank the following for their generous advice and feedback during the preparation of *Gateways to Art*. Special gratitude goes to: John Adelman, Lone Star College Cy-Fair; Fred C. Albertson, University of Memphis; Dan Boylan, Trine University; Andrea Donovan, Minot State University; Kara English, Tarrant County Community College; Trina Felty, Pima Community College; Ferdinanda Florence, Solano Community College; Rebecca Hendrick, University of Texas at El Paso; Bonnie Holt, Contra Costa College; Kathy Holt, Arapahoe Community College; Frank Latimer, Pulaski Technical College; Bridget Lynch, Simmons College; Patrick McNally, Community College of Aurora; Ken Magri, American River College; Erin Morris, South Mountain Community College; Carola Naumer, Truckee Meadows Community College; Kristin Powers Nowlin, Southeast Missouri State University; Elaine O'Brien, Sacramento State University; Margee Bright Ragland, Georgia Perimeter College; Mollie Rushing, Delta State University; Dennis Sears, Gadsden State Community College; Suzanne Thomas, Rose State College; Li-Lin Tseng, Pittsburg State University; Cathie Tyler, Paris Community College; Kathy Windrow, Eastfield College; Kathy Windrow, Eastfield College; Linda Woodward, Lone Star Community College Montgomery; Susan Zucker, Louisiana State University.

The publisher also gratefully acknowledges the following contributors: Wafaa Bilal, Tracy Chevalier, Mel Chin, Michael Fay, Antony Gormley, David Grove, Zaha Hadid, Zahi Hawass, Mona Hatoum, Hyo-In Kim, Steve McCurry, Melchor Peredo, Martín Ramírez, Colin Rhodes, Howard Risatti, Sonoko Sasaki, Richard Serra, Cindy Sherman, Paul Tacon, Dan Tague, Spencer Tunick, Bill Viola, and Robert Wittman.

Debra J. DeWitte
would like to thank the following for their scholarly assistance: Melissa Bowden, University of Texas at Arlington; Richard Brettell, University of Texas at Dallas; Annemarie Carr, Southern Methodist University; Juilee Decker, Georgetown College; Rita Lasater, University of Texas at Arlington; John McQuillen, University of Toronto; Jenny Ramirez, Virginia Military Institute; Beth Wright, University of Texas at Arlington; and her warmest thanks go to her family: Bill Gibney, Jaclyn Jean Gibney, and Connie DeWitte.

Ralph M. Larmann
would like to thank the following for their scholarly assistance and support: Ella Combs-Larmann, independent scholar and artist; Dr. Gordon Kingsley, Harlaxton College; Steven Ochs, Southern Arkansas University; Dr. Heidi Strobel, University of Evansville; University of Evansville, Office of Academic Affairs, Office of Alumni Relations, University Library, Department of Art; and for their patience and understanding: Ella, Allison, and Tip.

M. Kathryn Shields
would like to thank the following: Laura M. Amrhein, University of Arkansas Little Rock; Damon Akins, Guilford College; Maria Bobroff, Guilford College; Ingrid Furniss, Lafayette College; Rita Lasater, University of Texas at Arlington; Claire Black McCoy, Columbus State University; Jenny Ramirez, Virginia Military Institute; and express love and gratitude to her family: Barry Bell, Gillian Denise Shields Bell, Alden Emmerich Shields Bell, and Nancy Shields.

Index

50, 50–51

Herculaneum 310

Here Is New York: A Democracy of Photographs (exhibition) 221, *221*

Hermaphrodite with a Dog (Arbus) 575, *575*

Herschel, John 214

Hesse, Eva 157; *Hang-Up 156*, 156–57

hierarchical scale 130, *130*, 298, 299, 304, 324, 325, 526

hieroglyphics/hieroglyphs: Egyptian 204, *204*, 302, *302*; Maya 353

highlights 58, 78, 172

Hildegard of Bingen 321; *The Fifth Vision of Hildegard of Bingen 321*, 321–22; *Scivias (Know the Ways)* 321

Hildesheim, Germany: Church of St. Michael's doors *471*, 471–72

Hill, John 28

Hill, Holliday, Connors, Cosmopulos agency: Tyco advertising campaign 210, *210*

Hinduism 331, 332; in Indian art 122, 334, 488

Hine, Lewis Wickes 219; *Power House Mechanic Working on Steam Pump 569*, *569*; *Ten Year Old Spinner, Whitnel Cotton Mill* 219, *219*; *Work Portraits* 569

Hip Hop Project (Lee) 589, *589*

Hiroshige, Ando: "Riverside Bamboo Market, Kyōbashi" 141, *141*

Hirst, Damien: *The Physical Impossibility of Death in the Mind of Someone Living* 269, *269*

Hitler, Adolf 40, 41, 158, 431

Höch, Hannah 224; *Cut with the Kitchen Knife through the Last Weimar Beer-Belly Cultural Epoch of Germany* 224, *225*

Hodgkin, Howard: *Interior with Figures* 99, *99*

Hogarth, William 401; *False Perspective 518*, *518*; *Marriage à-la-Mode* series 402, 402–3

Hokusai, Katsushika 31; "The Great Wave off Shore at Kanagawa" (from *Thirty-six Views of Mount Fuji*) 81, *81*, 117, *117*, 195, *195*, 346, *346*; *Maple Leaves on a River* 26, 28

Holocaust, the 541

Holt, Nancy 107; *Solar Rotary* 107, *107*

Holy Virgin Mary, The (Ofili) 39

Holzer, Jenny 109–10; *Untitled (Selections from Truisms...)* 110, *110*

Homer, Winslow: *Prisoners from the Front* 41, 41–43

homosexuality 568, 576, 577

Hong Kong: Bank of China (Pei) 287, 287–88

Hopi, the 360; kachinas 490–91, *491*

Hopkins, Roger 460

Hopper, Edward: *Nighthawks* 159, *159*

Horse in Motion, The (Muybridge) 229, 229–30

Hotel Rwanda (George) 546, *546*

House (Whiteread) 71, *71*

House with the Ocean View, The (Abramovic) 242, 243

Houser, Allan: *Reverie* 154, *154*

Houses at L'Estaque (Braque) 426, *426*

Houston, Texas: Rothko Chapel 481, *481*, 483

Hudson River School 407

hues 92, 93

human body: and notions of beauty 557–59; and performance art and installations 562–65; *see also* nudes

Human Condition, The (Magritte) 519, *519*

human sacrifices 357, 357–58, 463, 488, 488–89

Humana Building, Louisville, Kentucky (Graves) 289, *289*

humanism 376–7, 509

Hummingbirds, The (Lostutter) 129, *129*

Hunefer (scribe) 492, 494

Hung Liu 186; *Interregnum* 186, *186*, 188

Hungry Tigress (Asuka period) 343, *343*

Hunters in the Snow (Bruegel the Elder) 146–47, *147*

Hussein, King of Jordan 323

Hutu genocide 546

hypostyle halls 278, 279

I Like America and America Likes Me (Beuys) *see Coyote, I Like America and America Likes Me*

Icarus (Matisse) 97, *97*, 178, *178*, 424, 424–25, 482, *483*

iconic 554

iconoclasm 550

iconographic analysis 154–56, 161

icons *318*, 318–19, 474–75, *475*, 550, *550*, 551

ideal, the 377

idealized 471, 557

identity, in art 571, 573, 585

ideograms 552, 553

Ife, Nigeria: Oni sculpture 132, *132*; ritual vessel 484, 484–85; terracotta head 558–59, *559*

Iktinos and Kallikrates: Parthenon 135, *135*, 305, *305*, 513, *513*

illuminated characters/illuminations 208, *208*, 320, 321; *see also* manuscripts, illuminated

illusionism 182, 259, 408, 508; in architecture 511–12, 513–14; in paintings and drawings 508–11, 514–19; in sculpture 512

Imagen de Yagul (Mendieta) 443, *443*

IMAX 228, 229

imitation 162–63; *see also* appropriation

Immediate Family (Mann) 226

impasto 186, 417, 503

implied line 52–53, 54, 86, 109, 141, 160, 395

implied texture 136, 199

impression (printmaking) 192

Impression Sunrise (Monet) 412, 412–13

Impressionism/Impressionists 99, 234, 344, 345, 411–13, 415, 427, 429

Improvisation #30 (Cannons) (Kandinsky) 428, *428*

In the Blue (Crest) (Mickett and Stackhouse) 69, *69*

in the round 66, 74, 260, 393

Inca, the 348, 351, 488; Machu Picchu 351, *351*, 353; mummified children 488, 488–89; tunic 352, *352*

incise, incised (decorative technique) 309

Inconvenient Truth, An (Guggenheim) 235–36, *236*

India 330, 331, 332; architecture 332, *332*, 333, 334, *334*, *335*, 335–36; Bidri ware huqqa base *143*, 143–44; cave paintings 333, *333*; Hinduism 331, 334; map *330*; painting 335, *335*; sculpture 334, 334–35, 488, *488*

Infinity (J. de Rivera) 153, *153*

Ingres, Jean-Auguste-Dominique: *Grande Odalisque* 157, 157–58

inks 174; brush and ink drawing 175–76; paintings 125–26, *126*, 189–90; *see also* pen and ink drawings

inlay 487

Inquisition, the 390

insanity and art 104, 416, 503–4, 505

installations 110, *110*, 111, 240, *246*, 246–47, *533*, 533–34, 584; human bodies as 562, *564*, 564–65, *565*; and identity *446*, 446–47, *447*; mixed-media 450, *450*; and multiculturalism *445*, 445–46; in public spaces 457, *457*; sculptural 273, *273*, 585, *585*; video 448, *448*, 450

Insurrection! (Our Tools Were Rudimentary, Yet We Pressed On) (Walker) 247, *247*

intaglio printmaking 192, 195–97, 199, 203

intarsia 259

intensity, color 83

interior design 118, *118*

Interior with Figures (Hodgkin) 99, *99*

Interregnum (Hung Liu) 186, *186*, 188

Ionic order 306, *306*

Irascibles, the 202–3

Ise Jingu (Grand Shrine of Ise), Japan 480, *481*

Isenheim Altarpiece (Grünewald) 387, *387*

Isfahan, Iran: Madrasa Imami mihrab *324*, 324–25; Masjid-i-Shah portal 480, *480*

Ishtar Gate, Babylon 300, *300*

Islam/Muslims 61, 103, 316, 331, 335; *see also* Koran, the; Muhammad, Prophet

Islamic art and architecture 316; *Banner of Las Navas do Tolosa* 61, *61*; calligraphy 61, *61*, 316, 324; huqqa base *143*, 143–44; kufic script 320, 325; manuscripts 320, *320*, 322, *322*; mihrabs *324*, 324–25; miniature 335, *335*; mosque lamp 100, *100*; mosques 148, *148*, 324, 368, 368–69; Taj Mahal *335*, 335–36

isometric perspective 84, *85*, 86, 537

Istanbul: Hagia Sophia 282, *282*, 318

ivory 43

Iznik pottery 100, *100*

Jahangir, Mughal emperor 335; *Jahangir Preferring a Sufi Shaykh to Kings* (Bichitr) 335, *335*

Japan 330, 331–32, 340; architecture 282–83, *283*, 342, *342*, 480, *481*; geishas 559; illusionistic artwork 511–12, *512*; literature 343; manga 49, *49*; map *330*; religions 331, 340, 343, 346; scrolls *343*, 343–44, 536–37, *537*, 559, *559*; shrine panel 343, *343*; tea ceremony 32, *32*, 37, 340, 342, *342*; textiles 340, 341; *ukiyo-e* prints 194, 344, *344*, 345; *see also* Hokusai, Katsushika

japonisme 345

jatakas 333

Jazz (Matisse) 97

Jeanne-Claude *see* Christo

Jefferson, Thomas 404; Monticello *404*, 404–5; Virginia State Capitol 30, *30*

Jerusalem: Dome of the Rock 322, *323*, 323–4; mosque lamp 100, *100*

Jesus Christ 105, *105*, 316, 317, *318*, 318–19, 325, 489, *489*

Jeunet, Jean-Pierre: *Amélie* 234, *234*

Jewish culture 103, 315, 316, 317; and Catacombs, Rome 478, *479*; Dura Europos synagogue *315*, 315–16, *317*

Johns, Jasper 502; *Flag* 502, *502*

Jonah 317

Journal of a Voyage to the South Seas, A (Parkinson) 370

Journey of the Sun God Re, The (Egyptian coffin painting) 26, 26–27

Joy of Life (Matisse) *423*, 423–24

Judaism 316

Judd, Donald 441; *Untitled* 441, *441*

Judith and Her Maidservant with the Head of Holofernes (Gentileschi) 583, *583*

Judith Decapitating Holofernes (Caravaggio) 394, *394*

Judith Decapitating Holofernes (Gentileschi) 139, *139*, 187, *187*, 394, 394, 573, *573*

Julie (Dijkstra) 485, 485–86

Julius II, Pope 381, 388; tomb (Michelangelo) 264–65, *265*

Jurisprudence (Raphael) 509

Justinian I, Byzantine Emperor 318, 319, 320, 520; Justinian mosaic 520–21, *521*

Kaaba, Mecca 324, *324*

Kabakov, Ilya and Emilia: *The Man Who Flew into Space from His Apartment* 273, *273*

kachina dolls, Hopi 490–91, *491*, 587

Kahlo, Frida 579; *The Two Fridas* 579, *579*

Kallikrates: Parthenon (with Iktinos) 135, *135*, 305, *305*, 513, *513*; Temple of Athena Nike 278, *278*

Kamehameha, King of Hawaii 372

kami 331, 340, 480

Kandariya Mahadeva temple, Khajuraho, India *334*, 334–35